THE SINGLE-PARENT FAMILY IN CHILDREN'S BOOKS:

An Annotated Bibliography

second edition

by
CATHERINE TOWNSEND HORNER

The Scarecrow Press, Inc.
Metuchen, N.J., & London
1988

Library of Congress Cataloging-in-Publication Data

Horner, Catherine Townsend, 1937–
    The single-parent family in children's books.

    Includes indexes.
    1. Children's stories--Bibliography.
2. Single-parent family in literature--Bibliography.
3. Family in literature--Bibliography. I. Title.
Z1037.H7793 1988   016.8093'9355   87-26403
[PN1009.A1]
ISBN 0-8108-2065-X

CONTENTS

ACKNOWLEDGMENTS

For Bert, indefatigable researcher, nonpareil literary assistant, willing--if not infallible--proofreader, patient helpmeet.

Special thanks to Kathy Boyd, San Jose Public Library, the Keeper of the Lists.

INTRODUCTION

When I was a little kid, a father was like the light in the refrigerator. Every house had one, but no one really knew what either of them did once the door was shut. My dad left the house every morning and always seemed glad to see everyone again at night. He opened the jar of pickles when no one else at home could. He was the only one in the house who wan't afraid to go into the basement by himself.... When anyone was sick, he went out to get the prescription filled.... He set mousetraps.... He signed all my report cards. He took a lot of pictures, but was never in them.... Whenever I played house, the mother doll had a lot to do. I never knew what to do with the daddy doll, so I had him say, "I'm going off to work now," and threw him under the bed. When I was nine years old, my father didn't get up one morning and go to work. He went to the hospital and died the next day.... I went to my room and felt under the bed for the father doll. When I found him, I dusted him off and put him on my bed. He never did anything. I didn't know his leaving would hurt so much. It still does.[1]

Erma Bombeck's poignant and moving encomium dramatizes the fact that a child takes his parents for granted. Bonded to him from birth, parents are the most reliable constant in his expanding but still sheltered world. The loss of a parent to death or divorce is often the child's first and most traumatic realization that life is a dynamic process of change and adaptation, denial as well as gratification, in the cycle of human experience.

TRENDS IN THE GENRE

The single-parent family has always been represented in children's literature. Prior to 1960 the cause of single parenthood in books was invariably widowhood or orphanhood with a single guardian. Nineteenth century examples of the genre, such as Margaret Sydney's FIVE LITTLE PEPPERS and Alice Caldwell Hegan's MRS. WIGGS OF THE CABBAGE PATCH, were usually lachrymose

v

and inspirational stories in which the brave and tragic widow would struggle on nobly in penury without sacrificing her integrity. She would finally triumph over adversity through patience, perseverance, rectitude, coincidence and Divine Providence.

These moral tales were gradually superseded in the twentieth century by adventure stories in which the phenomenon of single parenthood was employed as a contrivance to free young protagonists from close supervision, thus removing barriers to danger and providing them with greater latitude to seek excitement. This trend resulted in more suspenseful reading than the earlier moralism, but the condition of single parenthood was a fait accompli and only incidental to the plot. Never did it address the issue that the loss of a parent could be distressful to the child or that the problems inherent in single parenthood could be, in themselves, conflicts to be resolved.

At midcentury, Helen Daringer in STEPSISTER SALLY and Nancy W. Faber in CATHY AT THE CROSSROADS began pioneering the theme of the remarriage of the widowed parent as a source of conflict. But it was the sexual revolution of the 1960s and 1970s, the exponential leap in the divorce rate, and the concomitant emergence of the popular psychology movement that bred the new genre of the contemporary "problem novel." These narratives began appearing in the 1970s with predictable regularity and developed an instant appeal among young readers because of their use of the vernacular and their frank treatment of the subject matter. While they are considered essential for their bibliotherapeutic value, as literature they rarely soar because they are tethered inextricably to the prescribed formula necessary for helping the child to accept the unacceptable at a time of family crisis that may also coincide with the throes of his personal passage into puberty and adolescence. The need to neatly tie up all the loose ends by the final chapter takes precedence over the literary directive to stretch the reader's horizons, imagination and intellect.

The single-parent theme has come of age in the 1980s. Divorce has finally overtaken and surpassed widowhood as the primary cause of single parenthood, reversing the longstanding tradition and more accurately reflecting contemporary social conditions. Of even greater significance, many of the books which deal seriously and realistically with death, divorce, separation, desertion, remarriage, binuclear families, and never-married mothers have vaulted out of the mold of the self-conscious problem novel and become multidimensional, frequently with imperfect resolutions, and generally more literary. In her acceptance speech for the 1984 Newbery Medal for DEAR MR. HENSHAW, Beverly Cleary confided:

> Because I find life humorous, sorrowful, and filled with problems that have no solutions, my intent was to write about the feelings of a lonely boy and to avoid the genre of

the problem novel.... A couple of people said they liked the book themselves but expressed doubts about giving it to children because it wasn't funny and because Leigh's parents were not reconciled at the end--a conclusion I felt would be sentimental, dishonest, and a source of false hope to many children.[2]

The trend toward the complex plot is a salubrious compromise between the traditional adventure story and the deliberately cathartic "problem novel." At last there is a broad choice available for those who select books for the burgeoning ranks of children who, through capricious fate, are left with only one principal care-giver and who may benefit from reading about fictional characters in similar circumstances. The child from a single-parent home deserves to have access to a substantive body of literature--mystery, adventure, fantasy, contemporary realism, humorous stories, topical books, science fiction and historical fiction--in which the protagonist, like himself, has experienced family trauma and/or belongs to a nontraditional family group.

SCOPE OF THE BIBLIOGRAPHY

An attempt was made to identify and locate as many fiction titles as possible published between 1965 and 1986 pertaining to families fractured by divorce, desertion, separation, or the death of a parent; unmarried mothers or other single adults as heads of household; and the protracted absence of one parent from a traditional two-parent home. Included are books which deal with the restructuring of families by remarriage and the death or desertion of the single parent. Arrangement of the bibliography is by cause of single parenthood. The selection is limited to books which were available from public libraries in Santa Clara County, California, during the research period, and any omissions are therefore inadvertent. Out-of-print books are designated as such in the bibliographic data. Some modern classics and old favorites published prior to 1965 but still in print as of 1985 are also presented. Of the more than six hundred annotations incorporated in this bibliography, a total of 251 titles involving divorce, separation and desertion were located, as well as 231 on widowhood, 34 with unwed mothers, 34 on orphans or wards of the court having a single guardian, 23 characterized by protracted absence of one parent, and an additional 24 of indeterminable origin. In 1978, by comparison, the author found 95 books on widowhood, 56 on divorce, desertion or separation, 31 identified as orphans with single guardians, 23 involving the protracted absence of one parent, and only three having unwed mothers.[3]

The fiction bibliography can be approached through both the Subject/Author Index and the Title Index, which gives brief plot synopses and serves as a Ready Reference Profile. Nonfiction books are presented separately. Annotations are purposely expository rather than critical to enable the selector to judge for himself the relevance of the plot or situation to given circumstances. As an aid to selection, however, books were assessed according to their value to a single-parent book collection, not necessarily to a general fiction collection.

GUIDE TO EVALUATIONS

Because this is a nonselective bibliography which includes as many titles as could be found, a rudimentary evaluation was assigned to each book ranking its value specifically to a single-parent fiction collection. The evaluatory symbol was placed at the end of the imprint. The four ratings are described as follows:

R++ = highest recommendation.
> Exceptional literary quality and/or isolated books on sensitive contemporary social topics such as parental kidnapping, child molestation, incest and battered wives.

R+ = highly recommended.
> The core of the single-parent collection. Treatments are timely and trenchant; literary quality is above average. The "problem novel" is included in this expansive designation, along with others chosen for their relevance, immediacy and credibility.

R = recommended.
> Books of average literary quality as well as those with peripheral pertinence, insignificant conflict, or improbable plots. Into this category fall most works of science fiction, period pieces, pure adventurism, high interest/low vocabulary novels, and families headed by an adult who is not the child's biological parent.

NR = not recommended.
> Dated or didactic books, unrealistic resolutions, and caricaturization of the single parent. Very few books received the NR ranking because of poor literary standards. Such titles are rarely to be found in today's cost-conscious public libraries.

More than a selection tool, this bibliography provides a comprehensive and integrated record of the past twenty years and more in the history of American book publishing on the subject of the single-parent family in children's literature.

NOTES

1. Erma Bombeck, Field Newspaper Syndicate, June 21, 1981.

2. Hornbook 60:4, August 1984, p. 437.

3. Catherine Townsend Horner, The Single-Parent Family in Children's Books, Scarecrow Press, 1978.

1. Abercrombie, Barbara. CAT-MAN'S DAUGHTER. New York:
    Harper and Row, 1981. 154p. Grades 6-8. R+
    Being the daughter of a TV superhero is not glamorous for
Kate McAllister, 13. Following her parents' acrimonious divorce two
years earlier, they have only communicated via attorneys and have
abided strictly by the letter of the visitation agreement. Kate is in
California now only because her mother, a New York interior decorator, owes her father one week of Kate's time. She dreads it, because the latest of her father's Barbie doll girlfriends has the visit
programmed to impress her dad and doesn't include time for her beloved paternal grandmother, Riley, with whom she would rather
stay. Then, stupendously, she is "kidnapped" by Riley and taken
to her home in San Pedro from which she runs a service, staffed by
her endearing collection of outcasts and misfits, which entertains at
birthday parties. Disguised as a clown to deceive the police and
media, Kate joins the close-knit group. As Riley calculated, Kate's
mother arrives on the scene, and each parent blames the other publicly for Kate's abduction before appearing in tandem to confront
Riley. But the anticipated dialogue about Kate's welfare never materializes. It seems as if they will return to the status quo until Kate
suggests that she would prefer to live with Riley instead of going
to boarding school when her mother remarries. The idea proves
practical and agreeable to all.

2. Adams, Florence. MUSHY EGGS. New York: Putnam, 1973.
    (OP) Illus. by Marilyn Hirsh. Unp. Grades K-2. R+
    The lives of David, 7, and his brother Sam, 4, are enriched
by their devoted Italian-immigrant babysitter Fanny, who has mas-
tered the art of scrambling eggs exactly the way they like them.
Mom is a computer programmer who is also an adept home handy-
person. She built them a play ship in their Brooklyn backyard.
Daddy is a New Jersey accountant who visits every Sunday and
shares activities and excursions with them. But it is Fanny who is
their surrogate parent on weekdays. She is as much a playmate
and companion as she is a caretaker. When Fanny announces that
she is returning to Italy, the boys are distraught. David cries and
Sam throws a tantrum. Mom stays home with them for a week of vacation, but then a new babysitter arrives. David speculates upon
whether he will come to love Molly, too, someday.

1

3.   Adler, C. S. GOOD-BYE PINK PIG. New York: Putnam,
         1985. 176p. Grades 5-7. R+
        Amanda Bickett's brother Dale, 17, tells her that the minia-
tures she receives anonymously each birthday are from her fairy
godmother. With them, the timid, bright, lonely, imaginative girl,
now 10, creates a fantasy world that is far more real and less
threatening than her anxiety-ridden life. Her favorite miniature
is Pink Pig, who provides entree to the Little World where she
wields power second only to the evil Wizard. Amanda's critical,
ambitious, perfectionist banker mother goads her and Dale to be aggressive and competitive in achieving her lofty expectations of them.
At school, Mother orders Amanda to avoid the lady custodian Pearly,
who is also Amanda's paternal grandmother and whose weak, wife-
emasculated son deserted the family when Amanda was born. Mother
disapproves of Pearly because she is uneducated and uncouth, but
Amanda appreciates her for her tolerance and kindness. In defiance
of Mother, Amanda visits Pearly's ramshackle house every day after
school. There she is accepted as she is, enjoys the pets she has
always been denied, learns about her father, and discovers that
Pearly is her "fairy godmother." Bolstered with new confidence,
Amanda exiles the Wizard from the Little World. With that symbolic
act she asserts greater control over her own life, and her fantasies
vanish with her insecurities. The revelation that Mother has been
embezzling from a bank account to put Dale through college when
he fails to win a scholarship exposes her own human frailties. Dale
breaks the apron strings to join the army, and a humbler Mother
agrees to let Amanda live temporarily with her grandmother while
she starts a new life far away.

4.   Adler, C. S. ROADSIDE VALENTINE. New York: Macmillan,
         1983. 185p. Grades 6-10. R+
        Eight years ago when Jamie Landes, now 17, was only 9, his
mother ran off with a Jamaican sea captain. While he had difficulty
forgiving her for finding happiness, he enjoyed visiting her on vacations until she died in an auto accident. Thereafter he has found
it impossible to live up to his dedicated cardiologist father's rigid
standards and turned, in his mid teens, to alcohol and drugs. Now
clean, he still lacks motivation in school and cannot convince his
father of his sincerity in wanting to enter the medical profession
also. In the meantime, his feelings for longtime Schenectady friend
Louisa Murphy have changed from platonic to romantic. Not only
does she fail to take him seriously but she already has a steady
boyfriend. His quixotic gesture of sculpting a roadside Valentine
of snow only embarrasses Louisa. The public display, moreover, infuriates his father who subjects him to a diatribe on his puerility.
Unable to remain under the same roof and suffer such debasing
vituperation, Jamie moves out, takes a job, and invites his father
to dinner to prove his maturity and independence, hoping that their
frigid relationship will thaw. Dad finally bares his soul, divulging
his expectation that his beloved wife would return to him, and his
bitterness when she died. And to Jamie's jubilation, Louisa breaks

up with Vince and places an ad in the personals: "Louisa loves Jamie."

5. Adler, C. S. THE SILVER COACH. New York: Coward, McCann and Geoghegan, 1979. 122p. Grades 5-7. R
     As the older daughter, Chris, 12, feels that her newly divorced mother imposes upon her and shows favoritism toward her cute but temperamental little sister Jackie, 7. Now Mother has enrolled in intensive nurse's training and has brought the girls to spend the summer with the paternal grandmother they have never met in Vermont. Chris is apprehensive and plans immediately to leave with her father when he comes to visit. Grandmother turns out to be pleasant, frank, reassuring, intuitive and imaginative. She even shares with Chris the delicate filigreed ornamental coach that she has found useful for dispelling gloom when she is lonely. Chris takes many flights of fancy aboard the magic coach, always to blissful adventures with her father. Daddy eventually appears-- but with his new girlfriend and her three bumptious boys--and reveals himself as the shallow, selfish, immature person he is, a disappointment to his mother and a bitter disillusionment to Chris and even Jackie. In helping her sister adjust emotionally, Chris overcomes her jealousy of Jackie and learns to be more tolerant of and cooperative with her mother through Grandmother's insightful guidance. Mother is quick to appreciate the transformation in her girls.

6. Agle, Nan Hayden. SUSAN'S MAGIC. New York: Seabury, 1973. (OP) Illus. by Charles Robinson. 140p. Grades 3-5. R
     Imaginative, possessive, and sometimes selfish Susan Prescott, 9, acquires a cat which her freelance writer mother forbids her to keep. Old Mrs. Gaffney, an antiques dealer, offers to keep Sereena for her, but the cat escapes. Susan is distraught because everything dear to her seems to disappear, beginning with her father who left her mother for another woman and now lives in St. Louis, far from their Baltimore home. Sereena returns to Mrs. Gaffney, and Susan feels as jealous as her mother must have felt on losing her husband. Still, she goes to visit the cat at Mrs. Gaffney's, where she covets an old dollhouse that Mrs. Gaffney agrees to let her purchase for a pittance in exchange for work around the shop. A museum appraiser values the dollhouse at a fortune which would enable Mrs. Gaffney to afford repairs on her dilapidated house and keep her shop, but she loyally honors her commitment to Susan. Dad, who is cavalier in his promises to visit Susan, shows up unexpectedly but departs almost immediately without a backward glance. Susan is almost glad to see him go. She decides to yield to reality and let go of things. As her third major sacrifice, she allows her mother to talk her into giving up the dollhouse for Mrs. Gaffney's benefit.

7. Alexander, Anne. TO LIVE A LIE. New York: Atheneum, 1975. Illus. by Velma Ilsley. 165p. Grades 6-8. R+

As Noel Jennifer, 11, living with her father in a new town, begins junior high school, she resolves to start a new life based on fiction: to repudiate the first name her mother derided, to tell everyone that her mother is dead, not divorced, and to escape further heartache by making no friends. Mom, she reasons, never wanted her in the first place, blamed the separation on her, caused her to lose her old friends, and deserted the children, forcing Jennifer to keep house for Dad, Ronnie, and little Linda. The first two deceptions are surprisingly easy to carry off, but the decision to make no friends is difficult when everyone is so congenial. Only one girl goes out of her way to be disagreeable and inquisitive about her past, necessitating further obfuscations and compounding Jennifer's misery. When Mom sends her a present for her birthday, she returns it unopened in unspoken indignation for all she has suffered on her account, instigating repercussions that end in total catharsis, new revelations, and renewed relationships based on a firm foundation.

8. Ames, Mildred. PHILO POTTS OR THE HELPING HAND STRIKES
     AGAIN. New York: Scribner, 1982. 184p. Grades 5-7. R+
     In spite of the fact that Philo Potts, 11, and his dad, a school custodian, are buddies, Philo is often lonely and wishes for a dog to keep him company in their Los Angeles mobile home. While his babysitter, old Miss Jolly, is watching soap operas in her own trailer, Philo talks to his "photo-mother" whose presence is very real to him. He is annoyed with Poppy for committing himself to a woman friend, Marilyn, on Sundays when they habitually share an excursion. With a friend, he decides to kidnap a neglected pet dog to teach the owners a lesson. When Mopey gets loose and joins a pack of half-wild dogs, their problems escalate. They decide to tame all the dogs, which they are secreting in a condemned house, and find homes for them. It takes all their resources just to feed them, but when the dogs take sick, the vet bills are beyond their means. Miss Jolly sympathetically assists them, hinting to Philo that his father may marry Marilyn and that his mother deserted them and is not dead as he supposed. Poppy admits he lied to spare Philo's feelings and to cloak his own bitterness. The photo Philo worships is that of an anonymous actress. Disillusioned, he runs off to his hideaway where he is cornered by a gang of toughs. Following his rescue and the capture of the thugs, Philo becomes a celebrity. His dogs are adopted, and Marilyn takes the leader of the pack, Philo's favorite.

9. Ames, Mildred. WHAT ARE FRIENDS FOR? New York: Scrib-
     ner, 1978. 145p. Grades 5-7. R+
     Michelle Mudd, 11, spots Amy Warner, also 11, as a fellow child of divorce the moment she moves into her Redondo Beach apartment building. They become circumstantial friends in spite of their vastly different personalities. Amy is invited to join the popular clique until the group learns that she is Michelle's friend. Both are convinced that children from broken homes are automatically

ostracized. Amy is bitter that her father left her and her advertising writer mother to marry a woman with three children and refuses to visit him, but Michelle is positively vindictive about her
father's disloyalty. Not only does she manipulate his guilt for her
material benefit but she also works witchcraft on his girlfriend
Diana. When Amy gives her a prized "penny wooden" doll from
her antique doll collection, Michelle turns it into an effigy of Diana
and mutilates it. The two have a temporary falling out over the
incident; the voodoo, moreover, proves ineffectual when Michelle's
dad announces he is marrying Diana. Later Amy learns that Michelle
is a kleptomaniac when she is caught shoplifting and steals a valuable doll for Amy. Judged mentally ill, not criminal, Michelle is
sent to live with her psychiatrist father. Like divorced couples,
Amy knows she is better off without her. She decides to talk to
her dad when he calls on her birthday and to make friendly overtures to the neighborhood girls.

10.   Anderson, Mary. YOU CAN'T GET THERE FROM HERE. New
        York: Atheneum, 1982. 194p. Grades 9-12. R+
        Her father deserted to regain his lost youth and find fulfill-
ment with a 20-year-old waitress; her mother, a former housewife/
clubwoman/volunteer, now works as a receptionist and attends evening classes; her brother Jamie is away at college. Recent high
school graduate Regina Whitehall, 17, feels abandoned and rootless
in Larchmont. Her interest in the theater draws her to the New
York studio of hypnotic dramatist Adam Bentley, whose students
perform in extraordinarily intense and sensitive dark dramas which
he calls "organic theater." She begs to become one of his resident
students, all homeless like herself, begins private lessons which are
really provocative psychiatric counseling sessions, and is soon cast
in the leading role of a disturbing psychodrama. As she struggles,
with Adam's coaching, to reach the core of her character, she becomes increasingly depressed until she cracks under the pressure
during a performance. Her brother, who happens to be in the
audience, insists that she leave Adam's sphere of influence until she
regains her senses. Now armed with suspicion, she ransacks
Adam's office and finds evidence that he records his students' raw
emotions and fantasies, creating plays from them and casting the
disturbed actors as themselves. Instead of releasing them from
their problems in his mentoring sessions, he exploits and aggravates
their confusions. Regina returns home to seek a common bond with
her mother and compare rites of passage.

11.   Angell, Judie. TINA GOGO. Scarsdale: Bradbury, 1978.
        196p. Grades 5-7. R
        Tough, aggressive Bettina Gogolavsky, 11, attaches herself
like glue to sensitive, naïve Sarajane Punch, also 11, who helps her
family run a restaurant at a New York resort lake. Tina tells S.J.
that she is vacationing with Jim and Emily Harris while her wealthy
mother is traveling in Europe. Abrasive and obnoxious at times,
vulnerable and sympathetic at others, she seems to need Sarajane

more than S.J. needs her. When Sarajane learns from the Harrises
that Tina has been a ward of the court since the age of 6 and that
the Harrises, her fourth set of foster parents, plan to adopt her,
she compassionately does not betray Tina's harmless, face-saving
fiction. The two unlikely companions become close friends. Sarajane's parents put Tina to work in the restaurant, and she proves
to be a diligent and reliable helper. But one day Tina doesn't appear, and Sarajane discovers to her astonishment that she is in New
York City visiting her mother, a semi-invalid who lives on welfare.
Mrs. Gogolavsky belatedly wants to make a home for Tina after
shedding an unsavory lover, and the court is allowing the child to
make the choice between returning to her mother or remaining with
the Harrises who can offer her the opportunity for enrichment and
security that she craves. Tina accepts the challenge of aiding her
mother in her struggle for independence but also makes a commitment to visit the Harrises--and Sarajane--on weekends. As a parting gesture, she gives S.J. the locket her mother gave her years
before to which she has clung as a symbol of hope.

12.   Angell, Judie. WHAT'S BEST FOR YOU. Scarsdale: Brad-
       bury, 1981. 187p. Grades 6-9. R++
       Her three best friends only half-jokingly call themselves the
Shuffleboard Generation. All daughters of divorced couples, they
are shuffled between parents on weekends strictly at the parents'
convenience and often to the detriment of their own plans. While
Lenore Currie's parents are also divorced--her mother having moved
to New York where she conducts market surveys while attending
graduate school--they genuinely heed their children's needs and make
a real effort to do what's best for them. Lenore, 15, and her mother
have always had a personality conflict which escalates as she gets
older and more independent, so she is spending the summer in their
hometown of Long Branch with her more casual father who is in
broadcasting. Allison, 12, and Joel, 7, stay with their mother with
the expectation that Lenore will join them in the fall when she begins high school. Lenore and her father begin dating at about the
same time and, after some initial awkwardness, discover that they
can discuss candidly their changing social lives. Every visit with
her mother, however, ends with a misunderstanding and Lenore's
flight back home. Eventually they agree to make permanent her
living arrangements with her father. Allison, meanwhile, is taking
her responsibility for Joel and the apartment too seriously, usurping
the mother's role. Recognizing the danger signals, they arrange
psychological counseling for her. Unlike one-sided stories written
from the point of view of the protagonist only, this unusual book
probes the emotions of all the family members and the parents' flex-
ibility and willingness to compromise for the sake of the children.

13.   Angier, Bradford, and Barbara Corcoran. ASK FOR LOVE AND
       THEY GIVE YOU RICE PUDDING. Boston: Houghton Miff-
       lin, 1977. 151p. Grades 7-12. R
       His wealthy, imperious, vindictive grandmother refers to the

father who deserted him and his mother when he was 5 as an un-
faithful, irresponsible crook, "not one of us." Robbie Benson, now
18, lives with her and his grandfather, who has been non compos
mentis since his last stroke, while his alcoholic mother is drying out
in a European sanitorium. Despite his privileged status, Robbie is
an outcast at his Massachusetts high school where he not only has
been spurned by the girl he likes but has also been rejected by
every Ivy League school he has applied to, much to his grandmother's disgust. Having kept a journal since the age of 11, Robbie
is fascinated to find one belonging to his father, who has been incommunicado since his desertion. The entries reveal that his father
was deeply in love with his college sweetheart, who was forced into
an unhappy marriage by her father. Rex Benson married Robbie's
mother Della on the rebound but was always drawn back to his
former flame whenever she beckoned. Della was furious to learn
that she was pregnant, and their doomed union disintegrated when
Robbie's grandfather lost his investment in Rex's ill-fated business
venture. When Grandfather dies and Grandmother leaves to visit
relatives, Robbie follows an impulse to locate his father in San Diego.
He learns firsthand that Dad is decent and sentimental but weak and
ineffectual. He decides to defer college and, with his inheritance,
to go to Italy to become reacquainted with his mother.

14.   Avi.   SOMETIMES I THINK I HEAR MY NAME.   New York:
         Pantheon, 1982. 144p. Grades 7-9. R
         Conrad Murray, 13, thinks that his aunt and uncle, with
whom he has lived in St. Louis since his parents' divorce four
years ago, are deliberately preventing him from visiting his parents
when they plan to send him to England on spring vacation. At the
travel agency he tries to exchange tickets with Nancy Sperling, a
peculiar private school student whose parents also live in New York.
Failing that, he decides to jump plane during his layover there and
find his parents, whom he believes to be Broadway stars. Nancy
and her sister, who occupy their own apartment on a lower floor of
their parents' luxurious apartment building, allow him to stay with
them. With Nancy, a distant and seemingly emotionless girl, he
makes expeditions to track down his very elusive parents, knowing
all the while that his aunt and uncle are frantic with worry over his
disappearance. His father turns out to be pathetically nervous, ef-
fusive and apologetic, doing all his acting as a menial salesman.
His mother is glitzy and fatuous, pitching cigarettes at shopping
malls. Conrad's appearance is an acute embarrassment and annoyance to both of them. Bitterly disillusioned, he learns only later
that Nancy's opulent existence is merely a mask for a barren life
and parents who are stuntingly cold, superficial and pretentious.
The troubled girl is sent away to a Swiss school, but she and Conrad agree to think of one another at a certain time every day.
Conrad is relieved to return home.

15.   Bach, Alice. A FATHER EVERY FEW YEARS.   New York:
         Harper and Row, 1977. 130p. Grades 6-9. R+

Max Cartwright, who married Tim's mother when the boy was 6, was always more of a father to him than was Ben, his biological father who deserted them when Tim was a toddler. Now Max, too, an aspiring screenwriter, has departed unexpectedly. Tim, 12, can't help but notice his mother Margot's melancholia and he broods about her expenditures on her erratic income as a realtor. He is convinced that they both need a man to take care of them. At the same time he is disturbed by his best friend Joey's progressive hemophilia and by the fact that his older chum, Melanie, is seeing more of her pseudo-sophisticated, boy-crazy freshman crowd and ignoring him (although Tim himself has a normal, healthy curiosity about Melanie's increasingly obvious sexual development). When Margot proposes a trip to California, Tim demurs because of the expense, yet he fears that his mother will locate Max and stay with him, squeezing Tim out altogether. He remains behind with Melanie's family while Margot goes, and by her rosy reports he deduces that she has found Max and will be returning with him. Tim plans a welcome home party for Max and is badly deflated when Max does not appear. Mother and son have an earnest talk in which she affirms that she mourned Max but is now ready to be independent and self-reliant, even if it means taking a salaried job, and so can Tim be.

16.   Baehr, Patricia. FAITHFULLY, TRU. New York: Macmillan,
       1984. 203p. Grades 6-10. R+
       It is bad enough that Tru Price's mother, a teacher, opens their New York beach home to elderly Aunt Paige, who is irritating, illiterate and intrusive, but it is nearly intolerable when Tru has to give up her room when her mother compassionately takes in a cousin and her illegitimate son. Tru, 15, escapes to the beach to pursue her muse, poetry, and to give vent to her feelings of guilt over her uncharitable attitude toward the interlopers and to her doubts about her mother's rigid, stodgy Catholicism. There she meets a liberal-minded novelist who has rented a house for the off season and who urges her to reject the lockstep of religion in order to express her creativity. Tru learns that the writer, Jack Price, is none other than her father, whom she had been led to believe was dead and whom her mother never divorced because of religious scruples. He explains that he was compelled to sacrifice his family for the sake of his art. When her mother forbids her to see him, they quarrel. Tru decides that she would rather live with Jack, whose resemblance to her is both physical and intellectual. Jack and his girlfriend of the moment have different ideas, however, and when he brutally critiques her poetry, Tru recognizes his utter selfishness, exploitation of others, deification of his craft, and lack of empathy and responsibility. In her rejection and confusion she finds herself attracted to a boy who is as ambivalent about religion as she. Tru resolves to be her own person, neither a copy of her undemonstrative, dutiful mother nor her calculating, devil-may-care father.

17.   Barnwell, Robinson. SHADOW ON THE WATER. New York:

David McKay, 1967. (OP) 216p. Grades 6-8. R

While romantic, aristocratic, city-bred Mama and pragmatic, undemonstrative, country-bred Papa are bickering more and more acrimoniously over the disposition of money and other amenities, they are communicating less and less as the lingering Great Depression continues its siege of their South Carolina truck farm. Maternal grandmother Talbot prevails upon Mama to file for legal separation and move into her gracious Virginia mansion with the two younger children, Camden, 13, and Talbot, 6, much to the youngsters' dismay. Onetime tomboy Cammie adjusts to society life and the prospect of a new boyfriend better than brother Tal, but both miss home, father, and old friends. Beloved paternal grandfather Rutledge's death reunites the family, including attractive older sister Charlotte, 18, but a reconciliation between their parents seems hopeless until a posthumous letter is found from Grandpa to Mama, telling her that Papa has always loved her and needed her but is too stubborn to articulate it.

18. Bauer, Marion Dane. SHELTER FROM THE WIND. New York: Seabury, 1976. 108p. Grades 7-9. R+

For five years after her mother, loathing the heat, dust and wind of the Oklahoma panhandle, ran off with another man, Stacy, now 12, and her father managed to live comfortably. Suddenly her father remarried and his new wife is about to bear their child. Fulminating with fury at Barbara's intrusive presence and disgusted with the reproductive process, Stacy runs away to try to find her mother. Almost overcome by exposure and dehydration on the desert, she is led by pet dogs to the primitive abode of independent Old Ella, who takes her in until she is ready to go on, teaching her self-reliance and responsibility. Through encounters with unsentimental Ella and Mr. Henderson, who brings her supplies once a month, Stacy vaguely recalls that her mother was an alcoholic who probably wouldn't want her even if she found her. The bittersweet whelping of Nimue's pups and its aftermath teach her the miracle of birth and the futility of hating. She decides to return to her father and stepmother but to visit Ella often.

19. Beatty, Patricia. ME, CALIFORNIA PERKINS. New York: Morrow, 1968. (OP) Illus. by Liz Dauber. 253p. Grades 4-6. R

Rapscallion Uncle Hiram inveigles peripatetic Pa to sell the Perkins' comfortable home in Sacramento in the 1880s and seek his fortune in the silver mining hamlet of Mojaveville on the desert, "the Creator's dumping ground," according to Mama, who has followed Pa resignedly from California to Oregon to Washington and back again, naming each of their three children, 13, 11, and 10, for the state in which he was born. This desolation, however, is too much for Mama, who with the children moves into the only habitable domicile, a house made of whiskey bottles, leaving Pa to bunk in iniquitous bachelor diggings until he comes to his senses and is willing to move back to civilization. In the meantime she clerks in the mercantile

store and, with the collusion of the boarding house proprietress,
intrepidly conspires to bring law and order, running water, and a
schoolteacher to town.   Uncle Hiram almost sabotages the school by
conducting the board of trustees like a marriage brokerage, but
Mama prevails.   Pa is stubborn too, and it isn't until the eldest
daughter California is ready for high school that he recognizes her
need for higher education and rejoins the family.

20.   Benjamin, Carol Lea.   THE WICKED STEPDOG.   New York:
          Crowell, 1982.   Illus. by the author.   Grades 4-6.   R+
          After her parents divorced two years ago when her glamorous
mother started a career in soap operas, Louise Branford, 12, has remained with her architect father in their Manhattan apartment where
they have settled into a comfortable, laissez-faire routine.   No one
consulted Louise about the divorce, nor does Dad consult her before
announcing that he will soon be marrying Evelyn, his homely Jewish
cartoonist friend.   Louise confides her resentment to Carly Altman,
with whom she also shares her concerns about adolescence.   Not only
does Evelyn monopolize the bathroom and close the bedroom door, she
also asks Louise to shop for health food and walk her clumsy, ubiquitous retriever, carrying a pooper scooper.   As onerous as the dog
is, at least he gives Louise something in common with Ryan Bernstein,
the boy on whom she has a crush, who also owns a dog and extols
the virtues of health food.   Although Evelyn shows sensitivity toward Louise by buying her her first bra, Louise fears that Evelyn
and Dad will have a baby of their own who will supplant her, and
she even contemplates suicide as an attention-getting device.   On a
private breakfast date, Dad reassures her that she will be loved no
matter what happens, and when Ryan asks her to go dog-walking in
Central Park, she complies with alacrity.

21.   Bennett, Jay.   THE KILLING TREE.   New York: Watts, 1972.
          121p.   Grades 7-10.   R
          There is an ominous mood at the airport when Fred Wilk,
17, goes to meet Walter Carlton, longtime friend and associate of
Fred's anthropologist father, who is returning from Africa to bring
him a rare old Mende statue, sole legacy of the elder Wilk who died
in Sierra Leone.   Almost immediately Fred starts receiving death
threats from a black African who wants him to give up the statue,
claiming it is a sacred tribal relic.   Knowing that his father would
never steal such an object, Fred stubbornly ignores the African and
hides the figure in the Brooklyn Heights apartment he shares with
his undemonstrative, well organized mother, an account executive
with an advertising agency who had divorced his father years ago.
Fred had planned to leave his mother at 18 and go to share the excitement of his father's life; now he wishes that Walter could be his
companion.   A ride in the subway with a menacing white African
brings Fred hurrying to Walter's elegant Manhattan apartment for
reassurance, but upon leaving he is kidnapped and pistol-whipped
by desperate thugs determined to ferret out the statue which they
believe holds a fortune in diamonds.   He is saved only by the

intervention of the black African, but he is still in deadly peril
from the man he trusts, Walter Carlton, who had double-crossed
and killed Fred's father. Only when justice has been served does
Fred learn the shattering truth about his father and make peace
with his mother.

22.   Blue, Rose. A MONTH OF SUNDAYS. New York: Watts,
        1972. (OP) Illus. by Ted Lewin. 60p. Grades 3-5. R+
        Jeffrey, 10, returns from summer camp to learn that his
parents are divorcing and that he and his mother are moving to
New York City. He is disconsolate at leaving behind the suburban
pursuits of Little League, biking and bowling, and dismayed at
the melange of black, hispanic, and Jewish kids in his inner-city
classroom. Dad tries too hard to entertain him when he calls for
him on Sundays, and Mom is too tired when she gets home from
work to cook his favorite dishes or even talk to him. A dynamic
young teacher helps him adjust to his classmates and take an interest in school projects, but his other problems remain. He blames
his mother for taking him away from his father and being just a
part-time mom. He unburdens himself to a friend's mother who
tactfully alerts Jeffrey's mother to the boy's feelings. Mom makes
a special effort to contribute to the big block party, and Dad takes
him to the park just to play catch as they used to do. When his
old gang invites him back, he finds he is too busy making plans
with his new friends.

23.   Blume, Judy. IT'S NOT THE END OF THE WORLD. Scarsdale:
        Bradbury, 1972. 169p. Grades 5-8. R+
        Twelve-year-old Karen's paramount concern is to keep her
separated parents from divorcing. She finds it totally inconceivable
and unacceptable that her father should want to move away from
home and live apart from her and her brother and sister. It is
difficult to adjust to the change in daily routine, her mother's new
job, and the restaurant meals with Daddy, even though peace has
been restored since her father's departure. She tries every wishful
scheme to reunite her parents. Her brother runs away and precipitates a crisis she feels sure will reconcile them, but it only
leads to more recrimination and spite. When she recognizes how futile her mission is and how miserable her parents make one another,
acceptance becomes easier.

24.   Bond, Nancy. COUNTRY OF BROKEN STONE. New York:
        Atheneum, 1980. 271p. Grades 6-9. R+
        Because her stepmother, divorced American archaeologist
Dr. Valerie Prine, is on assignment on the Roman ruins near Had-
rian's Wall, Penelope Ibbetson's blended family is spending the summer there during the worst drought in memory. The step-siblings,
Penelope, 14, her brother Martin, 18, and Valerie's children, twins
Mark and Luke, 12, and Louisa, 8, get along well with each other
and also with attractive, humorous, straightforward Valerie. Pennie's father Ted, a temperamental mystery novelist, is serving as

househusband for the summer. While left alone to babysit Lou,
outgoing Pennie makes friends with a diffident, defensive local
boy, Ran Robson, whose tenant farmer family is hostile to the interlopers after being evicted from the site of the excavation. The expedition is plagued with ill fortune, and Pennie, knowing that Ran
may be unjustly accused of sabotaging it, keeps their friendship a
secret. A misunderstanding and poor judgment on Ted's part leads
to Lou's apparent disappearance on the day that the tinder-dry
fells catch fire. Valerie is frantic with worry, and everyone is
temporarily furious with Ted. When all is forgiven, Valerie confesses to Pennie that she married Ted not only for love but also because she was afraid of growing old alone. Although the expedition
has to be cancelled because of the arson-induced conflagration, the
summer has been a valuable experience for Pennie, who has learned
a great deal about love, loyalty, trust and maturity.

25.   Bond, Nancy. A PLACE TO COME BACK TO. New York:
        Atheneum, 1984. 187p. Grades 7-10. R+
        From the time of his mother's divorce when he was 8, Oliver
Shattuck, now 15, was consigned to boarding schools, his mother
being too career-oriented to make a home for him. Since her remarriage two years ago, Oliver has come to live with his great-uncle,
Commodore Shattuck, in Massachusetts, where the two share com-
patible bachelor digs with Oliver's ungainly mastiff Amos. Oliver
forms a tight quartet with contemporaries Charlotte Paige and Kath
and Andy Schuyler. Then the Commodore dies unexpectedly in his
sleep, and Oliver's future becomes uncertain. It seems inevitable
that he will be forced against his will to accompany his mother and
stepfather to London, and he bitterly blames his uncle for dying before he finished high school. Always taciturn and ticklish, Oliver
now becomes inscrutable and withdrawn, unburdening himself to
Charlotte only on the day he coerces her to cut school. He stoically
declares his intention of having the dog Amos put to sleep and
presses Charlotte to become engaged to him during his absence, a
promise that she is not ready to make. As a compromise, she
demonstrates her high regard for him by volunteering to make a
home for his beloved pet despite her antipathy for animals.
Oliver seems satisfied with her limited commitment.

26.   Bradbury, Bianca. BOY ON THE RUN. New York: Seabury,
        1975. (OP) 126p. Grades 5-7. R+
        Nick, 12, is a victim of smother love. His father is a remar-
ried Washington VIP who is too busy to act paternal, and he lives
with his over-anxious, self-indulgent mother in a prison of plush
and perfume. Feeling cramped one day, he opens the apartment
window and sends her cherished china crashing to the pavement of
Manhattan below, is diagnosed as severely disturbed, and is remanded to his mother's punctilious psychiatrist. Seeing an opportunity to escape his gilded cage en route to his grandmother's summer home, the astute boy turns some belongings into cash and
adroitly engineers his bid for freedom on a neighboring resort island.

There he dyes his hair to escape detection, buys a bike and survival gear, and enjoys a week of independence and adventure in
which he acquires his first pet and first friend and learns that he
doesn't need the tranquilizers Dr. Ada Carter-White so liberally dispenses. Arriving at his grandmother's house, he finds that he can
deal more effectively and incisively with both parents.

27. Bridgers, Sue Ellen. NOTES FOR ANOTHER LIFE. New York:
    Knopf, 1981. 250p. Grades 7-12. R++
        Bliss Jackson, tennis player, piano teacher, gardener, home-
maker, and wife of pharmacist Bill Jackson, has reared her two
grandchildren with sagacity, compassion, grace and competence since
her son was hospitalized by mental illness and their mother became
an interior designer in Atlanta. Wren, 13, has inherited her grandmother's gift for music and is introspective but well adjusted.
Kevin, 16, shares Bliss' athletic ability and works part-time for his
grandfather, but he is frequently moody--half fearful that his
father's illness is hereditary, half guilty that he, as the elder child,
may have caused it. Now their father has responded to treatment
and is coming home, and their mother is also returning with important news. Kevin is hopeful that they will become a family again,
but his chic and beautiful mother dashes his hopes by announcing
that she is seeking a divorce and moving to Chicago to accept a
promotion. Feeling rejected by both his mother and his girlfriend
who has just jilted him, Kevin tries to commit suicide by swallowing
a bottle of Seconal capsules from the pharmacy. Saved by Bliss and
counseled by an astute young minister, Kevin pulls himself together
even when his father relapses and has to return to the hospital.
With penetrating insight and highly credible dialogue, the author
probes the minds of her three major protagonists.

28. Brooks, Jerome. UNCLE MIKE'S BOY. New York: Harper
    and Row, 1973. (OP) 226p. Grades 5-7. R
        Since Barbara Lewen divorced her immature, pathetic, and
disgustingly drunk ex-college professor husband, she has become
fixated on psychotherapy, giving Pudge, 11, full responsibility for
his sister Sharon, 8. The two draw close in their mutual isolation
and emotional need, and when Sharon is killed accidentally while in
his charge, Pudge, already tormented by his peers for his obesity
and chafing at the injustices of his rigid, unsympathetic teacher, is
in danger of losing control. His astute, widowed paternal uncle
quickly stretches a safety net under the high-strung boy, offering
him a job in his Chicago shoe store, committing his dad to a hospital
for treatment of his alcoholism and depression, and becoming a substitute father and role model. His mother, who has gone back to
work, starts dating--and soon marries--the school's basketball coach
whom she met at Parents Without Partners and whose son, Pete, is
a school leader. Apprehensive, Pudge discovers that Pete is un-
pretentious and that he needn't feel inferior to him nor guilty for
his own shortcomings. He decides to accentuate his strengths and
minimize his weaknesses, and, while his father does not remain sober, Uncle Mike is still there to bolster Pudge when he falters.

29. Bunting, Eve. THE ROBOT BIRTHDAY. New York: Dutton,
        1980. Illus. by Marie DeJohn. 80p. Grades 2-4. NR
        Glum because of their parents' recent divorce and their
move to a new house, twins Kerry and Pam are convinced that this
birthday party, to which Mom has invited four unfamiliar and possibly hostile neighborhood kids, is going to be the worst in history.
Then, through the door, stalks a walking, talking, larger-than-
lifesize robot man! Mom, an electronics teacher, has made it with
the help of her students and equipped it with a tape recorder to
speak whatever the children record. Naturally Kerry and Pam are
the envy of their new acquaintances, who quickly cement their
friendship. Robot also proves his usefulness in routing a gang of
older bullies that monopolizes the playground equipment reserved
for kids under ten. Using the remote control button, the twins
guide him to clank through the gates and confront the gang, speaking sternly in the voice of the intimidating TV exercise man whom
their babysitter records. But Robot becomes a real hero on a
stormy Christmas Eve drive to their grandparents' house when they
come to a washed-out bridge and station Robot in the middle of the
road with lighted eyes flashing and voice box amplified to warn
other motorists of the danger.

30. Butler, Beverly. CAPTIVE THUNDER. New York: Dodd,
        Mead, 1969. (OP) 205p. Grades 6-10. R+
        Angry, rebellious Nancy Essen, 17, has convinced herself
that she is in love with the town's "misunderstood" lowlife, Wayne
Albrecht, 21, who mooches her babysitting money to buy cigarettes.
She begs him to elope with her so that she can escape from her
prying, suspicious, critical, recriminating mother, a creamery
worker. When Wayne weasels out of the responsibility, she runs
away to the home of her mother's younger sister in Milwaukee, intent on finding the father who left home when she was 2. Aunt
Barbara is relaxed, tolerant, trusting and companionable. When
Wayne comes to visit them she gives him enough rope to hang himself, and Nancy finally sees him as the churl he is. She takes a
summer job in a fast-food franchise to finance her prospective move
to another state to elude Wisconsin's truancy law. When the father
she has lionized in her dreams arrives unexpectedly, he is flashy,
shallow and sybaritic. He tells her what she wants to hear--that
her life is her own and she should do as she pleases--but strangely
she feels let down. She realizes that her mother's strict supervision and exacting standards demonstrate that she really cares.
Despite Aunt Barbara's offer of a permanent home, Nancy returns
to her mother to finish high school.

31. Byars, Betsy. THE CARTOONIST. New York: Viking, 1978.
        Illus. by Richard Cuffari. 119p. Grades 5-7. R+
        Pap, Alfie's grandfather, curses the bureaucracy by day
and reminisces incessantly by night. His mother is glued to the TV
except when she's haranguing Pap to shut up. His sister Alma
bears the brunt of household responsibility, and Alfie escapes the

discord by retreating to his windowless attic crawl space, reached
only by trap door, where he keeps the art supplies with which he
covertly draws wry scenes based on the acerbic life around him.
Then one day his mother informs him that his larcenous, unemployed,
scapegrace older brother Bubba, his mother's favorite, and his ex-
pectant wife are coming to live with them, and she intends to fur-
nish them Alfie's private domain. Stricken and angry, Alfie barri-
cades himself in the attic, and no threat or entreaty will bring him
down, though Pap and Alma secretly side with him. When Bubba's
plans change and Alfie is reprieved, his mother taunts him that he
has not been victorious but has won only by default. He decides
to bring his cartoons out of concealment and work in public.

32. Byars, Betsy. CRACKER JACKSON. New York: Viking,
       1985. 147p. Grades 5-7. R++
       Although she denies it, Jackson Hunter, 11, knows that
his beloved former babysitter, who now has a child of her own, is
being physically abused by her cruel and possessive mechanic husband. Alma, whose pet nickname for him is Cracker Jackson, has
warned him to stay away from her and the baby so he won't become
a target of Billy Ray's irrational violence. But Jackson knows he
must intercede somehow before the naive, optimistic young woman is
critically injured or worse. He can't appeal to his parents for help.
Alma, in shame, has exacted his promise not to tell his mother, a
stewardess. His father, divorced for three years and living far
away, forbids him to go to Alma's house out of concern for his
safety. When Billy Ray wreaks his anger on the baby, Alma agrees
to go to a battered wives' shelter in the next town. Jackson
"borrows" his mother's car for the suspenseful hour's drive--only
to have Alma renege at the last moment. When Alma fails to keep
an appointment with Jackson's mother, Mrs. Hunter concedes that
something is wrong and goes into action. She arrives in time to
call an ambulance for the seriously hurt mother and child. When
her adored baby finally recovers, Alma accepts the inevitability of
entering the shelter while still grieving over her broken marital
dreams.

33. Caines, Jeannette: DADDY. New York: Harper and Row,
       1977. Illus. by Ronald Himler. Unp. Grades K-2. R+
       When Windy's father comes to pick her up every Saturday
morning, he is always in a playful, loving, teasing mood. They are
greeted at his apartment by Daddy's wife Paula, who joins in their
camaraderie and sews new clothes for Windy. On a Saturday when
she is sick, Daddy comes to visit her and cheer her up, but she
looks forward to the following week and their plans to fly a kite
from his roof. During the week Windy develops "wrinkles" in her
stomach from worry and anticipation, but when Daddy arrives on
Saturday morning, her cares are dispelled by their special little
rituals and togetherness.

34. Calvert, Patricia. THE MONEY CREEK MARE. New York:

Scribner, 1981. 135p. Grades 7-9. R+

Saddled with a woods' colt when she was just 15, Rosanne
Carmody has always felt restless and unfulfilled. When her daughter
Ella Rae is herself 15, son Buster is 6, and baby Chloe is still in
diapers, she seizes the opportunity to follow her dream and hitches
a ride to Hollywood with a trucker who patronizes their Missouri
diner, leaving the family behind. An improvident toper, Cash
Carmody pins his own hopes of wealth on a mare he plans to breed
and is sorely disappointed to learn that the fee at the Puckett-
Smythes' stud farm is well beyond his means. Plucky Ella Rae secures a job with the Puckett-Smythes for the purpose of breeding
the mare covertly. When she is caught, she freely confesses and
promises to make restitution. Mrs. Puckett-Smythe, impressed with
her intelligence and integrity, wants to adopt her and make her over
into the daughter she never had. Although reluctant, Ella Rae cannot disappoint her for the sake of her family and courageously goes
off to finishing school. Her snobbish classmates, however, make
life miserable for her and eventually she runs away. No longer
wanted by the Puckett-Smythes, she returns to Cash, who has
stopped drinking and plans to marry the down-to-earth woman he
and the younger children love. Ella Rae replaces her flimsy hopes
for her mother's return with solid plans for the future.

35. Cameron, Eleanor. TO THE GREEN MOUNTAINS. New York:
     Dutton, 1975. 180p. Grades 6-9. R+

Kath Rule, 13, shares a room with her fastidious mother in
the shabby but respectable hotel she manages in Southern Ohio during World War I while her self-pitying husband doggedly works his
rundown farm, paying occasional conjugal visits and refusing to seek
gainful employment. A racial liberal as well as a feminist, Elizabeth
Rule encourages her Negro factotum, Will Grant, in his bid to study
law by buying him a set of secondhand law books. For this she is
ostracized by her bigoted brother-in-law, the Negro church is
burned, and a spiteful woman starts rumors about Elizabeth and Will
Grant. Devout, lighthearted Tiss, Grant's wife and good friend of
Kath and her mother, slowly but inexorably reacts to the slurs, the
torching of her beloved church, and finally to her husband's consuming and quixotic aspirations. She conducts an affair with another
man and is killed in an accident that some deem judgmental. Elizabeth is distraught and remorseful that her sterling intentions toward
the Grants backfired and caused them such tragedy. She decides
to cut her losses, divorce the husband who behaves boorishly to
her and Kath, decline the marriage proposal of the local doctor, and
move with Kath to her mother's home in Vermont, a dream Kath has
long held.

36. Carrick, Carol. WHAT A WIMP! Clarion, 1983. Illus. by
     Donald Carrick. 89p. Grades 3-5. R+

After her divorce, Mom moved with the boys, Russ, 13, and
Barney, 9, to her old rural hometown where she takes a job in a
real estate office while studying for her license. Transferring to a

new school where he is behind his classmates in math and has an
unsympathetic teacher is hard enough for Barney, but far more
traumatizing is the unwelcome attention he receives from Lenny
Coots, a sixth-grade bully, who bedevils him on the playground
and waylays him going home from school. When he reacts with fear,
anger, tears and flight, it only fuels Lenny's cruel streak. Barney
excels at art, but that only earns him more trouble when he draws
during academic periods. Both his teacher and his mother call him
on the carpet. He telephones his father for advice on handling
Lenny but is told that he must solve the problem himself. Russ
tries but fails to deter the bully, and Barney knows that if his
teacher intervenes it will result in worse harassment later on.
Driven to the limit of his endurance, Barney simply refuses to turn
tail the next time Lenny lies in wait for him. Mastering his tears,
he challenges Lenny to beat him up and get his kicks, even if he
is killed in the process. Suddenly the bully is embarrassed and
loses interest, and Barney proudly informs his father that he followed his advice.

37.   Childress, Alice. RAINBOW JORDAN. New York: Coward,
         McCann and Geoghegan, 1981. 142p. Grades 7-9. R+
         Told from the viewpoint of two disparate black women and
the perplexed teen who spans their worlds, this is the story of
three incongruously tangent lives. Kathie Jordan found herself
pregnant and married at the age of 15, but has been separated
from the child's father for most of Rainbow's life so as to qualify
for AFDC. Undereducated, unskilled, and unwilling to let her
daughter cramp her style, she disappears periodically with her boyfriend of the moment. During these periods of abandonment, Rainbow is placed in the foster care of refined, childless, middleclass
Josephine Lamont. Rainbow, now 14, is torn between loyalty to her
young, sexy, flamboyant mother and adherence to the high standards
of Miss Josie's staid household. Pressured by her boyfriend to
sleep with him and ashamed at school to admit that her mother has
abandoned her, Rainbow is often at loggerheads with Miss Josie, who
is trying to improve her potential by instilling the principles of moral
integrity, sexual responsibility, etiquette and scholarship. Then
Rainbow learns that Miss Josie has not been completely honest with
her and is less than perfect herself. When faced with her faults,
Josie softens. Rainbow admits to herself that Kathie is a poor role
model and that she can coexist with Miss Josie by cooperating more.

38.   Chorao, Kay. A MAGIC EYE FOR IDA. New York: Seabury,
         1973. Illus. by the author. Unp. Grades 1-3. R+
         Ida's only memory of the father who deserted her and her
family is the funny way he dipped his celery in butter. Her mother,
an artist who works at home, is preoccupied with her painting and
seems to ignore Ida. Her older brother Fred is absorbed in motion
pictures and exercising with barbells. In school she is overshadowed
by prissy, frilly Yolanda, whose doll collection makes Ida's worn
stuffed animal seem shabby indeed. Her mother seems oblivious to

Ida's request for a new doll and her threat to run away, so Ida
sneaks onto the subway to try to find Yolanda's house. Instead
she gets lost. Panicky, she is rescued by a friendly palmist who
invites her into her parlor and quickly ascertains Ida's strengths,
including her gift for poesy. After bolstering Ida's self-confidence,
Madam Julia gives her a magic eye necklace and drives her home.
Instead of the punishment she expects, Ida gets the undivided attention of both Mama and Fred, and at school the next day her
magic eye steals Yolanda's thunder.

39.   Christian, Mary Blount. GROWIN' PAINS. New York:
         Macmillan, 1985. 179p. Grades 6-9. R+
         Ginny Ruth Grover, 12, is convinced that her tight-fisted,
God-fearing mother drove away her light-hearted, free-spending
father three years ago. Since the cannery in their squalid, insular
Texas town closed, Maw has been cooking and cleaning at the
schoolhouse for a bare subsistence. Their only Christmas treats
are provided by a brain-damaged neighbor whose spasmodic move-
ments and halting speech Ginny Ruth used to fear. Mr. Billy
encourages her to publish her poetry in the newspaper for cash,
and she shows her appreciation by altruistically helping him with
chores. While Ginny Ruth enjoys visiting the many giddy Davis
sisters, she hates the way they mock Mr. Billy. In gathering
precious honey as a wedding gift for Alpha Davis, Ginny Ruth is
severely stung and is carried in shock to the home of her mother's
parents, who have been estranged from Maw since she married Paw
in defiance of their wishes. The crisis ends the feud, but she
and Maw decline the offer of a home with them, even though Ginny
Ruth no longer believes in her father's return as faithfully as she
used to. To achieve her goal of escaping Clemmons and getting
a proper education, she and Maw pick cotton in the searing heat.
Ginny Ruth becomes ill and wishes she were as strong and indomitable as her mother. To prove that she is a blend of maternal
pragmatism and paternal romanticism, she spends her first earnings
on a decent meal to reward her mother's toil. Maw surprises her on
her birthday by demonstrating that she can relax and compromise
also.

40.   Cleary, Beverly. DEAR MR. HENSHAW. New York: Morrow,
         1983. Illus. by Paul O. Zelinsky. 134p. Grades 4-6. R+
         Boyd Henshaw has been Leigh Botts' favorite author ever
since his second-grade teacher read his WAYS TO AMUSE A DOG
aloud to the class. When his sixth-grade teacher in Pacific Grove
assigns a report about an author, it is only natural that Leigh
write to Mr. Henshaw for background information. The author
turns the tables on him by replying with a list of ten questions of
his own for Leigh to answer. The boy is incensed, but his mother,
who works for a catering firm and studies nursing, insists that he
respond. This leads to an extended correspondence in which Leigh
unburdens himself about how his parents divorced when 'his father
became a cross-country trucker and how Dad sometimes forgets

support payments and never visits the lonely, diffident boy. Mr.
Henshaw eventually weans him from his dependence on the author
by suggesting that Leigh keep a diary to record daily events and
contemplations, including his anxiety that Dad might remarry and
acquire a more promising son. Leigh wins honorable mention in a
creative writing contest for his essay "A Day on Dad's Rig," and
suddenly his father appears to ask his mother for a second chance.
She firmly declines, but Leigh is relieved to know that while Dad
may be immature and unreliable, he misses his family and is proud
of his son.

41. Cleaver, Vera, and Bill Cleaver. ELLEN GRAE. Philadelphia:
       Lippincott, 1967. Illus. by Ellen Raskin. 89p. Grades
       5-6. R
       Eleven-year-old Ellen Grae Derryberry's custodial father
sends her to town each September to spend the school year with
the kindly McGruders, whom she alternately amuses and exasper-
ates with her tall tales and artful prevarications, particularly the
morbid ones that involve violent or bizarre death. When the silent,
simple swamp man Ira, who sells peanuts in the train depot, confides in her the gruesome circumstances of his parents' death, she
harbors his secret until she becomes physically ill, knowing that
the truth will mean either the penitentiary or the insane asylum
for the innocuous old man. Mrs. McGruder sends for Ellen Grae's
parents, who convince her that she has the moral obligation to make
a clean breast of it. When the sheriff demonstrates condescending
incredulity, she feels the mixed emotions of relief that Ira is safe
and indignation over her besmirched honor. Her effervescent elan
returns under Mrs. McGruder's warm affection, and she puts the
unpleasantness out of her mind.

42. Cleaver, Vera, and Bill Cleaver. LADY ELLEN GRAE. Phila-
       delphia: Lippincott, 1968. Illus. by Ellen Raskin. 124p.
       Grades 5-6. R
       Uninhibited Ellen Grae (see 41) is enjoying the summer of her
eleventh year when her divorced parents decide to turn her over to
her priggish aunt to learn the social graces and curb her fanciful
stories. To forestall such a fate she attempts to demonstrate that
she can behave like a lady on her own by donning false eyelashes
and getting a permanent, but her father is not fooled. Further efforts to prove her command of etiquette only succeed in nearly making
a tomboy of Cousin Laura, to Aunt Eleanor's dismay, and she whisks
both girls back to her ostentatious home in Seattle. Elegant as it is,
Ellen Grae cannot be acclimated to a life of cold and damp weather,
sleeping late, posh dinner parties, a maid to cook, clean and iron,
and worst of all, the onus of wearing gloves, nylons and a garter
belt. There is method in her madness of deliberately being struck
by the boom while out sailing, but it almost fails. It takes the
outpouring of affection from her many friends in her beloved
Thicket, Florida, to bring her home where she belongs, unspoiled.

43. Cleaver, Vera, and Bill Cleaver. ME TOO. Philadelphia:
         Lippincott, 1973. 158p. Grades 5-7. R+
     The fact that they are twins is only skin deep. Lydia
Birdsong is a precocious 12; her sister Lorna has been mentally
retarded since the age of 2, speaks her own peculiar language,
and marches to the beat of a different drummer. One day, in disgust at Lornie's immutability, their exacting scientist father deserts
the family, and their mother, a nurse, cannot afford to keep Lornie
at the school for exceptional children year 'round. She becomes
Lydia's responsibility for the summer, and the latter is determined
to succeed in reaching her twin where others have failed. While
her mother has been overprotective, Lydia institutes a strict daily
regimen of instruction designed to remake Lornie into a mirror
image of herself to show her father his error in having abandoned
them. Her patience wears thin after long, fruitless effort, and
she invokes love and prayer to no avail. Still she is unwilling to
accept the fact that Lornie has the mind of a 6-year-old. The
priggish and ignorant family of her best friend Billy Frank forbids
him to see her for fear the two may eventually marry and have a
child like Lornie. Billy himself turns traitor when he calls Lydia
a mother hen for her overzealousness. A brush with death in a
sinkhole puts life back into perspective, and Lydia can at last view
her sister with detachment as Lornie returns to the boarding
school with others of her kind.

44. Clewes, Dorothy. MISSING FROM HOME. New York: Har-
         court, Brace, Jovanovich, 1975. 150p. Grades 5-7. R+
     Their British parents loved the remote French wine country
of Provence and decided to make it their permanent home, where
Simon Grant, their father, paints and teaches art and their mother
Sara writes books. Now Simon has succumbed to the advances of
a wealthy 19-year-old art student and has run off with her to Paris.
Sara, hurt, lonely, and distraught, has flung an ultimatum after
them, prohibiting his return. Maxwell, 12, and Carrie, 14, after
several months of living in misery with Sara, decide to take a radical measure to reunite their parents by running away. They are
sheltered by a hippie commune whose young members seem sympathetic to their cause and hide them in an abandoned factory. One
of the company is avaricious, however, and plans to hold them for
ransom. They learn that their disappearance is involuntary only
when they hear a radio broadcast, and they try to escape but are
immediately apprehended. Eventually they are rescued by the
gendarmerie in an eventful and plausible climax, and the entire es-
capade has the desired effect of reconciling Sara and Simon, who
has long since become disenchanted with his selfish, callow paramour.

45. Clymer, Eleanor. LUKE WAS THERE. New York: Holt, Rine-
         hart and Winston, 1973. (OP) Illus. by Diane deGroat.
         74p. Grades 3-5. R+
     First his father went away after quarreling with his mother;
then his mother remarried and had a new baby; finally Mama's

second husband left her after more argumentation. After that Mama
went into a decline. Now she has to go to the hospital for surgery.
and a social worker takes Julius and his half-brother Danny to a
children's shelter. Julius becomes withdrawn until a cool new black
counselor named Luke earns his respect and awakens his interest in
constructive pursuits. Then one day Luke, a Conscientious Objector, is arbitrarily assigned to a V.A. hospital for his alternative
military service. Julius feels abandoned all over again and allows
himself to be drawn into a shoplifting, purse-snatching scheme.
Afraid of being arrested if he returns to the shelter, the inexperienced boy turns to the streets, parks, and abandoned buildings,
stealing, panhandling, and growing ever more hopeless. In Grand
Central Station he happens upon a small Puerto Rican waif who is
even more terrified than he and knows he must take him to the
shelter where he'll be cared for. There he finds that everyone is
frantic about his disappearance, including Luke who came back to
help search for him. Reunited with his mother, Julius always remembers that Luke was there when he needed him.

46. Colman, Hila. NOBODY HAS TO BE A KID FOREVER. New
        York: Crown, 1976. 117p. Grades 6-8. R+
        Sarah Grinnell turns 13 and becomes aware that the roles
of womanhood and parenthood, and the transition to both, are un-
clearly defined, subject to change without notice, and infinitely
baffling and aggravating. Her male-dominant father, who sacrificed
an art career to support his family, insists that his wife's place is
in the home looking after Sarah and her older sister, who is becoming seriously involved with her boyfriend. Her mother, itching to
resume the music career she mothballed for motherhood, attends
consciousness-raising meetings and grows increasingly resentful of
her husband's domineering attitude and her irksome household chores.
Meanwhile, Sarah and her former best friend develop a quasi-
rivalry over attentions from the same boy. The domestic feuding
culminates in Mrs. Grinnell's departure to establish a studio in a
seedy loft in downtown New York, even though she is still dependent
on her husband for support and sees Sarah only on prearranged
"dates." Then Mr. Grinnell loses his job, as well as his wife, and
succumbs to self-pity. Sarah's practical solution--to relinquish their
apartment and move permanently to their summer home where her
father can resume painting and her mother can also work--finds favor with her mother but not with her intransigent father until he
salves his ego by making it seem like his own idea. Sarah, interested in a new boy, contentedly puts finis to her diary and decides
to write a bona fide book.

47. Colman, Hila. WEEKEND SISTERS. New York: Morrow, 1985.
        169p. Grades 6-9. R+
        Jealousy and resentment well like bitter gall when Amanda
Maynard's father, with whom she spends every weekend, leaks the
news that he is marrying a woman with a daughter two years older
than she. Fern is mature and sophisticated for 16, popular, studious

and impeccably dressed. Not only does she have Amanda's dad to
herself full-time, but she also attends the private school where he
teaches and which Amanda's mother, a housewares designer, can no
longer afford. Amanda feels fully betrayed when her father tries
to adopt Fern and exhorts Amanda to dress like her. The only
thing the girls share is their mutual aversion to one another and to
their parents' relationship, Fern out of fealty to her dead father and
Amanda because Dad's new family has completely supplanted her.
Fern accepts the situation aloofly and stoically, however, while
Amanda is overtly sulky and hostile, especially when Fern also ap-
propriates her weekend boyfriend. When Fern wrecks Mr. May-
nard's car, he is inordinately solicitous instead of punitive, and
Amanda knows that her former intimacy with her father is defunct.
Her discovery that Fern shoplifts causes her unease and embarrass-
ment, but she doesn't tattle. When Fern spends a weekend with
Amanda and her mother and steals Mom's household money, however,
Amanda is forced to speak up. At first she is disbelieved until
Fern acknowledges that the model daughter has feet of clay. They
realize then that Fern is intensely troubled, and Amanda makes a
magnanimous gesture towards her. Her father apologizes for taking
their love and loyalty for granted, and a less fickle boyfriend materializes for Amanda.

48.   Cone, Molly. THE AMAZING MEMORY OF HARVEY BEAN.
        Boston: Houghton Mifflin, 1980. Illus. by Robert MacLean.
        83p. Grades 4-6. R
        The summer that his parents decide to split up, Harvey, 11,
already abstracted and depressed, is especially bedeviled because
neither parent seems to want him. Letting each think he has gone
with the other, he sets off on his own and soon encounters a very
stout but friendly older man, Mr. Katz, scavenging in a supermarket
dumpster. Mr. Katz invites the boy to his home, which is a motley
assemblage of materials scrounged from junkyards. The garage is
crammed to overflowing with others' useful discards. Mrs. Katz is
an equally amiable dumpling, just as forgetful as Harvey himself,
who creates appetizing viands from her husband's gleanings. She
is also a walking encyclopedia of mnemonic devices who gladly
teaches Harvey her system of memorization. When the health department threatens to evict the Katzes because of their untidy garage, Harvey quickly reorganizes it. And when his parents finally
track him down and accuse the Katzes of kidnapping him, Mr. Katz
rebuts that as a salvager, he hates to see anything go to waste,
including a scrap of a boy. Happy to know that he is wanted and
loved, Harvey decides to spend school days with his mother, weekends with his father, and vacations with the Katzes.

49.   Conrad, Pam. HOLDING ME HERE. New York: Harper and
        Row, 1986. 184p. Grades 6-10. R++
        Two years after her college professor father moved into an
apartment across town, boarder Mary Walker moves into the New
York home that Robin Lewis, 14, shares with her businesswoman

mother. Curiosity impels Robin to snoop through Mary's belongings
and read her diary. She learns that Mary has left her abusive husband and her two adored children in the care of their grandmother
in a neighboring town. Robin pedals there to discover that Timmy,
7, is an incorrigible bully but that Leslie, 12, is plainly pining away
for her mother. Empathetic Robin, who resents her mother dating
while she is spending weekends with her father and who believes that
under no circumstances should parents leave their children, arranges
to surprise Mary by bringing Leslie to her house and reuniting
them. Her good intentions backfire. Mary is furious with her for
jeopardizing her plan to start a career as a nurse and establish
residency before trying to wrest legal custody of the kids from the
man who conceals his Jekyll-and-Hyde nature behind a law officer's
badge. Robin, who has appeared brave and mature about her
parents' divorce, is finally moved to express her despair over her
father's defection. He explains that even though their marriage
seemed placid on the surface, there were emotional undercurrents
that she, as a child, could not expect to fathom. On a night when
her mother is out with her boyfriend Tom, Robin is terrified when
Mary's husband, drunk, breaks into the house in search of his
wife. Robin escapes to summon help while the irrational man wrecks
the place. When her mother and Tom return, Robin realizes how
comforting Tom's presence is.

50. Corcoran, Barbara. AXE-TIME/SWORD-TIME. New York:
        Atheneum, 1976. 204p. Grades 7-9. R
        Struck on the head by a golf ball as a child, Elinor, 18, was
left with a minor learning impairment that permits her to finish high
school but not to qualify for an Eastern Establishment college. Her
possessive, social-conscious mother will not acknowledge the disability and insists that she take remedial courses to pass College
Board exams. Upon her parents' separation, her brother's enlist-
ment in the armed services, and her boyfriend's departure for Dart-
mouth, Elinor is left to cope alone with her protective and domineering mother. Mother objects strenuously when a sympathetic teacher
asks her to be a Civil Defense plane spotter in the embryonic days
of U.S. involvement in World War II, but Elinor stands her ground.
The ultimate test of her self-reliance comes when her doctor father's
formidable new fiancee challenges her to quit school and take a job
with the Navy in a defense plant, and she and her mother almost
stop speaking. Everyone else, however, is proud of her initiative,
especially her boyfriend Jed, now in uniform himself. Her handicap
proves undetrimental.

51. Corcoran, Barbara. A DANCE TO STILL MUSIC. New York:
        Atheneum, 1974. Illus. by Charles Robinson. 180p. Grades
        6-9. R
        Left totally deaf from an untreated ear infection, Margaret,
14, is uprooted from her familiar New England hometown and brought
to the Florida Keys by her waitress mother who is a conscious martyr to the cause of rearing Margaret alone, compounded by the

burden of her handicap. Frightened and diffident in the hearing
world where she is easy prey to danger and derision, Margaret
alienates herself from human contact and refuses to speak because
she is afraid of making loud or peculiar noises as her deaf grandfather used to do. When her mother's prospective husband offers
to send her to a home for handicapped, it is anathema to Margaret,
and she decides to run away. Within a few miles she is providentially found by Josie, a motel chambermaid living in the isolation of
a houseboat. Josie accepts her as naturally as she does any of the
wild creatures sharing the swamp, and Margaret becomes increasingly relaxed and finally begins to speak again, her pent up emotions
tumbling out. Truant officers finally catch up with her, but
through a teacher friend of Josie's she is able to enroll in an experimental day-school program at the university and, best of all,
to continue living with Josie.

52.   Corcoran, Barbara, and Bradford Angier. A STAR TO THE
        NORTH. Philadelphia: Lippincott, 1970. (OP) 156p.
        Grades 6-10. R
        Feeling trapped by his arbitrary and peremptory father,
who has made unilateral plans for a summer job for him, and Eva,
his dipsomaniac ex-actress stepmother who is indifferent to the
children, Nathaniel Winslow decides to use the money his grandmother sent him for his sixteenth birthday and join his Uncle Seth
in the British Columbia wilderness. An experienced backpacker,
Nathaniel is dismayed to be saddled with his sister Kimberly, 14, a
tenderfoot who feels similarly constricted at plans to send her to
camp and stows away on the bus with him to his Canadian departure
point. To reach Seth's remote cabin, they must negotiate the untamed Bear River via canoe. When Kimberly sprains her ankle,
Nathaniel decides to shoot the rapids instead of portaging, but the
canoe sinks with their supplies and they are forced to continue on
foot through the trackless forests. Karen becomes feverish and
the two are overtaken by a summer snowstorm, but adversity draws
them closer and helps Karen to mature. When at last they reach
their destination, Nathaniel is disillusioned to find that Seth has
taken up with a cheap woman, rejecting them both. Nathaniel is
offered a neighbor's ramshackle cabin in exchange for restoring it,
while plans are made for Kimberly to join their sympathetic grandmother.

53.   Corcoran, Barbara. THIS IS A RECORDING. New York:
        Atheneum, 1971. (OP) Illus. by Richard Cuffari. Grades
        6-9. R
        Marianne is immature at 14 and resorts to hyperbole and oc-
casional prevarication for effect. At the beginning of her sophomore
year her parents send her to her grandmother in Montana, whom she
has not seen since infancy, while they travel in Europe in an effort
to repair a troubled marriage. Never having been west of the Hudson, Marianne is expecting cowboys, ranch houses and wild Indians.
She is surprised to find that her urbane grandmother lives in a

commodious Victorian mansion and hobnobs with educated Indians who are harassed by a bigoted redneck sheriff. When her class-mates react with hostility to Marianne's loftiness, Grandmother Katherine, who gave up an illustrious stage career to marry a rancher, comes out of retirement to give a vibrant performance that wins their respect. They, in turn, make friendly overtures to Marianne, who herself earns the respect of Katherine and her young Indian friend by saving his little brother's life. When her parents' marriage fails, Marianne resents returning to Boston with her mother who seems so insensitive, but she has acquired the maturity to handle it. She confides events and emotions to her tape recorder.

54. Corcoran, Barbara. THE WINDS OF TIME. New York:
        Atheneum, 1974. Illus. by Gail Owens. 164p. Grades 6-9.
        NR
        Teenage Gail becomes the ward of her disarmingly solicitous but malicious uncle when her mother returns to the mental hospital, and she seeks the first opportunity for escape. It comes when Uncle Chad's car crashes on a snowy mountain road in Colorado and he is pinned in the wreckage. Gail, unharmed, follows her pet cat down an overgrown lane straight into a fairyland of the forgotten splendor of the nineteenth century, the munificent wooded estate of the pioneering, financiering Partridge dynasty. Elderly Mrs. Partridge and her bachelor son, now recluses, graciously take her in without question, yet Mrs. Partridge's grandson Christopher, a serious naturalist, is suspicious of her until he becomes convinced that her story is true. While awaiting word from Gail's honorable but capri-cious father, whose last known address was Hawaii, Mrs. Partridge predicts her checkered future in Tarot cards, and they all connive to keep her out of the clutches of the underhanded, overbearing sheriff, the tool of wily Uncle Chad. When her affable father fi-nally appears, the Partridges offer him a job and a home for the summer.

55. Culin, Charlotte. CAGES OF GLASS, FLOWERS OF TIME.
        Scarsdale: Bradbury, 1979. 316p. Grades 7-9. R+
        The court, guided by the letter and not the spirit of the law, has taken custody of Claire Burden, 14, from her bohemian artist father and awarded it to her mother, a drunken waitress who physically abuses Claire and threatens to kill her if she indulges her proclivity for drawing. While she hates her mother Claire cannot divulge the truth about her wretched home life to anyone who might pity her and inform the authorities, fearful that they would be forced to live with diabolical Grandma Simmons, who batters them both while sober. Consequently, the lonely, terrified girl is hostile and aloof toward her rural Carolina classmates, who all spurn her but one, Clyde Bowman, who patiently tries to draw Claire out of her shell and eventually falls in love with her. She is also be-friended by an aging black man who tries to bolster her self-esteem to little avail. Driven by greed for Claire's inheritance from her paternal grandmother, Grandma Simmons brings matters to a head

by coming to claim custody of the girl. When Claire resists, she
is beaten senseless, as is her mother when she rises for once to
Claire's defense. Claire learns belatedly that genuinely concerned
people can be trusted to make fair and wise decisions when the
court appoints her high school art teacher to be her foster parent
and sends Grandma Simmons to jail.

56. Danziger, Paula. THE DIVORCE EXPRESS. New York: Dela-
     corte, 1982. 148p. Grades 7-10. R+
        For the first year after the divorce, Phoebe Brooks'
parents agreed that they should live in the same New York neighborhood to facilitate joint custody of their daughter. Fragmented
from spending half a week and alternate weekends with each parent,
Phoebe rebels by becoming the school prankster, whereupon her
father decides to move to their summer home in Woodstock to support himself as an artist, while her mother opens a design studio in
the city. Phoebe stays with her father during the week and com-
mutes via "the Divorce Express" to her mother on weekends, along
with dozens of other children of divided homes, including Rosie,
also 14 and an only child, who becomes like a sister to her.
Phoebe's first bad disillusionment with her split life comes when her
city boyfriend's loneliness overcomes his loyalty and he defects to
her former best friend. A campaign for better lunches in the
cafeteria at Kilmer High School where she and Rosie are freshmen
helps her make other friends and meet a new boy to date. A bus
breakdown on the Divorce Express brings the revelation that
Phoebe's father and Rosie's mother are seeing each other seriously.
Phoebe's mother also reveals that she is marrying an older man who
is anathema to Phoebe. Her anger at her mother is ameliorated by
the knowledge that if her father and Rosie's mother wed, the friends
will be true sisters. She agrees to attend the wedding but to visit
her mother less often.

57. Danziger, Paula. IT'S AN AARDVARK-EAT-TURTLE WORLD.
     New York: Delacorte, 1985. 132p. Grades 7-9. R+
        Best friends from the Divorce Express that plies between
divided homes in Woodstock and New York City (see 56), Rosie
Wilson and Phoebe Brooks, both 14, expect to become as close as
sisters when Rosie's mom Mindy, an aspiring writer, moves in with
Phoebe's artist father Jim. The informal new family declares itself
committed to respecting one another's originality and creativity,
but tension develops immediately when the girls move into the same
bedroom and all four are forced to share one bathroom. Phoebe
reacts with hostility when Mindy reproaches her for necking with
her boyfriend while parked in front of the house, believing that a
double standard exists because Mindy and Jim bill and coo overtly.
Rosie sides with her mother. A truce is declared when Phoebe's
mother and pompous stepfather take the girls on a vacation trip to
Canada, where Rosie meets her first boyfriend. The feud resumes
when temperamental Phoebe clouds Rosie's euphoria by petulantly accusing Rosie of neglecting her. Later Phoebe drops a bombshell by

announcing that she intends to live with her mother to express
her anger at Jim and Mindy's cohabitation. Gloom prevails in her
absence, even while they celebrate the sale of Mindy's first book.
Rosie resents Phoebe's attempt to sabotage the family, and when
Phoebe changes her mind and decides to return, Rosie finds it difficult to forgive her. Phoebe agrees to accept counseling, and
Mindy relinquishes her office as a bedroom for Phoebe.

58. Danziger, Paula. THE PISTACHIO PRESCRIPTION. New York:
      Delacorte, 1978. 154p. Grades 6-9. R+
      The shopping trip to buy clothes for her freshman year in
high school is fraught with tension for Cassie Stephens, 13, because
her chic mother always imposes her sophisticated tastes on Cassie
and then tries to make her feel guilty for her seeming ingratitude.
Her father, moreover, always picks a fight with her mother over
the expenditures, and her older sister Stephanie, a senior who has
also been warped by their mother, belittles, insults and denigrates
her. The emotional turmoil triggers Cassie's frequent asthma attacks
for which her panacea is surreptitiously eating pistachio nuts. Her
best friend nominates Cassie for class president, but because of her
inferiority complex she feels her bid is doomed to failure until she
challenges a tyrannical teacher and suddenly becomes the school
heroine. During the campaign she meets a mature boy who takes a
serious interest in her, and she develops greater self-confidence.
But the antagonism between her parents accelerates until the night
of Cassie's victory celebration, when an acrimonious exchange results in a severe asthmatic attack and her father leaves home.
Cassie and Stephanie, now allies, and their little brother Andrew, 7,
attempt a reconciliation to no avail, and Mom starts dating again.
Cassie decides that Twinkies may be more efficacious than pistachios.

59. Delton, Judy. ANGEL IN CHARGE. Boston: Houghton Miff-
      lin, 1985. Illus. by Leslie Morrill. Grades 4-6. R
      When Rags' and Angel's mom (see 61) is persuaded to take
a Canadian vacation with her sister, Mrs. O'Leary's friend and retired department store co-worker Alyce volunteers to stay with the
children in her absence. Angel, 10, is convinced that Alyce is incompetent after she loses her car in the airport parking lot, serves
burnt French toast for breakfast, and calls the police to find Rags,
4, who is only in his customary retreat under the porch. Her
opinion is reinforced when Alyce clumsily breaks her leg and is
whisked off to the hospital. Angel, afraid that she and Rags will
be sent to a foster home, notifies no one that they are on their own.
She takes Rags to school with her, where he lands in trouble by
proudly inscribing his name in wet cement. Together they weather
an attack by ghosts and/or burglars in the night. When Alyce returns on crutches, secure in the misconception that her charges
have been in the care of a neighbor who is, in reality, out of town,
Angel welcomes her with the realization that Alyce is not so inept
after all. She confesses all and is greatly relieved when her mother
arrives to take charge firmly and capably.

28   The Single-Parent Family

60. Delton, Judy. ANGEL'S MOTHER'S BOYFRIEND. Boston:
        Houghton Mifflin, 1986. Illus. by Margot Apple. 165p.
        Grades 4-6. R
        On returning from vacation (see 61 & 59), Rags' and Angel's
mother seems abstracted, inattentive, clumsy and giddy. That,
coupled with overheard conversations and several letters from Washington, D.C., leads Angel to conclude that the feds are after Mother
for being in arrears on taxes. Concerned, she tries to raise funds
by holding a Saturday dog-washing. To forestall her possible kidnap and arrest, she arranges a hideout in a friend's basement.
When she finally blurts out her fears to her mother, Mrs. O'Leary
belatedly informs her that she met a man on vacation who is coming
to visit them. That news is more unsettling to Angel, 10, than her
cloak-and-dagger fantasy. She reasons that mothers don't need
friends because they have families to do things with. She is prepared to dislike Rudy on sight, especially because he is preempting
her bedroom, and to be humiliated by his occupation as a professional clown. Instead, Rudy appears perfectly normal and takes a
genuine interest in the children, springing delightful surprises upon
all of them. When he takes a job with the TV station in their Wisconsin town, moreover, Angel becomes a celebrity by appearing on
his show. Rudy moves into his own apartment, and Angel begins to
miss having him around the house. The O'Leary family spends a
listless and doleful Christmas when Rudy goes to visit his family for
the holidays, and Angel worries that he may not return. At a
lively St. Patrick's Day party, he and Mrs. O'Leary announce their
engagement, to which Angel readily gives her stamp of approval.

61. Delton, Judy. BACK YARD ANGEL. Boston: Houghton Miff-
        lin, 1983. Illus. by Leslie Morrill. 107p. Grades 4-5. R+
        Mother insists that babysitting is not just a job but a re-
sponsibility for someone's very life, and Angel O'Leary, 10, has her
hands full keeping tabs on her energetic and inquisitive brother
Rags, 4, while their mother works, their father having deserted the
family before Rags was born. While they are enjoined from leaving
the block, Rags finds plenty of trouble near at hand, and the diversions she devises for his amusement as often as not get them both
in hot water. Angel concludes that Rags is the root of all her problems and ponders how to get rid of him. When he gets lost temporarily in the shopping mall while supposedly under her care, her
wish seems to have been fulfilled and she is conscience-stricken.
With a new appreciation of Rags, she now endeavors to do something
special to please her mother. The dinner she concocts turns out a
little differently than she had planned, but Mother seems to appreciate it anyway. When a classmate invites Angel to go swimming, she
is convinced that her mother will never allow her to shirk her Responsibility, but to her incredulity Mother agrees that she needs
friends her own age. Angel's horizon suddenly begins to expand.

62. Dexter, Pat Egan. ARROW IN THE WIND. Nashville: Nelson,
        1978. (OP) Grades 5-6. R+

Ben Arrow is 11 when he and his sister Kara, 10, learn the devastating news that their father is divorcing their mother and moving to San Francisco to recapture his lost youth. Mrs. Arrow takes a bookkeeping job, but her salary is inadequate for the upkeep of their modest Phoenix home, so Ben undertakes the self-sacrifice of a morning paper route, and Kara agrees to shoulder household responsibilities and babysitting. Ben stands up to the bully who has bedeviled him for years and, after learning of the reprobate's wretched homelife, tries to rehabilitate and befriend him. His faith appears to have been misplaced when he is accused of being an accessory to Joe's theft of a camera, but Ben's ingenuous defense of Joe falls on the ears of a sympathetic judge, and Joe promises to go straight. Mr. Arrow visits at Easter, as promised, having disappointed them at Christmas. Mrs. Arrow's first attempt at dating produces a negative response from Ben and Kara, but she handles it very sagely. Ben's new dog presents them with puppies, and when torrential rains create disastrous flooding, the Arrow family refuses to evacuate and elects to stay in their cement block house to save the puppies. They all come through unscathed and realize that they can weather any eventuality.

63. Dixon, Jeanne. LADY CAT LOST. New York: Atheneum, 1981. 193p. Grades 5-7. NR
    When her alcoholic writer husband leaves her to escape tedium, Betty Jo Fergusson uproots her family, Kenneth, 12, Oona, 10, Marlow, 7, and Angel to go live at her mother's Montana farm without announcing their arrival. To her dismay she discovers that her mother has moved to Phoenix and sold the farm to developers. Friendly neighbors, the Getzes, take them in while Mrs. Fergusson hunts for work, but the two eldest children have difficulty adjusting. Kenneth is distraught because his beloved Siamese cat has been frightened away by the developer's watchdog. Oona is self-conscious of her appearance and has trouble making friends because of her thin-skinned personality. In her dejection she hears voices beckoning her to a reputedly haunted cave. When they realize that she is missing, the Getzes mount a search, Mrs. Fergusson having gone to her new job as a department store clerk. But it is Kenneth who braves the dangers of the cave to search for his sister and in the quest also discovers his lost cat alive along with the skeleton of a boy who perished there a generation ago. When the developer learns that the cave undercuts his property, he revokes his contract, and Grandma writes to say that she is giving the Fergussons half of her profit so that they can buy a house. Oona's erstwhile friend Miranda Getz feels guilty for the part she played in her almost fatal disappearance and makes amends.

64. Donovan, John. I'LL GET THERE. IT BETTER BE WORTH THE TRIP. New York: Harper and Row, 1969. 189p. Grades 7-9. R
    Following his parents' divorce when he was only 5, Davy was sent to live with his grandmother, who reared him and his

dachshund Fred with love and laughter in a small town near Boston.
His complacent life is shattered eight years later by her unexpected
death, and he is uprooted and taken to New York to live in a tiny
apartment with the selfish, unstable, alcoholic mother he scarcely
knows. His shock and alienation are cushioned by his relationship
with the adoring dog and a new friend he meets at his private
school. Tentative sexual probings between the two boys result in
a confrontation with Davy's erratic mother, following which the dog
Fred is killed in a traffic accident. Seeking a scapegoat in his
silent rage, Davy heaps guilt and shame upon himself, engulfs himself in sports, and shuns his friend. The tension explodes in a
locker room fist fight which restores their friendship and Davy's
self-respect.

65. Dorman, N. B. LAUGHTER IN THE BACKGROUND. New York:
         Elsevier/Nelson, 1980. 158p. Grades 5-8. R+
         Mom, a library clerk, barhops on Friday nights to unwind,
brings home strange men who spend the night, is hungover and
malodorous on weekends, and is irrationally irritable with lonely
Marcie, 12, who does all the cooking and housekeeping. On mornings when Mom is particularly sick, she swears off drinking for
short periods and even attends Alcoholics Anonymous meetings for
a few months, while Marcie meets with Al-Anon which helps her
through the vituperation of Mom's "dry drunks." But Mom always
backslides, citing numerous excuses, becoming progressively worse
and blaming Marcie for causing her to age when Marcie plans a birthday celebration for her. Marcie consoles herself by eating glutton-
ously, inviting her mother's excoriating sarcasm about her weight.
She appeals to her divorced father to make a home for her, but he
demurs because of his impending marriage to a divorcee with three
boys. On the night that her mother's latest drunken and disoriented pickup almost rapes her in the dark, Marcie marches herself to
the assistant principal and demands authoritative intervention. The
court places her in a caring foster home where Marcie learns to un-
burden herself of the guilt, shame and self-pity inculcated by her
mother. When Mom, having lost her job, makes a mawkish call at
Christmas and, overhearing their happy laughter, accuses the foster family of stealing her affection, Marcie decides to quit reaching
for food for solace the way her mother embraces her bottle.

66. Dragonwagon, Crescent. ALWAYS, ALWAYS. New York:
         Macmillan, 1984. Illus. by Arieh Zeldich. Unp. Grades
         2-3. R++
         Every summer the little girl's mother drives her to the air-
port for the flight to her father's home in Colorado. She feels sad
at leaving her mother in New York for three months and reflects
upon their life together, remembering the time when her attractive
mother gave her a manicure but warned her that her father would
not approve of her painting her nails. Her dejection is tempered by
the anticipation of seeing her carpenter father again, and she recalls the time when he taught her to chop kindling, cautioning her

that her mother would disapprove of something so unfeminine. She
knows that at the end of vacation she will be unhappy to leave
Daddy but glad to be returning home. When she asks each of them
independently why, if they were so unsuited, they married in the
first place, their answers are identical. The reply is that they made
a mistake because they didn't know each other or themselves well
enough, but both agree that her birth was the best thing that ever
happened to either of them. She feels well loved.

67. Duncan, Lois. A GIFT OF MAGIC. Boston: Little, Brown,
        1971. Illus. by Arvis Stewart. 183p. Grades 5-8. R+
        When her mother gets the nesting instinct, deciding to di-
vorce her war correspondent husband and make a home for her
three fledglings in Florida where she grew up, Nancy, 12, rebels.
Her disapproval increases when her mother takes up where she left
off with her childhood sweetheart, Mr. Duncan, who is now Nancy's
junior high principal. Kirby, 13, has her gift of the dance to absorb her time and energy, and Brendon, 9, has a new friend plus
his gift of music. Nancy inherited from her sage grandmother another special gift, that of ESP, but she tries to conceal it because
she doesn't want to become a guinea pig. Her sister has an opportunity to study with a major ballet company, but Nancy doesn't
want her to leave home. When Kirby falls and breaks her leg,
Nancy believes she caused the accident by thought transference,
but when Brendon embarks in a homemade boat, her clairvoyance
saves his life. Mr. Duncan's part in the rescue reveals his firm
fiber, and her father's remarriage completes her catharsis and acceptance.

68. Dunnahoo, Terry. WHO CARES ABOUT ESPIE SANCHEZ?
        New York: Dutton, 1975. (OP) 152p. Grades 7-9. R
        Esperanza means Hope, but Espie Sanchez has precious little
of that when she is apprehended a third time for running away from
her apathetic mother, whose succession of degenerate boyfriends
makes life untenable. Juvenile Hall seems inevitable until fate intervenes to place her in Mrs. Garcia's foster home, an alternative Espie
accepts only because its minimum security affords the opportunity
to run again. The religious atmosphere of the house and her roommate's involvement with police training through Law Enforcement
Explorer Group (L.E.E.G.) are initially oppressive. Later Espie
herself becomes a L.E.E.G. recruit as an excuse to get out of the
house, but soon she becomes seriously involved and determined to
endure the rigorous training. When her brother dies of a drug
overdose, she cooperates with the narcotics squad at grave personal
risk to bring his supplier to justice. Against all odds but with the
encouragement and faith of several, Espie triumphs over her hostility. Espie's progress can be followed in two sequels, THIS IS
ESPIE SANCHEZ and WHO WANTS ESPIE SANCHEZ, where the
heroine, still tough, helps others and mellows.

69. Ellis, Ella Thorp. HUGO AND THE PRINCESS NENA. New

York: Atheneum, 1983. 178p. Grades 5-7. R+
    While her mother, divorced from her alcoholic playwright
father, returns to college in New York to pursue her M.A. in social
work, Nena Seelig, 11, is sent to live with her grandfather in Pis-
mo Beach, California, because of the threats of an obscene telephone
caller. Hugo, who is 80 and calls her Princess, loves the water and
swims daily; Nena is mortally afraid of it. Hugo, a poet, requires
total concentration in his work; Nena distracts him by her frequent
bathroom trips. Hugo's constant companion is an overweight boy,
Irving, of whom Nena is instantly jealous and resentful. Hugo solves
one of their differences, and endears himself to Nena, by buying her
a trailer of her own to park next to his. Irving's mother gives Nena
a job in her restaurant, and she helps another trailer park resident
detect metal on the beach. But Nena's antipathy toward Irving remains until she discovers that Hugo suffers from chronic anemia and
suddenly must be hospitalized for a transfusion. She learns then
that Irving has been monitoring his blood pressure and helping him
to conceal his ailment from her, and she is consumed with guilt.
When Hugo does not improve, all of Nena's self-doubts arise: could
she be responsible for her father's drinking, her cat's death, Hugo's
debility? In propitiation and an effort to please him, Nena conquers
her fear of the ocean and learns to swim.

70. Engebrecht, P. A. UNDER THE HAYSTACK. Nashville: Nel-
        son, 1973. (OP) 124p. Grades 6-7. NR
    The intricately stacked bales of hay disguise a maze of tun-
nels leading to the secret retreat which is their only refuge from
their mother's husband, who picks on June, 6, and Marie, 8, makes
sexual advances to Sandy, 13, and even slaps their mother around.
Suddenly their mother runs off with him, abandoning the girls, who,
fearing separation, devise the story that she is visiting a sick aunt.
Bravely, Sandy marshalls the younger girls into disciplined farm
hands on their primitive, dilapidated acreage. Now the hay must be
used to feed the cows, and the three have to hire themselves out as
crop pickers to earn money for expenses. Sandy handles each succeeding crisis with aplomb beyond her years, but as their food supply dwindles and their clothing grows shabbier, it is harder to hide
their plight from community busybodies. Their only outside support
comes from loyal and generous friend and neighbor Joe and his
mother. Joe defends them from dangerous harassment and becomes
Sandy's first romance. His mother discreetly provides sympathy, an
occasional treat to vary their fare, and an insight into their mother's
character. The girls hide when the sheriff first comes to collect
them, but Sandy knows they can no longer delay the inevitable.
When their mother reappears alone as unexpectedly as she left, seeking forgiveness, Sandy conquers the hatred she has harbored.

71. Ewing, Kathryn. A PRIVATE MATTER. New York: Harcourt,
        Brace, Jovanovich, 1975. Illus. by Joan Sandin. 88p.
        Grades 4-5. R+
    The people moving in next door are a friendly retired couple

who have plenty of time to give Marcy, 9, the attention she lacks because her divorced father lives in California and her realtor mother works most of the time. Marcy tags along everywhere with Mr. Endicott as he potters about his house and garden, and he gives her little jobs to do to make her feel important. Soon she begins to fantasize that he is her missing father. When her real father and his new wife want to take her on a weekend trip, she tries unsuccessfully to circumvent it and is relieved to return to Mr. Endicott and the school project he is helping with. But Mrs. Endicott's sudden death shatters their relationship. When the grieving man moves away, Marcy experiences the same sense of loss and grief. At the same time, she must adjust to the prospect of a new stepfather and the move to a new home (see 72).

72. Ewing, Kathryn. THINGS WON'T BE THE SAME. New York: Harcourt Brace Jovanovich, 1980. 92p. Grades 4-5. R+

In the sequel to A PRIVATE MATTER (see 71), Marcy Benson, 10, wouldn't mind her mother marrying Bill Compton if it didn't disturb the status quo. She resists the idea of moving to a new home, starting a new school, and of having to act friendly to Bill's daughter Carole Anne, also 10. While her mother and Bill are honeymooning, Nancy is shipped to San Francisco to stay with her father, his new wife, and his infant son. The Benson family maintains a far more casual lifestyle than Marcy and her structured mother, but she adapts easily and has a wonderful time. When she returns to Pennsylvania she discovers that not only has her mother changed to suit Bill, who is even more fastidious than she, but that their mother/daughter intimacy is gone. She frets when her mother disciplines her for impertinence. Then Carole Anne comes to visit and, as a guest, receives preferential treatment and attention. Angry, Marcy writes to her father to request that she come to live with them, then changes her mind and is horrified that it may become a fait accompli. Carole Anne suggests a solution, and Marcy reconciles with her mother after concluding independently that everyone must make adjustments for all to be happy.

73. Eyerly, Jeannette. THE WORLD OF ELLEN MARCH. Philadelphia: Lippincott, 1964. (OP) 188p. Grades 7-9. NR

Sixteen-year-old Ellen's parents' divorce strikes her like a thunderbolt. Her mother takes her and her little sister to live in a small town in the Midwest, where she transfers from private to public school and makes a friend but is afraid to join in group activities and cliques because of the imagined stigma of her broken home. She invents excuses for her father's absence while longing for such tangible evidence of his presence as the sound of his voice and the aroma of his pipe. Goaded by her friend and her own desperation to reunite her parents, she borrows the car and runs away with her little sister to a secluded vacation home. Her strategy goes awry and terminates in an auto accident. Awakening in the hospital, she joyously believes she has effected a reconciliation when she sees her parents holding hands, only to learn later that they were humoring

her, believing that she was in shock. Her disillusionment and de-
moralization are assuaged by an attractive male acquaintance who
offers understanding, encouragement, and affection. An episode involving the death of a classmate's father suggests that a divorced
dad is better than a dead one.

74. Fisher, Lois I. RACHEL VELLARS, HOW COULD YOU? New
        York: Dodd, Mead, 1984. 155p. Grades 5-6. R+
        Though reconciled to her parents' divorce, Cory Matthew-
son, 11, abhors their denigrating one another in her presence and
still feels insecure in her new private school in Port Hudson where
she lives with her dad, a computer salesman. While her mother, a
Manhattan fashion designer, has always been unmaternal, Cory is
proud of her success, enjoys visiting her showroom and wearing her
creations, and no longer cries over the fact that her mom puts
business first. Her only friend is raffish, irreverent Rachel Vellars, a pariah to the rest of the school because of her obnoxious
and bizarre behavior. Cory's parents are in accord in their disapproval of Rachel, who also embarrasses Cory occasionally. The
demise of classmate Beth's cat proves to be Cory's entree to the
popular clique. Though Rachel warns her that Beth's bunch are
snobs who will eat her alive, Cory finds them friendly and tuned
to her own wavelength except for their criticism of Rachel. As she
strives anxiously to gain the acceptance of Beth's friends, she feels
guilty for betraying Rachel and snubbing her. It takes Beth's remarkable maturity and insight to reassure Cory that each individual
can have her own personal friends independent of the group. Relieved, Cory makes the effort to regain Rachel's trust, win the kite
flying contest they have entered together, and confidently convince
her parents to accept Rachel.

75. Fisher, Lois I. RADIO ROBERT. New York: Dodd, Mead,
        1985. 128p. Grades 4-7. R+
        Now 12 (see 76), Robert seems to be standing still while
everything about him is changing. His best friend Clete has taken
an interest in girls; his aggressive classmate Josie is tormenting him
more than ever; his hard work in school is not being rewarded by
his new teacher; and his mother has begun dating again. The most
startling change of all is that his radio personality father, Drive-
Time Donald, is returning after two years in Baltimore and impetuously puts Robert on his talk show. His appearance is a hit with
the audience because of his spontaneity, and he becomes a regular
guest and celebrity among his friends. Then his father cavalierly
tries to edge out Robert's Adult Ally, Biff, who has become a surrogate father in his dad's absence. Robert is incensed at his father's insensitivity for Biff's feelings until he learns that Biff has
a girlfriend who will also be sharing Biff's time. He is stunned to
discover that nemesis Josie has a crush on him. On his final broadcast he exercises the first amendment of the Bill of Rights, which
his teacher has been inculcating, by talking about his parents' divorce. His father is not amused, but his teacher is finally

impressed. Embarrassed that he also inadvertently mentioned admirer Josie on the air, he is astonished to find that he, too, has
been changing and that Josie doesn't seem quite as obnoxious to him
anymore.

76. Fisher, Lois I. WRETCHED ROBERT. New York: Dodd, Mead,
        1982. 110p. Grades 4-6. R+
        Considered pleasant and predictable by his Maine acquaint-
ances, Robert Bailey, 11, seeks to change his reputaiton and thereby get some attention, choosing the adjective "wretched" from the
dictionary. A latchkey kid since his father departed and his mom
got a job as a realtor, he is dragged unwillingly to meetings of
Adult Allies by his mother, who belongs to its parent group, Match-
less Mates. There he is paired with brawny Biff Brunner who, as
a sports enthusiast, is anathema to pedantic Robert. When he rude-
ly informs Biff that he hates sports, the kind and gentle man is
miffed. He then alienates his neighbor by neglecting and killing
the prized plant collection he promised to tend for her. By far his
worst wretched act is to donate a blank check his mother had
signed, earmarked for paying bills, to the class library fund. Although his mother justifies his deceit as a reaction to the divorce,
Robert is nevertheless abject at losing favor with three trusting
people, and he suddenly comprehends the other meaning of the word
wretched. His misery is compounded when he carelessly allows his
cat to run away. Biff helps him rescue the cat and forgives him his
lapse of behavior. Robert decides to search his dictionary for an
image that will not distress his favorite people.

77. Fitzhugh, Louise. THE LONG SECRET. New York: Harper
        and Row, 1965. Illus. by the author. 275p. Grades 5-7.
        R
        Beth Ellen's blue-blooded grandmother, with whom she has
lived in luxury for all of her 12 years, has tutored her to be a lady
no matter what, and she has grown up timid, indolent and insipid.
Her friend Harriet is of the opposite temperament: brash, abrasive
and ambitious. She is determined to expose the originator of the
barbed, Biblical-sounding notes that have been surfacing around the
summer colony. Beth Ellen is unprepared for the descension of the
chic, brittle and sybaritic mother she hasn't seen in seven years and
the vacuous sycophant she married after shedding her first husband.
When Beth Ellen expresses a tentative desire to pursue an art career
and be a productive member of society, they are first amused and
then alarmed and decide to remove her from her grandmother's influence. When Beth Ellen finally asserts herself histrionically, they
lose interest and her grandmother even condones her single breach
of etiquette. Harriet finally finds the evidence she has been seeking,
but Beth Ellen's long secret has served its purpose.

78. Fitzhugh, Louise. SPORT. New York: Delacorte, 1979.
        218p. Grades 4-6. R+
        Since his parents' acrimonious divorce when he was 4, Sport

Rocque, now 11, has kept house and managed finances for his
absent-minded, impecunious and quixotic novelist father. His social butterfly mother, who was declared an unfit parent in the
settlement because of her international gambling and nonchalant
treatment of the boy, has suddenly returned because her father,
a multimillionaire, is dying. The old man truly loves Sport and
provides well for him in his will. Following the funeral, Mr.
Rocque carries through with his plan to marry Kate, a caring,
adaptable, down-to-earth woman whom Sport adores and who will
be an exemplary stepmother to him. While his father is honeymooning, Sport is parked temporarily with his mother, who tries
to make him over into a spoiled, foppish sycophant. Rebelling, he
insults an influential friend of hers and then invites three of his
classmates, including Harriet Welsh (see 77), to lunch, where by
mischievous prearrangement they offend Sport's meticulous and
prejudiced mother. With cunning and selfish determination to
wrest back his custody and thereby his inheritance, she has Sport
held incommunicado in a luxury hotel suite from which he is rescued by one of his multi-ethnic buddies. After another abortive
kidnap attempt, his mother finally gives up the chase and jets off
to Europe to avoid the nasty publicity.

79.   Fox, Paula. BLOWFISH LIVE IN THE SEA. Englewood Cliffs:
          Bradbury, 1970. 116p. Grades 6-9. R+
      Written from the viewpoint of his half sister Carrie, 12,
this is the story of Ben, 18, who has lived with his mother and
stepfather since his parents' divorce and who, a year earlier,
dropped out and turned off, his long hair and lassitude becoming
a bone of contention between him and his stepfather. Carrie, however, adores and defends Ben, and when his biological father, a
purportedly prosperous Arizona rancher, suddenly materializes in
Boston and wants to see him, he asks Carrie to accompany him.
The bon vivant father turns out to be nothing but a seedy, drunken
bum with a touch of engaging elegance, living in a flophouse hotel.
Ben's decision to remain in Boston and rehabilitate his father gives
him the direction he needs in life, but Carrie realizes that he has
grown up and left her behind. The present he leaves her explains
the significance of his cryptic slogan, "Blowfish live in the sea."

80.   Fox, Paula. HOW MANY MILES TO BABYLON? New York:
          David White, 1967. Illus. by Paul Giovanopoulos. 117p.
          Grades 5-8. R
      When James' father deserted them, he and his mother went
to live with his father's three aunts. Then his mother had to be
hospitalized and was lost to him also. The introverted boy seeks
desperately to find her. Playing truant, he goes to the basement
of a derelict house in his New York slum where he fantasizes that
his mother is an African queen and communes with her. The house
is also the headquarters of a tough teenage ring of dog thieves who
surprise him and, under duress, put him to work for them. That
night he makes a harrowing and abortive attempt to escape in the

dark, deserted funhouse at Coney Island. Later he manages to
elude the hoodlums, return the dog he took, and make his way
home--where his mother is finally awaiting him.

80a. Fox, Paula. THE MOONLIGHT MAN. New York: Bradbury,
        1986. 179p. Grades 7-10. R+
        Boarding school student Catherine Ames, 15, whose remarried
copy editor mother is traveling in Europe, anticipates with some
trepidation her first full-fledged vacation with her long-divorced
father. He disappoints and annoys her by inexplicably being three
weeks late in collecting her and then spending their first evening
together by passing out drunk with disreputable companions at
their Nova Scotia cottage. When Catherine expresses her disgust
at his insobriety, he pledges to go on the wagon for the duration
of their visit, revealing to her a rich, multifaceted personality. A
novelist who peaked early, he is now a nomadic travel writer, a
man's man who is untamed and unintimidated by social convention.
He is at once a philosopher, gourmand, sportsman, bon vivant,
scholar, libertarian, cosmopolite, romantic, pub crawler, eloquent
raconteur and compulsive charmer. Catherine's mother, a prosaic
"daylight woman," divorced him because she could not tolerate his
inebriation, irresponsibility, unpromising career, irregular hours
and footloose habits, but Catherine revels in his carefree vitality,
non-conformity and unfettered mind. When he backslides, Catherine's
anger at him for frightening her and endangering his life vie with
her pity and love for him. At their parting, she forgives the "moonlight man" his foibles and even prods her regimented, predictable
and hypercritical mother into admitting that she once loved him un-
reservedly.

81. Freeman, Barbara C. A HAUNTING AIR. New York: Dutton,
        1977. (OP) 158p. Grades 5-9. R
        Melissa Brown, 16, and her playwright father are persuaded
to move into old Miss Clayfield's Victorian mansion when the new
owner of the property next door razes its equally old structure and
hounds Miss Clayfield for her site so he can build a modern development. Frustrated by her refusal to sell, the developer constructs a
small house next door but has difficulty keeping it rented until a
young widow and her infant son move in. Lonely Melissa, whose
mother deserted them when she was small, makes friends with the
mother and her son Bobson. Their discovery of a cache of antique
toys and the sound of mysterious childish singing piques their
curiosity and leads Melissa on a voyage of discovery into the history
of the mansion through accounts in old newspapers and letters to
Miss Clayfield's grandmother. They disclose the tragic existence of
the mistreated bastard daughter of a mad serving girl who was befriended by the mistress of the house until her own death in childbirth. The unfortunate waif was doomed to wait eternally for the
lost infant. Her restless spirit finds peace when Bobson comes to
stay, and he and his mother seem to coexist amicably with the wraith.
Melissa's mother appears briefly before going away permanently, and

her father, free at last to put down roots, buys the venerable
house at Miss Clayfield's behest.

82. Gaeddert, LouAnn. JUST LIKE SISTERS. New York, Dutton,
       1981. Illus. by Gail Owens. 90p. Grades 4-6. R+
       Disappointed at being an only child, Carrie Clark is elated
to learn that her cousin Kate, only three months older than she,
will be coming to spend the summer at the Clark's home in New
York's Berkshires. Enthusiastically planning their activities, Carrie
is unprepared for Kate's resentment at being there, triggered by her
parents' imminent divorce. Her mother has abandoned her to start
a career in New York City, and her father has been transferred to
Tulsa. In contrast to Carrie, moreover, Kate is tall, blonde, athletic and reserved. She is particularly intolerant of Carrie's best
friend Alice, who is overweight and clumsy. Kate directs her hostility at Alice, whose mother is an unabashed homemaker with five
adored children. When she deliberately allows Alice to nearly drown
in the lake, Carrie loses her patience and makes a barbed riposte,
whereupon Kate runs away. Kate's parents arrive, and when the
troubled girl is found, Carrie's family makes the difficult decision to
offer her a permanent home. Kate, however, rejects their proposal
and chooses boarding school instead. As a good will gesture, she
concedes that she may come for cousinly, not sisterly, visits from
time to time.

83. Gerber, Merrill Joan. NAME A STAR FOR ME. New York:
       Viking, 186p. Grades 6-9. R
       The summer that she is 13, Evelyn Richards welcomes the
opportunity to accompany her mother from their Los Angeles home
to rural Kentucky, where her mother will be attending an artists'
workshop given by Rodney, an old flame, at his art colony. Evelyn,
who has a romantic picture of farm life and the South, will be staying with the family of another college classmate of her mother's whose
son Chet is her age. Left behind are Evelyn's older sisters and her
"patient, mild, cautious, reasonable" businessman father. Instead of
falling in love with sensitive Chet as she anticipated, Ev meets his
wickedly attractive older cousin Red, a scapegrace who grows pot
and raises fighting cocks, but who also stirs exciting new feelings
in her. Daily life on a working farm--outhouses, non-homogenized
milk, and the slaughter of animals--is quickly disenchanting, but her
infatuation with Red progresses until, after an afternoon of wine
drinking, she almost goes too far and suddenly realizes the danger
of their relationship. She runs away from the farm and locates her
mother, only to discover that Mom has become mesmerized with the
dashing Rodney and the lure of recovering her lost youth. Horrified, Ev carries out a plan to regain her mother's attention and makes
peace with Chet. Her mother ends her summer fling, but Ev returns
home with the promise of a long-distance romance with Chet.

84. Gerber, Merrill Joan. PLEASE DON'T KISS ME NOW. New York:
       Dial, 1981. 218p. Grades 7-10. R+

Leslie's libertarian mother divorced her reactionary father because he opposed women working outside the home. Now a fourth grade teacher, she is too absorbed in pursuit of new encounter group weekends and bed partners to pay any attention to the teen's changing needs, and her guidance is inconsistent and frequently sarcastic. Tough as it is to live with her mother, Leslie, 15, finds it preferable to living with her father and his vacuous new family. She feels platonic towards her old chum and fellow school orchestra member Ron, so when Brian, the male lead in the senior play whom all the girls worship from afar, singles her out to be his new conquest, she welcomes the opportunity to escape from her strife-torn home, even though Brian is disturbingly egotistical. He introduces her to the forbidden pleasures of beer drinking and heavy petting in his waterbed-equipped van. When her mother announces her plans to marry Kesey, a former teacher of Leslie's, and move to Sacramento, Leslie is resentful. With her mother's encouragement she becomes friends with Lois, the talented first chair violinist. When Lois is tragically killed in an auto accident, both Brian and Ron offer Leslie their individual type of solace. Suddenly Leslie realizes that she cannot be dependent upon anyone else for her own emotional stability and decides to cast her lot with her mother and Kesey in the new locale.

85.   Gerson, Corinne. HOW I PUT MY MOTHER THROUGH COLLEGE.
         New York: Atheneum, 1981. 136p. Grades 5-8. R+
         Soon after her father leaves the family home on Long Island and moves to an apartment in New York, Jessica Cromwell's mother makes the long-deferred decision to matriculate at the local college. The first change that Jess, 13, notices is the switch of apparel from suburban homemaker dresses to the collegiate uniform of jeans and boots. Jess takes over all the household chores so her mother is free to study, but what gives her the greatest sense of role reversal are the late night sessions when Mom wakes her to relate the events of the day and to ask for advice, oblivious of Jess' need to discuss her own difficult social transition to junior high. Jess is named assistant editor of the school paper; her brother Ben, 9, makes captain of his soccer team; and Mom is chosen college cheerleader. The children approve of Dad's new girlfriend, whom he eventually marries, but Mom brings home a succession of unsuitable male companions, the latest of whom runs an underground newspaper and convinces Mom to become an activist and participate in an illegal sit-in. Ben precipitates a crisis by running away to underscore his abhorrence of the hippie, and Mom takes them all to a counselor for family therapy. In her sophomore year, to Jess' relief, Mom gains the experience and confidence to make wiser, independent choices of friends and extracurricular activities just as Jess reaches the stage where she needs her mother to advise her about boy problems.

86.   Giff, Patricia Reilly. RAT TEETH. New York: Delacorte,
         1984. Grades 4-6. R+

Offense seems to Radcliffe Samson, 10, to be the best defense for the teasing he takes at his new school in Queens for his
awful affliction--buck teeth. Before his parents' divorce, he was
happy and respected at his old school. Now he lives three days a
week with his mother, a night school student, while he spends the
rest of the week with his father in his aunt's house ten blocks
away. Dad, who just received his chiropractor's license, cannot
yet afford orthodontia for Cliffie. In addition to his disfigurement,
there is the stigma of dragging a suitcase to school on the day he
switches houses. So Cliffie launches insults at his new schoolmates
in preemptive strikes and plans to show them up at the one activity
in which he excels--baseball. His cockiness betrays him, and he
becomes the goat as the fourth graders ignominiously defeat the
fifth graders. To save face, all he can do is to run away. His
first attempt goes awry when he is victimized by another truant who
is as tough as Cliffie only pretends to be. The second attempt is
more successful than he wants it to be. No one thinks of looking
for him in the vacant house where he is hiding, lonesome and bored,
with the stray cat he has come to love. When he finally gives up
and goes home to Aunt Ida, he is surprised and gratified to learn
that both parents would like to have him full time. And in his first
attempt to meet his contemporaries halfway, he discovers that they're
friendly after all.

87.   Goff, Beth. WHERE IS DADDY? THE STORY OF A DIVORCE.
         Boston: Beacon, 1969. Illus. by Susan Perl. Unp.
         Grades K-2. R+
         Janeydear loved to play with Daddy and Funny the dog, but
sometimes Daddy would scold if she made too much noise when he
wasn't in a playful mood. One day he wasn't there at all and Mommy
didn't know when he was returning. Janey wonders if he is angry
with her. When he does return and takes her to the beach all by
herself, she thinks that life has returned to normal because she
doesn't understand the word divorce. That evening her parents
quarrel and Daddy goes away again, promising that he will always
be her daddy. Janey and Mommy go to live with Grandma, who is
strict about dogs. Then Mommy gets a job and Janey is more lonely,
angry and bewildered than before. When she vents her frustrations
on Funny, the adults finally recognize her inarticulate fears and give
her the attention and reassurance she needs, and Daddy comes to
take her to the zoo.

88.   Goldman, Katie. IN THE WINGS. New York: Dial, 1982.
         166p. Grades 6-10. R+
         Jessie, 15, is thrilled to be cast in a major role in her Palo
Alto, California, high school play and to make exciting new friends
among the drama clique. At first she welcomes rehearsals as an opportunity to escape her parents' arguments. Her father, a cardiologist, refuses to take seriously, nor tolerate, her mother's burgeoning career as an author of children's books. Suddenly her
euphoria sours when her parents separate and then divorce, and

her best friend Andrea gives her the cold shoulder for putting the play first. Dad is out of touch with the children's preferences when he plans activities for the Saturdays he spends with Jessie and her brother Eric, and even Mom, with whom Jessie gets along famously, becomes furious with her when she stays for an impromptu meal with the cast when she is expected home for dinner. Her deepening depression takes the form of exhaustion, and soon she is dreading each day and mechanically going through the motions. When she fails a test and flubs a rehearsal a few days before opening night, she loses her control and breaks down in front of the director. Getting her anxieties off her chest and her tears shed, she begins to look at the situation objectively, calmly and positively, even volunteering to help her mother over her own emotional rough spots and asserting herself to force Mom to discuss openly their mutual concerns. Everyone relaxes, and on opening night Andrea is sitting in the front row along with Mom, Dad and Eric.

89.   Graeber, Charlotte Towner. THE THING IN KAT'S ATTIC.
         New York: Dutton, 1984. Illus. by Emily Arnold McCully.
         49p. Grades 2-5. R+
         Dad visits on Sundays, a whole week away. That does not help Kat, her sister Holly, or Mom when they hear nocturnal noises coming from the attic. Mom is convinced it is a mouse and is determined to discourage it without male assistance, but Kat is highly skeptical of the identity of the unwelcome visitor and of her mother's ability to catch it. A mousetrap and a cage borrowed from the animal shelter prove ineffectual. Aunt Kathy suggests an exterminator, but humanitarian Mom vetoes poison. The next-door neighbor volunteers to smoke out the intruder as it becomes bolder, but independent Mom declares that they need no masculine aid. On Saturday she hauls out the ladder, discovers a piece of loose siding, and, after driving three squirrels out the opening with help from the dog, nails it firmly back in place. When Dad arrives to pick up the girls the following morning, they proudly and triumphantly relate their victory over the invaders.

90.   Grant, Cynthia D. JOSHUA FORTUNE. New York: Atheneum,
         1980. 152p. Grades 5-8. R+
         Born of hippie parents in San Francisco's Haight-Ashbury, Joshua Fortune George, 14, despises his name and rootless existence. When his sister Sarah Sunshine, now 11, was small, their father, a born rover, left the family to pursue his fantasies in tropical lands. Josh's mother Suzanne, now divorced and teaching first grade, still practices the lifestyle of the counterculture. Their latest move has brought them to the lackluster town of Santa Rosa, where Suzanne's boyfriend Harley is a toy salesman. Intense, choleric Harley is critical of Suzanne's relaxed permissiveness, and he and Josh are instant adversaries. At school he gravitates toward two classmates who are even more unorthodox than his old city chums, and his relationship with Alexa waxes warm and very personal. Harley makes the first attempt at conciliation by giving Josh a bike for Christmas.

Josh's dad, whom he hasn't seen for three years and who continually
breaks his promise to visit, turns up unexpectedly and inopportune-
ly with his new wife on Suzanne and Harley's wedding day. Joshua
Fortune, no stranger to change and lack of protocol, decides to
quit fighting it.

91.   Greene, Constance C.   AL(EXANDRA) THE GREAT.   New York:
        Viking, 1982.   133p.   Grades 5-8.   R+
        Summer's heat is oppressive in their New York apartment
building, and Al, 13, having received an invitation from her father
and his wife to visit them on their farm in Ohio, is eagerly anticipating the change of scene, not to mention the expectation of renew-
ing acquaintances with Brian, the boy she met at her father's wedding (see 93, 95, and 97). Her chic mother, who works in Better
Dresses and is now dating a Mr. Wright (who is still not Mr. Right),
has had a cough that suddenly degenerates into pneumonia. While
she is hospitalized, the family of her best friend and foil invites Al,
still original and outspoken but maturing, to stay in their apartment
down the hall. As her mother's illness lingers, it becomes clear to
Al that her prospective trip will have to be postponed, and, suffering from acute disappointment, she calls to inform her father's new
family of her decision to remain at her mother's side. Her mother
conveys her pride in Al's unselfishness, and Dad and Louise send
her a T-shirt with the legend "Al(exandra) the Great."

92.   Greene, Constance C.   ASK ANYBODY.   New York: Viking,
        1983.   150p.   Grades 5-7.   R+
        Divorced after 15 years of marriage, Schuyler Sweet's
parents occupy opposite ends of their Maine farmhouse where her
father maintains his cartoon studio and her mother pursues nature
photography. Now Mother is off on assignment to Africa and to
meet Angus, the Australian hunter with whom she fancies she is in
love, leaving Daddy, Sky, 11, Tad, 7, and Sidney, 5, to keep
house. Opinionated Sky resents Pamela, the lazy, selfish art student whom her father frequently invites to dinner. She and her
two friends Rowena and Betty have formed the Chum Club, and
when Nell, a cocky new girl, moves into a rental property nearby,
an intrigued Sky insists that she be invited to join them despite
the others' misgivings. Nell, who sports green fingernails, boasts
of her transiency, and demonstrates that she knows how to turn
boys on, immediately dominates the organization of the Chums' yard
sale. Sky becomes disenchanted with Nell only when she runs over
the family pet in the truck she is too young to drive and shows no
remorse. She changes her opinion of Pamela when the latter gives
her empathetic advice and comfort. The sale is a success, but when
it is over they discover that Nell's trashy family has moved out in
the middle of the night, absconding with their profits and Rowena's
mother's fur coat. Mother returns minus Angus, and she and Dad
start making conciliatory noises. Sky resolves to be more discrim-
inating but not to make snap judgments.

93. Greene, Constance C. A GIRL CALLED AL. New York:
       Viking, 1969. Illus. by Byron Barton. 127p. Grades 4-6.
       R+
       When Al first moves to Apartment 14C, she is a conscious
nonconformist, compensating for her broken home. Her chic, svelte
mother works all day and dates most evenings. Her father sends
her plenty of money but never writes, calls or visits. Left to her
own devices, the lonely and intense seventh-grader gorges herself
to obesity, wears a homely hairstyle, and hates being called Alexan-
dra. She and the amusingly ingenuous narrator of the story, a
classmate who lives down the hall, become firm friends. With the
tactful help of the inimitable building superintendent, Mr. Richards,
a retired bartender and armchair philosopher, Al begins to think
positively about herself, make the best of the situation, and improve
her appearance. Mr. Richards' untimely death sobers and matures
both girls, but memories of shared camaraderie buoy their spirits.

94. Greene, Constance C. I AND SPROGGY. New York: Viking,
       1978. Illus. by Emily McCully. 155p. Grades 4-6. R+
       Adam, 10, whose parents divorced four years ago and now
make better friends than they did lovers, lives in New York with
his mother, an illustrator, and dreams of being a celebrity invited
to Gracie Mansion by the mayor. In the two years since he last saw
his father, Dad has remarried and this summer has brought his new
wife and stepdaughter, Sproggy, also 10, to visit. Charged by his
father with taking care of Sproggy, Adam takes an immediate dislike
to his British stepsister. Far from needing his protection, she is
a head taller than he, poised, dexterous, and competent. With
her leadership qualities Sproggy saves Adam from muggers, steals
his dog's affections, and organizes his best friends into forming a
chess club, a game Adam doesn't play. The more she encroaches
upon his personal interests, the more bitterly and spitefully he
lashes out at her. Sproggy has one point of vulnerability, however,
and when Adam surprises a group of bullies heckling her because
of her real name, Evangeline, he comes to her rescue and belatedly
makes friends. On the day that the building superintendent of
Adam's apartment house is honored at a reception at Gracie Mansion,
Sproggy wangles an invitation for all the club members through the
good offices of her influential uncle, and Adam finds himself on the
TV news.

95. Greene, Constance C. I KNOW YOU, AL. New York: Viking,
       1975. Illus. by Byron Barton. 126p. Grades 5-7. R+
       At 13, Al (see 93) is tired of waiting--waiting to be attrac-
tive, waiting to be popular, waiting to get her period. An unexpected telephone call from the father she hasn't seen in six years
forestalls her adolescent maunderings but plunges her into a sea
of ambivalence. Her father invites her to attend his wedding and
meet his new family, and while she is delirious about seeing him and
meeting her stepbrothers, she is nervous about making a good impression and is especially resentful that her father could just walk

out of her life and now just as casually reenter. Her fears are
abolished at the wedding. She takes compassion on her father and
anticlimactically gets her period. For a nonconformist she is pretty
predictable to her bosom buddy, who acts as foil for Al's wit and
records her trials and tribulations in droll prose.

96.   Greene, Constance C. THE UNMAKING OF RABBIT. New
          York: Viking, 1972. 125p. Grades 5-6. R
          Gran says that Paul's mother is impulsive, selfish, willful
and childish. Her first husband, Paul's father, was a cad who ran
off when the boy was 2. Now his mother is stalking her second
husband, and Paul, 11, even though he loves his sensible, perspicacious, down-to-earth grandmother, is just marking time till his
mother sends for him. Small for his age, lonely and timid, he is
teased and easily cowed by a gang of classmates who call him
Rabbit. Life takes a turn for the worse when his mother, an aging
model, after her marriage to a sometime artist/photographer, disappoints Paul by making excuses not to make a home for him, and the
bullies start pressuring him to join them for some ulterior and
probably disagreeable motive of their own. After a disastrous day
spent in the city with his mother and her husband, he learns the
reason for the boys' friendly overtures. Because of his size, they
want him to enter the window of a house so they can burglarize it.
Somehow he summons the gumption to refuse. The grandson of
Gran's best friend, whom she's been touting ad nauseam, comes to
visit, and Paul, prepared to hate him sight unseen, discovers that
Gordon is just an average, ordinary guy. With the confidence of
his first friendship, Paul settles into his life with Gran.

97.   Greene, Constance C. YOUR OLD PAL, AL. New York:
          Viking, 1979. 149p. Grades 5-8. R+
          Uninhibited Al (see 93 and 95) is moody and edgy, awaiting
an invitation from her father's new wife to visit them on summer
vacation and also expecting a letter from the boy she met at their
wedding in California. The narrator, Al's friend, sounding board,
and chronicler, is glad of the diversion when sophisticated Polly,
a friend from across town, inveigles an invitation to spend two
weeks with her and her family in their apartment across the hall
from Al and her mother, a department store saleswoman in New York
City. Al, at loose ends, writes a letter to Brian which she vacillates
about posting, makes overnight plans with a disgustingly crass con-
formist, is perversely pleased that Polly snores and disturbs her
friend's sleep, and speculates on her mother's breakup with her
most recent beau. As the tension mounts, a domino effect of quarreling ensues among the girls, extending even to the narrator's
parents, until Al receives one of the letters she has been awaiting
and consoles herself that one is better than none. Anticlimactically,
the second missive arrives, and a jubilant Al thanks her old pal for
bearing with her.

98.   Greenwald, Sheila. BLISSFUL JOY AND THE SATs; A MULTIPLE

CHOICE ROMANCE. Boston: Little, Brown, 1982. 143p.
Grades 8-12. R+
Because her divorced parents are "childlike, unreliable,
disorganized actors," Blissful Joy Bowman, 17, is planning a normal,
structured lifestyle for herself, beginning with a scholarship to
Vassar. To achieve the latter, she is obsessively cramming for the
forthcoming SATs until the day a stray dog adopts her and she becomes temporarily sidetracked. Both parents' romantic liaisons
present further distractions, not to mention being asked out by
Howard Oaks, wealthy and attractive stepbrother of her private
school classmate Sybil. Two final complications are the mysterious
girl in green, who follows Bliss whenever she walks the dog, and
her mother's latest conquest, a young actor named Colin who also
seems to be making a pass at Bliss while challenging her values
and aspirations. From Colin she learns that the girl in green is
Howard's little sister who recognizes the dog as belonging to the
mother who deserted them. She has been following Bliss in hope
that she will lead her to her mother. As Howard's date at Sybil's
birthday party, Bliss is mortified when Howard and Sybil, who
have been secretly in love for years, reveal their plans to elope
and confess that they have been using Bliss as a red herring. She
turns to Colin for comfort. Unwittingly, she locates the missing
mother and becomes a celebrity. After learning the tricks of test
taking at cram school, she aces the exam and relaxes in the knowledge that there is life after the SATs.

99.   Greenwald, Sheila. THE SECRET IN MIRANDA'S CLOSET.
Boston: Houghton Mifflin, 1977. Illus. by the author.
138p. Grades 4-6. R+
Chic, svelte, gregarious Olivia Perry, sociologist, critic,
magazine editor, and liberated woman since her divorce, boasts that
her daughter Miranda prefers trucks to dolls. Miranda Alexis Perry,
chubby, myopic and shy, feels uncomfortable with the organized
activities her mother arranges for her and would rather unleash her
own fertile imagination. When she is presented with a lovely and
valuable antique doll, she is immediately smitten but feels compelled
to conceal the gift rather than risk Olivia's disapproval. In the
rear of her commodious closet in their New York City house, she
constructs an elaborate dollhouse where she occupies herself for
hours. At a party hosted by Olivia, Miranda's secret is spitefully
revealed by the sophisticated daughter of the man her mother has
been dating. After her initial shock, Olivia assures Miranda that it's
perfectly acceptable for her to assert her own individuality without
having to wrestle for her independence as Olivia had to do with her
role-bound father, brother, and husband. When Olivia loses her
university post, Miranda offers to sell her valuable doll, but her
mother demurs, asserting that Dinah is a symbol of freedom of
choice.

100. Griffiths, Helen. GRIP, A DOG STORY. New York: Holiday,
1978. Illus. by Douglas Hall. 129p. Grades 5-7. R

"...Bill Kershaw could no more sell his dog than he could his son, although some people wondered which of the two he preferred." The dog is Madman, a bull terrior bred and trained for his ferocity. The boy is Dudley, reared in impassive solitude on the moors where his surly, aloof father repaired after his wife deserted him and where he stages his illicit sport. Dudley is 11 in 1930, and his father decides he must choose and train a brute of his own in the family tradition. He picks a pup sired by Madman and names him Grip for his tenacity in war games. In the course of their gambols, Dudley first experiences the emotion of love. In his baptismal badger-baiting, Grip gains a reputation for courage and endurance even though grievously wounded. But his early promise is merely the result of obedience to the boy. In subsequent dogfights he defends himself by fleeing. Dudley cannot bear to drown the cowardly dog, as his father decrees, and merely abandons him. A classmate and her brother adopt the wretchedly forlorn dog and gradually tame and humanize his alienated master, teaching him that pugilism only masquerades as valor. In an outing on the desolate moors, Dudley and Grip are suddenly set upon by the murderous Madman. Grip instinctively knows when it is time to take a stand, and the canine gladiator engages his sire in a battle to the death. Grip, the victor, earns his keep by being put to stud, and Dudley makes peace with his new friends.

101.   Gripe, Maria. PAPPA PELLERIN'S DAUGHTER. New York:
        Day, 1966. (OP) Trans. by Kersti French. 156p. Grades
        5-7. NR
        Mamma, who is in domestic service to wealthy people on summer cruises, has promised to return by October, but when she does not appear, Loella, 12 and fiercely independent, makes preparations for her and her small twin brothers to weather the Swedish winter in their cottage in the woods. She avoids the townspeople, who regard her as a hoyden, because she fears that the authorities will separate the little family. She rigs a scarecrow, dubbed Pappa Pellerin and attired in her long-absent father's old clothing, to frighten away trespassers, but the ploy fails when Mamma writes to say she has found permanent employment in America and the boys are to go to a friend in the city while Loella is to live in an orphanage. The ingenuous girl finds the urban environment alien and fantasizes wildly to the other children about her missing father until she and they believe her inventions. Her bubble bursts on an evening's escapade with her worldly wise roommate, and Loella painfully has to acknowledge that her parents are divorced. At the end of the school term she and her brothers are permitted to return home. Her fantasies come true when she discovers that her father, summoned to make a home for them, is waiting.

102.   Guernsey, JoAnn Bren. JOURNEY TO ALMOST THERE. New
        York: Clarion, 1985. 166p. Grades 7-10. R+
        In rebellion against her mother's undisguised approval of a suitable boyfriend, Alison O'Brien, 15, baits her by encouraging the

attentions of a totally inappropriate and degenerate boy, challenging
her bank officer mother's feminist liberality. When they almost come
to blows over the issue, Alison decides to leave her Minneapolis home
to find her father, who left when she was a baby to pursue an art
career in Massachusetts. She takes along her adored paternal
grandfather Oliver, the only father figure she has ever known, who
suffers from Parkinson's disease and whom she fears will be consigned to a nursing home by her mother. During periods of solitude
on the long drive, while Oliver naps, Alison reflects on her former
intimacy with her mother and begins to miss her. The trip is physically taxing, and Oliver has to be hospitalized only hours away from
their destination. His imbalance of medications is corrected, but the
hospital notifies Alison's mother of their whereabouts, and she in
turn alerts her former husband of their impending arrival. When
Alison and Oliver locate his seedy apartment, they discover him
missing, unable to face up to them because of the lies he has told
them in letters. Alison reconciles with her mother by phone and
heads home with a firmer grip on reality and the knowledge that she
is loved.

103. Hahn, Mary Downing. DAPHNE'S BOOK. New York: Clarion,
       1983. 177p. Grades 6-9. R+
       Jessica Taylor, 12, is short on self-confidence as she enters
middle school and is anxious about being accepted by the popular
clique. She is appalled, therefore, when her English teacher pairs
her, the best writer in class, with Daphne Woodleigh, the best artist, to enter a picture book writing contest. Daphne is a misfit
and the butt of cruel ridicule. Jessica's mother, a divorced librarian, encourages her to make the best of the partnership, and, indeed, when Jessica scratches Daphne's defensive shell, the two become close friends. Then Daphne's crotchety grandmother, with
whom she and her sister live in poverty on the outskirts of their
Maryland town, falls victim to senile dementia, and Daphne feigns
mononucleosis to stay home and watch her. The grandmother's
Social Security checks go uncashed, the utilities are turned off,
and the three are starving. Although sworn to secrecy, Jessica finally confides their plight to her mother, hoping that she will take
them in. But Mrs. Taylor, who has plans to remarry, alerts
authorities, and the sisters are taken to a children's shelter. Their
grandmother dies of pneumonia, and Daphne blames Jessica for her
guilt. Before the sisters leave for a new home with relatives, Jessica informs Daphne that their story has won first prize and forces
Daphne to talk out her emotions. They vow to remain friends, and
Jessica takes up where she left off with her former acquaintances.

104. Hall, Lynn. THE BOY IN THE OFF-WHITE HAT. New York:
       Scribner, 1984. 87p. Grades 5-6. R++
       A horse lover, Skeeter Long, 13, applies as live-in mother's
helper on summer vacation to Maxine Bates who runs a horse training and rental farm in Arkansas. Her charge is Shane, 9, whose
father abandoned Maxine during her pregnancy and who knows that

his birth was a mistake. Maxine, who moonlights as a grocery store
clerk, is undemonstrative and unconsciously critical of Shane.
When a stranger, Burgess Franklin, starts showering him with flattering attention, Shane responds like a puppy dog. Maxine interprets Burge's affection for her son as a signal that he is interested
in marriage. She makes friendly overtures to him, but Burge claims
he isn't free to marry. Following a fishing trip with Burge, Shane
starts acting fearful of him but refuses to discuss it with the observant Skeeter. When Maxine is hospitalized with a broken leg, she
gratefully accepts Burge's offer to move into the house in her absence, and later, still hoping he will propose, to stay permanently.
Shane pleads to sleep in Skeeter's bed and suddenly acts schizophrenic, claiming to be a boy named John and disavowing Shane as
a shameful boy. The light dawns on Skeeter that Burge has been
molesting him. She tells Maxine who almost kills Burge in attempting
to expunge her guilt over her selfishness and preoccupation. Shane
enters intensive therapy to repair his severely battered psyche.

105.   Hallstead, William F. TUNDRA. New York: Crown, 1984.
         121p. Grades 6-9. R
         Too proud to accept his wife's need for a part-time job as
an interior designer, Jamie Harwood's father left them a year ago
and has since remarried. Now 15, Jamie is tall, gangling, self-
conscious, insecure, and resentful of her mother's boyfriend Nelson
MacClellan. To compensate for the heartache of the divorce, her
mother buys her a Siberian husky, Tundra, from whom she derives
self-confidence and love. She is desolate when the dog digs under
the fence and runs away but refuses to accept the probability, as
the days drag on, that he is dead. In the meantime, the dog is
enduring numerous life-threatening mishaps, including starvation
and being struck by an auto. In his weakness, he is snatched by
dognappers to be used as live bait in training a fighting pit bull.
Using his wits he escapes the brutality, only to be snared by the
Animal Shelter and scheduled for euthanasia. In her distress during
Tundra's absence, Jamie finally makes friends with Nelson, the only
adult who understands her faith and hope in Tundra's return enough
to help her reinforce the dog run. Her fealty is rewarded when the
two are reunited coincidentally at a dog show.

106.   Hamilton, Virginia. THE PLANET OF JUNIOR BROWN. New
         York: Macmillan, 1971. 210p. Grades 6-9. R+
         Grossly obese musical prodigy Junior Brown is being driven
to distraction by the two domineering women in his life, his piano
teacher, who will not permit him to play her instrument because of
her own psychotic delusions, and his compulsive, overprotective
mother who has silenced his home piano so that his practice will not
disturb the rest she requires because of her chronic asthma. He is
even failed by his father who habitually breaks his promise to visit
him on weekends from his job in New Jersey. His only friend is
streetwise orphan Buddy Clark, fugitive from the courts and social
welfare system, and big brother to a group of younger black waifs

subsisting underground in New York City. The two are on the hook
from their eighth grade classes, abetted by the school custodian who
has constructed an elaborate model solar system in the secret basement room in which he harbors them. On a final visit to the piano
teacher, the frustrated Junior precipitates a crisis in which his
severely cracked facade splinters irreparably before Buddy's horrified
eyes. Fearing that commitment to a mental institution will do ir-
revocable damage to Junior's fragile personality, Buddy temporarily
adopts Junior as one of the lost boys he is rehabilitating in his own
covert "planet."

107.   Hamilton, Virginia. SWEET WHISPERS, BROTHER RUSH. New
           York: Putnam, 1982. 215p. Grades 7-10. R+
           While her mother, a practical nurse, is out of the home on pri-
vate cases, Teresa (Tree) Pratt, 14, has sole responsibility for her retarded but beloved brother Dabney, 17, a burden that sometimes taxes
her monumental patience and capability. In the tiny storeroom she
retreats to after an especially trying week, the ghost of her mother's
long-dead brother appears to her and reveals details of the past:
how her young mother abused Dab and how handsome black Brother
Rush himself ran numbers and died in an auto accident caused by
Tree's spendthrift father who later deserted them. Then Dab becomes deathly ill, and providentially Mama Vy arrives home to assist
Tree. M'Vy recognizes Dab's symptoms as those of congenital por-
phyria (from which Brother Rush suffered), aggravated by heavy
drugs with which Dab's many sleepover girlfriends have furtively
supplied him. Dab is hospitalized, but it is too late. Because of
her protracted maternal role, Tree is inconsolable and lashes out
at both M'Vy for her unavoidable neglect and at Vy's gentle, diplomatic male friend Silversmith. M'Vy hires an old friend as housekeeper to relieve Tree of her chores, but it is too little too late,
and Tree considers running away. The funeral services calm her,
and she takes a new interest in life when she meets Silversmith's
grown, congenial son. M'Vy acknowledges past mistakes and promises a better life when she and Silversmith marry and start a catering service.

108.   Harris, Mark Jonathan. WITH A WAVE OF THE WAND. New
           York: Lothrop, Lee and Shepard, 1980. 191p. Grades
           5-6. R+
           When Marlee Phillips' parents separate, Mom finds a job as
librarian and moves Marlee, 11, and Jeremy with her from an affluent
Los Angeles suburb to bohemian Venice. Marlee cannot adjust but
believes the arrangement to be temporary because Mom and Dad are
seeing a marriage counselor. Jeremy is her mother's favorite, while
Marlee prefers her father. She appeals to move into his Hollywood
apartment near his advertising office but he declines. Both parents
begin dating, creating awkwardness and resentment. Overhearing
his mother tell a friend, "If only we didn't have children," Jeremy
concludes that they are no longer wanted. They step up their efforts to effect a reconciliation. When exemplary behavior fails, they
pin their hopes on magic. Marlee consults their elderly neighbor,

Angelo Tomaro, a retired magician, but he knows only sleight-of-hand. In a book on black magic she finds an ancient potion, but the results are negative. Finally she resorts to will and determination, but on the eve of her birthday Dad drops the bombshell that he and Mom are getting divorced and he is moving to New York. Numb and furious, Marlee runs away to get even. She is found close to home by Mr. Tomaro and finally sheds the tears that have been accumulating for months. She makes peace with her father and decides to concentrate on learning Mr. Tomaro's brand of magic.

109. Haynes, Mary. WORDCHANGER. New York: Lothrop, Lee
        and Shepard, 1983. Illus. by Eric Jon Nones. 252p.
        Grades 5-8. R
        One of Martha Wilson's objectives in remarrying was to pro-
vide a father for her son William, 12, after her husband's death of a
heart attack two years earlier. William instinctively dislikes Bruno
Ashburton, but when his mother learns that Bruno, a millionaire
with powerlust, has merely been exploiting her to gain access to
physicist Bill Wilson's notes on a technique for changing words in
books by remote control, she drugs Bruno and escapes with William
in the car in which Bruno has stashed the Wordchanger. Knowing
that Bruno and his ruthless henchmen will stop at nothing to recover the machine, they switch their auto for an Airstream trailer
for the cross-country flight to find Stan Lee, Bill Wilson's former
friend and collaborator in San Francisco, only to discover later that
Bruno can trace them by means of a radioactive signal that is
emitted by the Wordchanger. A stowaway, Lily Maxwell, 12, who
has run away from home because she feels that she is a stumbling
block to her divorced artist father's career, joins them in Colorado.
Along the way, Martha, a physicist herself and textbook editor,
conducts research in a university library into the principles of the
device as Bruno closes in by helicopter. Lily and William hide the
trailer while Martha locates Dr. Lee. She realizes too late that Stan
has betrayed her for money when Bruno nabs her. The kids save
the day with great ingenuity, assisted by William's astute grandparents, and Lily reconciles with her father.

110. Heide, Florence Parry. WHEN THE SAD ONE COMES TO STAY.
        Philadelphia: Lippincott, 1975. (OP) 74p. Grades 5-7.
        R+
        Sara has come to live with her mother Sally, a successful,
sophisticated, stylish, snobbish social climber who is trying to remake Sara in her own image. When Sally collected her from her
father, a junk dealer, she discarded her old shabby clothes and
toys, bought her expensive new ones, deposited her and her finery
in a modern decorator apartment at a good address, and told her to
make friends among the pampered daughters of privilege and influence. Instead, the lonely girl befriends an equally lonely, impoverished, uneducated old woman who encourages her to delve into her
fading memory for reminiscences of her happy, carefree life with her

affable father and half brother. Sally, believing that the past
should be obliterated, gets an unlisted telephone number when
Sara's father tries to call. The repressed and beleaguered child's
last opportunity to assert herself comes when Sally decides to take
a short trip to New York. Sara, unfortunately, follows the course
of least resistance.

111. Helmering, Doris Wild. I HAVE TWO FAMILIES. Nashville,
         Abingdon, 1981. Illus. by Heidi Palmer. Unp. Grades
         1-3. R+
         When 9-year-old Patty's parents get divorced, she is afraid
that they will divide her and her little brother Michael like community
property, but instead they decide to share custody because of her
mom's irregular hours as an airlines reservation agent. Her dad,
because of his 9-to-5 schedule, will be the primary care giver.
Monday through Wednesday, Dad wakes them, gets them ready for
school and day care, and drops them off on his way to work. On
Wednesday, Mom picks them up and they spend the night with her,
returning to Dad on Thursday evening. Saturday is spent with Dad
and Sunday with Mom. Living primarily with Dad is not without its
difficulties. Tempers flare when disorganization in the morning
sometimes makes them late, and the children are initially frosty to
the attractive young woman Dad dates on Saturday nights. But Dad
stresses open communication and advanced planning as the methods
of solving their problems. Especially important is their game of
"Catch-up" in which each of them must relate at least two events
that happened in the course of his day. With chores shared three
ways to lighten Dad's load, Patty's worry is reduced to minor inconvenience.

112. Hermes, Patricia. A SOLITARY SECRET. San Diego: Har-
         court Brace Jovanovich, 1985. 135p. Grades 7-12. R++
         When the fighting stops and her mother starts packing, the
unnamed fourteen-year-old girl is optimistic that life will soon be
better for her and her already emotionally scarred brother Benjamin,
6, whom she's sheltered all his life from their indifferent parents.
But her mother takes only Benjamin, leaving her behind to keep
house for her father. That night he enters her bedroom and forces
himself upon her. The next night she attempts to lock her door,
but he punches a hole in it. Thereafter he rapes her routinely.
He snaps: "It happens all the time. Get used to it. This is our
secret." She can't bring herself to tell the sanctimonious nuns at
school or her rural neighbors because of the alarming realization
that this despicable man is the only relative she has left. The
knowledge nauseates her, and she is terrified that she may be pregnant. And he sneers: "You ask for it, you know. You love it."
Her hatred of him turns to self-loathing. When she makes friends
with a new girl in school, he forbids her to see Sheila whose
mother is so warm and empathetic. When she learns that Sheila is
dying of a rare disease, her fear and guilt that God is punishing
her for wishing her father dead add to her burden of anguish.

The longing to be rescued and loved finally impels the lonely,
frightened and distraught child to thrust the journal chronicling
her personal purgatory upon Sheila's mother following the funeral.
Four years later, after therapy and foster care, she becomes her
beloved Benjamin's guardian, and together they lay to rest the
nightmares of their past.

113.   Hoban, Lillian. I MET A TRAVELLER. New York: Harper
          and Row, 1977. 182p. Grades 6-9. R
          The only Jew in her Christian missionary school in Jerusa-
lem, Josie Hayden, 11, is lonely and obsessed with adolescent woes,
while her mother, a breezy and charismatic artist, is absorbed in
the exciting, exotic Israeli life and her new love affair. An aging
Russian immigrant couple moves to a nearby apartment, and when
the husband dies, Josie consoles his widow Mira. The grandmotherly woman becomes a surrogate mother to the unhappy girl in her
mother's frequent absences, even though they do not speak a common
language. Josie sees the possibility of returning to her old home in
Connecticut given the adult companionship of Mira, since her mother
has no intention of returning to suburbia. She quietly sets about
earning airfare, telling no one of her scheme. Her disillusionment
is unbounded when she learns that her beloved Mira is having an
affair of her own and has no desire to emigrate to America. Her
mother provides her with a book on sex after 60 and concedes that
she is a poor parent but a loving one and not about to change to
suit Josie. At the end of the school term, her mother ends her affair and begins a new one as she and Josie depart Israel for parts
unknown. Josie glosses her lips and decides to take a grown-up
interest in boys herself.

114.   Holland, Isabelle. THE EMPTY HOUSE. New York: Lippin-
          cott, 1983. 218p. Grades 5-9. R
          Upon their father's unjust imprisonment for tax fraud, hav-
ing accepted culpability for his firm's new accountant, Betsy Smith,
15, and her epileptic brother Rodney, 12, are sent to stay with
Aunt Marian and Uncle Paul on the Jersey Shore. Their mother,
divorced five years from their father, has remarried and works as a
roving reporter based in London. Defensive among the local snobbish teens, they make friends only with elderly, distinguished Mrs.
Whitelaw and her handicapped daughter who live alone in a dilapidated old house full of cats, and with Ted Lockwood, the friendly
soda jerk. Only later does Betsy discover that Ted's father is the
investigative reporter who hounded her father in the press. When
Roddy has a seizure on the beach with ghoulish newshawks televising
the episode, she believes that Ted, with whom she has fallen in love,
has leaked the news of their identity. She and Roddy seek refuge
with Mrs. Whitelaw and learn from her that their father salvaged her
ancestral home from repossession by a racketeer long ago. They
realize then that the mobster has waited till now to retaliate by in-
filtrating their dad's company. Ted proves his innocence and loyalty
by urging his father to expose the truth, and Betsy and Ted reconcile.

115.   Holland, Isabelle. HEADS YOU WIN, TAILS I LOSE. Phila-
          delphia: Lippincott, 1973. 159p. Grades 7-9. R+
          An undemonstrative, reactionary father with a cruel streak
and a progressive, critical, brutally frank mother create a volatile
environment for overweight Melissa, 15, who is already agonizing
over her inability to attract the boy she likes. The battered ball
in her parents' vicious game, she finally rebels against their chronic
withering derogation and exhorts them to get divorced. After her
father's departure, her mother resorts to alcohol in her self-pity.
Melissa filches her mother's diet pills to lose weight and her sleeping
tablets to offset the effect of the amphetamines. The weight loss is
dramatic, but she finally overdoses at rehearsal for a school play
and the truth suddenly emerges. A compassionate teacher and a
perceptive boy, her only friends, help her pull herself together
and grasp the reins of her own life. Melissa effects a reconciliation
with her father while coping maturely with her mother until she can
go her independent way at 18.

116.   Holland, Isabelle. THE MAN WITHOUT A FACE. Philadelphia:
          Lippincott, 1972. 248p. Grades 7-10. R+
          Charles Norstadt, 14, and his two half-sisters each have
different fathers. Their socialite mother has just dumped her fourth
husband and is about to annex number five. She makes no secret
of the fact that she made a mistake in marrying Charles' father.
Charles gets along well with his younger sister Meg, 11, but Gloria,
16, has always lacerated him with her tongue. To escape her vitriol,
Charles is eager to get to boarding school but has failed the entrance exam. In desperation he turns to a hideously disfigured man,
a former teacher who is now a virtual recluse, to tutor him. Because Justin McLeod is a stern taskmaster, their relationship begins
in antagonism. As their interchange thaws, McLeod discloses how
he received his affliction but rebuffs Charles' attempt at sympathy,
and the betrayed boy blurts McLeod's secret to his indolent friends
in a drug-induced stupor. When both apologize, their mutual respect and friendship finally flourishes, and McLeod becomes the
father figure Charles so badly needs. An unfortunate incident precipitates an isolated homosexual encounter between the two, and
Charles, having passed the test, goes off to school. Later he
learns that his father was a common drunk, and in distress he again
seeks out McLeod, only to learn that he has just died. Defeatism
almost engulfs him, but he opts to return to school and live up to
Justin McLeod's expectations.

117.   Holland, Isabelle. OF LOVE AND DEATH AND OTHER JOUR-
          NEYS. Philadelphia: Lippincott, 1975. 159p. Grades 7-10.
          R+
          In the same day, Meg Grant, 15, learns 1) that the father
whom her mother divorced before she was born and whom she has
never met is coming to Assisi to visit her, and 2) that her mother
has terminal cancer. As long as she can remember she and her
gamin mother, now married to Peter Smith, a serious scholar who

subsists by writing pornography, have vagabonded about Europe,
giving guided tours in summer to supplement their income. Suddenly she discovers that her father did not know of her existence
earlier because her mother was not sure at the time she left him
that he was, in fact, the father. His upper crust family, with whom
she was incompatible, snubbed her insufferably. He later became an
Anglican priest and remarried. Meg is initially hostile to her father
until she hears the circumstances of his long neglect, then confides
to him her fear of her mother's impending death. Meg finds it difficult to grieve when her mother dies and wants to remain with Peter
or their painter friend Cotton, with whom she is infatuated. Against
her wishes she is sent to her father in New York where she plots
her return to Italy, and, when thwarted, sinks into deep depression.
It is only when Cotton sends her a portrait of her mother that the
floodgates to her emotions finally open to bathe the festering wound.

118. Hopkins, Lee Bennett. MAMA. New York: Knopf, 1977.
         108p.   Grades 5-7.   R
         Mrs. Kipness is conscientious about rearing her fatherless
boys to be good citizens. Neighborly, considerate, industrious and
strict, yet fiercely protective of her two cubs, she is a model of
rectitude in every way but for the remarkable formula she has de-
vised for stretching their income. Her elder son, Mark, 10, is embarrassed when Mama forces him and his brother Chris, 5, to hide
in the rest room of the train while the conductor takes the tickets,
but he doesn't become really suspicious of Mama's pragmatic budget-
balancing devices until she asks him to bring home bags full of
merchandise which she has liberated from the latest of a long succession of employers (to whom she gives notice when things become
too hot). Mama calls it a game and has no difficulty justifying her
brazen shoplifting, but Mark knows it is larceny and is nervous,
frightened, and even ashamed of Mama. He lacks the courage to
confront her with her wrongdoing for fear of hurting her feelings
and spoiling her pleasure in providing Christmas treats for him and
his brother. After the holidays, he has hopes that in her new job
at the laundry she will find nothing to steal. In the meantime, his
love, loyalty and gratitude to her never waver.

119. Hopkins, Lee Bennett. MAMA AND HER BOYS. New York:
         Harper and Row, 1981. 149p. Grades 4-6. R+
         Not only does change of occupation cure Mama of her klep-
tomania (see 118) but it also brings an offer of matrimony. When
she makes the momentous announcement that she has the opportunity
of marrying her boss at the laundry, Mark, 10, reacts with incredulity and Chris, 5, with immutable negativity. Faced with her sons'
opposition to Mr. Jacobs, a decent man who puts business foremost,
Mama capitulates. As a substitute, Mark arranges for Mama to meet
his school custodian, Mike Carlisle, who impressed him favorably
when he interviewed the widower for the school newspaper. An
offer to fix a leaky faucet leads to an invitation to dinner, and the
romance is off and running. Mike takes the boys to the beach and

to the circus for the first time in their lives, endearing himself to
them. But Chris, while being punished for a prank that floods
the basement of the laundry, begins having misgivings about Mama's
new relationship, reasoning that if she marries Mike, he and Mark
will be displaced and perhaps institutionalized. As a result, he
starts acting rebellious and flouting his outspoken mother's uncompromising, if sometimes illogical and contradictory, standards. The
school psychologist advises Mama and Mike to declare their intention
of marrying. When they do, all of Chris' doubts and insecurities
vanish.

120. Hunter, Evan. ME AND MR. STENNER. Philadelphia:
         Lippincott, 1976. 157p. Grades 5-6. R+
         It is difficult to hate Mr. Stenner, but Abigail O'Neill, 11,
is committed to aggravating him, because it is he, formerly a mutual
friend of both her parents, who is responsible for the dissolution of
their marriage. While her mother is awaiting her final decree and
Mr. Stenner is seeking a divorce from his intractable wife, they are
living together openly as husband and wife. Abby lives with them
and visits her father on alternate weekends. Mr. Stenner, a fashion
photographer, is fair, amusing, self-deprecating and paternal, but
Abby remains defensively and belligerently loyal to her dad, a rigid,
stuffy architect. When she pushes Mr. Stenner's tolerance beyond
its limits, he draws firm guidelines governing her behavior and en-
forces them. Abby displays only token resentment because she
feels guilty for treating him shabbily. When her mom marries Mr.
Stenner (and her dad is occupied with an exotic South American),
Abby is invited to join them on their honeymoon abroad. In Italy
Mr. Stenner gives her a bracelet for her birthday which she adores,
but she can't resist giving one more twist to the knife by declaring
that she can't accept it because her father might object. Mr. Stenner's patience snaps, and in the aftermath Abby begs his forgiveness, confesses that she loves him, and casts about for a more personal appellation for him.

121. Hurwitz, Johanna. DE DE TAKES CHARGE. New York:
         Morrow, 1984. Illus. by Diane de Groat. 121p. Grades
         4-5. R+
         Divorced for a year, DeDe Rawson's father is looking for
perfection in a woman. DeDe, 10, spends only odd weekends with
him in New York while living in New Jersey with her mother who
has allowed herself to go to seed. An art student before marriage,
Mrs. Rawson hates her job as department store clerk and cannot
afford repairs on their house or car. DeDe persuades her to join
a vegetable co-op in hopes that she will meet an eligible bachelor.
The results are disappointing, and DeDe gives in to self-pity when
she and Mom are reduced to eating Thanksgiving dinner alone in a
restaurant. She makes a devious effort to play matchmaker between
Mom and her shop teacher, Mr. Evans, and is chagrined when it
fails. A friend's mother encourages Mrs. Rawson to go into business
making the ceramic planters she creates as a hobby. In the

56   The Single-Parent Family

meantime, she meets Mr. Evans under natural circumstances at a
school play. This time they strike a responsive chord, and Mrs.
Rawson informs DeDe that she can arrange her own relationships.
DeDe decides to measure time no longer as B.D. and A.D. (before
and after divorce) and concentrate on surviving braces instead.

122. Johnson, Annabel, and Edgar Johnson. THE GRIZZLY. New
        York: Harper and Row, 1964. Illus. by Gilbert Riswold.
        160p. Grades 5-8. R
            Sensitive and artistic like his mother with whom he lives,
David is alarmed when his rugged outdoorsman father Mark arrives
to take him camping at a remote wilderness site. His father's motive is to make a man of him, but David, intimidated by recurrent
nightmares, fears that Mark will harm him physically or abandon
him to test his mettle. Mark, however, saves him when a savage
mother grizzly protecting her cubs attacks him, then turns to maul
Mark. The stark question of survival necessitates David's trust and
cooperation, and gradually he dispels his diffidence and masters new
skills. At the same time, his father acknowledges that his method
of parenting may have been clumsy in his thinly veiled statement,
"Not all animals are born to be good fathers." The story closes
with David's unrealistic hope that his parents will be reconciled.

123. Jones, Rebecca C. MADELINE AND THE GREAT (OLD) ES-
        CAPE ARTIST. New York: Dutton, 1983. 112p. Grades
        5-7. R+
            When her mother decides for economic reasons to move from
cosmopolitan Chicago to her mother's home in the quaint town of
Sycamore, Indiana where she finds work as an insurance agent,
Madeline Marshall, 12, displays a large and tangible chip on her
shoulder. To compound her lack of enthusiasm in trying to make
friends, she is suddenly stricken with an epileptic seizure in class
and becomes the brunt of derision. She shares a hospital room with
aged Mary Gibson, 94, for whom she initially feels nothing but contempt until the "Old Lady" wins her over by her humorous affability.
Afraid to return to school, she feigns another attack, but back in
the hospital the Old Lady is not fooled. Madeline pleads with her
divorced father, an assistant professor at the University of Illinois
whom she visits on weekends, to make a home for her, but he neatly
sidesteps the issue. On a visit to Mary Gibson in her convalescent
home, the Old Lady suggests that they run away together; she will
provide the means while Madeline will be her traveling companion.
But Mary's "means" turns out to be an expired credit card, and their
escape ends at the bus depot. Later Madeline learns that Mary has
had a stroke and has made good her escape into the childish fantasy
of senility. Back in school, Madeline discovers that another classmate has been targeted for embarrassment and empathetically goes to
her rescue.

124. Jones, Adrienne. A MATTER OF SPUNK. New York: Harper
        and Row, 1983. 302p. Grades 6-9. R+

Discarded by her husband in 1921 (see 125), Mase Standfield, a Theosophist from Atlanta, takes her daughters Blainey, 9,
and Margery, 7, to the sanctuary of the Society's colony, Krotona,
in the Hollywood Hills. There the girls are enrolled at the School
of the Open Gate while their mother does volunteer work for the
movement, an ecumenical group that espouses the brotherhood of
man, reincarnation, and the reconciling of science with religion.
Margery is initially homesick, in spite of their exotic surroundings,
wishfully thinking that the family will eventually be reunited. Her
father writes to them and faithfully sends a monthly check. Her
goal in the Society's youth group is to conquer her timidity, which
she begins by standing up to a tough, sneaky classmate and completes by saving their neighbor, a glamorous movie star, from being
exploited by a false prophet. Their enchantment with Krotona palls
when they are asked to share quarters with a deranged psychic,
and Mase makes the momentous decision to rent a modest apartment
downtown where the girls suffer the stigma of attending public
school. Their dream of owning their own home is finally attained
when they find an affordable bungalow on the fringes of Beverly
Hills. In 1928 Mr. Standfield comes to visit, incidental to watching
Georgia Tech play in the Rose Bowl game. His monthly check continues until the Great Depression forces them to become totally independent at last.

125. Jones, Adrienne. WHISTLE DOWN A DARK LANE. New York:
        Harper and Row, 1982. 274p. Grades 6-10. R+
        Mase Standfield was 39 when her first daughter, Blainey,
now 8 in 1920, was born. She nearly died in childbirth with
Margery, now 6. Fearful of risking another pregnancy, she maintains a separate bedroom from her husband, a devoted family man.
When it is time for the family to repair to their summer home in the
mountains of Georgia, Mr. Standfield stuns Mase, who by breeding
and Southern tradition is a clining vine, by announcing that he has
other plans for himself. He ensures that they are ensconced comfortably and securely at Cloudacres, leaving with them the family
Hupmobile which Mase is terrified of driving. She and the girls
cope with the aid of faithful local retainers, Mase showing unaccustomed spunk. For innocent Margery it is a puzzling summer of trying to untangle the web of adult motivations and relationships, good
and evil, through overheard conversations and encounters with their
neighbors, including Ku Klux Klansmen. She sees her beloved father
only when he joins them for her seventh birthday celebration. At
the close of the summer when they return to Atlanta, Mr. Standfield
dashes their expectations of living together once again as a family
by moving permanently to his club. Close friends counsel Mase,
ordinarily the epitome of feminine decorum and self-control, to pull
herself out of her depression and make a new life for herself and
the girls by emigrating to California (see 124).

126. Jukes, Mavis. LIKE JAKE AND ME. New York: Knopf, 1984.
        Illus. by Lloyd Bloom. Unp. Grades 3-4. R++

Young Alex is slight, sensitive, uncoordinated and artistic
like his entomologist father, who has arranged for him to take ballet
lessons. He feels slightly intimidated by his stepfather Jake, a
brawny, bearded, tattooed ex-cowboy. Alex's offer to help chop
firewood with the heavy, well honed axe brings a visible wince of
pain to Jake's countenance. When Alex wonders whether the twins
his mother Virginia is expecting will resemble him or Jake, she
opines that they may be like both of them. Jake gently chides Alex
on fearing to deal the coup de grace to his loose tooth, but when
Alex observes a wolf spider and her babies crawling out of the wood-
pile into Jake's clothing, the seemingly invincible giant hastily strips,
revealing that he too has phobias. After Alex liberates the spider,
Jake swings him aloft in a dance of gratitude, and Virginia, patting
her ample abdomen, announces that the twins seem to possess Terpsichorean talent also--like Jake and Alex.

127.   Jukes, Mavis. NO ONE IS GOING TO NASHVILLE. New York:
        Knopf, 1983. Illus. by Lloyd Bloom. Unp. Grades 3-5.
        R+
        While spending the weekend with her father Richard and
stepmother Annette, Sonia Ackley, who aspires to be a veterinarian,
is adopted by a cunning brown and white dog with animated ears.
Unfortunately, her father will not let her keep him, not only because
he has an antipathy for animals but also because he or Annette will
have to care for Max between Sonia's visits. Annette is sympathetic
to Sonia's cause, but Richard is adamant. When no one responds to
his ad for a lost dog, he places another one offering Max for adoption. When a rancher arrives to take the dog for his little girl,
Sonia cannot hold back her tears. Annette suddenly intercedes in
her behalf, and Richard capitulates to the lachrymose females. Annette presents the dog to Sonia with love from her father and "Wicked
Stepmother."

128.   Karl, Jean E. BELOVED BENJAMIN IS WAITING. New York:
        Dutton, 1978. 150p. Grades 5-7. NR
        One older brother is in reform school and the other is
joining an older sister away at college on scholarships. Lucinda
Gratz, 11, youngest of the family, is not sure which she fears more:
her parents' hideous altercations or the retaliation of the juvenile
gang on whom her bad brother squealed. Then her father moves out
and her mother, preoccupied with her own problems, first ignores
Lucinda, then deserts her altogether. Now she has no defense at
all against the punks who take over the house, and she's afraid to
inform her big sister because she fears foster care. Her only
asylum is within the patrolled gates of an old cemetery nearby,
where she takes up residence in the former caretaker's cottage which
is deserted but for a voice emanating from the broken statue of a
long-deceased child. The voice is that of an extraterrestrial being
trying to establish contact with earthlings. She enlightens the dis-
embodied interstellar visitor, whom she calls Benjamin, about life
within her own galaxy while dodging the hooligans and researching

the history of the memorial park for her sixth grade class. When
the incorrigibles burn down her old home, she has no choice but
to contact her sister. The foster home that is arranged for her
is not as bad as expected, and she is relieved to know she is no
longer alone, but it is difficult to convince her brother and sister
of Benjamin's existence.

129. Katz, Welwyn Wilton. WITCHERY HILL. New York: Atheneum,
        1984. 144p. Grades 7-10. NR
        Although he lives with his mother in Wisconsin, Mike Lewis,
14, always spends summers with his journalist father. This summer
they are staying on the island of Guernsey with Mr. Lewis' old
friend Tony St. George and his homely daughter Lisa and beautiful
Titian-tressed second wife Janine. Mike encounters initial hostility
from Lisa, who believes that her detested stepmother is a witch in
the island's venerable but now illegal black magic cult. Mike's
father scoffs, convinced that Lisa is jealous of Janine, but Lisa's
conviction is borne out when her doctor father becomes possessed
following the poisoning death of an enigmatic patient. Skulduggery
results from a struggle for power between diabolical Janine and the
dead man's sinister nephew. Mike's father seems less distressed by
the fact that his dear old friend is obviously dying than petulant
that his vacation has been spoiled. He goes on a sailing expedition
with a livelier group, leaving Mike alone to deal with Lisa's own
devilish and horrifying possession upon her father's death. Mike
alone must thwart Janine's intention of offering Lisa as a human sacrifice while she is in a diabetic coma. Cheap thrills abound as the
boy bravely and craftily engages the full malevolence of the renegade
coven to save his new friend. Later Mike ruminates on his changing
relationship with the father who no longer seems infallible.

130. Keller, Beverly. NO BEASTS! NO CHILDREN! New York:
        Lothrop, Lee and Shepard, 1983. 124p. Grades 5-6. R+
        Mark Blank's clients lost confidence in him as a marriage
counselor when his wife left him to "find herself." He tried his
hand unsuccessfully at being a hippie and selling sports cars, and
now, since joining the county mental health clinic, he has hired
Mrs. Farisee, a veritable tartar, to be housekeeper for his children,
teen Desdemona and twins Antony and Aida, as well as their assorted stray pets. Resentful as the children are of Mrs. Farisee
and her intolerance of animals, imposition of chores, and general
fastidiousness, they positively loathe their avaricious landlord, Harley Grove, whose mild-mannered son Sherman, their friend, is the
antithesis of his father. Sherman runs away to protest the Blanks'
eviction notice. Mr. Grove tries to placate him with a sissy "yap"
dog named Precious, but the boy and dog become lost at the Fourth
of July picnic which Mr. Grove is attending as a local politician.
The Blanks, including Mark's down-to-earth girlfriend Shirley, comb
the woods to find them. The press extols the rescuers, after which
Mr. Grove can hardly evict them, and Sherman's dog undergoes a
change of personality after being renamed Jake. Mark reassures

Desdemona, who has feelings of inadequacy because of her mother's
departure, of his affection. He confides in her that he is not ready
for remarriage but doubts that he and her mother will ever reconcile.

131.   Kerr, M. E. IF I LOVE YOU AM I TRAPPED FOREVER. New
              York: Harper and Row, 1973. 177p. Grades 7-10. R+
              In spite of the fact that his father deserted his mother be-
fore he was born and that he and his mother, a Welcome Wagon hostess, must live with his grandfather, Alan Bennett, 16, a high
school senior in his New York Finger Lakes town, has the world on
a string. He is handsome, cool, athletic, popular, and goes steady
with stunning Leah Pennington. Incredibly, the arrival in town of
Duncan Stein, a born loser and Alan's antithesis, suddenly evokes
nagging self-doubts in Alan's mind. Duncan believes in old-fashioned,
sentimental romantic fantasy, quite the opposite of the practical,
sharing type of love that is the norm of the town's teens, and he
starts a newspaper devoted to the fulfillment of those fantasies to
which even Alan's girlfriend succumbs. To further shatter Alan's
complacency, the father whom he has never seen and whom he can
do nicely without, suddenly asks him to spend his holidays in New
York City with him and his wife, the high school sweetheart for
whom he dumped Alan's mother. He and his father inevitably clash
because of Alan's hostility over his father's disloyalty to his mother,
yet he can't help liking his father's wife. Once so self-assured,
Alan now turns for solace and understanding to Duncan's mother,
a woman who has herself loved and lost, while Duncan enjoys the
popularity that once was Alan's. Even Alan's mother changes as
she begins dating a newcomer.

132.   Kerr, M. E. IS THAT YOU, MISS BLUE? New York: Har-
              per and Row, 1975. 170p. Grades 6-9. R+
              When her mother runs off with her psychologist father's
research assistant, ten years her junior, Flanders Brown, 14, is
shipped off to Charles School in Maryland, a strict, church-
affiliated institution. Reared an agnostic and liberal, she is afraid
she cannot cope with the school's regimentation, her obsessively
devout housemother Ernestine Blue, or her deaf-mute dormmate Agnes
Thatcher, who is perverse, uncouth, and physically violent. But
her first friend, Carolyn Cardmaker, an irreverent, flamboyant, rebellious P.K. (Preacher's Kid), eases her transition. Flanders is
embarrassed and reproved by the stuffy administration when her
father is interviewed on television because of the faddish sex therapy farm he is establishing. She is not ready, however, to join the
Agnostics Club at Cardmaker and Agnes' behest because she has
grown to respect and defend Miss Blue, whom the others cruelly
deride. When Miss Blue, an excellent teacher, is forced to resign
because of her intense but harmless spirituality, even the Agnostics
are incensed at the injustice, and Cardmaker is expelled for her
part in their retaliation. At Christmas vacation, Flanders locates
her mother, whom she had earlier rejected, in New York City and

learns that she has left her young lover and is seeking her own
identity by working and attending university classes. They reconcile, and Flanders returns to Charles School with an open mind
about religion.

133. Kerr, M. E. LOVE IS A MISSING PERSON. New York: Har-
        per and Row, 1975. 164p. Grades 8-9. R
        When their parents divorced, Daddy chose vibrant individ-
ualist daughter Chicago to live in New York with him, while introverted Suzy remained with her mother. Suddenly Chicago, now 17,
a spoiled, self-styled revolutionary, returns and proposes that she
and Suzy, 15, change places. Her reason soon becomes obvious
when their father marries a sleazy redhead young enough to be his
daughter, in effect usurping Chicago's position. The two sisters
with such dichotomous personalities try living together in armed
truce at their mother's lavish beach estate, the one quietly pursuing
library volunteer work, the other ostentatiously and quixotically organizing her revolution to end oppression of minorities and equalize
the classes while paradoxically demanding and expecting the appur-
tenances of wealth. When Chicago proselytizes the class valedictorian, a black, and woos him from his former sweetheart, Suzy's
best friend, she triggers a tragedy that eventually drives the pair
underground. Suzy can't begin to comprehend her sister, but she
does develop compassion.

134. Kerr, M. E. THE SON OF SOMEONE FAMOUS. New York:
        Harper and Rowe, 1974. 226p. Grades 6-10. R+
        Overshadowed by the high profile of his famous father who
hobnobs with statesmen and movie stars, Adam Blessing, 16, after
being expelled from Choate, drops his celebrated surname and goes
to live with his maternal Grandfather Blessing, an alcoholic veterinarian, in a sleepy backwater of Vermont. At the local high school
he crosses paths with Brenda Belle Blossom, 15, self-conscious tomboy and only child of a prudish mother who was widowed young.
She has an inferiority complex to match Adam's own, and, innocently
supposing him to be as unsophisticated as she, suggests that they
form a coalition of "Nothing Power" and feign going steady to give
the appearance of normality. Meanwhile, Adam is secretly attracted
to another girl whose father, a young veterinarian in competition with
Dr. Blessing, is adamantly opposed to their dating. Brenda Belle is
called upon to front for them so they can sneak trysts. Adam's
former stepmother, a fading film comedienne, comes to visit the
Blessings at Christmas and first alienates and then charms Dr. Blessing. To further complicate matters, Adam's father's recently jilted
fiancee, a glamorous if vacuous starlet, arrives unannounced and
attempts suicide. In a funny scene in the school gymnasium at a
masked ball, Adam's cover is finally blown and the tragedy that
fueled the veterinarians' feud is bared. Dr. Blessing and the ex-
comedienne rendezvous in Hollywood, where Adam joins them, and
Brenda Belle makes peace with her physiognomy and quits courting
the popular crowd.

135. Kindred, Wendy. LUCKY WILMA. New York: Dial, 1973.
        Illus. by the author. Unp. Grades K-1. R+
        With a modicum of words, this picture story demonstrates
how a little girl's carefully planned and orchestrated Saturday outings with her divorced father are sterile, drab and humdrum as they
stalk silently through the Museum of Natural History, the Metropolitan
Museum and the Central Park Zoo. On the fourth Saturday, they approach the entrance to the Frick Collection and discover that children
under 10 are not admitted. Thrown off schedule, Dad is forced to
improvise, and a spontaneous romp through the park ensues. Wilma
launches herself onto her father's back for a piggyback ride, they
frolic to the notes of an alfresco flutist and serendipitously discover
a topic of conversation. When they part, their eyes sparkle and
they genuinely anticipate future Saturdays.

136. Klein, Norma. IT'S NOT WHAT YOU EXPECT. New York:
        Pantheon, 1973. (OP) 128p. Grades 7-9. R+
        The summer that Dad feels trapped and unfulfilled and
moves to an apartment in New York looms long and bleak to twins
Carla and Oliver, 14, and their mother until Oliver, an haute cuisine
chef, hatches a scheme for opening an expensive restaurant in a
neighbor's home, run entirely by the kids and their friends in their
sleepy corner of exurbia. Their venture is supremely successful
and makes the months fly, yet it affords Carla some private moments
for pondering the perplexities of life. Unlike her brother, who is
a pragmatist and almost as relaxed and unaffected as Mom, Carla is
idealistic and often depressed and pessimistic over the vagaries of
life, including divorce. She would like to live according to a pre-
conceived plan, but Oliver submits that life is fraught with unforeseen pitfalls. As if to prove his point, their older brother's girlfriend becomes pregnant and has an abortion. At the end of the
summer, his restlessness allayed, Dad returns to his family.

137. Klein, Norma. ROBBIE AND THE LEAP YEAR BLUES. New
        York: Dial, 1981. 154p. Grades 5-7. R+
        While his mother, a college art history teacher, flies to
Washington for the weekend, Robbie is supposed to stay with his
father, who lives in the same New York apartment building with his
young POSSLQ Jill, an aspiring clown. Dad has neglected to inform
Mom that he, too, will be out of town giving a lecture, and Jill has
an infectious virus. Mom's boyfriend agrees to take Robbie for the
weekend, along with his own two daughters who are near Robbie's
age, 11. With all the dissolutions, recouplings and casual cohabi-
tations going on about them, it is not remarkable that Robbie's
classmates are prematurely curious about sex and matrimony. It
being Leap Year, some of the girls propose trial marriage to the boys,
and in a lunch hour ceremony Robbie weds Eve, while his friend
Thor marries three of his admirers. Their parents approve because
it is practice for the real thing, but it is also a tacit license to go
as far and as fast as the participants choose. Robbie, who is still
sexually immature, is relieved when Eve decides to call it off and

remain his girlfriend. Mom's boyfriend's precocious daughter also
wants to be his girlfriend and invites him to her tenth birthday
party at which Jill the clown performs. Mom's boyfriend is smitten
with Jill, who responds, leaving both of Robbie's parents temporarily
unattached and on the prowl again. In their Child Care class, Robbie and Thor practice on a live, volunteered baby, and when school
is over both parents are on hand to see Robbie off to summer camp
and new fields to conquer.

138. Klein, Norma. TAKING SIDES. New York: Pantheon, 1974.
      (OP) 156p. Grades 5-8. R+
      A year in the life of Nell, 12, has its nadirs and zeniths,
its introspections and insights. Switching custody from her mother
in the country to her dad in the city is not onerous, because her
father is her favorite parent and she still visits her working mother
on weekends. Sharing a room with her kid brother who wets the
bed, accepting her father's girlfriend, and coping with the dilemma
of divided holidays require more difficult adjustments. Her father's
sudden heart attack reverses the plan and forces another adaptation.
Interludes with her first boyfriend and heart-to-heart confidences
with her best girlfriend are part of any girl's young teen experience.

139. Klein, Norma. WHAT IT'S ALL ABOUT. New York: Dial,
      1975. 146p. Grades 6-8. R
      Asian on her father's side and Jewish on her mother's,
Bernadette, 11, lives in New York with her mother and her mother's
new husband Gabe. The family expands with the adoption of Suzu,
a Vietnamese orphan who adores Bernie but who can be temperamental. Soon Gabe loses his job, grows surly, abusive and belligerent,
and finally disappears. In the meantime, Bernie is invited to her
father's wedding where she learns that his wife Peggy is already
seven months' pregnant. They offer her a home with them when
they hear of her mother's second divorce, but Bernie declines, knowing that she'd miss her mother and Suzu. After the baby is born,
her father and Peggy invite the three of them to visit. After a
pleasant vacation in California they return to New York to discover
that Gabe has returned with his daughter by his first marriage. He
has a new girlfriend, but they all remain amicable and Bernie becomes friendly with Gabe's daughter. Perplexed by conflicting loyalties, Bernie vows she will never marry, but her sagacious grandmother (who has just remarried at 62) tells her, "You can like a lot
of people, but you can only love a few."

140. Konigsburg, E. L. (GEORGE). New York: Atheneum, 1970.
      152p. Illus. by the author. Grades 6-9. R+
      Ben Carr was born a "concentric twin." All his life he has
had a little man named George living symbiotically within him who
communicates both audibly and inaudibly. When he was small, his
mother called George an imaginary playmate and hoped he would disappear when Ben's brother Howard was born, but George merely
internalized and survived even their parents' divorce. Now Ben is

12, and Howard, 8, is the only other person who is acquainted with
George. A serious student of organic chemistry, Ben is enrolled in
a sixth grade experimental science program at his special school in
Florida. He misguidedly curries favor with William, an opportunistic
senior, to the vociferous objection of George. Items mysteriously disappear from the lab, imperiling the program, and the teacher, Mr.
Berkowitz, who is also dating Mrs. Carr, suspects that Ben is the
thief. When the boys are sent to their father's home for the
Christmas holidays, Mr. Carr's second wife, an amateur psychologist,
ferrets out the existence of George and a psychiatrist is called in.
Acting on a hunch, Ben discovers just before Easter recess that
William and his partner have been manufacturing LSD to sell to the
expected influx of vacationing college students. Ben destroys the
substance and pragmatically lets George take the blame to avoid
adverse publicity to the school. In the ensuing year, William receives his just deserts, Mr. Berkowitz marries Mrs. Carr, and Ben's
voice deepens to match George's.

141.   Konigsburg, E. L.   JOURNEY TO AN 800 NUMBER.   New
            York: Atheneum, 1982. 144p. Grades 5-7. R+
            When Rainbow Maximilian Stubbs was 4, his mother, an ex-
hippie, divorced his father and eschewed commune life in New Mexico because she wanted a conventional life and consistent education
for her son.   After achieving a degree and an administrative post
at an exclusive private school near Philadelphia, she marries a
trustee of the institution to ensure Max's social status there.
While they are on their honeymoon cruise, Max, now 10, is sent to
visit his vagabond father who supports himself by booking gigs for
his obnoxious camel at state fairs, conventions, dude ranches, and
even Las Vegas cabarets.   During his summer's sojourn with his
father, he meets an interesting but disparate melange of people,
most of whom he considers his social inferiors.   He sports his school
blazer as a badge identifying him as different and superior.   Especially intriguing are a girl his age and her mother who pop up everywhere he and his father go but always under different names.   He
learns that Sabrina's mother is a professional convention crasher
during vacations to escape the boredom and anonymity of her job as
a telephone operator.   With Sabrina's help he recognizes that an
individual's value lies within, not upon phony labels of class consciousness, and that his unique, endearing, kind, loyal and patient
father is a pearl beyond price.

142.   Lasky, Kathryn.   BEYOND THE DIVIDE.   New York: Mac-
            millan, 1983. 254p. Grades 6-10. R+
            For the grievous sin of attending a non-Amish funeral ser-
vice and not repenting the transgression, Meribah Simon's father is
"shunned" by their community of plain folk: not permitted to live
with or speak to his family nor farm his land. With little recourse,
he decides to leave Pennsylvania and join the Forty-niners. Sympathetic Meribah, 14, begs to go along. Their journey by covered
wagon begins in St. Joseph, Missouri, where the disparate members

of their company share high spirits, optimism and camaraderie.
Gradually, however, the rigors, deprivation, misfortune and aridity
of the pilgrimage begin to warp, crack and peel away their veneer
of civility, revealing the pettiness, greed, jealousy, selfishness and
even bestiality lurking underneath. The supercilious belle from
Philadelphia is savagely raped, yet the rapists go free while the
victim is ostracized and driven mad until she wanders off into the
desert to perish. Meribah's staunch father injures his hand, and
the infection slowly spreads through his body. The others abandon
the two of them to die in the High Sierra after appropriating their
equipment and supplies in a frenzy of predatory self-preservation.
After burying her father, Meribah learns winter survival skills from
the gentle Yahi Indians whom the new settlers have falsely branded
as hostile in order to justify massacring them. When the opportunity
arises for Meribah to rejoin white "civilization," she declines and
opts to live in solitude in the mountain wilderness.

143.   Levine, Betty K. THE GREAT BURGERLAND DISASTER.
       New York: Atheneum, 1981. 104p. Grades 6-9. R+
         Because his mother was always an indifferent cook, Mike
Whitbread, 15, even before his parents' divorce, learned to cook,
earned a widespread reputation in Scarsdale, and went into business
as a caterer. Now the bike on which he makes his deliveries has
been stolen and he is forced to seek employment at the local fast-
food franchise. The bilious burgers they dispense prompt him to
convince the manager to diversify the menu with himself as chef.
The revamped Burgerland is a huge success, but Mike is burning
his candle at both ends for minimum wage, and his father is miffed
that Mike is too busy to spend his weekends with him and his girlfriend in New York City where he works as an ad agency artist.
Mike's presence at home on weekends, moreover, cramps the style
of "Ms.," his mother, an accountant who moonlights as a night
school instructor and takes in boarders to help put his sister
through college. But when Mike tries to assert his own social independence, he is chastised by his mother. The gourmet fare at
Burgerland makes headlines and the head office revokes the franchise, leaving Mike unemployed again. A solution is found to their
various dilemmas when his mother and dad switch homes, freeing
the family car for Mike's use to revive his catering service. Mike
considers seeing a psychiatrist to explain the games adults play and
plans a summer trip with a friend.

144.   Levy, Elizabeth. MOM OR POP. New York: Dell, 1981.
       Illus. with cartoons. 63p. Grades 3-5. R
         The new girl in class seems stuckup and carries with her
a pink plastic bag that piques the curiosity of Fat Albert and the
Cosby kids. Flora's secret, when revealed, is not the bomb they
suspected but a moth-eaten plush dog, her only memento of her
father who is separated from her mother. Albert and the gang try
to cheer her up, but every time her dad calls or appears, it touches
off another fight between her parents over the unhappy girl. Their

latest quarrel is over the celebration of Flora's birthday, and in the
middle of it the honoree disappears. While the Cosby kids strike out
on foot in search of her, the distraught parents shelve their differences temporarily and comb the neighborhood by car. Only when
she is found do her parents realize how they have been hurting her
and vow to correct their mistake. Flora invites everyone home for
birthday cake. A note from Bill Cosby confirms that the family may
not live happily ever after under the same roof, but that the parents
will now work together for the good of the child.

145.   Lexau, Joan M.   EMILY AND THE KLUNKY BABY AND THE
       NEXT-DOOR DOG. New York: Dial, 1972. Illus. by
       Martha Alexander. 38p. Grades 2-3. R+
       The last time there was new snow, Emily and her mother
made a snowman together, but since her parents' divorce Mama is
always too busy to play. Today she is doing income tax, and Emily
must entertain the klunky old baby. All their games are too noisy,
and a preoccupied Mama banishes them outdoors. Full of self-pity,
Emily resolves to run away to Dad's apartment. But the baby falls
off the sled and cries, the next-door dog follows them, and worst
of all, she becomes hopelessly lost turning corners. With the dog
leading, they complete the circuit of the block and miraculously
find themselves in front of their own house with Mama cheerfully
waving from the window, unaware of the tense drama and averted
disaster. She has finished the taxes and is ready for another
project with which Emily can help.

146.   Lexau, Joan M.   ME DAY. New York: Dial, 1971. Illus. by
       Robert Weaver. Unp. Grades K-2. R+
       Rafer awakens on the morning of his birthday feeling that
the world is his oyster. Gradually he becomes preoccupied with
thoughts of his divorced father and the letter he always receives
from him on his birthday. Soon his mood turns morose after the
mailman comes and goes with no missive for him. A mysterious
telephone message sends him on a grudging errand to the fruit
store, where he spies his father waiting for him on the street corner. "Did you undivorce me?" Rafer asks. Daddy replies slowly,
"Look, your mother and me are divorced. Not you kids. No way!
You and me are tight, buddy. Together like glue, O.K.?" "O.K.,
Daddy," Rafer beams. His world is rosy again.

147.   Lexau, Joan M.   STRIPED ICE CREAM. Philadelphia: Lip-
       pincott, 1968. Illus. by John Wilson. 95p. Grades 3-5.
       R
       Youngest of five children, four of them girls, Becky, 7,
is tired of the faded hand-me-downs she has to wear but accepts
her fate with good grace and pitches in on chores with the others,
Cecily, 14, Flo, 13, Abe, 11, and Maude, 10, while Mama works in
a button factory by day and moonlights as a domestic. The warm,
loving black family is dependent on others' discards but too proud
to accept welfare because it forced their father to desert them when

he didn't qualify for benefits yet didn't earn enough to support them all. They save their meager clothing allowance for school shoes and material to make new dresses for Cecily. All Becky wants for her approaching birthday are the traditional chicken spaghetti and striped ice cream, but Mama warns that things are leaner this year than last. Accustomed to basking in the attention of her older sisters, she is perplexed and peeved when they suddenly have no time for her and complain that she is always underfoot. When Abe takes her outdoors to play, she knows his motive is merely to keep her out of the way. She wallows in self-pity, and the summer seems interminable. On the morning of her birthday, Maude takes Becky swimming at the public pool. When they get home the others reveal the secret of their peculiar impatience: on the sly they have been sewing a brand new dress just for Becky in the very colors of her favorite Neapolitan ice cream.

148. Lisker, Sonia O., and Leigh Dean. TWO SPECIAL CARDS.
       New York: Harcourt, Brace, Jovanovich, 1976. Illus. by
       Sonia O. Lisker. Unp. Grades 1-3. R+
       Hazel Cooper, 7, thinks that getting a divorce is miserable because all her parents do is yell and fight. She wishes her 3-year-old brother were old enough to talk to. Then one night her father packs and moves out. Life is much more peaceful, but Hazel wonders if Daddy is ever coming back and whether Mom will leave, too. Then Daddy calls and arranges to pick up her and Billy to stay overnight with him in his new apartment in the city. After a wonderful weekend Hazel decides that divorce isn't all bad, because now she has two happy homes in exchange for one tense one. On their return they go shopping for cards for Grandma's birthday, and Hazel wants to get one for Mom and Daddy, too, expressing her love for them. She can't find one about getting divorced, so she makes one of her own and cuts it in half for each of her two special parents.

149. Lowry, Lois. THE ONE HUNDREDTH THING ABOUT CAROLINE.
       Boston: Houghton Mifflin, 1983. 150p. Grades 5-7. R+
       Caroline Tate's mother, a bank teller who was divorced by her husband nine years ago, is given to enumerating randomly and humorously her daughter's numerous strong points. The one thing that really aggravates her about Caroline and her mechanical genius brother, J.P., 13, is their constant bickering. Caroline's share of family responsibility is to do the laundry. Her ambition is to be a vertebrate paleontologist, and she haunts the nearby Museum of Natural History in New York. When she finds a sinister note to their upstairs neighbor in the lobby wastebasket, she leaps to the conclusion that the man, Frederick Fiske, has his cap set for her mother but plans to eliminate the stumbling blocks, her and J.P., by murdering them. Her best friend Stacy, who aspires to be an investigative reporter, helps her gather further evidence that points conclusively to the ulterior intentions of the man who has begun dating Joanna Tate. In a rare show of solidarity, Caroline conspires with J.P. to make a preemptive strike against Mr. Fiske at a dinner party hosted by their mother. They are hoist by their own petard

when an electrical short circuit darkens the building, and Mr. Fiske,
a history professor, reveals that he has been writing a novel, a fact
that would account for his purported skulduggery. In reality he is
a warm and sympathetic individual, and Caroline is embarrassed by
her suspicions.

150. Lowry, Lois. SWITCHAROUND. Boston: Houghton Mifflin,
        1985. 118p. Grades 5-6. R+
        Still confirmed enemies, Caroline Tate, 11, and her brother
J.P., 13 (see 149), declare detente while opposing a summer visit to
their father, a stipulation in the divorce contract which he has never
exercised since he left them nine years ago. The reason he wants
them this year becomes apparent as soon as they reach Des Moines.
While his wife Lillian attends classes, Caroline, who detests infants,
is elected to babysit identical twins Holly and Ivy. Electronics buff
J.P., who abhors baseball, is drafted as coach of half-brother
Poochie's inept Little League team which their dad sponsors. Both
plot a diabolical revenge: Caroline by switching the twins, who can
only be identified by the color clothing they wear; J.P. by accentu-
ating each team member's negative points to ensure their defeat in a
decisive game. Then Caroline learns that her father's buffoonery is
a mask to cover his concern over his failing sporting goods business
and that Lillian is only taking her real estate license under duress.
Caroline and J.P. are remorseful and try to reverse the harm they
have done. J.P. volunteers his computer skills to unravel the
firm's finances and discovers that a former disgruntled employee
sabotaged the programming to simulate insolvency. Caroline, a keen
strategist, gladly returns the babies to their mother, who is now
able to drop her classes, and takes over the coaching duties, giving
the team a sporting chance. But she agonizes over the uncertain
identity of the twins and the medical crisis it precipitates until
Lillian confides that she has a secret method of identifying them.
Caroline and J.P. are then free to relax and enjoy the remainder
of their visit.

151. Luger, Harriett. THE UN-DUDDING OF ROGER JUDD. New
        York: Viking, 1983. 137p. Grades 7-10. R+
        For six years after his parents divorced and his mother,
a recovered alcoholic, moved to New York, Roger Judd, now 16, and
his father led the bachelor's life in California. Then his father remarried and Roger suddenly acquired a precocious stepsister, Vanessa, also 16, who teases him sexually and ingratiates herself with his
father to get favors from him. Roger's grades and self-esteem plum-
met in direct proportion to his father's mounting favoritism for
Vanessa. When he uncharacteristically faces down hooligans, he
earns the friendship of classmate Julie, whose sexy twin sister is
pregnant. Gallantly, he goes out on a limb to help her get an abortion, but Vanessa maliciously hounds him to find out the name of the
girl, believing that Roger is the father. She succeeds in provoking
him into a fight with his father in which his dad sides with Vanessa.
Suicidal and branded incorrigible, he is sent like an outcast to stay

with his mother, who seems sympathetic at first. When a couple of errors of judgment arouse her suspicions, she grounds him while she is at work at her accounting firm, ignominiously confiscating his pants. No one believes his protests that he has nothing to hide until he finally blurts out his rage for her years of neglect, and she finally begins to listen. He returns home to finish school but chiefly to resume his budding relationship with supportive Julie.

152. Magorian, Michelle. BACK HOME. New York: Harper and
     Row, 1984. 375p. Grades 6-9. R
     Evacuated from England to the U.S. in 1940, Virginia Dickinson, called Rusty by her foster family for her red hair, and now 12 in 1945, returns home thoroughly Americanized. Her mother is a total stranger. A housewife before the war, she has joined the Women's Voluntary Service and become an auto mechanic, to Rusty's disapprobation. Mrs. Dickinson likewise disapproves of Rusty's American slang and informality. She is hurt and resentful that Rusty regards her American family with the affection that should be hers. To improve Rusty's etiquette and elocution, she enrolls her in an inflexibly proper British boarding school where the alienated child chafes under the artificial decorum and the heckling of classmates and faculty. Her only solace lies in clandestine nocturnal visits to a bombed-out house in the woods. Her situation deteriorates when her cold, punctilious, condemnatory father returns from the Pacific, expecting the family to return to its pre-war male-dominant status. He forbids Rusty to come home on weekends, driving her to extend her retreats to her private haven. When Rusty's secret existence is finally exposed and she is expelled, Mrs. Dickinson suddenly comprehends her daughter's desperation and empathizes, feeling equally stifled by her rigid husband. The parents separate, and Mrs. Dickinson takes Rusty and her baby brother to live an independent life in a house inherited from a wartime friend. Rusty and her mother relax in one another's company and discover that they have much in common.

153. Mahy, Margaret. THE CHANGEOVER. New York: Atheneum,
     1984. 214p. Grades 7-10. R
     Seeing her reflection in the mirror go old on occasion is a frightening premonition of danger to Laura Chant, 14, who lives with her mother, a bookshop manager, and little brother Jacko, 3, in a New Zealand suburb. It happened first when her father ran away with his girlfriend a year ago, for which Laura has never forgiven him. It happens again when an evil sorcerer, Carmody Braque, puts an indelible mark on Jacko, draining his vitality to sustain Braque's craving for immortality. Medical science is unable to reverse Jacko's mysterious decline, and Laura consults a schoolmate, Sorenson Carlisle, 16, whom she recognizes to be a male witch. Sorry, a genetic freak, is romantically attracted to Laura, but she is still too immature to respond. Sorry's mother and grandmother, also witches, counsel Laura to trick Braque into releasing her brother by becoming a witch herself. In a rite of sorcery that

corresponds with the rite of passage into womanhood, Laura, a sensitive, makes the complete conversion and, in a contest of white versus black magic, vanquishes Braque and draws Jacko back from the brink of death. At the same time her emotions for Sorry blossom into maturity, and she is able to return his affection. The experience also enables her to comprehend and forgive her mother's need for intimacy with her new boyfriend during the time of Jacko's crisis and to accept at last her father and his now pregnant wife.

154. Mann, Peggy. MY DAD LIVES IN A DOWNTOWN HOTEL.
          Garden City: Doubleday, 1973. Illus. by Richard Cuffari. 92p. Grades 4-5. R+
          When Joey's father storms out of the apartment one night and his mother is in tears next morning at breakfast, Joey knows it must be his fault. After school he takes the bus to his father's office and presents him with a list of resolutions for being a better son if only his dad will return home. Dad explains that the only good part of their marriage was having Joey, and the bad part was not Joey's fault. Then he arranges to take him to the circus. But his mom is still distressed, and Joey hates Dad for hurting her. At the circus Dad overcompensates by buying him too many sweets, making him sick, but still it is fun because Dad never had time to take him places before. Dad takes the old TV but replaces it with a color set, and the noise of it helps fill the void in the lonesome evenings. When Joey discovers that 53 kids on the block have no father living at home, he decides to form a secret club and at last regains a sense of belonging.

155. Matthews, Ellen. GETTING RID OF ROGER. Philadelphia:
          Westminster, 1978. Illus. by Pat Duffy. 96p. Grades 4-6.
          R+
          Immature Roger Ingels, 6, is the laughingstock of the school and the bane of his scholarly sister Chrissy's fourth grade existence. Each of his classroom misadventures--from biting the prettiest girl and flushing his underwear down the toilet to repeating first grade-- is juicy fodder for the sixth grade wags on the school bus and mortifying for Chrissy. She tries to ignore him, but he won't go away. Denying their kinship is useless because they look alike, down to the matching chicken pox he so generously bestows on her the night before Halloween. Worst of all, Roger jeopardizes their divorced mother's chances of marrying genial Mr. Davis when he damages the transmission of his new car, but Mom is upset, instead, with Chrissy for fibbing to Mr. Davis that Roger is adopted. Chrissy can't even interest her father in taking Roger off her hands when they visit him during Christmas vacation. On the night of a howling blizzard when Mom can't get home from her insurance company job and the two of them are alone in the house without power or telephone service, Chrissy acts responsibly and discovers that it's more reassuring to face crisis with companionship. And when Dad takes Roger on a weekend trip, Chrissy feels strangely lonely and abandoned. His injury in a schoolyard accident finally changes her mind about getting rid of Roger.

156. Mazer, Harry. GUY LENNY. New York: Delacorte, 1971.
        117p. Grades 6-9. R+
        Guy, 12, and his father have lived companionably since his
parents' divorce many years earlier until the advent of Emily who, to
Guy, constitutes the proverbial "crowd," and he doesn't attempt to
mask his sentiments. Then the mother he doesn't remember arrives
with her husband and starts making maternal overtures to him, compounding his confusion and resentment. When he learns that his
father has sent for his mother and asked her to make a home for
Guy so he can marry Emily and make a life of his own, Guy feels
bitter and betrayed. In his rage and self-pity he feels suicidal but
reasons that death might be lonesome and uncomfortable. He realizes
that he can survive on the strength of his individuality, no matter
which parent he decides to live with. Subplots include encounters
with the neighborhood punk and Guy's first sexual stirrings.

157. Mazer, Norma Fox. I, TRISSY. New York: Delacorte, 1971.
        176p. Grades 6-8. R+
        Even though she knows that the typewriter her father gives
her is a sop for his guilt about leaving the family, Trissy Beers, 11,
adores it because it enables her to express on paper the sentiments
which get her into trouble when she voices them. In her daily
stream-of-consciousness log she records her wry and frequently
unflattering observations and opinions about the people and events
in her life, starting with her imperfect parents and her two brothers, Mitch, 15, and Robert, 7. She is particularly upset when anyone sits in her father's former place at the dining room table, and
the ruse she uses to bring her father over on Robert's birthday
when her mother's boyfriend is visiting infuriates both parents.
Her attention-getting devices in school cost Trissy her best friend,
and on one of the children's weekly junkets with their father she
thoughtlessly wanders off, panicking her parents and earning another
punishment. In her father's apartment she accidentally discovers
the cake that his girlfriend left to surprise him and goes berserk,
smearing it all over the walls. Later she frightens her mother by
starting a fire in a wastebasket. Finally her father has a serious
talk with her about her identity crisis, and Trissy is at last able to
control her erratic behavior, give up her jaundiced typewritten
maunderings, and start a constructive handwritten diary.

158. Mazer, Norma Fox. TAKING TERRI MUELLER. New York:
        Morrow, 1983. 224p. Grades 6-9. R++
        Since her mother's death in an auto accident when she was
4, Terri Mueller, now 13, and her father, a carpenter and exemplary
parent, have been vagabonding all over the country. At her new
school in Ann Arbor, Terri makes friends with Shaundra, whom she
envies for her large family even though Terri and her father are
uncommonly close. Daddy refuses to talk about her mother and
keeps no family pictures. Their only relative is Daddy's sister, who
visits them once a year. An overheard remark of Aunt Vivian's
piques Terri's curiosity and prompts her to pick the lock on her

father's metal box. To her consternation she finds a document that
indicates that her parents were divorced and realizes that her father
has lied to her. When she confronts him about it, he very reluctantly discloses that, afraid of losing her after the divorce and her
mother's remarriage, he kidnapped her. Terri is stunned to learn
that her mother is still living. With Aunt Vivian's help Terri locates her mother in California. They have an emotional telephone
reunion after Terri exacts a promise that her mother will not prose-
cute her father. At Christmas vacation she goes to visit her and
get acquainted with a half-sister and grandparents she didn't know
existed. Suddenly she hates her father for depriving her of eight
years of the love and camaraderie of an extended family and decides
to remain with her mother. Later she changes her mind when she
visualizes how destitute and forlorn her father will be, having lost
his fiancee who feared that he might repeat his selfish act of love
should they have a child and an unsuccessful marriage.

159. McAfee, Annalena, and Anthony Browne. THE VISITORS WHO
        CAME TO STAY. New York: Viking/Kestrel, 1985. Illus.
        by the authors. Unp. Grades 1-3. R+
        With the exception of infrequent visits with her mom in
another town, Katy and her dad practice a comfortable and secure
routine in their seaside home, where they watch TV together, read
to each other, and take uneventful solitary strolls on weekends.
Katy can even tell what day of the week it is by the kind of sand-
wich Dad packs in her lunch. Then without warning, Dad brings
home fashionable Mary and her practical joker son Sean. Katy is
not amused by Sean's loathsome rubber animals, warty monster hands,
or disgusting whoopee cushion. Weekend outings at the beach and
amusement park become bizarre excursions. Mary's large, flashy
wardrobe overflows Dad's closet, and her culinary attempts are
failures. Dad doesn't seem to perceive the chaos, but when Katy
announces that she is fed up with sharing her room, her house,
and her father, the interlopers promptly move out. She and Dad
resume their normal activities, but Dad seems quieter than usual,
and even Katy notices that life has become humdrum. When Dad
suggests visiting Mary and Sean, Katy agrees and purchases a
trick water-shooting camera to turn the tables on Sean.

160. McCaffrey, Mary. MY BROTHER ANGE. New York: Crowell,
        1982. Illus. by Denise Saldutti. 86p. Grades 4-6. R+
        Since the death of their beloved Italian grandmother, Angelo
Tooley, 7, has been the responsibility of his big brother Mick, 11,
who feels that the youngster is an albatross about his neck. Not
only does he tag after Mick everywhere he goes, slow him down after
school, and curtail his activities with boys his own age, but the uninhibited, hyperactive lad also makes embarrassing noises that are a
cross between a duck's quack and an automobile horn. Waiting for
Mama on Friday nights is particularly onerous, because the shop
where she works in a flea market stays open late and she usually
arrives home with a headache. Saturdays are no fun either, because

Mama is not only busy with chores but inexperienced at household
projects that their truck driver father would have undertaken before he deserted them a year earlier. Fortunately, Mick's friend
Leon is both loyal and handy and is able to mount Mick's bulletin
board for him. In church Mick feels remorseful for resenting his
brother, but it is not until Angelo is struck by a car after Mick,
in a fit of pique, leaves him to walk home alone that Mick is filled
with love and contrition. Though seriously injured, Ange utters
his peculiar sound, and suddenly it is music to Mick's ears.

161. McCord, Jean. TURKEYLEGS THOMPSON. New York:
         Atheneum, 1979. 242p. Grades 6-8. R+
         She loathes her given name of Betty Ann. Her unflattering
nickname of Turkeylegs is no improvement, but it fits the image she
has projected since her parents' divorce three years earlier of being
tough, suspicious, independent and mean. She also despises
Brother, 7, a timorous bedwetter, but she adores Laura, 3, who is
still malleable and whom she is grooming to be a carbon copy of herself. Turkey, 12, is responsible for the two while her mother clerks
in a store. In addition to picking frequent fights with all the boys
in school, Turkey also has a history of truancy, and one day she
gets into serious trouble by stealing the bicycle she covets and fantasizes is her own. Given an ultimatum, she turns over a new leaf
for the rest of the term, but when her beloved sister dies that summer of a sudden and mysterious malady, Turkey is so grief-stricken
that she becomes an automaton. Her inebriate father returns, and
they move to a different part of town. The gifts of a dog and a
bicycle do not mollify her, and she contemplates suicide. She fails
to respond to the school psychologist and finally, in desperation,
goes in search of a fellow loner and Huck Finn type who befriended
her in her delinquent days as they roamed the bluffs overlooking
their Ohio tributary town. Charlie invites her to join him in his
cave, but Turkey realizes that dropping out of society is not the
answer to her problems and returns home to confront her guilt and
confusion.

162. McGraw, Eloise. HIDEAWAY. New York: Atheneum, 1983.
         217p. Grades 5-9. R++
         On the afternoon of his mother's wedding, Jerry Starbeck,
12, is supposed to be picked up by his divorced father. True to
form, his father forgets his obligation, and Jerry, feeling betrayed
by his mother's remarriage, dismayed by the prospect of living with
three strange stepsiblings, and knowing that he will not be missed
if he disappears for the week he is expected to spend with his dad,
takes a bus from his Portland home to the seaside community where
his paternal grandparents live, hoping that they will offer him a
permanent home. Letting himself in through the dog door, he
gradually comes to the awful realization that his grandparents have
moved without telling him and that their former home is being
watched by a teenaged girl while the new owners are away. At
first he tries to dodge the housesitter, but when he sprains his leg

on the precipitous stairs to the beach he desperately needs to attract her attention. Hanna Holderith, 16, is a tough, resilient
orphan, veteran of numerous foster homes. The frightened boy and
the lonely teen form a strong fraternal bond of respect and affection.
When Jerry proposes that they run away together, the idea is very
appealing to Hanna, but she knows realistically that it would never
work. The only way she can convince him that the venture would
be doomed to failure and misery is to pretend to proceed with it.
Then it is Jerry who demurs, deciding to return to his mother and
face up to the changes in his life. And Hanna, though regretful
of losing him, is flushed with new sensitivity and self-confidence,
thanks to Jerry's acceptance and trust.

163. McGraw, Eloise Jarvis. A REALLY WEIRD SUMMER. New
        York: Atheneum, 1977. 216p. Grades 5-8. R
        The ritualistic existence at their staid great-aunt and
uncle's old inn in Oregon, converted to residence and grocery store,
is stifling for the Anderson children, Nels, 12, Stevie, 10, Rory, 8,
and Jenny, 6. They want to go home, but there is no home to go
to. Dad, an air freight pilot, and Mom, who has a new job in a
dress shop, are making divorce decisions and have farmed out the
children for the summer. Nels, his father's favorite, is ambivalent
when offered a home with Dad in Alaska. Exploring a shuttered
section of the inn, he discovers a hidden closet that admits him to
the old tower, caught in a time warp and inhabited by a boy and
his parents who resided there fifty years ago. Nels develops an
easy rapport with Alan Reeves and his congenial family in their
idyllic and fascinating dimension. He slips away to join them every
morning, abandoning Stevie who depends on him for companionship.
Nels feels remorseful when Stevie buys the friendship of older boys
with cookies from the store and Nels forgets his birthday, but he
is reluctant to share his delicious secret with his brother. When
Alan implores Nels to join them permanently, he concludes that he
can no longer escape reality, but he almost becomes trapped as he
tries to return. Later he wonders whether he imagined the whole
adventure and decides that it is important for all four kids to stay
together.

164. Mearian, Judy Frank. SOMEONE SLIGHTLY DIFFERENT. New
        York: Dial, 1980. 197p. Grades 5-8. R+
        Marty Trevor, 12, is heckled by her wealthier seventh
grade classmates for being a latchkey kid whose mother drives a
cab for a living. Marty's father deserted them when she was 4, and
she yearns for him to return and once more make them a complete
family. Instead, her paternal grandmother Flossie comes to live with
them and contributes the warm touches of a homemaker which Mom
has never had time to be. Flossie seems antipodal to Mom, who is a
rigid fundamentalist. She is pragmatic, agnostic, drinks bourbon
temperately, and bets on the horses. Still, they blend harmoniously,
and Flossie informs Marty that her father is a rogue and a charmer
who is now remarried. Mom shows her that, as the offspring of two

divergent personalities, she can combine the attributes of both Mary
and Martha, the Biblical sisters for whom she was named. When
Marty contracts a rare case of scarlet fever, Flossie nurses her
through it before succumbing to it herself. She dies of anginal complications, and Mom, acceding to Flossie's preference for cremation,
reveals that there will be no funeral service or interment. Mom
makes a real effort to be more relaxed and sympathetic, and Marty,
with the friendship of Charlie, a serious student like herself,
doesn't miss the company of her snobbish acquaintances.

165. Meyer, Carolyn. C. C. POINDEXTER. New York: Atheneum,
          1979. 208p. Grades 6-10. R+
          Both her mother and her paternal aunt are divorced, but
while her mother is the domestic type and involved with a singles
group to meet men, Aunt Charlotte, an art teacher, is a militant
feminist and man-baiter. Aunt Charlotte's grown son Michael lives
in a commune, and C.C. (for Cynthia Charlotte), over six feet tall
at the age of 15 and the brunt of insensitive teasing, is convinced
that she wants to join him upon graduation. C.C. is hired as caretaker for her aunt's house while Aunt Charlotte attends a feminist
convention, and Laura, C.C.'s best friend who is also experiencing
the pain of her parents' divorce, takes refuge there. Meanwhile,
C.C.'s father is preparing to marry a woman whose children C.C.
and her sister Allison, 10, dislike, and her mother is buying a
stagnant business and attempting to turn a profit. C.C. takes a
second job at the shop to earn bus fare to the commune. At the
birthday party Laura throws for C.C. at Aunt Charlotte's, Michael
shows up and paints a less than idyllic picture of commune life.
Charlotte, having renounced her feminist crusade, also appears unexpectedly with a charismatic poet in tow. C.C.'s mother, once the
clinging vine, is now savoring her independence and has made a
success of her enterprise, and even C.C. has gained confidence in
her sales ability and no longer feels a need to retreat. Laura decides to join the commune instead.

166. Meyer, Carolyn. ELLIOTT AND WIN. New York: Atheneum,
          1986. 193p. Grades 8-12. R++
          Thrice married and divorced, Winston Kelly's mother has
recently moved to Santa Fe, where she has registered Win, 14, with
Los Amigos, an organization that pairs adult male role models with
fatherless boys. Win is dismayed to draw Elliott Deerfield, a geologist whose tastes run to epicurean food, classical music and exotic
art. Win's only friend, Paul, whose Amigo is comfortably plebeian,
tries to convince Win that Elliott is gay. Paul also stereotypes their
classmate Heather, a girl with unfortunately large breasts, as a person of loose morals. Win abhors Paul's cruel slurs toward Heather
and compensates by developing a close comradeship with her. Unexpectedly, he also enjoys his outings with Elliott as they attend
kayak races, go to the opera, photograph wildflowers, and learn
Kung Fu. In the meantime, Win's mother, an ex-hippie who supports
them in several ways while attending night school and who has vowed

never to remarry, falls in love again. This time it is with Win's
younger half-brother's Amigo. Paul returns from a visit to his dad
in Dallas devastated at learning that his supposedly virile father is
a homosexual with a live-in lover. While picnicking in a condemned
building, Heather and Win are ambushed by a gang of drunken
punks, and Win is a helpless witness to Heather's rape. Her mother
blames Win, and the family soon moves away. Win keeps his anguish
bottled up until a discerning Elliott helps him to work through his
emotions on a camping trip. Suddenly Win realizes that Elliott is his
best friend and that his sexual orientation, whatever it may be, does
not matter.

167. Miles, Betty. LOOKING ON. New York: Knopf, 1978. 187p.
       Grades 6-9. R
       Tall, gangling, prematurely developed and overweight for
14, Rosalie Hudnecker is self-conscious and lonely, yearning to be
thin and glamorous like the models in the magazines in the beauty
salon where her mother works in upstate New York. Her father deserted eight years ago, and the brother who provided attention
when her mother was too busy or tired has married and moved away.
The grove of pine trees that had been her haven next door, moreover, has been felled to make a clearing for a house trailer. The
attractive, trendy college couple who move into the trailer, however,
more than make up for the loss, and Rosalie finds herself living a
vicarious existence through Tony and Jill Judson and growing away
from her mundane contemporaries. Her mother disapproves of her
intimacy with the Judsons, and even Rosalie feels uneasy about neglecting her babysitting responsibilities when the newlyweds beckon
and beguile. But one day when she is alone with Tony and experiences unsettling undercurrents of sexuality, she realizes that
she is too young to handle adult sophistication. With a diet and
haircut to give her self-confidence, she plots her course for an academic program in high school and returns to her familiar circle of
friends to grow up at her own pace.

168. Moore, Emily. SOMETHING TO COUNT ON. New York:
       Dutton, 1980. 103p. Grades 4-6. R+
       Despite her father's assurances that she and her little
brother Jason will spend every weekend with him and that her behavior has nothing to do with the divorce, Lorraine Maybe, 10, has
the foreboding that she will never again see her father, an auto
mechanic. Her mother takes college classes in interior design while
also clerking at Macy's. Lorraine, who is black, has earned the
reputation of being willful, uncooperative and pugnacious at her
multiracial school in the Bronx, but this year she likes her new male
teacher and tries hard to please him. Still, her father habitually
breaks his promise to visit on weekends with the excuse that he is
too busy starting his own business in Queens. Pathetically trying
to overcome his indifference, she and Jason write him a letter pledg-
ing perfect deportment. Then, goaded by a manipulative new girl
in class, Lorraine falls into serious trouble at school and is sus-

pended. Her father again refuses to become involved, believing
that his duty ends with providing child support. Lorraine suddenly
ceases to pine for her father and begins to appreciate the fact that
her parents are no longer fighting. She makes peace with the new
girl and returns to school with greater maturity.

169. Morgan, Alison. PAUL'S KITE. New York: Atheneum, 1982.
        113p. Grades 5-7. R+
        Reared by his grandfather in a remote Welsh farmhouse,
Paul Evans, 11, has tasted nothing but the simple life except for a
brief sojourn with his aunt and uncle after Grandad's death. Now
the Dawkeses are sending him unescorted to London to locate the
mother who ran away with another man when Paul was a baby. His
father departed thereafter and is now presumed dead. His mother
has allowed her family to believe that she is a top fashion model,
while in reality she is just a hack who is past her prime. She has
no intention of suddenly acting maternal; indeed, she insists that
Paul call her Aunt Megan and introduces him as her little brother.
Oblivious to his wants and welfare, she pursues her personal
pleasures with the men in her life, leaving Paul to mooch about the
dingy flat and explore the teeming city by himself. His cousin
Joanna comes to visit, and, while the two are sightseeing on their
own, she is critically injured by a car. Megan cannot be found,
and Paul must keep the lonely vigil at the hospital until Joanna's
parents arrive. Paul is then struck by two startling revelations:
that his father is a former drug abuser who is now leading the as-
cetic life with an American religious sect, and that Uncle William is
about to serve a prison term for embezzlement. When Paul expresses
his loathing for living with his mother, Aunt Jean agrees to accept
him as man of the house while Uncle William is incarcerated. Paul
sails a kite in celebration past Joanna's hospital room window.

170. Morris, Judy K. THE CRAZIES AND SAM. New York:
        Viking, 1983. 136p. Grades 5-6. R+
        Sam Diefenback's divorced mother administers a Florida
health clinic. His dad, who has custody of Sam, is a dedicated
Washington bureaucrat who frequently works overtime generating
reports on low-income housing. In his absence he has strict but
fair and sensible rules for Sam, 11, to follow. Left to entertain
themselves, Sam and his friend Phillip pedal to the park to watch
the drunks and crazies, but sensitive Sam is uncomfortable when
Phillip ridicules the unfortunates. He makes friends instead with
an embassy boy from his class who speaks little English but who
communicates graphically with his artwork. Chafing at his father's
overprotectiveness and glutted with health foods supplied by their
grocery co-op, Sam yearns to be unfettered like his paripatetic
aunt and to devour the sweets he is forbidden. One lonely Saturday he contracts a case of "the crazies" himself and impulsively accepts a ride with the odd but seemingly harmless doughnut woman
from the park. Suddenly he finds himself a prisoner in her seedy
apartment, where she intends to keep him for companionship. It

is his new friend who secures his release through a detailed drawing for the police. Sam's experience teaches him that it is not so much that he misses his mother but that he is angry with her for leaving him. His dad plans to spend more time at home with Sam.

171. Myers, Walter Dean. MOTOWN AND DIDI. New York: Viking, 1984. 174p. Grades 7-12. R

An above-average student, Didi Johnson, 16, is seeking a college scholarship as a passport out of the Harlem she hates. Harlem--where her father deserted her mother to a life of daywork before a stroke incapacitated her physically and mentally. Harlem-- where her brother Tony, 15, has become a heroin addict. When Didi angrily and naively fingers Tony's pusher, Touchy, to narcotics agents who look the other way, Touchy, the real power figure in Harlem, sets his goons on her. She is saved from rape and possibly worse only by the intervention of Motown, a streetwise orphan who is living underground in a condemned building. In gratitude, Didi finds Motown a modest apartment where he can hide out from Touchy when the latter puts out a contract on him. Touchy wreaks his revenge on Didi, nevertheless, by providing Tony with uncut heroin on which he overdoses and dies. Hysterically, Didi persuades Motown, who has fallen in love with her, to execute Touchy. Intervening belatedly to keep Motown from either being killed or arrested for murder, she is wounded in the crossfire by Touchy, who is finally brought to justice. Didi, who had to turn down a scholarship to care for her dependent mother and brother, falls in love with Motown for his chivalry and integrity, in spite of his rough edges.

172. Naylor, Phyllis Reynolds. THE SOLOMON SYSTEM. New York: Atheneum, 1983. 210p. Grades 6-9. R+

The Solomon brothers, Nory, 16, and Ted, 13, have always had a special rapport and operate with instinctive teamwork. They are uneasy when their parents begin to communicate only through them and make no attempt to hide their dissatisfaction with one another. The boys are reluctant at first to leave for summer camp for fear that when they return to their Maryland home, Mom will have forced Dad to move out and everything will be changed. Once at camp, they wish they could stay forever and not have to face reality. Ted signs up for survival classes so that in case of a divorce the two of them could escape it by living off the land. He hopes to effect a reconciliation by wiring his mother flowers in his dad's name. Grandma Rose confirms their fears at Visiting Day. To add to Ted's misery, Nory has discovered girls and a rift develops between them. When they return home, their parents announce their decision to split the once inseparable boys, along with their community property, as the most equitable solution. Their mutual pain resolves the boys' differences, and they make an abortive attempt to run away together. Airing their grievances does not alter their parents' arbitrary and unilateral agreement, nor does Grandma Rose's intercession. It is their determination to share a newspaper route to earn money for camp next summer that convinces Mom and

Dad that they should not be divided. Mom becomes custodial parent, while Dad has liberal visitation rights, and Ted decides to stop anticipating trouble.

173. Neufeld, John. SUNDAY FATHER. New York: New American Library, 1977. 159p. Grades 7-10. R+
Although she harbors minor resentment that her mother sacrificed her career to be an asset to her husband's before he cast her off, relegating Mom and the kids to a downwardly mobile duplex, Tessa O'Connell, 14, of Denver, compares her parents' divorce to ripping off a bandage. The pain didn't last, and her father reserves Sundays for structured excursions with her and her brother Allie, 11. She objects obstreperously, however, when her father announces his intention of marrying the woman with whom he's been living. Tessa accuses Zandra of being a homewrecker and a slut instead of admitting that she is jealous of the chic woman and her sophisticated daughter Fran. She vows to make life hell for the other family in retaliation for her father's defection, but running away to dramatize her indignation does not elicit the guilt and pity she expects from them. By acting impassively toward her, they offer no resistance for her to fight against. Even her mother is unsympathetic. Because she still loves her ex-husband, she supports his bid for happiness. When Tessa beseeches her father to continue living with Zandra instead of marrying her, it is Fran who discerns her subconscious motivation. She tells Tessa that her hopes of a reconciliation are unrealistic and that she is selfish for trying to keep others from fulfilling their wishes because she is against it. Tessa suddenly realizes that her father is only a part of her life and that change and adjustment are inevitable. She decides to attend the wedding and to act aloofly gracious.

174. Neville, Emily Cheney. GARDEN OF BROKEN GLASS. New York: Delacorte, 1975. (OP) 215p. Grades 7-8. R+
Brian, 13 and white, leads a tangential existence with three black classmates in a St. Louis slum, brooding and drifting in a self-imposed vacuum because his problem seems so hopeless and insurmountable: an alcoholic mother who makes homelife intolerable with her open favoritism for his younger brother. He can't leave home as his dimly recollected father did, and his resentment aggravates the situation. In his loneliness and diffidence, he seeks the companionship of a stray dog. But his would-be human friends have difficulties, too, and two of them turn to him for solace: Dwayne, when his coolness lands him in trouble with housing project toughs and his father grounds him; and Fat Martha, when she fears she may be pregnant. As the long, emotionally turbulent summer closes, Brian's older sister brutally confronts him with the fact that their mother's illness is permanent and they must learn to cope with it. Martha, Dwayne, and Dwayne's girlfriend Melvita accept Brian into their circle.

175. Newfield, Marcia. A BOOK FOR JODAN. New York:

Atheneum, 1975. Illus. by Diane de Groat. 48p. Grades
2-4. R+

The first eight years of Jodan's life overflow with the camaraderie of family togetherness and mutual cooperation. When she is
9 her parents begin arguing. Jodan isn't sure which is worse--the
unhappy silences or the noisy quarrels. Then her mother announces
their separation, and she and Jodan move back to California. Her
father writes to her, but she misses their bedtime conversations and
hugs and eventually begins to forget what he looks like. When she
visits him at Easter, he gives her a special looseleaf scrapbook he has
been creating for her when she is lonesome for him. It contains a
potpourri of remembrances, incidents, anecdotes, advice and activities, as well as old photos. Best of all, this intimate communion between father and daughter can be supplemented as time goes on and
is physical evidence of his love. She decides to make one for him.

176. Norris, Gunilla B. LILLAN. New York: Atheneum, 1968.
        (OP) Illus. by Nancie Swanberg. 136p. Grades 5-6. R+
        Lillan was the pet name given to Ingalill, 10, by extrava-
gant Papa before he deserted her and Mama a year ago, and now
Lillan is assailed by doubts that if her father and mother could stop
loving one another, it follows that her mother might also stop loving
her. To make ends meet in post-war Sweden, Mama must rent out
the best rooms in the house and take a job, leaving her little time
and energy for companionship with Lillan. When her mother begins
keeping steady company with Jon, a man she met at work, Lillan's
fears are intensified. In her shame over the divorce, she is reluctant to go to school and make friends but eventually overcomes that
stigma. The tug of war at home for her mother's affection continues,
however, and in her anxiety she begins taking things that don't belong to her just for the feeling of possession. But Jon proves to
be a gentle and understanding compadre, and he and Mama gradually
allay her fears. Her birthday becomes a real family occasion, and
she decides to use her real name, relegating thoughts of Papa to
childhood memories.

177. Nostlinger, Christine. MARRYING OFF MOTHER. San Diego:
        Harcourt Brace Jovanovich, 1978. Trans. by Anthea Bell.
        140p. Grades 5-7. R+
        Their parents, who have been quarreling with increasing
venom, finally split while the family is vacationing on the Yugoslavian
seacoast, and Mrs. Kauffmann takes Susanna, 12, and Julia, 14,
home to Vienna to live with her mother, maiden aunt, and single
sister. Domestic tranquility is doomed from the start in that three-
generational household of women dominated by matriarchal Grandmother, who is also known as the Sergeant Major, and nervous,
fussy Great Aunt Alice who serves as housekeeper and spouts platitudes eternally. Poetical Sue's solution is to marry off Mother, a
clothing boutique buyer, to someone who will whisk them all out of
the house. Her first candidate is her German teacher on whom she
uses a subliminal suggestion technique garnered from her father's

advertising agency, but she overdoes it, causing Dr. Salamander to suspect an unhealthy mother fixation and to recommend psychiatric treatment for Sue. Her second victim is their next-door neighbor with whom Grandmother has a time-honored running feud. Sue arranges what she hopes will be a private tryst between the two adults at a ski lodge at Christmas, but her plans go comically awry when Grandmother peremptorily invites herself and becomes apoplectic on discovering her nemesis at the same hotel. Mother comes unglued until Julia, the quiet one, saves the day by calling Father to come to the rescue. A reconciliation is effected, and the family sense of humor is restored.

178. Okimoto, Jean Davies. IT'S JUST TOO MUCH. New York:
        Putnam, 1980. 126p. Grades 5-7. R+
        One thing that Cynthia Browne, 12, has noticed about parents divorcing is that they seem to give the children almost anything they ask for. In her case it has been numerous pets. Now her mother is remarrying a doctor whom Cynthia likes (see 179), but she and her little sister Sara are dubious about inheriting two built-in stepbrothers. Moreover, while Cynthia is still one of the last "no-bra" girls in her Seattle sixth grade class and is developing acne as well, her best friend Trae is becoming gorgeous and turning heads. Cynthia reaches the nadir when she learns that she is not included on the honeymoon and must stay with Great-aunt Gertrude whose archaic ideas indirectly cause the death of Cynthia's hamster and canary. Events start improving when she goes to summer camp and Mom sends her a training bra, but they decline again when she goes to visit her dad and his tactless girlfriend. All the injustices seem to shrink, however, when Cynthia starts seventh grade and gains the attention of an attractive new boy with whom she shares a predilection for sports. Her contentment is complete when she finally makes friends with the stepbrother who is her own age.

179- Okimoto, Jean Davies. MY MOTHER IS NOT MARRIED TO MY
80.   FATHER. New York: Putnam, 109p. Grades 5-6. R+
        When her mother tearfully announces her imminent divorce, Cynthia Browne, 11, feels physically sick at the news, but her little sister Sara, 6, is too young to comprehend the enormity of the changes that will occur in their lifestyle. Cynthia thinks it is unjust that the kids don't get a vote in this family-shaking decision. Her father, a traveling boat salesman based in Seattle, takes an apartment nearby to which he brings the girls on weekends, along with the receptionist he has been seeing. The girls are confused by the two different sets of rules in their two homes, but they concede that their lives are filled with more activities than ever before. They pull a practical joke on Daddy's girlfriend in an effort to discourage her but are only forced to apologize. Mom assuages Cynthia's fears that her shortcomings caused the divorce but develops a case of nervous jitters when asked on a date. The girls decide she should marry a man who owns a horse because Cynthia likes to ride, but

the man's political conservatism is immiscible with Mom's liberalism.
Mom, who teaches ceramics, finally meets a mature political activist
doctor, with whom she falls in love. Cynthia is strongly drawn to
Sam but feels disloyal to her dad until Mom explains that one's
supply of love is inexhaustible and self-perpetuating. The girls
prepare to meet their future stepbrothers with open minds (see
178).

181. Oppenheimer, Joan L. GARDINE VS. HANOVER. New York:
        Crowell, 1982. 152p. Grades 7-10. R+
        Abby Gardine, 10, accepts her mother Frances' remarriage
to Berk Hanover as a situation she cannot change and becomes a
pal to her stepbrother Drew, 11. Her sister Jill, however, is distressed by her parents' recent divorce when her mother returned to
teaching, and she is antagonistic at having Caroline Hanover, also
16, move into their San Diego home. Jill is diminutive, dark, attractive and casual, a B student who is gregarious, accustomed to having
her own way, and has a steady boyfriend. Caroline is a tall, lanky
redhead, obsessively neat and intellectual like her divorced oncologist
mother, and an introvert who has never dated until she meets a boy
who works for her father, a former New York accountant who became
a landscape architect after his divorce. The two stepsisters cannot
resist the overpowering urge to snipe at one another constantly,
while the tension created by their polemics creeps like a malaise over
the total family. To air grievances, Berk calls a conference which
turns into an accusatory insult exchange. While Jill and Abby are
in San Francisco visiting their father, Berk and Frances quarrel over
the girls' selfish, intransigent animosity, and the Hanovers move into
an apartment. Both teens should be glad but instead feel guilty
over their parents' pain. When a virulent strain of flu fells Jill and
her mother, a panicky Abby calls Caroline, who responds to the
crisis. When Jill recovers, it is her turn to minister to Caroline.
Later, they talk until midnight, confessing their sins and agreeing
to coexist.

182. Orenstein, Denise Gosliner. WHEN THE WIND BLOWS HARD.
        Reading, Mass.: Addison-Wesley, 1982. Illus. by Linda
        Strauss Edwards. 102p. Grades 3-5. R+
        Only slightly less devastating than her parents' separation
is the news that her mother is moving from New York City to Prince
of Wales Island in Alaska, where she will teach at the native Tlingit
school. The few things Shawn likes about the wilderness town of
Klawock are the totem poles and the tiny seaplanes that are its only
link with civilization. About everything else she is defensive, including her backward and bashful classmates who stare at her red
hair and from whom she remains aloof. Her oral report on seaplanes
wins the respect of the others and encourages shy Vesta, the girl
who sits next to her, to proffer her friendship. Her relationship
with her peers thaws, but Vesta's independent grandfather seems to
resent Shawn's presence. Her mother sends her on an errand of
neighborliness to deliver venison stew to the old man, and she dis-

covers that he is not as forbidding as she imagined. He shows her how totem poles are carved, and the three become an intergenerational triumvirate. Shawn is stricken when she learns that Vesta's family is moving to Ketchikan because the hunting season has been poor. Now it is Shawn's turn to reassure Vesta about her adjustment to a new environment. She and Grandfather console one another in Vesta's absence.

183. Orgel, Doris. MY WAR WITH MRS. GALLOWAY. New York: Viking/Kestrel, 1985. Illus. by Carol Newsom. 74p. Grades 3-5. R+

Rebecca Suslow, 7, has never had a war with any other babysitter. The last one was so preoccupied with her studies that she was oblivious to Rebecca's most imaginative shenanigans. Mom, a doctor, thinks they were fortunate to find Mrs. Galloway, but Rebecca knows otherwise. Mean and bossy, the new sitter won't let Rebecca's cat Whiskers roost on top of the refrigerator or in the dresser drawers, and she reprimands Rebecca and her neighbor Michael when they make a mess in the bathroom. At least Mrs. G. doesn't snitch on their mischief to Mom, and she does seem sort of sympathetic when Rebecca has a tiff with Michael while playing divorce (Rebecca's father lives in faraway Oregon). But the battle lines are drawn on the day that Mrs. Galloway refuses to let her and Michael crawl under Rebecca's own bed to watch Rebecca's own cat having kittens. When the dust settles, Rebecca learns that Mrs. G. really loves cats and is only concerned for their welfare. She even agrees to adopt one of Whiskers' babies and names it Reb after Rebecca.

184. Osborne, May Pope. LOVE ALWAYS, BLUE. New York: Dial, 1984. 183p. Grades 6-9. R+

Self-conscious because of her height, Blue Murray, 15, is socially insecure, unsophisticated and intellectual. She lives in North Carolina with her mother, an independent heiress and social butterfly whose superficial friends Blue dislikes. Blue writes impassioned letters to her father, a temperamental playwright who has lived in New York City since he was invited to leave a year before. She is surprised when her mother, who is now dating a phony, agrees to let her visit her father on summer vacation. Far from being successful, as he has intimated in his letters, Dad has been driving a cab for a living and resides in a cheap apartment while hoping to have his play produced off-off-Broadway. Nonetheless, Blue is exhilarated to be with him, exploring the metropolis and meeting her first boyfriend, Nathaniel, whose mother formerly dated her dad. When her father's deal falls through, Blue suddenly sees his dark, immature, emotional side, the depression that her mother regards as incapacitating instability. In panic over locking herself out of the house while going in search of her father, Blue calls her mother and instantly regrets it when Mom sends officious Uncle Walter after her. Her dad agrees that she should return home while he seeks psychological help. Blue promises to write to both him and Nathaniel.

185.   Park, Barbara. DON'T MAKE ME SMILE. New York: Knopf,
         1981. 114p. Grades 4-6. R+
       His dictionary defines divorce as a "complete separation,"
but to super-sensitive Charlie Hickle, 10, divorce creates the same
visceral feeling as watching your mother back the car over your
brand new bicycle. He reacts by sobbing hysterically, begging off
school, running away to live in a tree, and letting his grades slip.
Subconsciously he is trying to punish his parents for ruining his
life by eliminating family vacations and Christmases and the convenience of being able to talk to his father on impulse. When his
father can no longer stand Charlie's sniveling on a weekend outing,
he takes him to a child psychologist of whom Charlie is suspicious.
Against his will he finds himself liking the personable young doctor,
himself the product of a broken home, who surprisingly agrees that
it seems unfair for the innocent victim to have to bear the pain of
the divorce. He assures Charlie that the wound will heal in time
and that he can speed his recovery by telling, not yelling, his
feelings to his parents and by calling him at any time to discuss his
problems. Still, Charlie schemes to reunite his parents and pleads
for a family picnic on his birthday. It is a fiasco, and the only way
to restore peace is by asking his father to leave. His relationship
with his father changes from filial to friendly, and even his attitude
toward his mother alters as she starts job-hunting.

186.   Park, Ruth. PLAYING BEATIE BOW. New York: Atheneum,
         1982. 196p. Grades 6-8. R
       When her adored architect father runs off with a younger
woman, Lynette Kirk, 14, angry and disillusioned, abjures her given
name and take the name of a witch, Abigail. A good student, reserved, composed, independent, but aloof and unpopular, she is
further isolated by her resentment toward her dad. While in this
state, and wearing an item of apparel from her mother's trendy antique shop in Sydney, Australia, Abigail espies a strange child observing other neighborhood children in a game called Beatie Bow.
Out of curiosity she follows the girl home into an unfamiliar part of
the city and is suddenly and inexplicably transported to the year
1873, where she learns that the waif is the Beatie Bow for whom the
game was named. While searching for a way back to her own time,
Abigail lives with the Bows and experiences their joys and sorrows,
as well as the hardships, inconveniences, social inequities and political barbarities of nineteenth-century Australia. Beatie's grandmother, who is possessed of "the gift," is certain that Abigail is
there for a purpose. The reason becomes clear when Abby is able
to save the family from a disastrous conflagration that would have
precluded the fulfillment of their destinies. Back home at last, her
wayward father asks to return to the family, and both she and her
mother forgive him. Some years later Lynette meets a young man
who bears an uncanny resemblance to a seaman Abby loved and lost
in 1873.

187.   Peck, Richard. DON'T LOOK AND IT WON'T HURT. New

York: Holt, Rinehart and Winston, 1972.   173p.   Grades
6-9.   R+

Carol, 15, narrates the saga of the unhappy homelife of the
Patterson family, whose father deserted them when her younger sister, now 9, was a baby and whose shrewish mother barely supports
them in a grim hand-to-mouth existence by working the night shift
at a diner.   Carol is the sensible one, though gawky, who earns
good grades and shoulders responsibility.   Her older sister, 17, is
uncontrollable, runs with a fast crowd, becomes pregnant, and goes
to a home for unwed mothers.   Thereupon their mother transfers her
suspicions to Carol.   Carol's maturity, insight, and decisiveness
save the family from total disintegration and restore a modicum of
peace and hope.

188.   Peck, Richard.   FATHER FIGURE.   New York: Viking, 1978.
        192p.   Grades 7-12.   R+

Jim Atwater, 17, has been very conscious of his role as a
model for his kid brother Byron since their father's defection nine
years earlier when their mother brought them to live with their impersonal and resolute grandmother in Brooklyn Heights.   Now their
mother has taken her own life in the face of terminal cancer, and
Jim shoulders Byron's emotional burdens as he continues to run
physical interference for him.   But imperious, patrician Grandmother
has an emotional crisis of her own, and dealing with an outspoken
teenager and a broken-armed adolescent only aggravates it.   She arranges to send the boys to Florida to their father, a stranger to
both of them, for the summer.   Jim is resentful when his dad makes
fatherly overtures to Byron, who seems receptive to them.   He also
develops a sexual rivalry with his father.   These feelings erupt into
open warfare, then lapse into uneasy armistice before open dialogue
and catharsis can erase the tension.   Jim returns to Grandmother's
to make college plans, but Byron remains behind to spend the school
year with his father.

189.   Peck, Richard.   REMEMBERING THE GOOD TIMES.   New York:
        Delacorte, 1985.   181p.   Grades 7-10.   R+

Suburbanization of rural Slocum Township is the catalyst
that forges the friendship of three unlikely companions.   Kate Lucas
has lived there all her life with her divorced mother in an old farmhouse in the middle of a pear orchard belonging to her grandmother,
Polly.   Buck Mendenhall arrived in seventh grade when his mother
remarried and he came to live with his father, a construction
worker, in a trailer behind a service station.   The following year
brought Trav Kirby with his affluent parents who moved into an exclusive new subdivision.   Diffident Buck and privileged Trav gravitate toward the friendly, accepting, well adjusted and nonjudgmental
girl.   Trav is intense, anxious, idealistic, intelligent, and driven to
achieve by the lofty expectations of his attorney father with whom he
has a love/hate relationship.   Insecure in his changing adolescent
world, he retains sentimental links with childhood that Buck and Kate
have long discarded.   Family and friends alike are shocked when Trav

is caught shoplifting from a toystore at the end of their freshman
year. Trav's father sends him away for the summer, while Polly
makes the sacrifice of selling her orchard to developers to ensure
Kate's college education. On his return, Trav is distressed by the
sale of the orchard and the impending loss of their secluded grove.
After making gifts of his most precious toys to Kate and Buck,
Trav hangs himself from a pear tree. Polly's stirring eulogy helps
unite the disparate elements of the community and bring catharsis
to Kate and Buck.

190. Perl, Lila. THE TELLTALE SUMMER OF TINA C. New
          York: Seabury, 1975. 160p. Grades 6-7. R+
       Since their parents' divorce, Tina, 12, and Arthur, 9,
have remained with their father in their expensive Long Island
suburb. Now their less conventional mother and her new husband
Peter have returned to Manhattan, where they have taken an apartment and want the children to spend the summer. Arthur is delighted, but Tina, who disapproves of Peter and their new lifestyle,
wants to remain at home with her friends, the Saturday Sad Souls
Club. The SSSC was formed as a self-help beauty club for girls
with problems (Tina is a lanky stringbean with a nervous habit of
wrinkling her nose when self-conscious), but the induction of a
new member causes strife and Tina drops out. She decides to
spend the remainder of the summer with her mother and Peter after
all. In the city she meets her first boyfriend, discovers that personal appearances are not nearly as important as she thought, and
comes to like Peter. She returns home more self-confident and
learns that her father has reconsidered his own plans to remarry.

191. Peterson, Jeanne Whitehouse. THAT IS THAT. New York:
          Harper and Row, 1979. Illus. by Deborah Ray. Unp.
          Grades 2-4. R+
       Emma Rose LaRue watches silently as her weeping father
lets himself out the front gate, suitcase in hand, declaring, "I am
tired of all our shouting and fighting. I need to find my own
happiness." Inside, her mother, also crying, prepares supper.
When Emma Rose describes her father as a grouchy old bear to her
little brother Meko, Mother contradicts her. If he is still her father,
she ponders, why did he leave her? Her magic dance fails to bring
him back, and she is melancholy because she didn't even say goodbye. On her desk she arranges a "Remembering Place," a shrine of
mementos, but as time elapses and he does not return, the trinkets
get shoved into a drawer. When the teacher asks for fathers to
help build a treehouse, Emma Rose volunteers hammer and nails
instead. She composes a very mature song which expresses the
hope that he is not sad and lonely. When winter comes, she and
Meko put Father's old hat on their snowman and, "That is that!"

192. Pfeffer, Susan Beth. THE BEAUTY QUEEN. Garden City:
          Doubleday, 1974. (OP) 134p. Grades 7-9. R+
       Impelled by an overbearing mother seeking to fulfill her own

wishes, gorgeous Kit Carson half-heartedly enters a local beauty
pageant determined to lose. Her competitive spirit prevails, however, and she places first. Her jubilant mother, basking in reflected glory, insists that she continue to the county, state and
national finals, delaying 18-year-old Kit's personal desire to pursue
an acting career. After winning the county contest, she is nagged
by the fear that her looks, not her talent, have been responsible
for her success in the theater. Philosophically, she resigns herself
to the knowledge that while her dramatic ability is genuine, her
physical attributes afford her an entree. With equanimity she cuts
the maternal apron strings, abdicates her title, and strikes out to
test her talent with a new acting company.

193. Pfeffer, Susan Beth. MARLY THE KID. Garden City:
        Doubleday, 1975. (OP) 137p. Grades 7-9. R+
        At 15, Marly Carson also runs away from her harridan of a
mother (see 192) to live with her father and his new wife, and
gradually she begins to emerge from the cocoon she has woven about
herself in self-defense. She makes her first best friend, develops
a crush on her English teacher, who is not only an outstanding instructor but is a Robert Redford lookalike, and gets suspended for
daring to retort when her sarcastic, chauvinistic history teacher
calls her (accurately) "plain, plump and pimply." Her bluff father,
diplomatic stepmother, and laudatory schoolmates rally to her defense,
and her self-confidence is replete.

194. Pfeffer, Susan Beth. STARRING PETER AND LEIGH. New
        York: Delacorte, 1979. 200p. Grades 7-10. R+
        A child actress whose mother has managed her career since
babyhood, Leigh Thorpe, 16, was most recently seen on a family TV
sitcom, then filmed a controversial TV movie before retiring upon her
mother's remarriage and moving to Long Island where she wants to
become an average teenager. Her stepfather, Ben Sanders, has a
son Peter, 17, who is a housebound hemophiliac. Peter and Leigh become friends quickly, but the kids at school are aloof until Peter
coaches her on how to act like a typical teen. It is his way of
living vicariously through Leigh. But when her dramatic role as a
teen alcoholic and rape victim airs, she is snubbed again, especially
by Andy, the boy she is most attracted to. That crisis eventually
is surmounted, but Leigh refuses to accept the lead in the class
play, not wishing to risk offending her classmates once more. Her
long anticipated first date with Andy is a disappointment because she
was expecting it to be script-perfect. When she and her actor father
are offered starring roles in a road company production of THE
DIARY OF ANNE FRANK, her professionalism overcomes her desire
for anonymity, much to Peter's dismay. He confesses that he has
fallen in love with her, and Leigh admits that she is confused about
her feelings. They agree to part for the duration of the play and
Peter's first year of college and to reassess their emotions afterward.

195. Pfeffer, Susan Beth. STARTING WITH MELODIE. New York:

Four Winds, 1982. 122p. Grades 6-10. R+

Elaine Zuckerman, 15, is torn between loyalty to long-time chum Melodie Ashford and the entreaties of her first boyfriend Steve to spend more time with him. Melodie, in spite of her wealth and material accoutrements, has the greater need. Her mother Connie, a stage actress, spends most of her time in New York and is divorced from Melodie's father Travis, a philandering British producer with whom she is waging a melodramatic battle over custody of the kids. Melodie wishes her parents were like Elaine's, whose dentist mother works out of their home and whose father is a manufacturer's representative for his computer chip company. At least they love one another and are concertedly solicitous of the welfare of Elaine and her brothers. Elaine, on the other hand, yearns for a homelife like Steve's. His mother is a professional housewife, and his father does not travel. When Melodie's sister Lissa, 7, runs away to dramatize her unhappiness at being ammunition in her parents' guerrilla warfare, the Ashfords refuse to notify authorities because of the adverse publicity, leaving the task of finding her up to the Zuckermans. In an acrimonious confrontation in the Zuckermans' living room, Melodie's parents finally listen to her solution to their problems: to move to New York where she and Lissa will be accessible to both parents. Elaine will be losing her best friend but gaining more quality time with Steve.

196.   Platt, Kin. THE BOY WHO COULD MAKE HIMSELF DISAP-
       PEAR. Philadelphia: Chilton, 1968. (OP) 215p. Grades
       6-9. R

Ignored by his preoccupied Hollywood producer father and verbally brutalized by his self-centered artist mother, Roger has developed a speech impediment which grows more acute as he gets older and more self-conscious. It is aggravated when his parents divorce when he is 12 and his mother takes him to live in New York, where a sarcastic teacher at his private school ridicules him and his mother's abuse grows more vitriolic. But others accept and befriend him: the glamorous model who lives in the penthouse, her French boyfriend who overcame his own vocal impairment, the crippled girl in the opposite wing who takes no quarter, and above all, Miss Clemm, the psychiatrist and speech therapist at school. With her encouragement Roger makes such dramatic progress that he tries to share the good news with his father by telephone, only to receive another rebuff. It is enough to drive the unwanted, unloved boy into schizophrenic withdrawal and eventually into a regressive, infantile autistic state. With the aid of Miss Clemm and the Frenchman, he begins the long road to recovery.

197.   Platt, Kin. CHLORIS AND THE CREEPS. Philadelphia:
       Chilton, 1973. 146p. Grades 5-7. R+

Chloris, 11, and Jenny, 8, can scarcely remember their profligate, philandering father who divorced their mother six years before and committed suicide three years later. When their mother starts dating other men (the creeps) and contemplates remarriage, the girls are not sure they need a new father. Jenny keeps an open mind, while Chloris is adamantly opposed to any change in the status quo. She becomes chief proselytizer in the cult to deify her father of which her paternal grandmother is high priestess. When their mother decides to marry Fidel Mancha, a Chicano sculptor, Chloris reacts with stony negativism and open hostility, blackballing Fidel's bid for legal adoption. When her mother erupts in anger and exasperation, Chloris goes on a rampage of deliberate destruction, climaxing in the torching of Fidel's studio. Psychiatry fails to overcome her stubborn rejection, but Fidel's saintly forbearance, wisdom and compassion finally triumph.

198. Platt, Kin. CHLORIS AND THE FREAKS. Scarsdale: Brad-
    bury, 1975. 217p. Grades 5-8. R+
    Chloris, now 14 (see 197), resurrects her father's spirit and perniciously plots her mother's divorce from Fidel. Jenny, 12, who adores Fidel, consults the stars to try to reverse the portent, perceiving that Chloris reserves the epithet "freak" for those of whom she is jealous. But Jenny's astrological machinations and Fidel's pontifical patience fail to curb her mother's restlessness, and she takes up with a business associate while Fidel is away at an art exhibit. Chloris appears receptive to the new inamorato to hasten her mother's decision, and it is Jenny's turn to play devil's advocate. But when the divorce plans are announced, Chloris unmasks her single-minded vituperation for all the men in her mother's life except her own father, taking grim satisfaction in making others unhappy to gain her perverse ends. Jenny is no more successful in preventing her teacher's and her best friend's parents' divorce. They both feel wretched.

199. Platt, Kin. CHLORIS AND THE WEIRDOES. Scarsdale:
    Bradbury, 1978. 231p. Grades 5-9. R+
    Jenny Carpenter, now 13 (see 197 and 198), has never really forgiven her mother for divorcing Fidel Mancha, whom she came to regard as her true father. But she has a new interest, her first boyfriend Harold, whom her sister Chloris, 15, refers to as a weirdo because of his predilection for skateboarding. Chloris' hostility has mellowed somewhat since the divorce, while her mother is between boyfriends, but when Mom suddenly starts dating again, Chloris parades her dormant rancor as punishment for her mother's daring to try to replace the girls' self-martyred father and to attempt to find happiness and self-fulfillment in middle age. If she is only going to be a part-time mother, Chloris reasons, she will retaliate by being just a part-time daughter. She makes clan-destine plans to embark on an illicit weekend tryst with a boy who has been hanging around the pizza parlor where she works. Her flight mars her mother's own weekend junket with her boyfriend, as Chloris intended, and leads to an early morning altercation between the sisters when the prodigal returns. Chloris palliates her mother by apologizing, but she concedes to Jenny later that she's unre-pentant. Jenny derives consolation from her wholesome relationship with level-headed Harold.

200. Potter, Marian. THE SHARED ROOM. New York: Morrow,
         1979. 192p. Grades 4-6. NR
              As she enters fifth grade, Catherine Doyle, 10, who occu-
      pies the same bedroom in her grandparents' house in which her
      mother grew up, develops an obsessive curiosity about her parents,
      whom her grandparents adamantly refuse to discuss: pleas for in-
      formation only elicit tears and accusations of ingratitude from Nana,
      while Pop retreats behind the noise of his electric tools. A fabri-
      cated story of idyllic family life leads to the revelation by petty,
      gossiping small town classmates that her mother is incurably insane.
      Catherine's pugilistic reaction to the news earns her the sobriquet
      of Ali. When she learns of her grandparents' annual Christmas pil-
      grimage to the nearby mental hospital, she demands to be taken
      along. When that ploy fails, she sends her mother a surreptitious
      gift. The correspondence this produces convinces Ali that her
      mother is normal. Intercepting a letter from the hospital director
      declaring that her mother is rehabilitated and can function at home
      precipitates Ali into bringing her home without permission. Nana
      is furious and almost persuades even Ali's mother that living outside
      the institution is hopeless. Pop explains to Ali about her mother's
      nervous breakdown and subsequent suicide attempts after Ali's birth
      and her husband's desertion, the cause of Nana's heartbreak. Ali's
      mother realizes that her mother will never forgive her for failing to
      fulfill her expectations, and she makes her own decision to move to
      a local halfway house where she can be part of Ali's life.

201. Rabin, Gil. FALSE START. New York: Harper and Row,
         1969. (OP) Illus. by John Gundelfinger. 139p. Grades
         5-7. R
              Richard Gould's mother condones the abusiveness and in-
      ebriation of her husband, an unemployed bricklayer in Depression-
      era New York, because he was the product of a broken home in his
      Eastern European boyhood. Richard, hating him, feels that life
      would be much pleasanter if Pop would just disappear. Pop views
      Richard as a coward because he is not aggressive enough, but Rich
      is simply cautious, especially about competing in a foot race against
      Cock-a-boy Indian, the biggest kid in their Jewish ghetto. When
      Pop can no longer dodge the landlord, the family is evicted from
      their apartment and forced to find a more squalid one, and Pop ful-
      fills Richard's wish by exiting without notice. Rich can't help com-
      paring him with wealthy, flashy Cousin Jack, a friendly, outgoing
      fight promoter. He can't understand why his mother not only
      hopes that Pop will return but also refuses to rely upon Cousin
      Jack's largesse. Herself illiterate, she pawns her rings so that Rich
      will not have to leave school and take a job. When a race is finally
      arranged between Rich and Cock-a-boy, Richard learns that it has
      been rigged by crooked gamblers so that he will win. Unwilling to
      back out, he uses his ingenuity to preserve his integrity. He is
      later crushed to learn that Cousin Jack is a phony. When a drunken
      "John Doe" fitting Pop's description turns up at a local hospital,
      Richard reluctantly identifies him for his mom's sake.

202. Rabinowich, Ellen. ROCK FEVER. New York: Watts, 1979.
        85p. Photos by Mauro Marinelli. Grades 5-10. Hi-Lo. R
        Always a heavy drinker, Doug's mother has become violent
and irrational, venting her resentment for her husband's divorcing
her after her family put him through medical school. To escape her
fury, Doug, 16, tries to immerse himself in the amateur rock group
of which he is the vocalist, but his tension breaks his concentration
and another member, Alex, offers him downers to calm his nerves.
An agent wants them to cut a demonstration record for which each
member of the group must put up $100, but when Doug asks his
father for a loan he gets a lecture on applying himself to academics
instead of frivolities. He snatches several bottles of pills from his
father's office, intending to sell them to a drug dealer but keeping
a handful of Quaaludes for himself. He begins dating Valerie, a
girl he met at rehearsal, but when his mother invites her to dinner,
Ma gets drunk and makes an ugly scene. Doug, depressed, gets
stoned and assaults Alex, jeopardizing the group's chance of going
pro. Remorseful, he decides to straighten himself out but is con-
fronted by his mother, who falls down the stairs and loses consciousness. At the hospital, his father appears to show more concern for
his welfare. The band and Valerie welcome him back, and Doug
flushes away the remaining pills.

203. Riley, Jocelyn. CRAZY QUILT. New York: Morrow, 1984.
        215p. Grades 6-9. R+
        Back in her grandmother's home in suburban Chicago after
being kidnapped and taken to the boondocks of Wisconsin for four
months by her mother (see 204), Merle Carlson, 13, finds that she
has lost touch with her trendy adolescent classmates. Her best
friend Kayla has matured and outgrown her, and the class bully,
Jinx, picks on her. Her mother, committed to a mental hospital by
her grandmother, petitions for a sanity hearing at which Merle tes-
tifies in behalf of her grandmother because life with Mom was so unstable and substandard. She hates being the eldest, because both
her mother and self-sacrificial working grandmother depend on her
to be responsible for siblings Ron, 11, and Diane, 9, both of whom
resent her authority. Merle's grandmother contends that her
daughter's mental problems are the result of escapism and a lack of
self-discipline. When Merle's mother, whose husband deserted her
long ago, comes home for a trial weekend, the two adult women
battle over control of the children. Grandma, a widow, wants to
marry the man she's dating in the unlikelihood that her daughter
will improve enough to be discharged and take custody of the kids.
In the meantime, Merle's period starts and she is relieved to know
that she is normal. She learns that her nemesis Jinx is abused by
her father. The editor of the school newspaper asks her to be
poetry editor because he likes her verse, then asks her to the
eighth grade dance because he likes her personally.

204. Riley, Jocelyn. ONLY MY MOUTH IS SMILING. New York:
        Morrow, 1982. 222p. Grades 7-10. R

Elaine Carlson is a chronic mental patient. Between hos-
pitalizations she works as a bookkeeper and lives, along with her
three children, in the home of her working mother who treats her
as a fourth and rebellious child. When her mother kicks her in the
head in a fit of pique over non-payment of rent, Elaine liquidates
her secret savings account and sneaks away by bus to Wisconsin,
taking the kids, Merle, 13, Ron, 11, and Diane, 9. There they set
up camp like gypsies. Elaine's mother eventually locates them, but
the grandchildren refuse to return with her to Chicago out of loyalty to their mother. At the end of the summer they move into an
unfurnished house with inadequate heating and plumbing. The
children start school and make friends, but Merle is too embarrassed
about their living conditions to invite anyone home with her. A
popular boy takes a romantic interest in her, but she finds out later,
to her chagrin, that he is only using her to make his former girlfriend jealous. Elaine becomes increasingly paranoid and loses her
job. When her condition can no longer be concealed from authorities, Merle calls her grandmother, who arrives to collect them as
Elaine is being taken away in a straitjacket. The children blame
their grandmother for causing their mother's breakdown, but Grandma reveals that Elaine refuses to take the medication that maintains
her equilibrium.

205. Rinaldi, Ann. BUT IN THE FALL I'M LEAVING. New York:
        Holiday House, 1985. 250p. Grades 6-9. R
        When Brieanna McQuade, 14, is caught vandalizing the
house of wealthy, elderly Miss Emily on a dare, her father is convinced that Brie's rebellion can be traced directly to her mother's
desertion to become a California career woman when Brie was 2.
A liberal newspaper publisher in suburban New Jersey, Dad harbors
antipathy for elite, conservative Miss Emily but cannot object when
the judge orders Brie to make reparation by working for Miss Emily
to learn good citizenship and community involvement. Brie is extremely resentful of Amanda, a model whom her father is dating and
who officiously tries to exert a maternal influence over her. She is
determined to remain with her mother on her next visit to her in the
fall, thus terminating her fights with her father over Amanda. Her
opinion of Miss Emily as a selfish, eccentric old fool gradually
changes as she learns of her unheralded philanthropy. When Miss
Emily dies suddenly, the girl's distress is exacerbated when her
mother cruelly informs her that Miss Emily was her grandmother,
estranged from her daughter because of her opposition to her marriage. Stunned, Brie refuses to forgive her father for withholding
the information and denying her a normal relationship with her
grandmother. Brie's older brother Kevin, a Roman Catholic priest,
reveals in their father's defense that Dad has always been a more
stable and loving parent than Mom. Difficult as that is for Brie to
accept, she forgives her stubborn father and decides to stay with
him.

206. Rinkoff, Barbara. THE WATCHERS. New York: Knopf, 1972.

(OP) 130p. Grades 5-6. R

Wary of becoming involved in his parents' cat-and-dog fights over his dad's compulsive gambling debts, Chris Blake, 11, has developed the safe pastime of people-watching in his New York apartment building. He watches nervous, skinny, misfit Sanford Townsend, 10, moving in and discovers that Sandy is also an astute observer. The older boy with the leathery veneer becomes friend, protector and mentor to the neurologically impaired and overprotected younger one. Sandy's father is appreciative of Chris' therapeutic effect on his maternally dominated son, and, over his wife's objections, starts treating them both as real people. Tension at home mounts when Chris' mother takes a temporary typing job she hates to compensate for her husband's profligacy. After Chris' dad admits that the horses are more important to him than his wife and child, she insists that he move out. Chris assuages his bitterness and rancor over the loss of his father by playing big brother to Sandy.

207. Roberts, Willo Davis. THE GIRL WITH THE SILVER EYES.
     New York: Atheneum, 1980. 181p. Grades 4-6. R

Katie Welker, 9, has the power of telekinesis with which she can move inanimate objects at will. Adults as well as children treat her as a freak because of her powers coupled with her peculiar silver-colored eyes. Katie has only recently come to live with her mother Monica. Her parents were divorced when she was 3, and, because her mother could not hold a job and care for her at the same time, she lived with her father and paternal grandmother until he deserted her and her grandmother died. In the cramped apartment she now shares with Monica, she overhears her mother telling her boyfriend that Katie's peculiarities may stem from her former job working with experimental drugs for a pharmaceutical company during her pregnancy. Monica has been in touch with former co-workers who have reported similar symptoms in their offspring. Friendly but inquisitive Adam Cooper moves into the apartment building and tries to ingratiate himself with Katie. She is afraid that he may be investigating her for the murder of her grandmother, because superstitious neighbors circulated a rumor that the death may have been unnatural. Katie flees, gravitating towards the addresses of the other similarly afflicted children, and discovers that they are as lonely, misunderstood and miserable as she. Together they confront Adam Cooper and learn that he is not a detective but a representative of the Institute of Psychic Phenomena. He hopes to recruit all the special children, who, having found one another, know they will never feel isolated again.

208. Robinson, Barbara. THE BEST CHRISTMAS PAGEANT EVER.
     New York: Harper and Row, 1972. Illus. by Judith Gwyn
     Brown. 80p. Grades 4-6. R

"The Herdmans were absolutely the worst kids in the history of the world. They lied and stole and smoked cigars (even the girls) and talked dirty and hit little kids and cussed their teachers

and took the name of the Lord in vain and set fire to Fred Shoe-
maker's toolhouse." Their mother could qualify for welfare but
works a double shift at the shoe factory because she's afraid to be
at home alone with the kids after their father hopped a train one
day and disappeared. Needless to say, they intimidate all of their
classmates, and the only place the other children find refuge from
the six stairstep Herdmans is in Sunday School. But one day the
Herdmans get wind of the fact that refreshments are sometimes served
at church, and they show up en masse just as the Christmas pageant
is being cast. Naturally, they aggressively grab all the lead roles
for themselves and, never having heard the Christmas story, set
about revising theology by zapping the bad guys and giving the
good guys a better shake. Rehearsals are a disaster, but the actual
performance is much more realistic and meaningful than the staid
committee envisioned, and the spirit of Christmas strikes the Herdmans like a bolt of lightning in spite of the fact that Mary has a
black eye and the Angel of the Lord yells, "Hey! Unto you a child
is born!"

209. Sachs, Marilynn. THE BEARS' HOUSE. Garden City: Double-
     day, 1971. Illus. by Louis Glanzman. 81p. Grades 5-6.
     R
     After her father's desertion and her mother's ensuing mental
illness, Fran Ellen, 10, has only two things to live for: her beloved
baby sister, for whom she has sole responsibility, and the Three
Bears' dollhouse in her classroom into which she escapes in fantasy
when the pressures of reality overwhelm her. Tormented by siblings
and peers alike, she lives a deception, trying to keep the family intact. Her world dissolves when the baby becomes ill and a discerning
teacher discovers their tragic plight. Left with only the dollhouse
family (a gift from her teacher for breaking her thumb-sucking habit)
for solace, acceptance and love, her daydreams supply the rationaliza-
tion for giving up her precious baby before she dies. In the end,
retreat into her fantasy family becomes her only defense, her only
tolerable recourse.

210. Sachs, Marilyn. THE FAT GIRL. New York: Dutton, 1984.
     168p. Grades 7-12. R+
     When his mother, a nurse with a martyr complex, berates
him, she accuses him of being selfish like his father, who moved out
on her when Jeff Lyons, now 18, was 7. His dad is remarried and
has two other sons who now share the good times that Jeff is denied.
His sister Wanda, 14, is also unhappy with their critical, melancholy
mother and decides to move in with Dad's new family. In her bitterness and self-pity, Mom tries to commit suicide with barbiturates.
Jeff blames Wanda for her disloyalty to the mother who reared her.
He falls in love with Norma, the most ravishing girl in his ceramics
class, and callously ridicules Ellen, the clumsy, inept fat girl, until
he discovers that she is threatening suicide also. Suddenly compassionate, he drops Norma unceremoniously and devotes himself to improving Ellen's self-respect, dressing her in dramatic caftans, heavy

jewelry and bold makeup. He is motivated less by love than by altruism and the subconscious need, like his mother's, to control. His insecurities recede in the glow of Ellen's dependency and adoration. As she loses pounds and gains friends through Weight Watchers, she becomes more confident, but Jeff is jealous of his creation and furious with her for rejecting the outfit he chooses for her to wear to the prom. He regards her sudden independence as ingratitude, and his old disgust for her resurfaces. Ellen ends the warped romance. Jeff and his mother are linked in their misery over disappointing relationships, but he vows not to brood over it as he goes off to college.

211. Sachs, Marilyn. VERONICA GANZ. Garden City: Doubleday, 1968. Illus. by Louis Glanzman. 156p. Grades 4-6. R
    Accustomed to winning the deference of her entire school through intimidation, gangling, aggressive, pugnacious, insolent Veronica, 13, is nonplussed and intensely aggravated when Peter Wedemeyer, the puny new kid, taunts, outwits and humiliates her at every juncture. She feels compelled to be the tough one of the family because the others seem to be such weaklings, from her defenseless half-brother Stanley, 5, and her cry-baby sister Mary Rose, 11, to her browbeaten, conciliatory stepfather whom her mother married eight years ago during the Depression. Even Mama is preoccupied, tense and overworked at the cleaning establishment she convinced her husband to open. Veronica harbors no respect, either, for her dimly remembered father whom her mother divorced long ago, and she is not disappointed when he reneges on his promise to visit. In spite of her intelligence, she is an indifferent student because of her devotion to wreaking revenge on Peter. When Peter and two cronies gang up on her in order to overpower her, she suddenly discovers the power of tears as a weapon when sympathetic adults come to her defense. Instead of retaliating when the opportunity arises, she decides she prefers to be a girl teased by a boy.

212. Sallis, Susan. AN OPEN MIND. New York: Harper and Row, 1978. 139p. Grades 6-9. R+
    Although he and his divorced father are very companionable, David Winterbourne, 15, pities his defenseless mother and resents his dad for leaving her to a dismal life as a geriatric nurse in their small English town. One day his father takes him to a performance of paraplegic and spastic children and introduces him to the woman in charge of the program whom he is dating and plans to marry. David is outraged because he never viewed his parents' split as permanent. As a ruse to spy upon Margaret Daly, he decides to volunteer at the school for the handicapped where she works. There he befriends a spastic boy, Bruce, whom he learns later is Margaret's son. Even though his mother appears to accept his father's planned remarriage, David, for her sake, plans to prevent it. He makes an elaborate excuse not to join his father for the Christmas holidays while his mother is hospitalized for a hysterectomy, and instead he hides out in his own house. There he also harbors

wheelchair-bound Bruce, who is ostensibly running away for the
same reason, while the parents mount a frantic search. Bruce's
motivation, however, is far nobler. Fearing that his mother will
sacrifice her happiness because of her reluctance to bring a severely handicapped child to the marriage, he plans to do away with himself. A shamed and sobered David, when he learns that Bruce will
die without his medication and special diet, struggles valiantly to
keep the boy alive so that they can become stepbrothers.

213. Sanderlin, Owenita. TENNIS REBEL. New York: Watts,
         1978. Photos by Chuck Freedman. 95p. Grades 5-8.
         Hi-Lo. R
         Kelly Anderson, 15, hates leaving the green hills of Maine
for the smoggy desert wastes of Southern California, but her father,
a doctor, is marrying the woman for whom he divorced Kelly's
mother, and Kelly has chosen to live with her mother. Mom is offered a job by Mr. Morgan, a wealthy old friend, at the beach and
tennis club he owns in her hometown of Palm City. There Kelly
vents her frustrations--the unfriendliness of the girls her age and
her disapproval of her mother's chumminess with her benefactor--
on the fuzzy yellow ball. Her only friend, Mike, a protege of Mr.
Morgan's, also seems to prefer playing mixed doubles with Kelly's
chief rival, even though Kelly is the better player. When her
mother marries Mr. Morgan, Kelly, now 16, spends the summer with
her father, resenting both stepparents for rendering her homeless.
Back in California she muffs the big tournament she is scheduled to
play with Mike, but in spite of the loss he asks for a reprise the
following year. He reminds her tenderly that tennis stars lead
nomadic lives independent of their parents, giving her a goal to aim
for and the prospect of a long-term romance.

214. Schuchman, Joan. TWO PLACES TO SLEEP. Minneapolis:
         Carolrhoda, 1979. Illus. by Jim LaMarche. Unp. Grades
         2-3. R+
         Dad's housekeeper, Mrs. Andrews, says of David's parents'
divorce, "David, some things you can't change. You may not like
them, but you just have to learn to live with them." David, 7, resides with his dad in the familiar home he's grown up in, while his
mother has taken an apartment in the city and works in a downtown
office. When she picks him up on Saturday to go kite flying, he
notices that she is a better listener now than she used to be. He
proposes to her that if he strives to be neater and less clumsy,
perhaps she will get "undivorced" from Dad. She explains to him
simply the reason for the divorce and the continuity of their love
for him. He begins getting accustomed to his second place to sleep.

215. Sebestyen, Ouida. IOU's. Boston: Little, Brown, 1982.
         188p. Grades 6-9. R++
         Annie Garrett has been a firm, fair, fun, loving and
highly principled single parent since her husband's desertion when
her son Stowe was a baby. She has imbued the boy, now 13, with

her integrity and values with which, as an adolescent who is longing
to experiment and take risks, he is sometimes uncomfortable.   An
underpaid day care center operator, Annie depends upon the monthly
check sent by her father who has been estranged from her since his
favorite son was killed going to her wedding.   Suddenly a relative
calls Stowe to inform him that the ailing grandfather he has never
met wants to see him--but not his mother--before he dies.   Resentful over the peremptory summons and the rebuff to Annie which
would only cause her more heartache, Stowe makes the agonizing
decision to withhold the information and decline the invitation.   He
wishes that he were capable of providing for Annie to repay her
for her years of nurturing and sacrifice.   When his life savings is
accidentally lost, Stowe can no longer keep his secret.   Annie swallows her own pride and pain in her elation over her father's conciliatory gesture to Stowe, and the two make the pilgrimage from
Colorado to Oklahoma to visit him.   They arrive too late.   Relatives
offer Annie a job and a home with them to compensate for her
father's truculence, but the independent pair decide to resume their
contented subsistence in mutual trust.   Stowe resolves to contact
his father before he will regret the omission.

216.   Sharmat, Marjorie. HE NOTICED I'M ALIVE ... AND OTHER
          HOPEFUL SIGNS. New York: Delacorte, 1984. 146p.
          Grades 7-10. R+
          Although they have a part-time maid, artistic but domestic
Jody Kline, 15, whose mother departed two years ago to "find
herself," acts as hostess for her suave, cosmopolitan attorney father. He is pursuing a divorce while dating divorcee Gossamer
Green, whose handsome son Matt, 18, he has hired as a summer in-
tern. Smitten, Jody attempts to attract Matt's attention with the
help of Opal Spiegel, a market researcher who becomes her surrogate
mother and adviser. When Matt finally asks her for a date, she
agonizingly has to decline because of a prior commitment and fears
that her rebuff will drive him into the arms of her rival. Her anxiety is unwarranted, however, when Matt asks her out again in
spite of the fact that he is trying to discourage their parents' romance in the hopes that his parents will reconcile. In the meantime, Opal remarries and moves away, while Jody's mother writes
that she has solved her identity crisis in Switzerland and will soon
be returning.

217.   Sharmat, Marjorie. TWO GUYS NOTICED ME ... AND OTHER
          MIRACLES. New York: Delacorte, 1985. 149p. Grades
          7-10. R
          After two years of globe trotting in search of self (see
216), Jody Kline's mother returns home expecting to take up where
she left off before abandoning the family. For Jody, love and resentment wrestle for supremacy. For her father, on the verge of
marrying Gossamer Green, the situation is equally awkward. Matt
Green, who is Gossamer's son and Jody's boyfriend, has become
reconciled to his mother's impending marriage to Jody's father.

Angry that Jody's mother is trying to reclaim his mother's territory,
he drives Jody into the arms of a new acquaintance, Travis Cameo,
vice-president of the senior class and her fellow artist. In the meantime, Jody suspects her mother of attempting to make her father
jealous by having an affair with "Uncle Mike," whom she coquettish-
ly refers to as her financial adviser. Jody abhors her mother's
machinations and is stunned when Matt's parents remarry, leaving
the field open to her mother. Jody eventually learns that "Uncle
Mike" is a private detective hired by her father to keep tabs on her
mother but who actually took advantage of both of them. Reluctantly, Jody makes peace with her mother and makes up with Matt after
Travis reveals his true colors as an insincere charmer.

218.   Simon, Norma. I WISH I HAD MY FATHER. Niles, Ill.:
       Whitman, 1983. Illus. by Arieh Zeldich. Unp. Grades
       K-2. R+
       The boy dreads the approach of Father's Day, because he
knows that he will be expected to complete the class art project
even though his gift will lack a recipient. He and his classmate
Grace never see or hear from their divorced fathers and do not
even know their whereabouts. He generally winds up giving his
artwork to his grandfather or his elderly downstairs neighbor.
When he sees his friends with their fathers it feels like "bumping
a sore and making it hurt again." His mother tells him that before
he remembers they all used to be happy together but that later his
parents started fighting and yelling. She doesn't like to talk about
his father and doesn't keep any pictures of him around the house.
He hopes that he'll meet his dad when he grows up but wishes that
his dad could see him now with his four front teeth missing and
wonders whether he thinks of him at all. He would settle for having his father just one day a year.

219.   Slote, Alfred. JAKE. Philadelphia: Lippincott, 1971. 155p.
       Grades 5-6. R
       In his Detroit suburb, Jake Wrather, 11, is a tough black
smart aleck. Since his mother deserted him two years ago, he has
lived with his Uncle Lenny, 24, a cool, preoccupied rock musician
who rehearses all night and sleeps all day. Left to his own devices, Jake stays up late watching TV and is habitually late for
school. The only thing he cares deeply about is his Little League
team, nominally coached by a team mother who knows nothing about
the sport. Suddenly his abnormal but complacent existence is in
danger of being destroyed when the school threatens to have him
placed in a foster home because of his tardiness, and the league
president delivers an ultimatum that his team must get a male coach
or disband. Lenny shows him how strongly he feels about their
remaining a family by establishing and enforcing strict new rules
for Jake, but the breakup of the team hangs over his head like
Damocles' sword. Uncle Lenny, a former high school athlete, would
make the ideal coach, but his long commute to rehearsals downtown
begins just at game time. The team locates an unused warehouse

nearby that would make a suitable studio for Lenny, but unfortunately it is owned by the sponsor of the team's archrivals. Reason
eventually prevails, and a deal is struck. Jake is finally free to devote himself wholeheartedly to baseball without fear of his family or
team being split.

220. Slote, Alfred. MATT GARGAN'S BOY. Philadelphia: Lippincott, 1975. 159p. Grades 5-6. R+
Danny's parents were divorced because his mom hated being
a "baseball widow" married to a major league player, but now his
father is on the verge of retirement, and Danny, 11, hopes he will
return to their small town so the three of them can take up where
they left off. When his mother starts seeing a man whose daughter
wants to join his Little League team, he reasons that the two parents
would attend games together and might get serious about one another, so he heads the delegation opposing girls on their team.
Susie is given a tryout anyway and passes handily. The other boys
accept her, but Danny quits the team. He is jolted when his mother
attends the next game without him, and he calls his dad for advice,
only to discover that his father is planning to remarry. His defenses
in tatters, Danny surrenders to the inevitable, but he is still proud
to be the son of a celebrity.

221. Smith, Doris Buchanan. KICK A STONE HOME. New York:
Crowell, 1974. 152p. Grades 6-9. R+
To compensate for the trauma of her parents' divorce three
years ago, Sara Jane concentrated on excelling at sports and remaining aloof from her classmates so no one would suspect her shame.
Now, at 15, she has suddenly developed an interest in boys that is
not competitive, but her tomboy image is difficult to eradicate in Atlanta where a premium is placed on femininity. The boy she has a
crush on is friendly but impersonal, while, of the two who are attracted to her, one wants to proceed too fast and the other is a
male chauvinist. Her mother regards her interest in sports and her
ambition to be a veterinarian as manifestations of immaturity, and a
personality conflict with her history teacher proves a nagging frustration. Even her dog's death while she is visiting her father and
his wife heightens her insecurity. Most days she makes a ritual of
kicking a stone home from school. When her one girlfriend, Kay,
confesses that her parents are also divorced, it creates an atmosphere for honest self-appraisal. With Kay's help she strives to overcome her awkwardness and self-consciousness. At a party she surprises herself most of all by displaying a natural savoir-faire and
attracting a sincerely interested young man. With new self-confidence
she makes peace with her teacher, adopts another dog, inducts Kay
into the intricacies of stone kicking, and takes up football again.

222. Smith, Doris Buchanan. TOUGH CHAUNCEY. New York:
Morrow, 1974. (OP) Illus. by Michael Eagle. 222p.
Grades 7-8. R
Chauncey, 13, would never hurt defenseless animals, only

people, because humans inflict pain on him. His thrice-divorced
mother whom he adores can't make a home for him because of her
succession of boyfriends, so he lives with his grandparents who ad-
minister brutality in the guise of stern moral guidance. His grandfather believes that it is sinful to attend movies but cold-bloodedly
shoots kittens and beats the boy and locks him in the closet when
he is ten minutes late from school. Calculatedly, Chauncey has become the toughest, meanest kid in his Georgia town, cutting a
swath of malicious mischief and destruction. In a last-ditch effort
to live with his mother, he is badly hurt jumping from a train and
returns to his grandparents on crutches. When his grandfather
tries to shoot his last kitten, Chauncey has no recourse but to run
away despite his incapacitation. He is aided by his erstwhile arch-
enemy and fellow scapegrace, a black youngster who tells him of
his own intolerable home life and suggests a foster home as an alternative in Chauncey's bid to make good.

223.   Snyder, Anne. FIRST STEP. New York: Holt, Rinehart and
       Winston, 1975.   128p.   Grades 7-9.   R+
       It is common knowledge that Cindy Stott's mother is an al-
coholic, but Cindy continues to protect and defend her, finally with-
drawing from her friends in an attempt to avoid hurt and humiliation. When she commands the lead in the high school play, and
leading man Mitch along with it, a jealous cast member cruelly baits
Cindy about her mother's drinking problem, and the defensive girl
responds with the desired effect every time. Mitch discloses that
his parents are both alcoholics and invites her to Alateen meetings,
but she remains skeptical. When her mother injures her younger
brother in alcoholic anger, she calls her father in New York to ask
if he will send for them, but while he is willing to send support payments, he makes it clear that he wants no further commitments. On
opening night her mother makes a sensational performance of her
own, eclipsing Cindy's stellar one and plunging her to a nadir of
mortification. At last she is receptive to the ministrations of Alateen
and loyal, long-suffering Mitch.

224.   Snyder, Zilpha Keatley. EYES IN THE FISHBOWL. New York:
       Atheneum, 1968. Illus. by Alton Raible. 168p.   Grades 7-
       9.   R
       Dion, 14, is vaguely dissatisfied with his impecunious fa-
ther's lethargic lifestyle after his mother left and wants to pursue
for himself the conventional materialistic life. Between his many
part-time jobs, he slips into the city's most sumptuous department
store to savor its aura of luxury. One day he sees an exotic girl
there with enigmatic dark eyes, and when he is accidentally locked
in the store after closing hours, he discovers that she and some unseen companions are responsible for ghostly occurrences and unex-
plained voices that are unnerving customers and employees alike. It
is only after he has developed a close attachment to Sara that he
learns she and her friends are spirits who have been materialized
there by an elderly psychic, and he is in mortal jeopardy of joining

them. After Sara departs and the store is closed, Dion realizes that
his father would feel stifled in a regular occupation. He renews his
latent interest in music and savors success as part of a dance combo.

225. Snyder, Zilpha Keatley. THE FAMOUS STANLEY KIDNAPPING
       CASE. New York: Atheneum, 1979. 212p. Grades 5-8.
       R+
       When Amanda Randall's artist mother receives an inheritance
that can only be spent in Italy, it becomes an opportunity for the
entire blended Stanley family (see 226) to spend a year in Florence.
Belligerent Amanda, 13, announces that she would prefer to stay
with her father, a flamboyant Hollywood public relations man, but
finally agrees to go. At their rented villa they make friends with a
local girl, and Amanda boasts that her father is "molto ricco." Soon
after, she is abducted by three hooded men who also grab the four
Stanley kids, David, 12, Janie, 7, and twins Esther and Blair, 5,
when they attempt to rescue her. The five children are held hostage
in a deserted farmhouse cellar while "Red Mask," the most vicious
of the kidnappers, makes ransom demands. Amanda tearfully admits
to herself and David her doubts that her father really cares enough
about her to ransom her. After numerous imaginative but abortive
strategies for convincing the kidnappers to release them, the three
youngest children overpower "Red Mask" with the aid of the more
timorous abductors, and Amanda learns to her astonishment and
gratification that her father was concerned enough about her to rush
to Italy. The adventures of the Stanley family continue in BLAIR'S
NIGHTMARE.

226. Snyder, Zilpha Keatley. THE HEADLESS CUPID. New York:
       Atheneum, 1978. Illus. by Alton Raible. 203p. Grades
       5-8. R
       Amanda, 12, has been living in California with her di-
vorced father and is resentful when her mother Molly, a newly remarried artist, brings her to live in New England with the Stanley
family, including David, 11, Janie, 6, and twins Esther and Blair,
4, whose mother died a year earlier. Arch, sophisticated, mysterious, and exhibitionistic, Amanda comes laden with occult paraphernalia and exercises influence over her stepsiblings by initiating them
into supernatural rites. Once they have demonstrated their good
faith by successfully completing their bizarre trials, Amanda becomes
more friendly. When Mr. Stanley, a college professor, is out of town
on a long field trip and the electrical system of their large old
country house goes haywire, they learn from the handyman that
Westerly House was haunted seventy years ago by a poltergeist.
Amanda holds a seance, goes into a trance, and contacts the spirit.
Suddenly the manifestations resume, much to Molly's alarm. David
suspects that Amanda is perpetrating the pranks. The eeriest occurrence happens on a night when the children are alone in the
house, and they are all genuinely frightened. Amanda confesses to
the earlier incidents, but she is as mystified as David about the
reappearance of the long-missing head of the decapitated newel post
cherub. Is young Blair the truly psychic one?

102   The Single-Parent Family

227. Snyder, Zilpha Keatley. THE WITCHES OF WORM. New York:
        Atheneum, 1972. Illus. by Alton Raible. 183p. Grades
        4-7. R+
        While visiting her secret San Francisco cliffside cave, latch-
key kid Jessica Porter, 12, whose father deserted when she was a
baby and whose mother Joy works as a secretary, discovers an orphaned kitten. Though she hates cats, she adopts the fascinatingly
ugly creature, which her elderly neighbor Mrs. Foster says resembles an ancient Egyptian Abyssinian, and names him Worm.
From the beginning Jessica thinks Worm is unearthly and devilish.
Soon he begins talking aloud to her, suggesting ways of getting
even with those who have slighted her. She is terrified to be alone
with him, and when Joy announces her plans to meet her boyfriend's
parents over the weekend, Jessica ruins her mother's new dress, at
Worm's instigation, to keep her at home. Worm directs her to mu-
tilate her ex-friend Brandon Doyle's trumpet in retaliation for his
defection to music lessons. Joy sends her to an ineffectual psychologist, but Jessica wants to dispose of the demon cat. Perspicacious Mrs. Fortune counsels her to destroy the demon but not Worm,
who is only a cat. She declares that everyone invites his own
devils and must exorcise them himself, which Jessica proceeds to do
with complete sincerity in her own way. Brandon proves to be a
real friend in the clutch and vows to help her rehabilitate Worm
from a feral animal to a trusting pet.

228. Springstubb, Tricia. WHICH WAY TO THE NEAREST WILDER-
        NESS? Boston: Little, Brown, 1984. 166p. Grades 5-8.
        R
        Aggravated by her parents' aggressive sniping at one an-
other and her own assigned role as patient, sensible middle child
between a temperamental older sister and a sensitive, neurotic
little brother, Eunice Gottlieb, 11, decides to drop out of the human
race in Sandusky, Ohio, and embrace primitive self-sufficiency.
Along with her friend Joy, who harbors a grudge against a fellow
ballet student, she establishes a phenomenally successful enterprise
designing poison-pen greeting cards for school clients as a fund
raiser for her retreat into the wilderness. A particularly acrimonious exchange between her methodical, predictable, impassive father,
who believes sulkily and inflexibly in his own infallibility, and her
short-fused mother, an adult education student who lashes back
snappishly, prompts Eu to invent an especially malicious card for
her parents. She is overcome with remorse when Mrs. Gottlieb
leaves home. Though she learns later that the breakup is not her
fault, she still decides to dissolve the business that foments spite
and inhumanity. Her mother returns after a week's absence, but
Eunice realizes that her mother has needs that the family can't provide and that eventually they will all go their separate directions.
She dismisses her plans of running away to be on hand to keep
house for the family if Mom abdicates. Even Thoreau returned to
society.

229. Stolz, Mary. GO AND CATCH A FLYING FISH. New York:
          Harper and Row, 1979. 213p. Grades 6-9. R+
          Taylor Reddick, 13, relishes her family's individuality. Her
father Tony is a gourmet chef, mother Junie has an eye for art and
collectibles, brother Jem, 10, is an amateur ichthyologist who wants
to be a mariner, she herself is a budding ornithologist, B.J., 4, is
a precocious appreciator, and all are expert kite flyers and sand-
castle builders. But matters are not rosy at their unique Florida
home. Tony and Junie feud bitterly over Junie's extravagant spending, lax housekeeping and yoga exercises, and over Tony's irregular working hours. After a particularly acrimonious quarrel over a
coromandel screen, independent Junie takes the family car and leaves
for New York, citing her need for time and space. Tony becomes
self-absorbed and withdrawn, leaving the care of the household, and
especially of uncontrollable, inconsolable B.J., to the two older
children in the oppressive summer heat. Taylor's best friend Sandy,
who despises and ignores her own parents, is poor consolation. A
letter arrives from Junie announcing her intention to study law, and
Tony sends for his regimented mother to keep house for the free-
spirited Reddicks. Jem reflects that their beloved Junie is as mercurial as a flying fish.

230. Stolz, Mary. LEAP BEFORE YOU LOOK. New York: Harper
          and Row, 1972. 260p. Grades 8-9. R+
          At Christmas, Janine, 14, reviews the events of the past
year: the trivial and profound discussions with family and friends,
the eventful bus trips to and from school, the fateful slumber party
when she got her first period, but most of all the events surrounding her parents' divorce and the changes it effected in all their
lives. Although her parents are a study in contrasts and discord,
her mother intellectual and impassive, her father warm and responsive, Janine is totally unprepared for their split and reacts
with acrimonious recrimination. Her father quickly remarries, and
she and her mother and brother Goya, 5, go to live with the grandmother Janine considers a snob and who belittles her father's den-
tistry practice. While she never develops a closer relationship with
her mother, she comes to appreciate her grandmother more. Time
dulls her rancor, as does her first boyfriend, and on Christmas
Day she finally forgives her absent father.

231. Stolz, Mary. WHAT TIME OF NIGHT IS IT? New York:
          Harper and Row, 1981. 209p. Grades 7-9. R+
          On Florida's Gulf Coast, Taylor Reddick's family is falling
apart (see 229). Her mother Junie has abruptly terminated the
parental squabbling by bolting for New York City to take a job.
Her father Tony, loner and night chef at a restaurant, says they
must pick up the pieces and rebuild their lives. Brother Jem, 10,
acts as if nothing has happened. B.J., 4, has become a headstrong
terror, while Taylor, 13, feels hollow inside and merely goes through
the motions of living. Tony sends for his overbearing mother from
Massachusetts to take charge of B.J., but Grandmother Reddick is

a fastidious housekeeper who can tolerate neither their casual lifestyle nor the summer heat and bugs. She pacifies B.J. by turning
him into a TV zombie in the dwelling's lone air-conditioned room
and puts the older children under heavy constraint which they try
to bear for their father's sake. Preoccupied with her frustrating
homelife, Taylor dreads the start of high school and ponders the
problems of her best friend's unstable family. When a monumental
hurricane is predicted, Tony receives a phone call from Junie urging
them to evacuate. When he stubbornly refuses, she returns to
weather the storm with them and deliver them from their grandmother's tyranny. While Tony and Junie work out a compromise,
Taylor realizes she does not have to depend on them for her own
happiness.

232. Stone, Bruce. HALF NELSON, FULL NELSON. New York:
      Harper and Row, 1985. 218p. Grades 7-10. R
         Always optimistic that his dream of becoming a professional
wrestler will soon materialize, Nelson Gato's father refuses to take
a steady job. His mother abhors living on her mother-in-law's
charity at the Florida trailer park she owns. When her husband accepts a demeaning job wrestling alligators and goes berserk, killing
his opponent, she takes daughter Vanessa, 7, and goes to live with
her sister in Georgia. The sensational publicity assures Mr. Gato's
reputation for pugnacity, and he joins the legitimate wrestling tour
as the Gator Man. With the encouragement of Heidi Tedesco, a
worldly but vulnerable acquaintance with whom he's fallen in love,
inexperienced Nelson, 16, plans to kidnap his sister as a theatrical
device to reconcile his parents. The ad-libbed abduction makes
headlines when Vanessa's wealthy friend insists on tagging along.
The snatch proves effective in convening the family, but Nelson
learns to his chagrin that Heidi, the flippant punk teen queen whose
licentious mother doesn't want her, has been using him to effect a
rendezvous with a drug dealer who has promised her the good life
in Key West. Nelson and his father, who decides to give up wrestling for his health and learn a trade, move into his grandmother's
trailer, while Mom and Vanessa return next door. On a visit to
Heidi at a correctional facility, Nelson regains hope that even if he
fails to save his parents' marriage, they still may be able to offer
Heidi a foster home.

233. Thomas, Ianthe. ELIZA'S DADDY. New York: Harcourt,
      Brace, Jovanovich, 1976. Illus. by Moneta Barnett. Unp.
      Grades K-2. R+
         Eliza's parents are divorced and her father has remarried.
He lives across town with his wife, their baby and a stepdaughter
who is about Eliza's age, but he spends every Saturday with Eliza.
One night she has a dream that her father's stepdaughter is an accomplished equestrienne, beautiful and smart, a "Wonderful Angel
Daughter." The next Saturday when Daddy asks her what she wants
to do, she vows to ask him to take her to his new house and meet
his new family, but she loses her nerve. The following week,

however, she is resolute and finds that her stepsister is an ordinary, friendly sort of girl like she is. Daddy takes them pony riding together.

234. Thompson, Paul. THE HITCHHIKERS. New York: Watts, 1980. Illus. by Susan Kuklin. 83p. Grades 5-10. Hi-Lo. R

Shawn Michaels, 17, is a big, clumsy underachiever with an oversize appetite who is unappreciated by his mother, a Pittsburgh secretary, and considers himself a millstone around his family's neck. He runs away to find his father, now living in California, who deserted them fourteen years before. In the Midwest he befriends a fellow hitchhiker, Val Wortman, 16, from New York, who seems as tough and self-assured as Shawn is diffident and insecure. Val, pregnant, is also bound for California to locate her boyfriend, whose family moved away deliberately to separate them. They accept a ride from a rancher and almost lose their lives when his pickup is washed off a bridge in a flash flood. They save the rancher from drowning, and he rewards them with bus tickets to Los Angeles. Shawn discovers his father, a drunken derelict who wants nothing to do with him. Val, rejected also, decides to return to her family and convinces Shawn, when he offers to take care of her and the baby, to try to make a go of it at home. They promise to keep in touch.

235. Tolan, Stephanie S. THE LIBERATION OF TANSY WARNER. New York: Scribner, 1980. 137p. Grades 6-9. R+

Tansy, a freshman, is the only black sheep in a family of goal-oriented achievers. Her sister is the senior class intellectual who plans to emulate her father's successful career in law. Her brother is the school's star athlete. Only her mother, the quintessential homemaker who keeps the Warner family machine oiled and operational, is pleased that Tansy is playing the title role in the school play. Then without warning her mother disappears without a trace, citing her need to find her own values in life. Mr. Warner, to whom appearances are paramount, sulks for a week, refusing to acknowledge that his wife has abandoned him, while the children, accustomed to being catered to, bumble about helplessly. Tansy's best friend organizes the unraveling Warners and helps Tansy search for her mother in order to ask for an explanation for her desertion. Through old telephone records she finally locates her in Chicago, where she is working in an interior design shop. On a visit to her mother, Tansy learns that she is no longer satisfied with being chattel to a regimented husband and nearly grown children. Tansy, too, steels herself to fulfill her own destiny independently, with or without the approbation of her critical family. Mother sends her roses on opening night.

236. Van Leeuwen, Jean. TOO HOT FOR ICE CREAM. New York: Dial, 1974. Illus. by Martha Alexander. Unp. Grades 2-3. R+

Sara is sitting on her apartment house steps on a hot summer

day, waiting for her father to come and take her to the beach, when
he phones to say that his car had to be towed to a garage and they
will have to postpone their outing. Disappointed, Sara begs her
mother to take her to the beach by subway, but Mama is preoccupied
with writing poetry as usual. Instead, Mama suggests that Sara
take her little sister Elizabeth to the park. They stop for ice cream
on the way, but Elizabeth rides off on her toy motorcycle and the
ice cream melts before Sara finds her. They stop to watch a parade
and again Elizabeth disappears. A mounted policeman discovers her
bringing up the rear of the procession. No sooner do they get to
the park than it clouds over and they have to rush for home. The
rain overtakes them, and they get their swim after all in a big
puddle by the curb. At home, Mama reads a poem she wrote especially for them about rain.

237. Vigna, Judith. DADDY'S NEW BABY. Niles, Ill.: Whitman,
        1982. Unp. Grades K-2. R+
        Things have changed since Daddy and his new wife had a
baby. Mommy (who has custody and is receiving child support)
says there won't be as much money now that Daddy has another
mouth to feed. The girl still visits him on weekends, but now she
has to share her room there, and it is cramped, noisy and smelly.
When there is an emergency in his wife's family and Daddy has to
cancel plans to take her, alone, to a professional puppet show, he
offers to take her to the park instead--with the baby in tow. The
girl helps to prepare the baby for the excursion and pushes the
stroller, but accidentally the carriage almost rolls into the duck pond.
She grabs it in the nick of time and is declared a heroine by all the
bystanders for saving her little sister. Suddenly she feels possessive, and when they get home she stages a private puppet show just
for the appreciative baby. Big sis is glad they like the same games
and have the same daddy.

238. Voigt, Cynthia. A SOLITARY BLUE. New York: Atheneum,
        1983. 189p. Grades 7-9. R++
        His mother Melody, dilettantish champion of the environ-
ment and the underdog, deserted Jeff Greene and his professor
father when the boy was 7. Since then Jeff has essentially reared
himself with maturity beyond his years in their university enclave
in Baltimore, isolated from the Professor by the latter's stolid preoccupation, perfectionism, and neglect. The summer that he is 12,
Melody unexpectedly invites him to stay with her and her elderly
relatives in their gracious ancestral home in Charleston. There he
receives all the affection, attention and stimulation he has missed
and returns home with plans to live permanently with Melody. His
second visit is far less rosy. Melody abandons him while she goes
crusading with her boorish boyfriend, and when he indicts her for
lying to him to serve her own selfish purposes, she excoriates him.
Shocked, betrayed, and emotionally battered, he learns that the
Professor was also a victim of her mental cruelty, trying to bury his
pain under a veneer of indifference but loving Jeff nonetheless in

his own blundering, undemonstrative way. Still traumatized, Jeff
is expelled from school and counseling is advised, but the Professor
elects to try to heal the brooding, disillusioned boy by moving to an
isolated refuge on the Eastern shore where Jeff makes his first
friends in the Tillerman family (see 510 and 511). But Melody has
not given up her bid for control of the family fortune which was be-
queathed to Jeff. She sues for his custody, forcing him to fight
fire with fire. To rid himself of her, he pays her off and at last
feels pity for the superficial, scheming woman.

239. Wagner, Jane. J.T. New York: Van Nostrand Reinhold,
        1969. Illus. by Gordon Parks. 63p. Grades 2-4. R
        J. T. Gamble steals a radio from a parked car because he
knows he won't get one for Christmas, but he has to run for his
life to escape Claymore and Boomer, bigger bullies who are also after
the radio. His mother accuses him of "turnin' bad" like the father
who deserted them. Amid the rubble of a razed tenement he finds
a starving, injured cat for which he makes an elaborate shelter out
of junk, cutting school to care for his pet and scrounging food for
it by charging it to his mother's account until she discovers and
puts an end to it. Boomer and Claymore find the cat's sanctuary,
and the terrified feline runs into the path of a car and is killed.
The inconsolable boy is comforted by the wisdom of his grandmother, who also helps his mother to understand him better. For
Christmas the grocer brings him a stray kitten which his mother allows him to keep. More mature and secure, he returns the radio,
faces down the bullies, asks the grocer for a job, and returns to
school.

240. Walker, Mildred. A PIECE OF THE WORLD. New York:
        Atheneum, 1972. Illus. by Christine Price. 218p. Grades
        5-7. R
        Her father, a novelist, is casual and unstructured; her
mother, a TV interviewer, lives by schedules. After their divorce,
Calder Bailey, 12, would rather live with Dad and his vivacious
fiancee, but Dad says her mother needs her. Mother, however, requires time alone and sends Calder to spend the summer in Vermont
with her grandmother, Mardie, who believes that Calder's father is
erratic and undependable. The two hardly see eye to eye. Exploring, Calder discovers a massive boulder looming out of the woods on
a farm belonging to diffident Walt Bolles' aunt. Their mutual reverence for the rock formation, deposited by a glacier eons ago, draws
them together in spite of their differences. Mardie hopes to create
a tourist attraction of the monolith, a plan which Calder and Walt
adamantly oppose. A wealthy urban contractor has grandiose plans
for quartering the serpentine stone with dynamite and cementing it
back together on the town common. Walt is impotent in dissuading
his aunt from selling it. When the rock is laid naked to the public,
it loses its awesome secrecy and significance for Calder and Walt.
As the pieces of the rock arrive in town, he clandestinely carves
their initials on its interior surface. When the boulder is reassembled

they both feel more optimistic, and Calder resignedly returns to
California with her mother and her tactful new husband, Calder's
former pediatrician.

241. Walker, Pamela. TWYLA. Englewood Cliffs, N.J.: Prentice-
      Hall, 1973. (OP) 125p. Grades 9-12. R
      When Wally Bell goes away to college he begins receiving
daily missives, egregiously misspelled, from a maladroit high school
acquaintance, Twyla Krotz, 15, declaring her undying love for him
and imploring him to respond. Wally, one of the few people who
has been kind to her, wants to discourage Twyla without hurting
her feelings. Her actor father deserted years earlier, while her
mother now works in a cafe. Though Wally never replies to her pathetic, intimate, soul-baring letters, she continues to write faithfully, inflating her pyrrhic victories and rationalizing her numerous
disappointments. Twyla is elated to learn of the availability of an
affordable Chevy, and she is euphoric to be nominated for homecoming queen. Both these upswings in her fortunes turn out to be
cruel hoaxes perpetrated by malicious mischief-makers whom she sim-
plemindedly trusts. Even her teachers turn quislings when they
conspire with her mother to send her to a trade school 300 miles
from her Midwest home. Her final humiliation comes at Christmas
when she is wishfully expecting Wally to attend her party and prove
her popularity. She learns instead that he is spending the holidays
with his girlfriend and has never loved Twyla. Wally receives her
last letter in the same mail as a newspaper clipping from his mother
describing Twyla's death in a suicidal accident while driving a
stolen auto.

242. Williams, Barbara. MITZI AND FREDERICK THE GREAT.
      New York: Dutton, 1984. Illus. by Emily Arnold McCully.
      113p. Grades 4-5. R+
      Her stepbrother Frederick, 11, has persuaded Mitzi's ar-
chaeologist mother Patricia (see 244 and 245) to allow them both to
accompany her on a summer dig at the site of a thousand-year-old
Chaco pueblo in New Mexico, but once there Mitzi, 8, is not so certain that it's a privilege. On top of the heat, hard labor, and unexpected wildlife, there is know-it-all Frederick rhapsodizing over
an ancient civilization (which to Mitzi is just dead Indians), over-
shadowing Mitzi at fly-casting, and entertaining the adults with his
guitar in the evening. Mitzi, who is fascinated by the lizards,
arachnids and skunks that invade the camp, and who wants to become a biologist like her stepfather Walter, decides that Frederick
is a coward for being squeamish about the native fauna and the
frigid swimming hole. When Mitzi undertakes an illicit expedition
into the desert to capture a collared lizard to take home to stepbrother Darwin, 3, she is startled by a rattlesnake. Frederick,
who has been following her protectively, is bitten while killing it.
In guilt and gratitude, Mitzi lets him take the credit of sharing with
Patricia a rare arrowhead that Mitzi herself unearthed.

243. Williams, Barbara. MITZI AND THE ELEPHANTS. New York:
     Dutton, 1985. Illus. by Emily Arnold McCully. 101p.
     Grades 4-6. R+
     Married two months to Mitzi's mother (see 244, 245, and
242), biologist Walter Potts is too busy writing a manuscript to
build the strong fence required for the St. Bernard puppy that
Mitzi, 8, has been offered. His friend the zoo director, however,
invites Mitzi to appear on a local zoo TV program. There Mitzi develops an affinity for the elephants and decides to become a biologist
specializing in large animals. When she is asked to present a birthday cake to the baby giraffe, an opportunity in which her stepbrothers Darwin and Frederick for once cannot eclipse her, it is
Mitzi's ingenuity that saves the occasion from disaster. She earns
further accolades by using her pachyderm telepathy to save the
life of one of the elephants who has contracted pneumonia. Nana
Potts, Walter's mother, believes that Mitzi deserves to have the dog
for her heroic deed. Walter, also impressed, agrees, and hires out
the job of building the fence so that Mitzi can get her puppy.

244. Williams, Barbara. MITZI AND THE TERRIBLE TYRANNOSAU-
     RUS REX. New York: Dutton, 1982. Illus. by Emily
     Arnold McCully. 102p. Grades 3-6. R+
     Mitzi McAllister's pride in being promoted to the highest
reading group and "living up to her potential" is deflated when her
divorced mother, an archaeologist, is too nervous and preoccupied
preparing to entertain her fiance Walter Potts and his family to appreciate her accomplishment. Mitzi, 8, would like to cancel the
wedding. She dislikes Walter, a biology professor, because he never
speaks directly to her, is planning to convert her porch into a room
for his mother, and has two sons who are thorns in her side.
Frederick, 11, is nosy, bossy, garrulous, superior and opinionated.
Mitzi is jealous of him because her mother plans to take him into the
field with her on summer vacation. But it is Darwin, 3, who is the
greatest annoyance. A spoiled, attention-seeking, thumb-sucking
genius, he pretends to be a ferocious dinosaur, stalking about
monosyllabically and meddling with her belongings. Because of his
photographic memory, he is given Mitzi's role of reciting a poem at
the wedding. But when Mitzi wants to visit her ailing friend, the
school custodian, it is Darwin who finds his address in the phone
book and takes her there. And when he obstinately refuses to re-
cite the poem at the rites, Mitzi saves the day by repeating it flaw-
lessly. Her mother rewards her for her maturity by allowing Mitzi
to join her and Frederick in the field, and even Walter is impressed.

245. Williams, Barbara. MITZI'S HONEYMOON WITH NANA POTTS.
     New York: Dutton, 1983. Illus. by Emily Arnold McCully.
     104p. Grades 4-6. R+
     The day after the wedding, while her mother is honey-
mooning with Walter Potts, Mitzi McAllister's stepgrandmother moves
into Mitzi's remodeled porch and patronizingly and peremptorily takes
over. She assigns Mitzi the task of riding herd on the terrible

tyrannosaurus rex, alias stepbrother Charles Darwin, 3, (see 244)
whose superior and devious intellect is forever spawning imaginative
new mischief. To add insult to injury, Nana Potts criticizes Mitzi
while exonerating and extolling her precocious and ingenuous grandson, no matter how devilish his behavior. His brother Frederick,
11, cannot tolerate Darwin either, but instead of sharing the burden
with Mitzi, he arbitrarily saddles her with keeping Darwin out of his
hair. Mitzi feels unappreciated and imposed upon until an irate
neighbor shrewishly accuses her of poisoning her dog with jelly
beans, and both Nana Potts and Darwin charge to her defense.
They celebrate their victory over the dog's crabby owner by planning a picnic, and when Nana Potts insists on picnicking in the
cage of a friend's cherry picker, Mitzi decides that she has acquired
the best grandmother around.

246. Windsor, Patricia. DIVING FOR ROSES. New York: Harper
        and Row, 1976. 248p. Grades 9-12. R
        Having spent her life in unnatural isolation on her mother's
sequestered estate, morbidly bound to the chronic invalid she believes to be mad and accustomed to being mocked in the town for her
mother's eccentricities, Jean, 17, is self-conscious, introspective,
abstruse, and preoccupied with disturbing sexual fantasies, a result
of the androphobia her mother subjects her to. Her father, who
deserted years earlier, makes expiation on the altar of guilt and
duty by spending his annual vacation with them and beseeching Jean
unsuccessfully to return to the mainstream of life with him in New
York City. The insecure girl comes upon a young man camping in
their woods and inexorably allows herself to become the sacrificial
lamb to the predatory male. Their love affair lasts the summer, and,
too reticent to seek contraception, Jean becomes pregnant. Simul-
taneously, she is informed that her mother is a closet alcoholic, and
Jean's obstetrician dispatches a delegation from Alcoholics Anonymous
to rehabilitate her. With her mother's recovery, Jean is suddenly
thrust into social situations she is unequipped to handle. When an
auto accident hospitalizes her mother, Jean decides to be assertive
and purposeful. As she nears parturition, however, her old amorphous fears return to haunt her, and sessions with a psychologist
do little to alleviate them. Following the birth of a baby girl, Jean
and her mother move away from the brooding abode for a new beginning, and Jean leaves her dark dreams behind.

247. Wolitzer, Hilma. OUT OF LOVE. New York: Farrar, Straus
        and Giroux, 1976. 146p. Grades 7-8. R+
        Reading her father's old love letters to her mother, Teddy,
13, wishes dowdy Mother would lose weight and take an interest in
clothes and cosmetics to lure Daddy away from his glamorous new
wife Shelley, the Enemy. Her sister Karen, 11, doesn't share her
resentment but has a campaign of her own to make Mother stop
smoking. Teddy's attitude toward Shelley thaws when she asks
Shelley's advice on beauty matters and gets a flattering haircut, but
it isn't until Shelley and Teddy's father announce that they are

expecting a baby that her hopes for repairing the family rift go aglimmering. She learns that beauty is in the eye of the beholder, and if she turns out to be like her mother it won't be half bad. She has learned to accept what she cannot change, while her best friend Maya has valiantly changed a situation she cannot accept.

248. Wolkoff, Judie. HAPPILY EVER AFTER ... ALMOST. Scarsdale: Bradbury, 1982. 215p. Grades 5-8. R++
    The problem is not Seth Krampner. Kitty Birdsall, 11, adores the unpretentious Jewish photographer her mother is engaged to. She and her younger sister Sarah also like their father's new wife, his ex-office nurse, and her children by a previous marriage with whom they play "musical kids" on weekends. The sticking point is R.J., 11, Seth's diffident, intellectual, and emotionally unstable son who lives with his wealthy, deprecating, and manipulative mother Kay. When Kitty irritates him on their first meeting, he calls her an exhibitionist. Her dislike of him intensifies when he and Sarah become chummy. It is only after she defends him against his aggressive, macho cousin that they declare a wary truce. After the wedding they move into an old factory loft in Soho that Seth and their mother, a jacket designer for a book publisher, are renovating for studio and living quarters. R.J. is sent to camp while his mother goes abroad, but when they learn of her secret scheme to spirit him away permanently in violation of the divorce contract, Seth goes to court to sue for custody. The whole family, including Kitty, rallies conspiratorially to wrest him from possessive Kay, who wants him only because she hates losing to Seth. Later they learn that Mom is expecting a baby who will balance the new half-brother on Dad's side. Kitty draws a family tree to diagram the complex relationship among the wholes, halves, steps, in-laws and outlaws of her extended and revised family.

249. Young, Miriam. NO PLACE FOR MITTY. New York: Four Winds, 1976. 123p. Grades 4-6. R+
    In 1896 when Mitty is 10, her religious fanatic father overtaxes Mama's pontifical patience, and she bundles Mitty and the boys off to her parents' farm near San Francisco. A tomboy, Mitty loves the harum-scarum life at Emeryville, already teeming with relatives. Grandpa races horses for a haphazard living, and Grandma, who crossed the country by covered wagon alone with two small children, contributes to the commotion and conviviality by clanging on a dishpan for reveille, playing practical jokes on Grandpa, and faking punishment for infractions by thwacking a trunk and telling the kids to yell. At the divorce proceedings, Papa's wealthy sister offers Mitty a home and education. Mama sees it as the opportunity of a lifetime, and Mitty trades her life of abandon for an oppressive one of rigid decorum and stifling supervision. She lives only for vacation visits to the farm. One day Grandma pays an impulsive call on Mitty at Aunty Bowman's house and discovers that she is being transformed into a mincing prig. Instantly, she packs her back to Emeryville.

250. Zolotow, Charlotte. A FATHER LIKE THAT. New York:
        Harper and Row, 1971. Illus. by Ben Shecter. Unp.
        Grades K-2. R++
      "I wish I had a father. But my father went away before
I was born. I say to my mother, you know what he'd be like?
'What?' she says." Thus a little boy launches into a description of
his fabulous fantasy father who plays checkers with him, helps
around the house, goes to PTA meetings, comforts him, disciplines
him gently, understands and supports him. Mother replies, "I like
the kind of father you're talking about. And in case he never
comes, just remember when you grow up, you can be a father like
that yourself!"

251. Adler, C. S. FOOTSTEPS ON THE STAIRS. New York:
        Delacorte, 1982. 151p. Grades 5-8. R
        After thirteen years as a single parent since her husband's
death in an auto accident, Dodie's mother, a successful computer
analyst, has married Larry, a divorced realtor. Dodie is delighted
because after years of bearing her svelte, serious mother's criticism
about her weight, histrionics and hyperbole, she now has a stepfather who loves her the way she is and appreciates her natural
ebullience. Unfortunately, Larry has chosen this summer for his
own children, Chris, 7, and Anne, also 13, who reside with their
mother, to get acquainted with their new family in the sprawling,
rundown house they have rented on a Cape Cod marsh. Dodie gets
off to a bad start with them when she pretends to be a ghost haunting the creaky structure. Sober, delicate, beautiful Anne treats
her with animosity and disdain despite Dodie's efforts to make
amends. Then Dodie begins hearing footsteps on the stairs at
night, and of course no one believes her until Anne, who shares
her attic bedroom, also hears them and sees an apparition. The
two become allies as they trace the nocturnal disturbances to the
ghosts of twin girls who inhabited the house at midcentury and
died in the marsh after quarreling over a man. In attempting to
lay the restless spirits, Anne and Dodie themselves nearly drown.
The experience draws them closer and they are able to conquer their
innate jealousy and share Larry's affections.

252. Adler, C. S. SHADOWS ON LITTLE REEF BAY. New York:
        Clarion, 1984. 176p. Grades 5-9. R
        It should have been a lark: living on an idyllic Caribbean
island as the guest of her mother's boyfriend John Reilly, proprietor of the Little Reef Bay Hotel, while her widowed mother is
on sabbatical from her teaching job in upstate New York. But
Stacy, 14, is homesick and feels out of place among the native hotel
employees and her elderly fellow guests. Her sole friend, an old
islander, has been arrested and accused of drug trafficking. Stacy
is convinced of his innocence. Her curiosity and sense of justice
prompt her to launch an investigation to find the true culprit and
clear his name. As the trail gets hotter she confides her evidence
to John, initially relieved to place the burden of responsibility on

him until she realizes that he is in league with the drug smugglers
and is bent upon silencing her. She cannot entice her naive
mother, who has a history of disastrous love affairs and trusts John
blindly, to leave the island, and she cannot reveal to her mother
John's duplicity for fear of imperiling them both. Suspense builds
as the child, mature beyond her years, wrestles mentally with her
host and enemy to defend her friend and save herself and her unsuspecting mother.

253. Aiken, Joan. THE SHADOW GUESTS. New York: Delacorte,
        1980. 150p. Grades 5-7. NR
        When his mother and older brother become lost in the
Australian desert and are presumed dead, Cosmo Curtoys, 11, is
sent back to England to live with his adult cousin. From Cousin
Eunice he learns of the ancient family curse in which firstborn sons
die in battle and their mothers of grief. Hazed mercilessly by his
boarding school mates, he makes friends on weekends with boys who
appear from nowhere at his cousin's historic millhouse and whom only
he can see. Gradually he comes to realize that these are incarna-
tions of long-dead members of his family tree who met the fate
prophesied in the curse. Two other supernatural manifestations,
however, grow suddenly hostile and menacing, disrupting life at
the mill and causing Cosmo's near-drowning in the millrace. During
his convalescence, his father, a doctor, returns to England to stay,
revealing that Cosmo's mother had insisted on moving to Australia
to try to escape the curse, and when that failed, had made a pact
with Cosmo's brother to die peacefully together in the outback and
thus break the pattern of violence and grief. Cosmo's schoolmates
become more receptive to him when they learn of his exotic adventures.

254. Alcock, Vivien. THE STONEWALKERS. New York: Delacorte,
        1981. 151p. Grades 5-8. R
        Unconvinced that her mother loves her, Poppy Brown, 12,
invents imaginary parents. Her father died when she was 3, and her
frail mother, who is frequently hospitalized, is an impersonal and
awkward parent. Her mother, whom she calls Mother Brown as if
she were one of her many foster mothers, is a cook, now in service
on a country estate where Poppy, ostracized for her fabrications,
communes with a statue in the garden which she names Belladonna.
On a stormy night, a bolt of lightning topples Belladonna before
Poppy's eyes, and to her amazement the statue comes to life. She
locks it in the basement overnight, but it breaks out of its hateful
captivity and lumbers off, disgruntled. Poppy and a new friend,
Emma, who is intrigued rather than skeptical of her farfetched story,
set off in pursuit. Before they catch up with Belladonna, it has
liberated all the statuary in a graveyard and struck out for the
desolate moors. Intrepid Poppy and Emma follow, but Emma injures
her ankle, and the statues impassively fall upon the terrified children
and carry them into an old mine shaft. When Poppy and Emma climb
onto a high ledge to avoid their rough play, they become enraged

and destroy each other in a cataclysmic clash of titans. When the
girls are rescued the following day, Poppy's mother is remorseful
for her rigidity and dispassion, and Poppy atones for not meeting
her halfway by at last calling her Mom.

255. Ames, Mildred. CASSANDRA-JAMIE. New York: Scribner,
        1985. 135p. Grades 6-9. R+
    When the new long-term substitute teacher takes over her
English class, Jamie Cole, 12, immediately notices her physical resemblance to her mother, who died of congenital heart disease three
years ago. She is further captivated by Ms. Schuyler's winning
personality which brings out the best in everyone, including class
clown Gavin MacLaren, for whom Jamie has no patience. Ms.
Schuyler pairs Jamie and Gavin in a dramatization from IDYLLS OF
THE KING for which Gavin shows a serious flair, earning them
plaudits from the teacher. It seems foreordained that Ms. Schuyler
should be the ideal mate for Jamie's attorney father. Jamie dismisses Dad's relationship with divorcee Sylvia Dennis, whom she dislikes, as merely therapeutic. When his need to discuss his loss
with someone who has experienced a similar one is over, she reasons,
he will quit seeing her. Meanwhile, she connives to link Dad and
Ms. Schuyler at every opportunity in their small California community and fantasizes about her future companionship with her stepmother. Jamie's carefully conceived plans disintegrate when she
learns that Ms. Schuyler is leaving to accept a post elsewhere and
already has a daughter. Her father, moreover, has proposed to
Sylvia, who has refused him. Jamie decides it would be foolish to
immolate herself on the pyre of her broken dreams as did the character she played in IDYLLS. She resolves to get to know Sylvia better and discover why she would decline someone as debonair as her
dad. She agrees to start a drama club with Gavin.

256. Angell, Judie. RONNIE AND ROSEY. Scarsdale: Bradbury,
        1977. 283p. Grades 6-9. R+
    Ronnie Rachman survives the normal new-girl-in-school
routine, including the explanation of her unusual given name, and
soon forms a triumvirate with Evelyn Racanelli and Robert Rose
(Rosey), fellow Long Island eighth grade classmates. Their new
friendship rallies after a brief strain when Ronnie and Rosie develop
a romantic attachment, and their comedy act at the Halloween show
is well received. Ronnie's tranquility is shattered, however, when
she learns of her father's death in an auto accident. Her acute
grief gradually subsides, but her normally scintillating mother collapses into a morose zombie, giving up her hobby of painting and
putting a stranglehold on Ronnie. When Ronnie tries to resume
her new life, Mom turns into an obdurate martinet, forbidding her
to see Rosey or even speak with him on the phone. With Evelyn's
connivance they manage to meet secretly, but the constriction and
duplicity cause Ronnie to develop migraine headaches. The suspicious Mrs. Rachman eventually catches them and descends upon
Ronnie like an avenging angel until Ronnie's pent up emotions spill

forth and she wishes her mother dead. She flees the untenable
house and her mother's wrath. An understanding teacher takes her
in until she and her mother can talk rationally about their feelings.
A summer's separation--Ronnie to stay with a friend in California--
enables them to reach new perspectives and Mrs. Rachman to rejoin
the living.

257. Arthur, Ruth M. THE WHISTLING BOY. New York:
         Atheneum, 1969. (OP) Illus. by Margery Gill. 201p.
         Grades 6-9. R
         Although her twin brothers Gregory and Marcus, 12, accept
their stepmother Lois without reservation, Kirsty Newton, 16, develops a crippling and irrational resentment for the young, attractive,
competent woman who has taken the place of her mother, who died
of a heart attack a year earlier. Their sympathetic housekeeper
suggests a summer vacation from Lois with her sister and brother-in-
law in Norfolk. In their historic Old Manor Farm, the Dillons install
her in an attic bedroom from which Kirsty hears mysterious music.
She soon meets and falls in love with a diffident boy, Jake Meryon,
who whistles the same eerie melody but appears to be deathly afraid
of the old house. Then she learns of the legend of the ghost of
the lonely French youth and his connection to the farmhouse. He is
said to lure susceptible young men to their deaths in the sea at the
site of a long-submerged town and to warn the countryside of
further impending floods. On the eve of a storm, Kirsty is called
home when her brother is injured by a panicky Lois, who also announces that she is expecting a child. Once confident, she now
seems vulnerable and helpless, and Kirsty suddenly feels superior
and benevolent. When she finally returns to Norfolk, the environs
lie inundated and Jake is missing. It is Kirsty who locates him,
saves him from fate, and lays to rest the ghost of the lovesick
French lad.

258. Asher, Sandy. MISSING PIECES. New York: Delacorte,
         1984. 136p. Grades 7-10. R+
         Affable Mr. Connelly is the adhesive that cements his
family together, and when he dies suddenly of a heart attack at age
50, Heather, 15, and her mother, never close, drift inexorably
apart. Accustomed to hospital volunteer work, Mrs. Connelly now
seeks gainful employment as dispatcher for a meals-on-wheels program
and immerses herself in self-improvement courses at night. Heather,
meanwhile, becomes involved with her first boyfriend, Nicky Simp-
son, who teaches her to bowl and to drive. Nicky chafes under the
impositions of his stepmother and her small children and, in spite of
his love for Heather, decides to move out at the end of the semester
to search for the mother who deserted him and his father when he
was 8. Distraught at losing him and uncertain about divulging the
secret of his whereabouts to Nicky's father, Heather has no adult
she can confide in. When Nicky cannot locate his mother he returns,
and it is only then that Mrs. Connelly learns of Heather's duplicity.
Dismayed, she confesses her feelings of inadequacy, insecurity, and

inability to display emotion, all seated in her early childhood. With
new maturity, Heather encourages her mother to start sharing her
feelings and to heal their hurt at their mutual loss by together
openly recalling their beloved husband and father.

259. Baird, Thomas. FINDING FEVER. New York: Harper and
        Row, 1982. 213p. Grades 7-10. R+
        Benedict O'Bryan, Jr., 15, has an aversion to the nipping,
nervous dog, Fever, belonging to his sister Polly, 10, but when
Fever is missing along with other dogs in their rural Connecticut
neighborhood he goes in search of him, joining a classmate, Robert
Striller, who theorizes that the dogs were stolen to sell to labora-
tories. Benny dislikes Strill, who is wealthy, supercilious and condescending, and whose arch-conservative father opposed the humani-
tarian causes that Benny's lawyer father espoused. His dad, who
succumbed to cancer two years ago, kept a notebook of his dying
contemplations, and Benny draws on the wisdom of his aphorisms on
interpersonal relations for forbearance as he and Strill team up to
trace the dognappers. After days of following clues, during which
Benny loses his summer job at a nursery, they catch up with the
criminals in a neighboring town. Benny, cautious and prudent,
wants to take their evidence to the police, but Strill insists on ap-
prehending them himself and forcing them to name the lab they
supply. To avenge the abduction of his own dog years ago, Strill
brutalizes the ringleader until Benny intervenes. Benny fails to
recover Polly's dog but uses his severance pay to buy her a new
puppy. He has mixed feelings when his mother, a paralegal, accepts
a better job with Mr. Striller's investment firm, but when Strill requests his company on a cross-country drive, he accepts uncondi-
tionally.

260. Bates, Betty. THAT'S WHAT T.J. SAYS. New York: Holi-
        day, 1982. 133p. Grades 6-8. R+
        Her brother T.J. is a self-confident and popular 13-year-
old at their suburban junior high, but Mouse (a childhood nickname
for Monica Sue) Brinker, 12, wears braces, plays the cello indif-
ferently, is klutzy at sports, and feels inferior and insecure among
her classmates who manipulate her. Since their mother's death eight
years earlier, they have lived with their socially prominent paternal
grandparents while their father travels extensively as a stock
analyst for Grandpa's Chicago brokerage. From snatches of furtive
conversation they overhear, they deduce that their father is planning to remarry, and they are apprehensive and resentful. Then
Mouse takes notice of Roland, a fellow orchestra member who is far
more diffident and socially inept than she. In trying to draw him
out of his shell, she gains the courage to stand up to their hecklers.
When Dad reveals his secret--that he's leaving Grandpa's firm, taking a new job in Sioux City, and relocating the family at the end
of the school term--Mouse discovers to her astonishment that stalwart
T.J. harbors more trepidation and regrets than she. With the prospect of a new friend her age nearby, a puppy to replace the rabbit

she gives to Roland to remember her by, more attention from Dad, and the intention of dropping her demeaning sobriquet, she faces her future with anticipation.

261. Bawden, Nina. THE ROBBERS. New York: Lothrop, Lee
          and Shepard, 1979. 155p. Grades 5-6. R
          Philip Holbein, 9, has always lived contentedly with his
grandmother in a "Grace and Favour" apartment in an English seaside castle provided by the Queen for widows of military commanders,
while his widowed father, a television newscaster, has followed current events around the globe. His long association with elderly ladies has matured him beyond his years and sensitized him to the
physical and emotional problems of the aging. Suddenly his cool
and remote father remarries, settles in London, and decides to make
a home for the boy. Although he and his grandmother both resent
the upheaval in their lives, Philip tries to make the best of it for
her sake and makes friends with his stepmother and a neighbor boy,
Darcy, whose father is crippled and cannot work. When Darcy's
brother, the family's sole support, bends the law and is sentenced
to prison, the boys try several abortive money-making schemes before Darcy persuades Philip to break into a haughty rich woman's
house. The two are caught, and Philip's unbending father prescribes
harsh punishment. His grandmother indignantly marches to Philip's
defense, spirits him back to their castle home, and offers to intercede in a musical career for Darcy.

262. Beatty, Patricia. EIGHT MULES FROM MONTEREY. New
          York: Morrow, 1982. 192p. Grades 6-8. R+
          Partly to ensure her mother of a job upon graduation from
library school and partly to delay her decision about marrying her
dead husband's law partner, Fayette Ashmore, 13, campaigns and
connives to have Mrs. Ashmore appointed emissary of the Monterey,
California, library in 1916 to extend service to isolated residents of
the Santa Lucia mountains. Although it is a journey that makes
strong men blanch, independent and indomitable Mother dons male
attire and climbs astride one of the cantankerous pack mules, along
with Fayette and Eubie, 10, determined to establish library outposts.
The trip at first seems like a lark with minor annoyances and inconveniences, but after their first muleteer axes his foot while drunk,
the mission becomes one of survival. Their second guide looks even
more disreputable and has a dark, mysterious past. Along the way
they befriend an orphan who is kept as slave labor by foster
parents, bury victims of a typhoid epidemic, and are shot at by
moonshiners, but Mother never loses her ladylike aplomb or dogged
determination. When she has to dismiss the second muleskinner, the
situation becomes critical, but alone they press on till they reach
Big Tree Junction which boasts two houses, a saloon, a general
store, and two ladies desperate for reading materials. With self-
reliance born of accomplishment, Mother decides not to marry Mr.
Herbert.

263. Beatty, Patricia. JONATHAN DOWN UNDER. New York:
        Morrow, 1982. 219p. Grades 6-9. R
        In 1851, en route to China with another get-rich-quick
scheme of importing silk to California gold miners' wives after his
own disappointing stint as a Forty-niner, Charlie Cole hears of the
gold strikes in Australia and is bitten anew by the gold bug. With
his loyal son Jonathan, 13, he stakes a claim at the frontier camp
of Ballarat, where they soon learn that, while strictly regulated by
the government, the gold fields are just as rough and tumble, corrupt and brutal as those in California. Most of their fellow prospec-
ters are Irishmen who were transported down under for minor crimes
in their homeland. The Coles are befriended by gentle Molly Quinn,
respected "Queen of Ballarat" and proprietress of the grog tent,
but even her benevolence is not enough to change their luck, and
unfortunate Charlie dies of pneumonia following a cave-in at his small
claim. Jonathan, whose mother died when he was an infant, is taken
under Molly's wing where he becomes a witness to her murder by an
extortionist who then takes him into the bush to die. He is saved
by an aborigine boy, and later, by virtue of his small stature, he
is hired by former rivals to work their deep mineshaft. There he
discovers the enormous nugget that will make their fortunes, though
he nearly loses his life when the shaft floods. In their gratitude
they reward Jonathan for his pluck by buying him return passage to
his aunts in Massachusetts.

264. Beckman, Delores. MY OWN PRIVATE SKY. New York:
        Dutton, 1980. 154p. Grades 4-7. R+
        When Arthur Elliott, 11, and his mother, widowed in a
plane crash, move from St. Paul to Southern California because of
his allergies, his mother places him in the care of aging Mrs. Kearns
while she starts her new job as hospital administrator. Arthur is
insecure because of his small stature, buck teeth, and asthma, but
Mrs. Kearns, an unorthodox widow, draws him out by showing him
how to make rubbings and peekaboos of ancient Indian petroglyphs.
He is somewhat intimidated by cocky Norrie Willis, another young
friend of Mrs. Kearns, but he is terrified of the swimming lessons
that his mother, a repository of predictable parental platitudes, has
committed him to, as well as of neighborhood bullies who learn of
his weaknesses. Then Mrs. Kearns loses her leg in an auto accident, and in despair and self-pity refuses to cooperate in the rehabilitation therapy that will restore her independence, despite the
efforts of Mr. Halverson, the physical therapist and his mother's
new boyfriend, who also wears braces to straighten his teeth. Mr.
Halverson's affirmative masculine influence has a galvanizing effect
on Arthur, who faces down the bullies, but he is still afraid of
failing the diving test just as Mrs. Kearns is fearful of trusting her
prosthesis. On the day of the test, Arthur draws from his new
reservoir of courage and dives headlong into the pool, surfacing to
find Mrs. Kearns standing unaided at poolside.

265. Bellairs, John. THE CURSE OF THE BLUE FIGURINE. New

York: Dial, 1983.   200p.   Grades 5-7.   R
    Because his mother died of cancer just six months ago and
his father is away fighting the Korean War as a jet pilot, bookish
Johnny Dixon, 12, is living with his grandparents in Massachusetts
and attending St. Michael's school. His eccentric neighbor and
friend, Professor Childermass, recounts a ghost story of the evil,
insane Father Baart, and soon afterwards Johnny finds an Egyptian
talisman in the church basement purportedly cursed by the former
priest. He is immediately afflicted with nightmares, invasions of
spiders, and the eerie feeling of being followed. When he claims to
have seen and spoken to Father Baart's ghost, the professor takes
him to a psychiatrist who tells Johnny that it is a figment of his
imagination caused by "insufficient grievement" over his mother's
death. But the ring that the alleged ghost has given him lends
him strange powers over a bully who harasses him. The professor
prescribes a change of scene and takes him for a vacation to the
White Mountains, but when Johnny disappears on a stormy night,
Professor Childermass belatedly realizes that the apparition is real.
He and Johnny must battle the forces of evil alone atop a mountain,
and when their harrowing ordeal is over, the professor offers an
astonishingly simple explanation of his adventure for Johnny to tell
his dad.

266.   Blos, Joan W.   A GATHERING OF DAYS.   A NEW ENGLAND
           GIRL'S JOURNAL, 1830-1832.   New York: Scribner,
           1979.   144p.   Grades 6-8.   R+
    In the year 1899, Catherine Hall Onesti of Providence, R.I.,
presents to her great-granddaughter the journal she kept from ages
13 to 15 while growing up in rural New Hampshire. In it the young
Catherine recalls the death of her mother from a fever four years
earlier, leaving her to keep house for her farmer father and younger
sister Matty. Though their nearest neighbors, the Shipmans, try
to make a match between Mr. Hall and a relative of theirs, Father,
on a trip to Boston to barter for winter provisions, meets a widow
and former school teacher, Ann Higham, whose son Daniel is
Catherine's age, and marries her after a brief courtship. Catherine
tries valiantly to sublimate her resentment at being usurped by her
refined and proper stepmother. Their only serious confrontation
arises when Catherine finds it necessary to confess to Ann that she
and her best friend Cassie Shipman gave away a worn quilt of her
mother's to a freezing runaway slave. Her punishment is to piece
a new quilt (in the Mariner's Compass pattern), a long, arduous
task. Tragedy strikes again when Cassie succumbs to a fever, but
Catherine learns later that the slave whom they befriended made it
safely to Canada. She reflects upon her choice of pattern for the
quilt as symbolic for navigating the joys, sorrows, and unknowns
of the ocean of life. When Aunt Lucy Shipman marries and has a
baby, Catherine enters her service temporarily as mother's helper
and leaves home for the first time with both regret and anticipation.

267.   Blume, Judy.   TIGER EYES.   Scarsdale: Bradbury, 1981.

222p. Grades 6-10. R+

Only weeks before Davey Wexler, 15, is to start high school in Atlantic City, her father is shot to death in a holdup of his market. The devastated and angry girl withdraws and masks her emotions, which escape in hyperventilating spells. When the doctor recommends a change of scenery, the family, including Jason, 7, flies to Los Alamos, New Mexico, to spend the winter with their paternal aunt and uncle, Bitsy and Walter. Starting school there, Davey makes friends with a girl who is a high achiever but who has an alcohol problem and also with a young man whom she meets in an isolated canyon who calls himself Wolf and names her Tiger Eyes. Although still denying to others that her father was murdered, Davey quickly overcomes her physical symptoms of bereavement, but her mother, controlled until now, suddenly goes to pieces and requires therapy. When a favorite patient at the hospital where she is a candy striper dies of cancer, Davey learns that it is Wolf's father. The two console one another before Wolf leaves for college. As Davey's mother responds to counseling, she starts dating a friend of Walter and Bitsy whom Davey dislikes, and Davey and her uncle are frequently at odds because of his peremptory overprotectiveness. Her long repressed hostility is targeted at her family until Davey herself accepts therapy and finally unburdens herself. When her mother is ready to go home, Davey is eager to return to New Jersey.

268. Bond, Nancy. A STRING IN THE HARP. New York: Atheneum, 1976. 370p. Grades 7-10. R

Following his wife's tragic death in an auto accident, David Morgan, English professor at Amherst, accepts a teaching position at a university in Wales to try to escape his grief, taking with him his two younger children, Peter, 12, and Becky, 10, leaving Jen, 15, at home with relatives to finish high school. Jen joins the family at Christmas and discovers tension and irritation dividing them. Peter is spiteful and truculent at being torn from friends and familiar foundations to be transplanted to the desolation of the Welsh seacoast, while Dad has severed communications by becoming absorbed in his work. Then Peter finds an ancient artifact that makes him act yet more aloof and peculiar. It is an enchanted harp key that produces trancelike visions of the legendary bard Taliesin and embroils the family and their friends in a sixth-century adventure. When an impersonal museum director asks Peter to relinquish the relic, Peter decides to restore it to its rightful owner instead, and sets about finding Taliesin's final resting place. Having learned so much of Welsh history and accomplished his mission, Peter becomes sympathetic to Wales, and with trust and communion restored the entire family decides to stay another year.

269. Bonham, Frank. VIVA CHICANO. New York: Dutton, 1970. 160p. Grades 5-8. R+

His laborer father taught Joaquin Duran pride in La Raza, high aspirations, and, by example, the dignity of integrity and hard work. But his father died in an accident when Keeny was 6, and

his life went into a tailspin. His introduction to juvenile hall occurred at age 7 when he ran away from home because his first stepfather abused him. Since then he has had a history of truancy,
theft, drug abuse and gangfighting. Now 17, he is on parole from
the CYA, anxious to go straight, and hoping for foster care to get
away from his termagant mother and felonious new stepfather. But
when his infant half-brother accidentally falls from a window in
their housing project, Keeny is accused of pushing him. On the
run again, he takes refuge in an abandoned police station in the
heart of Los Angeles' barrio, stopping en route to snatch a cardboard statue of Mexican hero Emiliano Zapata from a theater marquee
for company. Immediately the imposing figure begins talking aloud,
spouting nuggets of Mexican history and giving sage advice.
Against Emiliano's better judgment, Keeny leads his stoned former
gang members on a grim foray against their arch rivals. As the
police noose tightens, Keeny turns himself in after a dramatic demonstration of how people jump to conclusions through mass hysteria,
circumstantial evidence, and guilt by association. His parole officer
manages to place him in an enlightened halfway house, and Keeny
realizes that Emiliano's admonitory voice is actually that of his
father stored in his subconscious memory.

270.   Bonsall, Crosby. THE GOODBYE SUMMER. New York:
          Greenwillow, 1979. 148p. Grades 5-6. R+
          To avoid eviction from her room in the big house her
mother converted to a boarding house after her father's death in
Vietnam when she was an infant, Allie Pratt is forced to weed her
lifetime collection of memorabilia that everyone else calls junk.
Allie cannot bear to bid farewell to her treasures and jumps aboard
the garbage truck for the trip to the dump, creating such a dis-
turbance that she is confined to quarters and sentenced to hard
labor for two weeks. Adding insult to injury, her best friend Molly
leaves for a summer of adventure at camp, and the baby she strolls
with in the park moves away. Reprieve appears in the form of
theatrical Wanda Lenya, a new boarder formerly with the circus,
whose wild imagination and bizarre behavior match Allie's own.
Life suddenly becomes a lark as they romp through a memorable
Independence Day celebration and other frolics. As the new school
term approaches, Allie plans a surprise for Ms. Lenya which backfires when she comes home one day to find that the boarder has
been called away without saying goodbye. When Allie rails at her
mother over the loss of everything near and dear to her, Mrs. Pratt
for the first time discloses her own deep sense of bereavement and
tells her that "for every hello there is usually a goodbye sooner or
later." Molly returns, and Allie realizes that everyone who departs
leaves behind something of himself to be remembered by.

271.   Brady, Esther Wood. THE TOAD ON CAPITOL HILL. New
          York: Crown, 1978. 139p. Grades 5-6. R
          The War of 1812 is being fought in distant Canada when
Dorsy McCurdy, 11, describes her new family as an appetizing but

inedible cake. The volatile ingredients consist of her stepbrothers
Tyler, 10, a "sour pickle," Brandon, 5, a "wiggly weevil," and
herself, the "pepper" in the concoction. After her mother died in
the "long white-sickness" three years ago, she and her father lived
in Mrs. Pringle's boarding house for congressmen in the new capitol
at Washington where she was free to follow her tomboyish instincts.
But then Papa marries Ardis Trowbridge, a widow from Philadelphia,
and everything changes for the worse. Her stepmother calls her
a hoyden and tries to transform her into a lady; Tyler belittles her
and boasts of the superiority of Philadelphia; while Brandon clumsily
breaks all of her treasures. She fervently wishes upon a rare white
toad that they would return from whence they came and leave her
in peace. When the British unexpectedly invade Washington, Papa
tells her to take the others to safety while he joins the city's defense forces. But Brandon runs back to the house, and Dorsy
staunchly stays with him. There Tyler, and later Mama, locate
them and together they weather the burning of the federal buildings
and two wild thunderstorms. She learns that Tyler has been just
as unhappy as she, and when Papa finally rejoins them he finds that
their mutual adversity has turned them into allies at last.

272. Bragdon, Elspeth. THERE IS A TIDE. New York: Viking,
         1964. (OP) 192p. Grades 6-9. R+
         As Nat, 15, is about to be expelled from yet another of the
succession of private boarding schools to which his pedantic, punctilious father has consigned him, the perceptive headmaster suggests
that father and son make a pilgrimage to the school's retreat on an
island off the coast of Maine to get acqainted with one another, the
crux of the rebellious boy's problem. Nat loves the old house on
sight but is less enthusiastic about the taciturn islanders until he
makes an honest effort to understand and appreciate their distinctive
quality and earn their respect and acceptance. While Nat is groping
and growing, his father seems impervious to the rest-cure, continuing to work in aloof condescension until the death of a peculiar
old man, grandfather of Nat's elusive orphan friend Sue. In a brief
spate of recollection and confession, like the click of a shutter, Nat's
father reveals a glimpse of his emotions that signals optimism for the
development of a normal relationship.

273. Branscum, Robbie. ME AND JIM LUKE. Garden City:
         Doubleday, 1971. (OP) 140p. Grades 5-6. R
         Deep in the Arkansas Hills, Sammy John, 10, and his
youngest uncle and constant companion Jim Luke, 12, make the eerie
and grisly discovery of a dead body in a hollow tree. Sammy John,
who has been living with his maternal grandparents for the two
years since his father died and his mother went to the city to earn
a living, wants to keep the discovery secret so that the two of them
can do the sleuthing and earn the reward that would reunite him
with his mother. When his mother remarries and starts a new
family that does not include him, he is more determined than ever

to become rich and outshine the city man she married. The discovery that the murder was perpetrated by the secretive and vindictive Ku Klux Klan, that Jim Luke's older sister's husband is
strongly implicated, and that the local law enforcement is a corrupt
tool of the Klan, makes their mission fraught with peril, especially
when Klansmen learn their identity and the stalkers become the
stalked. When the nefarious rednecks are finally brought to justice,
the boys learn that there is no reward money, but Sammy John receives something even more precious: an invitation from his mother
for him and Jim Luke to visit her in Colorado the following summer.

274. Branscum, Robbie. SPUD TACKETT AND THE ANGEL OF
       DOOM. New York: Viking, 1983. 124p. Grades 5-7. R
       Because his mother left the farm when he was 3 and his
father was killed before his birth, Spud, now 15 during World War
II, has always lived in Christian charity with his strict but fair
grandmother. Spud's strutting, streetwise cousin Leroy from Detroit joins them when his father enlists in the army and his mother
goes to work in a defense plant. Leroy immediately begins casting
aspersions on their homespun way of life in the Arkansas hills, and
in a fight picked by Spud in defense of Grandma, Spud is pulverized
by Leroy who employs his gang-fighting techniques. Leroy, however, impressed with Spud's ability to take a licking, declares a
truce. Spud exacts sweet revenge by telling Leroy that a classmate is a girl of easy virtue. Leroy makes a pass and gets decked
by the irate tomboy. Their differences are soon forgotten when
a fanatical evangelist arrives to hold a revival and exhort the hard-
scrabble farmers to repent their sins, sell their property, and follow
him deeper into the hills out of reach of enslaving Germans and
Japanese while awaiting the call to Glory. When Spud and Leroy
fall victim to the mass hysteria and incendiary oratory, Grandma reassures them that he is not the Angel of God as he claims. She
courageously exposes him as the exploitative and avaricious charlatan
that he is, and Spud and Leroy, whose soldier father has died in
the war, accept Grandma's humble faith.

275. Branscum, Robbie. TO THE TUNE OF A HICKORY STICK.
       Garden City: Doubleday, 1978. 119p. Grades 4-7. NR
       Following her husband's death, Nell and J. D. Tucker's
mother left the children in the care of an aunt and uncle in the Arkansas hills while she emigrated to California to seek her fortune,
sending monthly checks for their support. Nell, 12, detests life
with Uncle Jock, who is exploitative, punitive and niggardly. She
lives to go to school, but when the school is closed for fall planting
and Uncle Jock announces that their ma has died in an auto accident,
circumstances go from bad to worse. Nell knows that they must run
away when Uncle Jock beats J.D., 13, half to death. They take
sanctuary in the deserted, isolated schoolhouse where they are
eventually discovered by sympathetic teacher, Mr. Davis, who aids
and abets their escape. He feeds, teaches and harbors them
through the snowed-in months while making inquiries about their

mother. Nell develops a crush on Mr. Davis until she learns that
he snores. January thaw brings Uncle Jock blustering about in an
attempt to regain control of the children, accusing Mr. Davis of
moral turpitude. The school board and the sheriff convene to hear
the children's testimony, and their mother appears to unmask Uncle
Jock as an avaricious swindler, child abuser and perjurer. Uncle
Jock gets his comeuppance, Ma marries Mr. Davis, and the reunited
family repairs to ShangriL.A.

276. Brenner, Barbara. A YEAR IN THE LIFE OF ROSIE BERNARD.
        New York: Harper and Row, 1971. Illus. by Joan Sandin.
        179p. Grades 4-6. R
        Rosie's actor father promised her that they would never be
separated when her mother died of pneumonia eight months before,
but he has had to break his pledge because "hard times" in 1932
have forced him to take work where he can find it. Rosie, 10, is
sent to live with her maternal grandparents and extended family in
Brooklyn. She makes friends with her relatives quickly and is intimidated only by her stern but loving grandmother who is as intractable as Rosie herself. On a brief visit at Easter, her father
brings her a puppet theater with which she and her cousins amuse
themselves, but on his next visit he is accompanied by a beautiful
but affected actress, Lydia, to whom Rosie takes an immediate dislike, making malicious mischief to discourage her. When they
eventually announce their marriage, Rosie retaliates by running away
in the dead of winter, and by the time she is found she, too, has
contracted pneumonia. Her own strong will, plus Grandma's ministrations, pull her through. During her recuperation she makes an
effort to be fair to her stepmother and decides to make her home
in California with Daddy and Lydia.

277. Bridgers, Sue Ellen. HOME BEFORE DARK. New York:
        Knopf, 1976. 176p. Grades 7-10. R+
        Though her mother thrives on the anonymity of life as a
migrant farm laborer, Stella Willis, 14, yearns to quit the cramped,
stifling, swaying old station wagon she has to share with three other
siblings, William, 10, Earl, 4, and baby Lissy, and put down roots.
When her father, black sheep James Earl, strikes a truce with his
younger brother Newton who inherited the family tobacco farm in
North Carolina, Stella seizes her opportunity. Newton grants them
the use of the tenant house which Stella, with the grudging aid of
her first friend, Toby, refurbishes. But domesticity is anathema to
defeatist Mae Willis, who, in a horrifying, foreordained scene is
killed by lightning. Stella turns for solace to Toby, whose rivalry
with another boy over Stella's attention escalates into violence.
James Earl finds comfort in Maggie Grover, prim spinster, childhood
friend, and proprietress of the mercantile establishment her father
founded. When James Earl marries Maggie and takes the family to
live in her substantial home, Stella, her surrogate mother role
usurped, stubbornly persuades her elders to let her remain in the
tenant house alone under the supervision of her aunt. With time to

ruminate, she realizes that stability comes from within, that home is
where the heart is, and she goes to take her place in the new
family structure.

278. Brink, Carol Ryrie. WINTER COTTAGE. New York: Mac-
         millan, 1939. Illus. by Fermin Rocker. 178p. Grades 5-6.
         R
         When his grocery business fails at the beginning of the
Great Depression, Pop, an improvident but eloquent poetry lover,
loads his unsold inventory into the trailer and his daughters Ara-
minta, 13, and Eglantine, 10, into the battered auto and departs
for Aunt Amy's grudging charity. The car breaks down in the Wisconsin woods near a summer cottage closed for the winter. Lacking
funds to repair the car, they elect to spend the winter at the cozy
former farmhouse where a runaway boy joins them. Minty, the pragmatic one of the family, attempts to extract Pop's secret recipe for
his stupendous pancakes, sockdollagers, gollwhollickers, and whales
in order to enter in a flour company contest and win the prize to
pay rent for the cottage. She is abetted by her sister Eggs and
the runaway, Joe. Unexpected visitors arriving in a blizzard arouse
mutual suspicion until Pop's friendly hospitality palliates it. Minty's
suspected Chicago gangsters are nothing more than the cottage's
rightful owners, who soon abandon their design to have the interlopers arrested. Minty's check comes through in the spring with
enough left over after rent to fulfill Pop's dream of opening a
secondhand bookstore.

279. Brooks, Bruce. THE MOVES MAKE THE MAN. New York:
         Harper and Row, 1984. 280p. Grades 7-10. R
         Court-ordered desegregation places bright, jiving Jerome
Foxworthy, 13, as the only black at his North Carolina high school,
where the only overt prejudice he encounters is being barred from
the basketball team. When his well organized mother, widowed when
Jerome was an infant, is hospitalized following an elevator accident,
he signs up for a cooking class in which he meets Bix Rivers,
skittish, defensive, literal, and agonizingly honest. Slowly Jerome
draws out his diffident white classmate at the basketball court deep
in the woods where Jerome goes to practice. Bix hates subterfuge
of any kind. As a natural athlete he easily picks up the mechanics
of basketball but refuses to learn the feints of which Jerome is
so proud. Eventually Bix reveals that his beloved mother, whom
his stepfather will not allow him to visit, is a mental patient under-
going shock treatments. Bix challenges his stepfather to a basketball duel for the right to visit his mother, a contest he almost loses
until in desperation he is forced to employ the fakery he abhors.
Jerome witnesses the corruption and collapse of his friend's rigid
standards when he is invited to a meal with the Foxworthy family at
which Bix acts the suave phony. Bix's backwards metamorphosis is
complete on the anticipated visit to his mother when she fails to
recognize him and, to save face, he pulls the most cynical "move"
of all and runs away afterward. Jerome's distress is ameliorated by
the hope that Bix will start a new life elsewhere.

280. Brown, Irene Bennett. BEFORE THE LARK. New York:
        Atheneum, 1982. 191p. Grades 5-8. R
        Summer and winter, Jocelyn Belle Royal, 12 in 1888, wraps
a heavy muffler around her head. Born with a harelip, she is persecuted by taunting street gangs and repulsive to ignorant adults.
Reared by her grandmother, a Kansas City washerwoman, since her
mother's death six years ago, Jocey longs to retreat to the farm
in Kansas owned by her father, who has been roaming the country
in his grief. She finally convinces Gram, who is suffering from a
chronic cough and certain she is dying, that departing the stock-
yard miasma would be beneficial to her health. Once on the farm,
Jocey toils indefatigably to plant a truck garden, but she resists
Gram's efforts to socialize with their rural neighbors for fear of
exposing her deformity and inviting revulsion or pity until the son
of a nearby farmer demonstrates that he sees beyond her handicap
and appreciates her as a person. The young man's declaration gives
her self-confidence, but she is still receptive to the news, delivered
by a peddler, of a new surgical procedure that can correct her affliction. Courageously, she returns to Kansas City alone and undergoes the operation free of charge at a teaching hospital. During
her recovery she is reunited with her father, looking older but content at last, who has returned from Mexico seeking her.

281. Buchan, Stuart. WHEN WE LIVED WITH PETE. New York:
        Scribner, 1978. 147p. Grades 5-8. R
        Adjacent to the Hollywood apartment building where Tommy
Bridges, 13, lives with his long-widowed mother, a would-be TV
commercial actress, lies an abandoned and overgrown estate. Bored
with city life, Tommy explores the precipitous grounds of the former
showplace and meets Joel, a streetwise runaway battered boy from
Wyoming, and Little Horse, a greenhorn New York cabbie discovering
his Indian roots. The two make their camp in the upper reaches of
the wooded canyon and try to elude the young but dangerous drifters
that tinsel town attracts. Tommy taxes their credulity with frequent
allusions to the happy years when he and his mother lived with Pete,
an abalone fisherman, in a shanty near Santa Barbara. He becomes
increasingly agitated as Susan Bridges, in an attempt to further her
career, becomes involved with a flashy, lecherous, balding man. To
distract his mother, Tommy runs away and hitchhikes to Santa Barbara. There Pete tells him that, contrary to his belief, he and Susan split up not because he ceased liking them but because Susan
wanted marriage, a commitment he couldn't make. Pete returns Tommy to his mother just in time to rescue Joel and Little Horse from an
incendiary blaze set by the malicious punks. Reunited with Susan,
Pete decides that marriage surpasses loneliness, and Susan easily
eschews the notion of a film career.

282. Bulla, Clyde Robert. THE CARDBOARD CROWN. New York:
        Crowell, 1984. Illus. by Michele Chessare. 79p. Grades
        3-5. R
        A knock in the night announces the advent of a girl

introducing herself as a princess in need of a place to sleep for the
night. Adam, 11, accepts her without question. His dour, dispas-
sionate father is more skeptical. He dismisses the princess as a
vapid daydreamer. Adam believes that he must be more akin to his
dead mother than to his stern, suspicious, literal father. The girl
turns out to be imaginative Olivia, whose beloved actor father
brought her to live with her despised Aunt Jen who lives up the
road from Adam and his father. Olivia fears that her father left
her because he is going to die. Critical Aunt Jen, however, views
her brother as irresponsible and her niece as a troublemaker.
Olivia requests Adam's assistance in running away to find her
father. Adam sells his adored calf to finance the venture, and his
father disavows him. Olivia returns disillusioned. Her father, far
from being terminally ill, abandoned her in order to remarry and
callously told her that she will recover from her heartache. The
castoff girl and the shutout boy decide to find their own happiness
in each other through exercising their imaginations.

283. Bulla, Clyde Robert. A LION TO GUARD US. New York:
       Crowell, 1981. Illus. by Michele Chessare. 117p. Grades
       3-5. NR
       In Elizabethan England a returning sailor leaves a terse
message for the wife and children of James Freebold that he has
built a house in Jamestown, Virginia, and hopes that they will be
reunited soon. Weeks later Mistress Freebold is dead of a long illness, and the children are at the mercy of the haughty and par-
simonious dame to whom they are in service. Doughty Amanda, 11,
marshals Jemmy, 8, and Meg, 5, to escape their bondage and seek
their father in America. They are fortunate enough to be taken
under the aegis of old Dr. Crider, whose fondest dream has been
to go to the colony and who outfits them for their venture. During
the voyage Dr. Crider is swept overboard in a storm, and the remainder of the ship's company is shipwrecked on the island of Bermuda. After a year on the enchanted island (about which Shakespeare wrote THE TEMPEST), the little band completes work on another ship and sets sail once more for the New World. There the
children find and rescue their sick and starving father, one of the
few survivors of the original settlement. Their talisman, the brass
lion-headed door knocker given them by their father before he left
London and which was stolen and then recovered in Bermuda, has
guarded their passage.

284. Bulla, Clyde Robert. OPEN THE DOOR AND SEE ALL THE
       PEOPLE. New York: Crowell, 1972. Illus. by Wendy
       Watson. 69p. Grades 3-5. R
       When their rented farmhouse burns to the ground, JoAnn,
7, and Teeney, 6, can save nothing, not even their dolls. With
money from the sale of the cow, their mother decides to move to the
city, where an old friend finds them modest lodgings and Mamma a
job as a chambermaid. They have nothing left over for frills, and
Teeney is miserable without her doll until a neighbor girl tells them

of the magical Toy House where dolls can be borrowed for two weeks like library books and can even be adopted permanently if the little girls prove their solicitude. JoAnn and Teeney are model mothers for the six-week probationary period until the day before the formal adoption ceremony when the neighbor's dog kidnaps Teeney's Baby and licks its face off. The kindly Doll Man solves the problem and even Mamma gets the doll she never had.

285. Burch, Robert. CHRISTMAS WITH IDA EARLY. New York:
        Viking, 1983. 157p. Grades 4-6. R+
        This Depression holiday season will be the first for the
Sutton family (see 286) since losing their mother. Twins Clay and
Dewey, 5, have made a pet of the Thanksgiving turkey, and their
outrageously unconventional housekeeper, Ida Early, humors them by
planning an alternate menu. Among her accomplishments is ventriloquy, with which she makes the animals appear to speak. Fussy
Aunt Earnestine arrives and immediately begins carping at Ida for
impropriety. When Earnestine contracts flu, Ida, with the patience
of Job, becomes chief nurse. The twins try to make a match between
Ida and the new preacher, Brother Preston, but it is doomed to
failure. The good cleric is scandalized when Ida conducts a Sunday
School class and, with her penchant for telling tall tales, embellishes
and modernizes the Bible stories. Ida's miraculous knack with animals earns her a role as a Wise Man in the Christmas tableau against
the reverend's better judgment. When she enlivens the carol
singing at rehearsal by adding a chorus of yodels, the apoplectic
preacher replaces her. Of course the animals run amok at the
evening performance until Ida graciously and coolheadedly corrals
them. Earnestine surprises Ida on Christmas Day with the lounging
pajamas she has long admired.

286. Burch, Robert. IDA EARLY COMES OVER THE MOUNTAIN.
        New York: Viking, 1980. 145p. Grades 4-6. R+
        Chores become games and conventionality flies out the win-
dow when Ida Early, six and one-half feet tall, tramps over the
Blue Ridge mountains of Georgia and appoints herself nanny and
housekeeper to the four motherless Sutton tykes, Ellen, 12, Randall,
11, and twins Clay and Dewey, 5. With her tall tales, homespun
logic, and odd antics, she captivates the youngsters, who scramble
to do her bidding, but scandalizes officious Aunt Earnestine, who
soon hies herself back to Atlanta. Ida even enters into the spirit
of the children's practical jokes, and it appears that she is unflap-
pable until the day in the schoolyard when their classmates ridicule
Ida's appearance, and Ida is visibly hurt that Ellen and Randall
cravenly allow it. She disappears, and in her absence the children
and their father, 43, a lumberyard foreman, flounder. When she returns, she is garbed in unaccustomed finery, a caricature of confor-
mity. Her personality has degenerated, too, and the Suttons decide
that they can no longer take Ida for granted. When Randall learns
that her dazzling rope tricks are not imaginary, he volunteers her
for the school pageant, and Ida becomes a heroine when she saves

the very girl who mocked her from a berserk bear. Ida restlessly
moves on, and after months of struggling to cope by themselves,
the Suttons are overjoyed when the old ebullient Ida Early rejoins
them permanently on Thanksgiving Day.

287. Burton, Hester. TO RAVENSRIGG. New York: Crowell,
        1977. 143p. Grades 6-8. NR
        Living with her sanctimonious aunt while her father, a cap-
tain with the East India Company, is at sea is hateful to Emmie
Hesket, 14, whose mother died in childbirth over a year ago in the
1780s. On his next voyage, she begs to be allowed to accompany
him. The ship founders in a raging storm off the Dover coast, and
Emmie, one of few survivors, is taken in by a vicar's family. Before going down with his ship, Captain Hesket cryptically and enig-
matically tells Emmie to go to Ravensrigg, and now, with the help
of James Kendall, a visiting Quaker proselytizing for an end to the
cruel and illegal slave trade, she sets out, riding pillion, in search
of the strange locale. Along the way they are grievously persecuted
by the greedy and brutal slave ship masters and their minions, and
Emmie, now 15, falls in love with James. At Ravensrigg she learns
to her horror and sorrow that her true father is not the benevolent
Captain Hesket but one of the most wicked and dastardly of the
slave captains. Gentle but valiant James declares his unspoken love
for Emmie and plans to marry her before she falls into her execrable
parent's clutches.

288. Byars, Betsy. THE ANIMAL, THE VEGETABLE AND JOHN D.
        JONES. New York: Delacorte, 1982. Illus. by Ruth
        Sanderson. 150p. Grades 4-6. R+
        Although John D Jones, 12, accepts with ill grace his fate
of spending summer vacation with the family of the radio sports an-
nouncer his widowed Chicago advice columnist mother has been dating,
he vows to be as disagreeable as possible. Deanie and Clara Malcolm,
14 and 12, bicker incessantly but always look forward to their two
weeks with their divorced father at his beach house in the Carolinas.
When they learn at the last moment that John D and his mother will
be sharing it with them, their vacation is instantly spoiled, and
they agree to shelve their antagonisms (and pet epithets for one
another--Animal and Vegetable) in order to fight the common enemy.
In spite of Sam Malcolm's and Delores Jones' efforts at cheerfulness,
mediation, conciliation and activity-planning, their offspring manage
to make themselves miserable. In her subconscious need to escape
the distress, Clara paddles out beyond the surf on a flimsy plastic
raft and is swept into the open sea. John D is the first to notice
her absence and spread the alarm. When she is given up for lost,
a penitent and distraught Deanie allows Delores to console her. But
with great tenacity Clara clings to life and is rescued, and John D
surprises even himself by being the most solicitous of all.

289. Byars, Betsy. THE NIGHT SWIMMERS. New York: Delacorte,
        1980. Illus. by Troy Howell. 131p. Grades 4-6. R+

A country-western singer awaiting stardom, Shorty Anderson works nights and sleeps or composes all day. Since his wife
died two years before in a plane crash, his oldest child Retta, named
for Loretta Lynn, has been keeping house for him and rearing her
two brothers, Johnny, 9, and Roy, 5, also named for C&W luminaries.
Keeping the boys entertained during the summer is Retta's chief
onus, and her latest inspiration is to take them swimming at a nearby
estate after the owner, a retired colonel, retires for the night.
When Johnny insubordinately strikes up a secret friendship with
another boy, resentment boils in Retta over the responsibility she
has had to bear for the boys and her immature, superficial father.
A sibling squabble rouses the pool's proprietor, who very nearly
apprehends them after a chase. Later, Johnny sneaks out of the
house to rendezvous with his friend, shadowed by suspicious, possessive Retta. Little Roy, awakening alone in the house, imagines
that the others have gone swimming without him and resolves to make
a splash of his own. He is saved from drowning by the Colonel,
who then confronts Shorty Anderson. Shorty's perennial, long-
suffering girlfriend Brendelle, who is genuinely fond of the children,
seizes the sudden leverage to make the family a fivesome, releasing
Shorty from the inconvenience of fatherhood and Retta from the
burden of premature adulthood.

290. Byars, Betsy. THE NOT-JUST-ANYBODY FAMILY. New
          York: Delacorte, 1986. Illus. by Jacqueline Rogers.
          149p. Grades 4-6. R+
          A domino effect of comic errors results when the Blossom
family's grandfather "Pap," who cares for them while their mother
is traveling in Texas on the rodeo circuit, is jailed for inadvertently
disturbing the peace while collecting aluminum cans for recycling.
Aspiring stuntman Junior, 7, is startled by the police into falling
instead of flying off the barn roof, thereby breaking both legs,
and Pap's dog Mud is stranded miles across town from his master.
With their private birdcall signal, Vern, 11, locates Pap and stages
a daring jailbreak-in to join him. It is up to Maggie to spring the
wheelchair-bound Junior from the hospital in time for Pap's hearing,
which she pulls off with the help of Junior's irrepressible amputee
roommate. The fourth estate sinks its teeth into the human interest
story, and public sympathy is clearly on the Blossoms' side. The
judge suspends Pap's 60-day sentence, and the four are free to return home where Mom, having seen the publicity in the media, catches
up with them. Even the disreputable Mud providentially negotiates
the hazardous crossing of Interstate 85 and, after running afoul of
a skunk, rejoins the family for a joyous reunion. Mom, a trick
rider whose husband was killed by a steer, considers changing her
occupation to hairdresser so that she won't have to travel.

291. Byars, Betsy. THE SUMMER OF THE SWANS. New York:
          Viking, 1970. Illus. by Ted CoConis. 142p. Grades 5-7.
          R+
          At 15, Sara is feeling very ambivalent and self-conscious

about both her appearance and her brother Charlie, 10, who has
been mentally retarded since a serious illness in infancy. Her older
sister Wanda, 19, is popular, attractive, and well adjusted with no
problem more serious than cajoling Aunt Willie, their guardian, to
loosen the apron strings. When their mother died six years ago,
their father lost interest in the family beyond support payments.
One day Sara takes Charlie to see migrating swans that are stopping
at a nearby lake. They make such an impression on him that he
wanders off in the middle of the night to try to find them again.
In Sara's desperation to find him, she learns that the boy she believes to be her enemy is really a stalwart friend. She also realizes
that everyone has obstacles to surmount of one magnitude or another
and that moping over them is non-constructive.

292.   Byars, Betsy. THE TV KID. New York: Viking, 1976.
         Illus. by Richard Cuffari. 123p. Grades 4-6. R+
         In the odd moments when Lennie isn't physically parked in
front of the television set at the struggling rural Tennessee motel
his mother inherited from her father, his fertile imagination is busy
inventing and casting new scenarios and commercials. Even when
his mother curtails his viewing because of failing grades, he cannot
concentrate on his studies because of his absorbing daydreams in
which he plays principal roles in his favorite shows. When he fails
the science test after letting his mom think he memorized the material, he is ashamed to face her with the news and rows across the
lake to the deserted summer colony where he likes to pretend he
owns one of the lodges. Startled by a cruising police car, he crawls
out of sight under the house, disturbing a rattlesnake which sinks
its fangs in his leg. TV magic and miraculous endings forsake him
in his desperate plight, and he pictures all too realistically his untimely demise. The suspicious police return, however, to rescue
him, and he begins his excruciatingly painful recovery. Suddenly,
real life has much more immediacy than TV contrivance. Lenny's
teacher allows him to improve his dismal test score by submitting a
report on rattlesnakes, and at last he finds science more engrossing
and meaningful than indiscriminate television addiction.

293.   Callen, Larry. SORROW'S SONG. Boston: Little, Brown,
         1979. 150p. Grades 5-7. R
         Sorrow Nix has always been mute but not deaf, but what
she lacks in elocutionary skills is more than recompensed in intelligence, sensitivity and compassion. Her disposition, moreover,
belies her given name, and she does not view her voicelessness as
a handicap. Sorrow has been friends all her life with Pinch Grim-
ball, with whom she communicates in writing, a pillar of strength to
her when her father died a year earlier. Now near their Southern
backwater town a rare, endangered whooping crane with a broken
wing has been sighted which will soon become prey, if not to alligators, then to the Zoo Man or to the Sweet brothers who simply
want to eat it. Sorrow and Pinch determinedly trap the big bird
and spend all their spare time catering to its voracious appetite.

Before long, others learn the whereabouts of the bird and steal it.
The children are obliged to highjack the whooper again and row it
to safety on an island. Sorrow takes cold on their damp nocturnal
outing, and all the avaricious, would-be crane snatchers pay her get-
well visits before resuming the hunt for the bird and squabbling over
it after its capture. Sorrow's expressive eyes communicate her an-
guish, and the repentant captor frees it to soar like Sorrow's spirit.

294.   Cameron, Eleanor. JULIA AND THE HAND OF GOD. New
        York: Dutton, 1977. Illus. by Gail Owens. 168p. Grades
        5-7. R+
        When her improvident journalist father was killed in World
War I (see 295), Julia Redfern and her mother and brother moved
into her maternal grandmother's cramped house in Berkeley. Gramma's open favoritism of Greg has always rankled, but now that Julia
is 11, their antagonism flares into conflict. Julia, who is imaginative
and absentminded like her father, is judged irresponsible by her
pragmatic fundamentalist grandmother. When she is punished for
scorching a pot while trying to cremate a dead mouse, Julia meets a
retired professor who encourages her to write creatively of her impressions and daydreams. She further distresses her family when
she disappears on the day Berkeley burns in a disastrous brush
fire and in one of her abstractions is almost incinerated. Gramma
calls it the hand of God that saved her, but Julia knows it is her
sixth sense that spared her. She ponders this and other "strange-
nesses," and when she, Mother and Greg finally move to a little
house of their own, Julia is inspired to begin filling the pages of
the journal that sympathetic Uncle Hugh gave her.

295.   Cameron, Eleanor. A ROOM MADE OF WINDOWS. Boston:
        Little, Brown, 1971. Illus. by Trina Schart Hyman. 271p.
        Grades 7-9. R+
        Adolescent Julia (see 294 and 296) shares with her dead
father the burning compulsion to write. She follows her muse at
the desk he made for her in her private sanctuary and window on
the world. Her endeavors are encouraged by her new friend, an
elderly neighbor who is an accomplished musician and kindred spirit.
When her mother reveals her plans to marry an old family friend,
Julia reacts negatively in rage and rebellion, burnishing her father's
tarnished image and succeeding in distressing her mother and older
brother. One of her fears is that of leaving her beloved room and
neighborhood friends near San Francisco. Part of that concern is
assuaged when two of the friends leave first and she makes advance
friends at the new location nearby. Julia is gradually shown that her
selfishness and obstinacy benefit no one, not even herself.

296.   Cameron, Eleanor. THAT JULIA REDFERN. New York: Dut-
        ton, 1982. Illus. by Gail Owens. 133p. Grades 4-6. R+
        Julia works hard at being a model of decorum but fails
spectacularly because she is imaginative, inquisitive, impetuous and
irrepressible. There is the time she borrows her big brother Greg's

bicycle and nearly plows into Aunt Alex; the time she pursues a
king snake and slides over a cliff at Yosemite National Park; and
the time she appeases the dread "grinling" in the garden with the
gift of an expensive doll. Her adored father, a would-be author
with copious rejections, prophesies that she will be a writer and
constructs for her a marvelous desk before he leaves Berkeley to
be an aviator in World War I. One day, in a tumble from a jungle
gym, she loses consciousness and has a vision of meeting her
father in which he imparts a cryptic message for her mother. Shortly after her recovery a telegram informs them of his death. Julia
refuses to believe it and convinces herself that he landed safely
among trees. Her distraught mother falls victim to a flu epidemic
and is snatched from the jaws of death by Julia's determined grandmother. Later Julia remembers her father's psychic message, and
when they examine his effects they find a saleable manuscript that
brings in a most welcome windfall.

297.   Carlson, Natalie Savage. THE FAMILY UNDER THE BRIDGE.
          New York: Harper, 1958. Illus. by Garth Williams. 97p.
          Grades 3-5. R
          The jaunty old hobo Armand, who has an antipathy for
both children and work, returns to his roost on the quay under
one of Paris' famous bridges, only to find that his niche has been
usurped by three homeless, fatherless moppets. The little "star-
lings" suffer him to stay, although their mother is mistrustful of
the disreputable beggar. The children quickly endear themselves
to him, and he takes them to petition Father Christmas, a friend
seasonally employed at a fancy department store. They ask for
nothing but a real home. When two officious society matrons
threaten to send the children to an orphanage and their mother to
jail, he hastily removes them to the camp of gypsy friends, to their
mother's initial horror. When the gypsies move on, he is forced to
consider gainful employment. Transformed by a bath and a mend,
he is engaged as concierge of an apartment building, the perfect
sinecure since the emolument includes living quarters where he can
nest his new brood.

298.   Cavallaro, Ann. BLIMP. New York: Dutton, 1983. 166p.
          Grades 6-10. R+
          In the year since her mother's death of cancer and her
father's subsequent remarriage, Kim Lunde, 17, has become a compulsive eater. Her svelte stepmother and her equally petite older
sister encourage and cajole Kim, unsuccessfully, to lose weight.
Kim is highly flattered to receive the attention of an attractive new
student, Gary Bellmore, who confides to her that he lost his twin
brother in an auto accident and that his alcoholic mother saddles
him with guilt over it. With the incentive of holding onto Gary,
Kim begins dieting, helps Gary with his homework, and worries
about his frequent absences from school. When he disappears for
weeks, she suspects him of exploiting her for having turned in her
book report as his own. Confronting him about it, she learns that

he is recovering from one of repeated suicide attempts out of despair over his brother's death and his parents' indifference to him. Kim, who has been seeing a psychiatrist to help her control her weight, convinces Gary to seek counseling for his own more serious problem and urges her father to give him a job in his hardware store. To her frustration, their friendship remains platonic, and, when invited to the senior prom by a fellow yearbook staff member, she accepts, feeling disloyal yet gratified by her increasing popularity since her dramatic weight loss. She remains in love with Gary who, still lacking self-confidence, doesn't declare himself until she confesses her feelings first.

299. Clark, Margaret Goff. THE LATCHKEY MYSTERY. New
      York: Dodd, Mead, 1985. 128p. Grades 4-6. R+
      Minda Carr, 11, and her brother Joey, 5, have been latch-
key kids since their mother moved the family from Buffalo, where their father died, to the house in Florida which she inherited from her mother and took a temporary secretarial job. After a rash of burglaries in their neighborhood, they join a group of fellow latch-key kids in organizing a Neighborhood Watch with the advice of the police department. The youngsters suspect and report everyone they see, from the junkman and gardener to a jogger and a nosy furniture polish saleswoman. When Mom gets a permanent job, she arranges daycare for Joey so that Minda can join a swimming club and participate in other after school activities. But before that transpires, their group decides to smoke out the thief on a halfday holiday from school by not answering their telephones and making it appear as if their homes are empty. When the telephone rings at the Carrs' house, Minda and Joey have been coached to exit immediately and go next door, but an accident delays them, and the burglar walks in on them. Minda's quick thinking in setting off an emergency signal helps avert serious danger and capture the surprising culprit.

300. Cleaver, Vera, and Bill Cleaver. GROVER. Philadelphia:
      Lippincott, 1970. Illus. by Frederic Marvin. 125p. Grades
      5-6. R+
      Eleven-year-old Grover's well meaning family shields him
from the fact that his mother has terminal cancer. Only his mother herself tries to prepare him in an oblique way for her eventual death by reminding him that he favors her side of the family which doesn't "howl" over misfortune. Soon afterward she calmly ends her life with a gun. His father suffers overtly and refuses to accept or condone her premature passage. Grover stoically pursues his daily rounds with friends Ellen Grae and Farrell, allowing his emotions to escape only once, when he angrily and clumsily decapitates a neighbor's turkey and struggles to plumb the unfathomable depths of mortality. On a visit to his mother's grave, Grover realizes that his father pities himself, not her, and allows his mind to "turn a corner." A fish head in the chowder cracks his father's mask of grief just enough to admit the first glimmering of hope.

301. Cleaver, Vera, and Bill Cleaver. A LITTLE DESTINY. New
        York: Lothrop, Lee and Shepard, 1979. 152p. Grades
        6-9. NR
        Adding to the shock of her father's sudden death by goring
at the horns of a bull he was auctioning is the growing suspicion
that the tragedy was not entirely accidental. Lucy Commander, 14,
vows revenge on the crass parvenu Tom Clegg, the Georgia town's
most influential citizen and moneylender who was Lucy's mother's
former suitor as well as her father's creditor. After a second rebuff by the proud widow, the remorseless Mr. Clegg calls in their
debts, forcing the destitute but self-respecting family to retreat to
their ramshackle farm at Jewel Sink. Brother Lyman, 28, a doctor,
tries to set up practice in town but is harassed by Clegg's cohorts.
Their only salvation is Ryder Tuttle, a rough diamond, erstwhile
trunk peddler and aspiring Western writer, who joins them as general
factotum and soon makes the shabby abode habitable and the acreage
productive. Then Lyman is abducted, and spunky Lucy sets out
alone to track him. She, too, is captured by Clegg's heinous henchmen until Ryder comes to deliver them in a harrowing and suspenseful denouement. Remembering her father's gentleness, Lucy stops
short of taking Clegg's life in retribution for all their suffering.

302. Cleaver, Vera, and Bill Cleaver. THE MIMOSA TREE. Phila-
        delphia: Lippincott, 1970. 125p. Grades 5-8. R+
        Following a feud with their backwoods neighbors, during
which their hogs sicken and die and their crops rot in the fields,
the five Proffit children, 4, 7, 9, 10, and 14, and their blind father
are persuaded by their blowsy, vulgar stepmother to pull up stakes
in rural North Carolina and move to a better life in Chicago. Their
tenement is barren of any living thing, so Marvella, 14, invents a
mimosa tree in the alley to placate sightless Pa. Of more immediacy
is the fact that the stepmother deserts them, leaving the naive hill-
billies, who have never heard of crime, drugs, welfare, or broken
homes, unprepared for survival in the slum jungle. Reared in the
Christian work ethic, they look for jobs but are told it is illegal to
hire children, yet bureaucratic indifference snarls financial assistance.
Purse snatching becomes their sole means of livelihood. When the
street urchin who taught them the trade pushes his mother in front
of a bus, it shocks Marvella into realizing that returning home is
the only way of regaining their pride and integrity. The neighbors
welcome them back warmly.

303. Clements, Bruce. ANYWHERE ELSE BUT HERE. New York:
        Farrar, Straus, Giroux, 1980. 152p. Grades 6-8. R
        The only object of value that Molly Smelter's mother was
able to carry out of Poland while fleeing from the Russians in 1944
was a portable dollhouse, a scale model of her fine home in Krakow.
It is the only thing that Molly, 13, wishes to keep when her father,
long a widower, is forced to auction all their possessions to reduce
their debts when his printing business goes bankrupt. Molly and
her father live with Aunt Aurora, and Mr. Smelter is resigned to

taking a demeaning corporate job just to make ends meet. But
Molly finds it galling to depend on the largesse of Aunt Aurora
and her opportunistic fiance and longs for her dad to leave Schenectady and start a new printing shop in Willimantic. Their situation
worsens when an avant-garde friend of Aunt Aurora's descends upon
them, thrusts her noisome son Claude on Molly to mind, and sets
her cap for Mr. Smelter. Molly consults an investment counselor
who was an old friend of her mother's. Generous Mr. Potrezeski
buys the beloved dollhouse, and with the proceeds Molly makes a
down payment on the new shop, compelling her conservative father
to commit himself to the move. When Claude is abandoned by his
mother, Mr. Smelter and Molly take him along to rear properly as
they start their new venture.

304. Clifford, Eth. THE KILLER SWAN. Boston: Houghton Mifflin,
          1980. 114p. Grades 5-9. R+
          His calm and quiet stepfather Steve Mebbin, a science
teacher, is the antithesis of Lex's mercurial father, now dead.
So is the environment to which Steve brought Lex and his mother
from the city a year ago. Lex, 14, has remained stoic, aloof, angry
and brooding. Even the swans which nest on their lake do not interest him. His only friend is Caleb Tyne, whom he rescued from
bullies as his father would have done just to prove his toughness.
Then Lex witnesses the cob, demented by blinding pain in his head,
murder one of the two male cygnets, and instinctively he endangers
his own life to rescue the other one, with whom he forms a strong
bond. It is Steve who solves the problem of giving the young bird
the freedom of its natural habitat while protecting him from his homi-
cidal father by constructing a screened enclosure out into the water.
As Lex's memories of his father, an ironworker who built skyscrapers
before losing his arm in an accident, keep surfacing unbidden, he
begins to associate the crazed cob with his tormented father. He
recalls his rage and self-pity and finally his own guilt and resentment when his father abandoned him by committing suicide. When
the destructive cob kills Caleb's dog, Lex is forced to shoot it. The
act proves cathartic, and he is able to forgive his self-destructive
parent.

305. Clifton, Lucille. ALL US COME CROSS THE WATER. New
          York: Holt, Rinehart and Winston, 1973. (OP) Illus. by
          John Steptoe. Unp. Grades 1-3. R
          Ujamaa's inner-city black teacher mistakes his confusion
over his origins for shame in his African heritage when she asks her
students to name the country of their ancestry. The elementary
school boy knows that Africa is a continent, not a country. When
he asks his family where they originated, they respond literally.
Sister Rose reports that Mama was from Georgia and Daddy from
Alabama. Daddy, tired from working all day for the city, replies
that they moved North from Birmingham after Mama died. That does
not satisfy Ujamaa. He goes to his great-grandmother, who informs
him that he is a Whydah from Dahomey on his mother's side and

probably an Ashanti from Ghana on his father's side. He then consults an old friend who tells him that country of origin is immaterial since all Africans crossed the water in the same slave boats. Black brothers' identity, he maintains, lies in their African given names. Ujamaa's means "Unity."

306. Clifton, Lucille. EVERETT ANDERSON'S CHRISTMAS COMING. New York: Holt, Rinehart and Winston, 1971. Illus. by Evaline Ness. Unp. Grades 1-2. R
        Everett Anderson starts the countdown to Christmas, savoring the metropolitan sounds of the season and Mama's tantalizing winks and smiles, though he daren't wish for the train set or bicycle that Daddy would know he wanted if he were alive. Apartment 14A rings with the merriment of an adult party and even sports a Christmas tree that came up on the elevator. On Christmas morning, exuberant black Everett, secure in his mother's love and pleased with his new pet guinea pig, considers himself happier than other boys who have many gifts to open.

307. Clifton, Lucille. EVERETT ANDERSON'S FRIEND. New York: Holt, Rinehart and Winston, 1976. (OP) Illus. by Ann Grifalconi. Unp. Grades K-2. R+
        Everett Anderson hopes that a new playmate, "an almost brother," will move into Apartment 13A, but the new tenant is a girl named Maria who can beat him at ball and running and who is no fun at all. He'd still rather play with Joe and Kirk in 14A and shut Maria out. But one day while Mama is at work, Everett locks himself out of the apartment and feels sorry for himself, wishing Daddy were alive to let him in and make him a peanut butter and jelly sandwich. Maria and her mother invite him into their apartment to wait, offering him tacos, a new experience. Of course Mama scolds him for losing his key, but he has gained a friend in Maria.

308. Clifton, Lucille. EVERETT ANDERSON'S GOODBYE. New York: Holt, Rinehart and Winston, 1983. Illus. by Ann Grifalconi. Unp. Grades K-1. R++
        Young, black Everett Anderson suffers through the five stages of grief in a modicum of simple words for the youngest child, accompanied by strong, evocative, eloquent drawings. In the denial stage he sees his father alive everywhere he looks and even in his dreams. In the anger phase he rejects candy, Christmas, Santa Claus, and even his mother. In the bargaining stage he promises to learn his times tables and never sleep late if his daddy can be restored to him. His depression in the fourth phase drives away his appetite and ability to sleep. After time passes, he reaches the fifth stage of acceptance and realizes that "whatever happens when people die, love doesn't stop, and neither will I." He is able to remember without pain.

309. Clifton, Lucille. EVERETT ANDERSON'S 1-2-3. New York:

Holt, Rinehart and Winston, 1977. Illus. by Ann Grifalconi.
Unp. Grades K-1. R+

Everett Anderson thinks that One is a lonely number, and
he's perfectly content with the twosome he and his mother make.
Mama, smiling her special smile, explains that she misses his daddy
and that Two is sometimes a lonely number for her. She has been
seeing a lot of Mr. Perry recently who tells Everett that he can't
take his daddy's place but that "Three can work and sing and dance
and not make a crowd in 14A." Everett decides that he can get used
to a threesome again if it makes everyone happy.

310.   Clifton, Lucille. EVERETT ANDERSON'S YEAR. New York:
       Holt, Rinehart and Winston, 1974. Illus. by Ann Grifalconi.
       Unp. Grades 1-3. R

The year that he turns 7, the small black boy savors the
four seasons month by month, occasionally recalling outings when his
father was living and fantasizing that his mother will soon be able to
quit working and stay home to play with him. At the end of the
year she explains to him that there will always be a new beginning to
come. He can follow her admonition to walk tall in the world, even
if his world is just an inner city tenement, because he is loved and
knows it.

311.   Clifton, Lucille. SOME OF THE DAYS OF EVERETT ANDERSON.
       New York: Holt, Rinehart and Winston, 1970. (OP) Illus.
       by Evaline Ness. Unp. Grades 1-3. R

"Being six/is full of tricks/and Everett Anderson knows it.
Being a boy/is full of joy/and Everett Anderson shows it." This up-
beat story in verse depicts the always lively and sometimes introspective black, inner city boy's adventures through an entire week,
including his unique way of losing his umbrella on a rainy Tuesday,
being lost in a candy store on Wednesday, cogitating upon his color
at bedtime on Thursday, and waiting for widowed Mama to come home
from work on Friday. Friday evenings after payday are best of all,
relaxing with Mama, but Saturday night sirens can be frightening
and Sunday mornings are definitely lonely without the daddy he misses so much.

312.   Cohen, Barbara. GOOSEBERRIES TO ORANGES. New York:
       Lothrop, Lee and Shepard, 1982. Illus. by Beverly Brod-
       sky. Unp. Grades 2-4. R

Fanny is only 8 when her widowed father emigrates to
America, war breaks out, and a cholera epidemic decimates the
Jewish population of their small Eastern European village, claiming
the aunt with whom Fanny has been living. Papa sends for the remaining family, who cross the ocean in steerage, subsisting on
moldy bread and cheese. Fanny is fascinated with the fragrant
orange ball she sees a fellow passenger peeling and eating. Another
passenger drowns himself rather than face deportation when he discovers that he is tubercular. The others are roughly poked and
prodded upon their arrival at Ellis Island, and Fanny is quarantined

with a rash. There, in "the cleanest white rooms in the universe," she is reunited with her father, who takes her home to a street paved not with gold but with garbage where he lives with his second wife. Fanny makes her first friend in the new land and is introduced to the wonders of the free library. And when she earns her first two nickels, she immediately spends them on succulent oranges, one for herself and one for her father.

313.   Cohen, Barbara. THE INNKEEPER'S DAUGHTER. New York:
          Lothrop, Lee and Shepard, 1979. 159p. Grades 6-10. R+
          Given to ungainliness and faux pas, such as lodging her
finger in the neck of a Coke bottle and wearing a glamorous cocktail dress to a preppy party, Rachel Gold, 16, yearns for a boyfriend and is attracted to a traveling businessman who registers at the inn her mother has managed in Connecticut since her husband's death of a heart attack seven years earlier in 1941. Rachel resents relinquishing her room to Mr. Jensen, another guest, when the inn is full, and sharing 10-year-old Rosie's digs. She abhors the monstrous oil portrait of a Scottish laird that her mother, an antiques collector, buys for the lobby. But aside from occasional irksome chores, Rachel enjoys life at the inn, reading English literature, listening to classical music, and even discussing sex with her mother. The tranquility ends, however, when a conflagration caused by faulty wiring on the old inn's landmark neon signs destroys the building. Mr. Jensen, who plans to marry Mrs. Gold, offers them his commodious home in Morristown, but Rachel and Dan, 13, who miss the bustle and bonhomie of the inn, are not placated. Rachel researches the value of the painting, ironically the only item salvaged from the fire, and finds it to be substantial enough to rebuild the inn. Mrs. Gold will still marry Mr. Jensen, but she and the family will not have to forgo their unusual lifestyle after all.

314.   Cohen, Barbara. THANK YOU, JACKIE ROBINSON. New
          York: Lothrop, Lee and Shepard, 1974. Illus. by
          Richard Cuffari. 125p. Grades 4-6. R+
          Sam, 10, lives and breathes baseball, has memorized the
record books, roots for the Brooklyn Dodgers, yet has never attended a game because his mother and three sisters do not share his enthusiasm. When elderly, black Davy becomes chef at the inn Sam's mother manages singlehandedly since his father's death three years earlier, shy Sam finally finds a friend and boon companion. Davy is a fan of the Dodgers in general and of Jackie Robinson in particular, and together they travel to as many games as time permits. When a heart attack hospitalizes Davy, Sam courageously makes the pilgrimage to Ebbets Field alone to get a ball autographed for him. But the ball isn't a powerful enough panacea to save his friend, and Sam is inconsolable at his death. He turns on the radio just as Jackie comes to bat and whispers, "Hit it for Davy," and is rewarded for his faith.

315.   Collier, James Lincoln, and Christopher Collier. JUMP SHIP

TO FREEDOM. New York: Delacorte, 1981. 198p.
Grades 5-8. R
Slaves in 1787 to a Connecticut sea captain, Daniel Arabus,
14, and his mother are hoping to buy their freedom with the soldier's
promisory notes that husband and father Jack Arabus, now dead,
earned fighting in the Revolution in his master's stead. But avaricious Captain Ivers has confiscated the papers and plans to sell
Daniel in the West Indies for being "uppity." Daringly, Daniel
steals them back and plans to jump ship at the first opportunity.
This presents itself following a devastating storm when the ship
must put in at New York for repairs. He is befriended by an ailing,
aging Quaker who is a delegate to both Congress and the Constitu-
tional Convention meeting in Philadelphia and is seeking a compromise
on the issue of slavery in order to forge a new nation. The solution is reached when Congress, meeting in New York, decides to
bar slavery north of the Ohio River in exchange for a fugitive slave
law agreeable to the South. When Mr. Fatherscreft dies en route
to Philadelphia, Daniel is sworn to deliver the message, knowing
that Captain Ivers is in hot pursuit and that the proposed legisla-
tion will enslave him forever. General Washington and William
Samuel Johnson intercede for him, and history is made.

316.   Colman, Hila. ELLIE'S INHERITANCE. New York: Morrow,
        1979. 190p. Grades 6-10. R
        Eileen Levine's parents had been poor Jewish immigrants,
but through her mother's flair for design, shrewd head for business,
and diligence, they became wealthy moguls in the garment industry,
rearing Ellie to a life of leisure and luxury (see 318). Then her
mother died when Ellie was 10, and her father, a self-described
shlemiel who had once been the dashing salesman for the enterprise,
lost their assets through poor investments. Now 18 in 1932, Ellie
is forced to abandon her rich friends, leave college, and seek
clerical employment for which she is utterly unprepared. She meets
a Communist organizer and becomes deeply embroiled in anti-Fascist
politics. Lionel wins the grudging approval of her emotional, arch-
conservative father only because he is the scion of a prosperous, influential family. Shortly before they are to be married, Lionel is
killed in the Spanish Civil War. During her mourning period, Ellie
decides to pursue a career in design and befriends an old acquaintance from their salad days, a German Jew who fled for his life,
leaving behind his family and fortune. Their budding romance survives the obstacles of Paul's pride and guilt and of Ellie's father's
objections to Paul's unpromising future.

317.   Colman, Hila. THE FAMILY TRAP. New York: Morrow,
        1982. 190p. Grades 6-10. R+
        Double tragedy has befallen the Jones family of Connecticut.
Their father has been killed in an industrial accident, and their
mother attempts suicide and is institutionalized. The two older girls
have always bickered, but with Nancy, 18, acting dutiful and officious, Becky, 15, chafes and the friction increases. To assert her

independence she takes a job as waitress at Mr. Kowalski's coffee
shop and begins dating a responsible and sympathetic boy. But
when school recesses, Nancy orders her to give up the job in order
to babysit Stacey, 9, and Becky smolders. She researches day
camp for Stacey, earning Nancy's grudging approval. Nancy, who
works for an interior decorator, starts dating David Cimino, the
young attorney who is handling their suit against their father's company. When Becky throws a party in Nancy's absence which gets
out of control, Nancy is furious and severely curtails Becky's social
life. Mr. Kowalski apprises Becky of the legal status of emancipated
minor, which seems tailor-made for her, and through David, she petitions juvenile court on her sixteenth birthday. A wrenching visit
to the hospital confirms Becky's fears that her mother will never
again function as a parent, and a bitter courtroom exchange between
the two sisters convinces the judge that Becky would be better off
living separately. A favorable settlement from their father's firm
guarantees her a small income, and Mr. Kowalski rents her a modest
apartment.

318. Colman, Hila. RACHEL'S LEGACY. New York: Morrow, 1979.
      190p. Grades 6-9. R
         Rachel Ginsberg, 12, intrepid and extroverted, is the only
member of the family who is eager to emigrate to the U.S. from Russia after Papa died of lung disease and fear of Cossacks in the early
1900s. Clever and adroit, she finds work in the garment industry
and eventually starts her own enterprise designing and manufacturing
children's dresses. A matchmaker arranges a wedding for her timid
older sister, but Rachel and her younger sister Inez believe in marrying for love. When Inez weds an Italian Catholic, intransigent
Orthodox Mama disowns her and dies shortly thereafter of tuberculosis accelerated by a broken heart. At 20 Rachel marries sincere,
suave, sophisticated Abe Levine, a fabric salesman who adores her
but who has no business acumen. Rachel continues to run the family
firm even after her daughter Ellie is born, but before long she, too,
contracts TB and dies an untimely death, secure in the knowledge
that she has provided well for her husband and child in the will
drawn by her nephew Nathan, an attorney by dint of Rachel's far-
sightedness and diligence. Seven years after her death, when
Ellie is 17, it is discovered upon Nathan's death that the will was
never executed and the assets were lost in the Depression. With
her mother's pride and fortitude, Ellie decides to lift her father and
herself out of destitution (see 316).

319. Colman, Hila. SOMETIMES I DON'T LOVE MY MOTHER. New
      York: Morrow, 1977. 190p. Grades 8-12. R+
         The Davis family revolves around their dynamic, gregarious
husband and father. His sudden death of a heart attack at 41 stuns
Dallas, 17, a recent high school graduate, and her sheltered and
introverted mother. Family friends seem to overlook Dallas' grief in
their concern for her mother, and the first sacrifice that Dallas makes
for her sake is to forgo her college plans. Instead of rising slowly

out of her despair, her mother becomes mired in it and clings to
Dallas like a drowning person, reining her in with a harness of
guilt. Dallas stands by helplessly while her mother monopolizes her
friends, including her boyfriend Victor, and at Thanksgiving her
mother makes a fool of herself over Victor's older brother. Mrs.
Davis' memories are so painful that she forces Dallas to spend
Christmas in isolation with her, and when Dallas and her friends
plan a ski trip, she insists upon going along to chaperone but acts
more like a teen. She resists Dallas' decision to take a part-time
job, and in her absence she pouts and vegetates. She even proposes that they both begin college together as roommates. Dallas
tries valiantly to be sympathetic and patient but inevitably resents
the incursions upon her youth and the right to her own life. It
takes the arrival of Mrs. Davis' domineering mother to show the
young widow that she is stifling her own daughter and to let go before she kills all love and friendship between them.

320. Conford, Ellen. LENNY KANDELL, SMART ALECK. Boston:
        Little, Brown, 1983. Illus. by Walter Gaffney-Kessell.
        120p. Grades 4-6. R+
        Since the summer of 1941, when his family vacationed in
the Catskills and a Borscht-circuit comedian caused his cautious and
reserved mother to laugh aloud, Lenny has wanted to be a stand-up
comic. Now 11 in 1946, Lenny is appreciated by his classmates for
his quips, puns and riddles but not by his superior sister Rosalind,
15, or his pragmatic mother, who, since his father's death in the
armed services, has been working at an unremunerative job. Occasionally and unintentionally rash and careless, Lenny gets in
trouble by stabbing his aunt's fur piece and tripping the school
bully, who vows his revenge. He is then faced with the problem
of raising money to repair the stole while evading Mousie Blatner,
who is reputed to have killed for a comic book. He decides upon
giving a one-man show on the roof of his Flushing apartment house.
The attendance is gratifying, but unfortunately Mousie gate crashes.
Without hesitation, Lenny leaps to the ledge of the roof and dares
his Nemesis to follow him, acting courageously in his father's memory.
The bully backs down, but when the crisis passes, Lenny learns
that his father died an ignominious, not heroic, death. Somehow it
does not matter, because he has proved something to himself and
earned the admiration of the girl he has been trying to impress.

321. Constant, Alberta Wilson. DOES ANYBODY CARE ABOUT LOU
        EMMA MILLER? New York: Crowell, 1979. 278p. Grades
        5-8. R
        Now that Papa and Miss Kate have wed (see 322) and pro-
duced a half-brother Barney, now 3, for Maddy, 14, and Lou Emma,
15, the latter is chafing under her additional responsibilities, at
being overshadowed by vivacious Maddy who has been invited to
join the debate team, and at always being taken for granted as the
"well-behaved young lady." She especially longs to be noticed
romantically by Tommy Biddle, whose father is president of Eastern

Kansas Classical College, but Tommy seems smitten by the worldly
new girl in school. When Tommy's mother Lavinia electrifies and
polarizes the town of Gloriosa by announcing her candidacy for
mayor, Lou Emma thinks she should add a plank to her platform ad-
vocating a public library, but Lavinia believes that paved streets
should come first. While Miss Kate and other progressives and suf-
fragists are preoccupied in promoting Lavinia's campaign, Lou Emma
quietly summons the nerve to approach the town's richest citizen
and ask for the use of a building for her pet cause. Her success
in achieving her goal earns headlines, donations toward a permanent
collection, and personal adulation. Lavinia opportunely endorses
Lou Emma's project and wins the election, and Tommy belatedly sees
that Lou Emma's virtues are more than skin deep. She decides
that she likes growing up after all.

322.   Constant, Alberta Wilson. THOSE MILLER GIRLS! New York:
          Crowell, 1965. (OP) Illus. by Joe and Beth Krush. 303p.
          Grades 5-6. R
          When Papa accepts the position of history professor at
Eastern Kansas Classical College in 1909, Lou Emma, 12, and Maddy,
11, persuade him that they don't need a housekeeper but can manage
on their own. Lou Emma, who takes most of the responsibility,
wishes secretly that Papa would remarry. In fact, she has already
picked out their stepmother, the attractive new milliner in town.
Miss Kate saves the day when Papa forgets until the last minute
about the obligatory reception staged annually by the college
president's wife, connives with the girls to keep a pet goat over
Papa's objections, devises a scheme to make a telescope for the college so Papa can teach astronomy, and shares in family frolic, triumph and ignominy at the Chautauqua held by the river that summer. Logical Papa doesn't appreciate what an enduring jewel Miss
Kate is until his maiden sister visits, but he quickly amends past
oversight, and Miss Kate gets a ready-made, not secondhand,
family.

323.   Corbin, William. SMOKE. New York: Coward-McCann, 1967.
          (OP) 253p. Grades 6-8. R
          Chris Long's father swept his mother off her feet and mar-
ried her, but when John Long died three years ago, her childhood
sweetheart, Cal Finch, who had remained a bachelor, left his own
prosperous ranch and returned to Oregon to woo and wed her.
Chris, 14, bears icy ill will toward the benevolent despot who has
supplanted his easygoing father, and he retreats to his treehouse
perch in the forest above the ranch. There he finds a feral German
shepherd, starving and riddled with parasites, and tames him with
pilfered food. But he soon realizes that the dog's advanced malnutrition will be deadly unless he seeks professional help, and it is
only then that he acknowledges his perfidy in harboring a predatory
pet on a sheep ranch. Cal surprises him by not only assisting in
restoring Smoke to health, but permitting Chris to keep him provided that his former owner does not claim him. Against his hopes,

the owner answers their advertisement, but when Chris' mom tries
to assuage his disappointment with the promise of another dog,
Chris blurts out his pent-up hostility towards Cal by telling her
that Smoke can't be replaced the way she replaced his father. He
absconds into the mountains with Smoke, and Cal wisely refrains
from sending the authorities to locate him. In the throes of a rite
of passage into manhood, Chris decides on his own to return, make
peace with Cal and call him "Pop" as his sister Susie, 11, does.

324. Corcoran, Barbara. THE PERSON IN THE POTTING SHED.
        New York: Atheneum, 1980. 121p. Grades 5-8. R
        While Dorothy and Franklin attend boarding schools in
New England, their mother spends a year in England recovering
from deep depression resulting from her husband's death in an auto
accident there. Then she marries Englishman Ian Staniford-Jones
and arranges to meet the children in New Orleans, where Ian will
be teaching architecture at Tulane. The children's first encounter
with their stepfather is strained and inauspicious. They rent a
rundown but historic plantation from diffident Eva DuPre who, with
her half-brother, resides in a more recent addition. Exploring the
eerie environs, the children meet Eva's dour maid, a drunken old
gardener, a mad crone, and a friendly black teen. Then the gardener disappears, and the children suspect foul play. Snooping
about, they locate his body buried in a snake-infested field, but by
the time Ian summons the gendarmerie someone has removed it. Ian,
furious, decides that the children are deliberately trying to make a
fool of him by inventing the corpse. They continue to try to solve
the mystery in spite of Ian's hostility, knowing that someone is
watchfully trying to thwart them. When they finally locate an
elusive clue and find themselves in deadly peril, Ian rushes to
their defense. After learning the muddled history of the DuPre
family, Ian apologizes for his mistrust, and Dorothy and Franklin
begin to appreciate his good qualities.

325. Corcoran, Barbara. SASHA, MY FRIEND. New York:
        Atheneum, 1969. Illus. by Richard L. Shell. Grades 7-8.
        R+
        In the plane crash that claimed his wife's life, Hallie's
father sustained lung damage. On his doctor's advice he and Hallie,
15, leave their amenable home, friends, and the accoutrements of
civilization in smoggy Los Angeles and move to a tiny trailer without
plumbing or electricity on the Christmas tree farm in the Montana
wilderness where he grew up. Miles from the nearest settlement,
their only neighbors are an old Indian and a frontier family with a
vicious son and a crippled daughter who becomes Hallie's only
friend. She strives unsuccessfully to cope with the solitude, danger,
inconvenience, and rigor of a wilderness winter until she finds the
orphaned wolf cub, Sasha, who puts meaning back into her life.
Sasha saves her life one day when Hallie is attacked by a wounded
lynx, but she is unable to save his when the spiteful neighbor boy
sees him as a menace and lays a trap for him. The cub's death

plunges her back into despair. She reacts with plucky resolve, however, when her father contracts pneumonia on the eve of the Christmas tree harvest, and she discovers how supportive and interde-
pendent the denizens of the northern woods must be. Boarding in
the nearest town solves Hallie's correspondence school problem, and
she will see her father on weekends.

326. Dahl, Roald. DANNY THE CHAMPION OF THE WORLD. New
         York: Knopf, 1975. Illus. by Jill Bennett. 196p. Grades
         4-6. R+
         Danny's mother died when he was an infant, and the boy
was reared happily if somewhat unconventionally in a gypsy-style
encampment behind his father's small country filling station and
garage. Only when he is 9 is his father's peculiar proclivity for
poaching pheasants from the forest preserves of Squire Hazel revealed, a hobby shared by the vicar, the doctor, and the constable.
Each has his own method of snaring the prize fowl, and Danny is
soon inducted into the intricacies of the sport. After rescuing his
injured father from the gamekeeper's diabolical trap, Danny becomes
world champion poacher, employing his wit and a product of modern
medical science, and comically spoiling choleric Mr. Hazel's posh annual turkeyshoot.

327. Daringer, Helen F. STEPSISTER SALLY. New York: Har-
         court, Brace, Jovanovich, 1966. Illus. by Garrett Price.
         160p. Grades 3-7. NR
         Salubrious Sally has lived all her young life since her
mother's death in her grandmother's small-town home with infrequent
visits from her father, a hardware dealer who remained in the city.
Father has remarried and acquired a built-in family and now wants
Sally to join them, uprooting her from her secure and complacent
life with Gran. Sally combines the patience of Job with the wisdom
of Solomon in eventually earning the acceptance of her fractious
stepsister Dorothy without much assistance from her unintentionally
vacuous, equivocating father. Her new brothers and stepmother respond more sympathetically.

328. Davis, Gibbs. FISHMAN AND CHARLY. Boston: Houghton
         Mifflin, 1983. 166p. Grades 5-8. R+
         To compensate for the frigidity of their father, a colonel
and instructor at a Florida military academy, Charlene Hawkins, 16,
has been ministering to Tyler, 11, since the death of their mother
in a sailing accident four years before. Tyler, who tries pathetically
to please his stiff and exacting father, has his own defense mechanism
for rejection and antidote for bereavement: his pet fish. In addition to the aquarium he keeps in his room, he and his wealthy friend
Byron have tamed one of the ponderous, defenseless manatee sea cows
that inhabit the bay and named it Piety. Byron's uncle is campaign-
ing to have the manatee declared an endangered species to save them
from poachers and malicious speedboaters. When Tyler introduces
his sister Charly to Byron, he doesn't count on their falling in love

and neglecting him, and when Piety's calf is wantonly slaughtered
Tyler feels bereft. He overhears Byron tell Charly that she is
overprotective of him, galvanizing him into seeking the attention
and approbation he craves from his father by swimming the mile to
Macaroon Island. When he begins to founder, Piety telepathically
appears to buoy him up, and he reaches the island where he inadvertently flushes the poachers, becoming an overnight hero to
everyone but his obtuse and insensible father. While searching for
his father's soul, Tyler basks in the paternal warmth of Byron's
cosmopolitan uncle.

329. DeAngeli, Marguerite. THE LION IN THE BOX. Garden City:
          Doubleday, 1975. Illus. by the author. 63p. Grades 3-5.
          R
          Papa is in the "Great Beyond" and Mama works night to
make ends meet for her brood of five in New York City at the turn
of the century. Christmas is approaching, and Lili, 7, longs for a
doll to replace her makeshift folded tea towel doll, but her hopes are
not high. Mama sets them to work making paper ornaments for their
donated Christmas tree, reminiscing all the while of her girlhood in
Austria and of the events that have occurred to them as a family.
On Christmas Eve while Mama is gone, a deliveryman brings a huge
box that he warns contains a lion. When Mama opens it on Christmas
Day, the wonderful carton disgorges treasures for them all, including
dolls for Betsy, 11, and Rosie, 9, clothing and toys for Ben, 5, and
Sooch, 1, and at the very bottom a beautiful Chinese doll for Lili,
all gifts from a chance acquaintance.

330. Derman, Martha. AND PHILIPPA MAKES FOUR. New York:
          Four Winds, 1983. 150p. Grades 5-6. R+
          Though still disturbed by dreams of the auto accident in
which her mother was killed, Philippa Catlett, 11, is content living
with her architect father and paternal grandparents. A minor
irritation--the arrival of a new girl, a pretty platinum blonde who
captures the role Philippa covets in the class play--becomes a per-
vasive problem when she discovers that Libby Barber's mother is a
new partner in her father's firm. Philippa is expected to be a one-
person welcoming committee to Libby while her dad and Libby's mom,
a divorcee, start acting very chummy. Resentfully, Philippa goes
out of her way to be nasty and inhospitable to Libby and is banished
from the Barber's house. She feels like an outsider because of her
father's intimacy with the Barbers. Philippa's worst fears are
realized when her dad announces that Mrs. Barber is going to become a mother to her when the four of them move into a remodeled
apartment above the office. She makes peace with Libby, but the
two are ostracized by most of their former friends because of the
small-town attitude toward cohabitation. To compensate, the adults
plan a family outing at the ice-skating rink. Libby, an accomplished
skater, welcomes the opportunity to show off, but clumsy Philippa is
less than enthusiastic until her father and Mrs. Barber clasp her
between them for a three-way skate, and she feels comfortable and
secure at last.

331. Duncan, Lois. DOWN A DARK HALL. Boston: Little, Brown,
        1974. 181p. Grades 6-8. NR
        The night her father died seven years ago, Kit, now 14,
saw him standing by her bed, but everyone insisted she had been
dreaming. Now her mother has just remarried, and while she and
her new husband are honeymooning in Europe, Kit is parked at an
exclusive boarding school run by a mysterious French woman and
her son in a secluded, foreboding mansion. The four students have
nothing in common but ESP and soon begin experiencing oppressive
dreams and composing masterful poetry, paintings, music, and
mathematical formulae far beyond their capacities. When they realize
what is controlling their minds and the insidious consequences, they
struggle to break the grasp but recognize that they are powerless
prisoners of the evil headmistress. Pitting their wills against hers,
they succeed in exorcising the spirits who, in a fit of pique, destroy
Blackwood Mansion. Kit almost loses her life when she saves another
girl and is rescued herself by her father's protective spirit.

332. Duncan, Lois. LOCKED IN TIME. Boston: Little, Brown,
        1985. 210p. Grades 6-10. NR
        Nore Robbins, 17, senses something sinister about her
waxenly beautiful stepmother, Lisette Berge, the moment she enters
her exotic and secluded plantation house in Louisiana fresh from
boarding school in New England, where she has lived since her
mother's death in an auto accident a year earlier. Her attractive
stepbrother Gabe, 17, and his adolescent sister Josie, 13, seem normal and friendly until Gabe deliberately leaves her to drown on a
river expedition. Lisette subsequently drugs Nore, but when the
frightened girl tries to articulate her fears to her novelist father,
he dismisses her accusations as rude and childish backlashes at his
remarriage. Nore then launches an investigation of the mysterious
Berges, blocked at every turn by the watchful Lisette. The awesome secret that she finally unearths of their eternal youth and
Lisette's need to prey upon a new and unsuspecting husband every
generation seals her own fate. She is spared from immolation on her
own funeral pyre by an unlikely source in the ironic denouement of
this chilling fantasy.

333. Dunn, Mary Lois. THE MAN IN THE BOX: A STORY FROM
        VIETNAM. New York: McGraw-Hill, 1968. (OP) 155p.
        Grades 5-8. R
        His father, chief of the Montagnard village, died in the
cruel bamboo cage, confined and tortured by the Viet Cong. Long
empty, the symbolic box has remained in the village as a deterrent
to other South Vietnam sympathizers. Now it is filled again with a
tall and grotesquely contorted naked white man. Chau Li knows he
must avenge his father's spirit by somehow releasing the defenseless
American so that he can at least die with dignity. He knows that in
doing so, even if he lives, he will never be able to return to the
family for whom he provides, for they must disavow him in order to
survive themselves. By sampan he spirits the broken body of the

man he calls Dah Vid to a cave in which provisions were left by the
retreating French soldiers. Viable morphine ampoules ease the man's
pain. Chau Li develops a deep affection for the big, gentle warrior
who wants to adopt him if they manage to escape. Alone, armed
only with resourcefulness, cunning and courage, Chau Li must tra-
verse the sabotaged jungle trails teeming with pursuing Cong to seek
help for David, whose feet were smashed to prevent his escape. Finally he reunites David with his fellow Green Berets, and the injured
man is airlifted through hostile fire to safety. But in the savage
melee the two are separated, the other Americans are killed, and
Chau Li stoically presses on alone for Da Nang.

334. Enright, Elizabeth. THE FOUR-STORY MISTAKE. New York:
        Holt, Rinehart and Winston, 1942. (OP) Illus. by the
        author. 177p. Grades 5-7. R+
        Nostalgia for their comfortable old city house is swept away
by delight in their new/old country home, an architect's nightmare,
but as unique as the four Melendy children, their father, Cuffy,
Willy, and Isaac the dog (see 335). Exploring the brook and woods
by bicycle and ice skates, gifts from Mrs. Oliphant, provides hours
of winter diversion, but it is the cupola and concealed room with its
unfolding mystery of the girl who once occupied it that really in-
trigues the children. A Christmas talent show leads to a radio acting job for Mona, and Rush teaches piano lessons to buy Defense
Bonds. Randy makes her contribution by spying a real diamond in
the brook, and Oliver discovers a treasure trove in the cellar.

335. Enright, Elizabeth. THE SATURDAYS. New York: Holt,
        Rinehart and Winston, 1941. (OP) Illus. by the author.
        175p. Grades 5-7. R+
        The motherless Melendy menage is managed efficiently and
benevolently by housekeeper Cuffy, handyman Willy, and Father, a
busy professor of economics. Bored with dreary Saturdays in their
aging and temperamental New York brownstone and cramped by
meager allowances, the four resourceful and independent children
decide to pool their assets so that each one can have a memorable
experience of his choice every fourth Saturday. Stagestruck Mona,
13, electrifies the family with a glamorous coiffure and manicure;
musical Rush, 12, chooses an opera at Carnegie Hall; artistic Randy,
10, opts for an art exhibit; while Oliver, 6, naturally gravitates
toward the circus. All get more than they bargained for. Among
their adventures they acquire a dog and strike up a new rapport
with an old friend, Mrs. Oliphant, who offers them an idyllic summer
vacation in her very own lighthouse after an accidental fire in the
attic makes a shambles of their stuffy city house.

336. Enright, Elizabeth. SPIDERWEB FOR TWO: A MELENDY
        MAZE. New York: Holt, Rinehart and Winston, 1951.
        (OP) 209p. Grades 5-7. R
        The school year looms interminable to Oliver and Randy,
the two youngest Melendys (see 335, 334, 337) who are suffering

from ennui as their older brothers and sister go away to school and
Father returns to the lecture circuit. A trip to the mailbox produces
a surprise message in the form of a rhyming riddle directing them to
the next clue in a treasure hunt that they soon surmise will last all
year. One verse points to another that grows progressively more
difficult to decipher, leading them by trial and error, wit and hunch
into intriguing and sometimes hazardous situations. They speculate
on the author of the riddles but discover the secret only at the end
of the rainbow trail, along with a special pot of gold from Mrs.
Oliphant.

337.   Enright, Elizabeth. THEN THERE WERE FIVE. New York:
            Holt, Rinehart and Winston, 1944. (OP) Illus. by the
            author. 241p. Grades 5-8. R
            It is summer vacation at the Four-Story Mistake (see 335
and 334) and Father is absent for long periods supporting the war
effort in Washington. The precocious, imaginative and versatile
Melendy children dam the brook to create a swimming pool, conduct
a scrap drive, befriend Mark, an orphan neighbor living with his
malicious second cousin, and with him share the adventures of
swimming in an old quarry, searching for Indian arrowheads, and
spelunking. When his cousin dies violently, the Melendys joyously
and officially adopt Mark, and they cap the summer by staging a
Children's Fair for charity.

338.   Estes, Eleanor. THE MIDDLE MOFFAT. New York: Har-
            court, Brace and World, 1942. Illus. by Louis Slobodkin.
            317p. Grades 4-6. R+
            The self-proclaimed "mysterious middle Moffat," shy, sen-
sitive Jane, concocts her own cures for the middle-child syndrome
(see 340). Blind faith and the luck o' the Irish help her muddle
through them triumphantly. Her chief mission is to preserve the
health of Cranbury's Oldest Inhabitant in anticipation of the spry
and spirited Fellow's hundredth birthday. An organ recital and a
play at the Town Hall are redeemed from the brink of disaster by
spectacular quirks of fate, and when she ventures into basketball
she is simply phenomenal! Together with her best friend Nancy,
as gregarious and vivacious as Janey is bashful, she witnesses a
solar eclipse and bathes stray dogs. The centenary birthday celebration inadvertently showers honor and glory on the modest Moffats
through Jane.

339.   Estes, Eleanor. THE MOFFAT MUSEUM. San Diego: Harcourt,
            Brace, Jovanovich, 1983. Illus. by the author. 262p.
            Grades 4-6. R+
            It is imaginative, ingenuous Jane who conceives the idea of
transforming the old barn on Ashbellow Place into a repository for
Moffat memorabilia (see 340, 338, 341). As it is the only museum in
Cranbury (pop. 3,000 in 1919), it becomes a highlight on the annual
tour of the town led by superintendent of schools Mr. Pennypacker.
The piece de resistance is the wax figure of solemn, earnest Rufus,

who models a paraffin mask while giving a good impression of a
statue as the students file by. Her office as flower girl at the
wedding of sweet, diaphanous Sylvie to the Rev. Ray Abbot inspires
Jane to gather all the loose rose petals along the block and have
Rufus rain them upon the radiant bride from the church balcony,
creating a fragrant and romantic spectacle. Jane holds a rehearsal
to allay her apprehensions over her first solo train trip, but when
things go awry she acts coolly and is rewarded with an exciting
ride in a handcar. Rufus and stolid, industrious Joey seize the opportunity to buy for one dollar the antique streetcar they have long
admired in the depths of the carbarn, only to learn that someone
has been having sport with them. After participating in the traditional ritual of casting straw hats in the ocean on Labor Day, Joey,
now 16, must drop out of school to become chief breadwinner and
start a correspondence course in draftsmanship. Rufus becomes a
Saturday Evening Post carrier, and Jane closes the Moffat Museum.

340.   Estes, Eleanor. THE MOFFATS. New York: Harcourt, Brace
          and World, 1941. Illus. by Louis Slobodkin. 290p. Grades
          4-6. R+
       The yellow house on New Dollar Street in Cranbury, Connec-
ticut, lies under the shadow of a For Sale sign, but the inimitable
Moffats, Sylvie, 15, Joe, 12, Jane, 9, Rufus, 5, and their seamstress
mother make the best of it. Commonplace occurrences such as Rufus'
first day of school, a saunter to Sunday school, and a junket to the
beach assume an aura of adventure. Together they hatch a Halloween plot that thoroughly rattles the neighborhood bully. The boredom of quarantine (and another ominous sign on the house) when
Rufus contracts scarlet fever is relieved by Mama's entrancing tales
of her childhood in New York. The hovering specter of privation
during that grim winter fades into the background with the onset of
spring, and the family moves into their tiny new house with the
promise of a best friend for Jane.

341.   Estes, Eleanor. RUFUS M. New York: Harcourt, Brace and
          World, 1943. Illus. by Louis Slobodkin. 320p. Grades
          4-8. R+
       The country is in the throes of World War, and the town
of Cranbury is contributing its share. The youngest Moffat, Rufus,
7, (see 340 and 338) knits a somewhat grimy and ungainly washcloth
for one of the boys in the trenches (and receives a treasured card
of thanks clear from France), plants an eminently successful Victory
Garden of green beans, and helps the rest of the intense and energetic Moffats make and market popcorn for Victory Buttons. But
there's time for diversion as well: Rufus' awed encounter with a
player piano, a bittersweet Fourth of July, a spooky adventure at
a deserted, fog-shrouded amusement park, an abortive attempt at
ventriloquy, and a spectacular softball game of just one inning in
which he saves his sister's team from disgrace. Rufus becomes the
family hero on a bitter winter night when the water pipe bursts by
propitiously producing the money to pay the plumber, buy more
fuel, and provide supper all around.

342. Fanning, Robbie. ONE HUNDRED BUTTERFLIES. Philadelphia:
        Westminster, 1979. 187p. Grades 6-7. R+
        Following her father's death of Hodgkin's disease at age 52,
Ristyn Anne Ward, 13, is sent to spend the summer with her maternal
grandmother in New York's Thousand Islands. Grandma Lee is blunt,
gruff, tough and mean, but she affords Risty the freedom to come
and go as she pleases among the resort habitues. Risty, who dis-
passionately tells herself that life is for the living and each moment
should be lived to the fullest, revels in the flattering, flirtatious
attention of the teenage males and their sophomoric escapades while
partying, picnicking, boating and water skiing. Then her devilish
bon vivant older cousin Shawn Lee blows in, captivating both Risty
and Grandma Lee. Despite his jocularity, Shawn Lee is practical and
perspicacious enough to recognize that Risty is bottling her emotions
over her father's death and sagely helps her release them. Risty
has been dreading the school assignment of collecting 100 butterflies
during vacation because it would mean depriving them arbitrarily of
life. Shawn Lee suggests that she photograph them instead, and
when he departs Risty is devastated. When she learns that beneath
her grandmother's bluff facade she is truly caring and concerned,
Risty strikes a truce.

343. Farley, Carol. THE GARDEN IS DOING FINE. New York:
        Atheneum, 1975. Illus. by Lynn Sweat. 185p. Grades
        6-9. R+
        Corrie's generous, impetuous, imaginative, and beloved
father is dying of cancer at the close of World War II. He is like
the frivolous flower in his cherished garden, while her sensible,
pragmatic mother is akin to the prosaic but vital vegetable. Corrie,
14, rails against a capricious fate that would pluck the bloom of such
a kind and beautiful soul while sparing others less deserving and
appreciative of life. She lights prayer candles for intercession at a
Catholic church, reasoning that prayers that cost money are bound
to be more efficacious than free Protestant ones. She experiences
pangs of guilt on recognizing her annoyance that his lingering illness is disturbing her social life. Her mother and an elderly neighbor help her to realize that a part of him has been perpetuated in
her and her brothers, and that as long as they remember him and
speak of his memory, he will live on. The physical garden may die,
but the symbolic garden has been sown with strong seed, nurtured
with love and integrity, and weeded of malice, pettiness and dis-
content.

344. Feagles, Anita MacRae. THE YEAR THE DREAMS CAME BACK.
        New York: Atheneum, 1976. 146p. Grades 7-9. R+
        In the year since her mother's psychosis-induced suicide,
Nell Carpenter, 13, and her freelance artist father have been leading
an unstructured, mutually tolerant existence, treading lightly on
emotional eggshells. Their placid, casual lifestyle is interrupted only
by the frequent, officious visits of Nell's fastidious maternal grandmother, whose flaying criticism nettles them both. Then Gordie, a

neighbor boy two years older than Nell, re-enters her life and fills
a gulf created when she and her childhood chums start maturing at
different paces and in divergent directions. At the same time, Amy
Traynor appears, a sensible, sympathetic and companionable woman
who has just opened a bookstore in their small New England town
and who dovetails comfortably into their little family. They even
vacation together, and Nell's father is palpably more relaxed and
youthful. Nell is unaccountably horrified, however, when her
father announces that he and Amy plan to marry. She runs back to
the borrowed Connecticut vacation house, accompanied by Gordie who
is concerned for her welfare. In the isolation of the old farmhouse,
she assesses her emotions and realizes that subconsciously she is
afraid of losing another mother to mental illness. When Amy and her
father catch up with them, Amy explains that Nell was not responsible for her mother's chronic depression, and at long last Nell's recurring nightmares are replaced by the pleasant dreams she used to
have.

345. Fenton, Edward. DUFFY'S ROCKS. New York: Dutton, 1974.
      (OP) 198p. Grades 5-8. R
      Gran Brennan reared Timothy's father so permissively that
he grew up to be wild, restive and irresponsible, stirred with the
wanderlust that brought him to visit his motherless son, now 13, only
once when the boy was 6. Gran is determined not to make the same
mistake with Tim, who loves her in spite of her severity that forbids
him friends outside of their dingy milltown suburb of Pittsburgh during the Great Depression. But Tim is longing to know this magnetic,
enigmatic man who is his father. By stealth, he finds Bart Brennan's
last known address, already two years old, among his grandmother's
personal effects. Boarding a bus to New York, he traces Bart to a
dead end, gaining insight into his character from two kind women he
has discarded. Returning home, he discovers his grandmother on the
brink of death, waiting to succumb only to extract Tim's promise not
to follow in his father's footsteps, a pledge easily vowed.

346. Fenton, Edward. THE REFUGEE SUMMER. New York: Dela-
      corte, 1982. 261p. Grades 6-8. NR
      Greece is at war with Turkey in 1922, and Nikolas Angeliki,
12, gets a realistic, firsthand view of what army life must have been
like for his dead father when he is asked to read aloud the journal
of a fellow fallen comrade to his unlettered widow. When two American children whose author father has rented the villa where Nikolas'
mother, a seamstress, is caretaker, he is flattered that they demo-
cratically treat him as an equal. Together with the French girls at
the neighboring villa whose mother is an aspiring opera singer kept
by a succession of wealthy "uncles," they form a secret society, the
Pallikars, for doing good deeds. While Nikolas enthusiastically enters
into their games, he realizes that from their remote plane they cannot
conceive of the real poverty of the Greek peasant, just as their
parents' peers, the military and political establishment to whom the
meaning of the war is a noble, idealistic abstraction, are out of touch

154 The Single-Parent Family

with the suffering, grieving masses they manipulate to fight for
them. The Pallikars' first object of charity misunderstands their
motives, but when millions of Greeks are evacuated from Asia Minor
after a defeat at Smyrna, they have the opportunity to be true
benefactors to three young refugee children. The group disbands
at the end of the summer, but Nikolas keeps their pact and remembers it fifty years later.

347. First, Julia. MOVE OVER, BEETHOVEN. New York: Watts,
1978. (OP) 121p. Grades 6-8. R
On their first day in seventh grade, Gina Barlow's friends
enthusiastically sign up for several of the plethora of extracurricular
activities available at their Boston junior high, but Gina must eschew
all outside interests because of her rigorous piano practicing
schedule. Her mother, who has operated a health spa since her husband's death five years earlier, is sacrificing to buy Gina the baby
grand her teacher insists she needs to fulfill her potential and Gina,
torn between her love of the instrument and her desire for social
affairs, feels obligated not to disappoint her mother. She meets a
remarkably well-rounded eighth grade boy who seems able to juggle
all his diverse avocations with impunity, and Gina is persuaded to
begin a dual life, skimping on her practice time to participate in the
school orchestra without her mother's knowledge. Still unilaterally
planning Gina's career, her mother decides to sell her business and
move to New York to enroll Gina in a special school, and Gina is
finally impelled to confess her duplicity and her need for greater ver-
satility and choice in her life. She and her new friend, Joshua, learn
to make intelligent compromises, and Mrs. Barlow astonishes Gina by
acquiescing.

348. Fleming, Susan. TRAPPED ON THE GOLDEN FLYER. Philadelphia: Westminster, 1978. Illus. by Alex Stein. 123p.
Grades 4-6. NR
Six weeks after Paul's mother's death from cancer shortly
before Christmas, his father, a Chicago policeman, decides it is un-
safe for the boy to stay alone after school in their apartment and
entrains him for California to live with his maternal aunt and uncle.
Already nervous about the long solo train trip and keeping his emotions tightly reined because of the kindly but garrulous grandmother
who is his seatmate, Paul is uneasy when the Flyer suddenly stops,
only hours from its destination, in a blinding blizzard high in the
Sierra Nevada. Reassured by a seasoned traveler that rotary plows
are on the way to dig them out of the snowslide, Paul makes friends
with a girl his age who is traveling with her mother and baby sister. Agonizing hours later they learn that the plows have become
trapped, the train is out of fuel, food is exhausted, the relief train
cannot get through, a gas leak has rendered the emergency
heaters unserviceable, and the banking snow makes the cars even
more frigid. Paul saves the day for Kathy's baby sister by
bringing out the powdered milk his father packed and scrounging

makeshift fuel to melt snow to mix it with. Their rescue three days
later breaks the bond that united the disparate passengers in their
common emergency, but Paul finds that his worries about being met
in Oakland are groundless.

349. Flory, Jane. THE GOLDEN VENTURE. Boston: Houghton
        Mifflin, 1976. 232p. Grades 5-6. R
        Minnie Welden, 11, stows away on her father's wagon as he
follows the Forty-niners to California to make his fortune and establish his independence from his spinster sister so that he can remarry.
He leaves Minnie in the care of respectable Mrs. Stanhope in the
brawling shanty town of San Francisco. An independent, enterprising young school teacher, sans school, joins their menage and organizes a bakery in Mr. Haywood's Emporium and a laundry at the
Stanhopes' house. The cash accrues, but a gang of felons, the
Sydney Ducks, rapaciously pursue it. When Mr. Haywood is burned
out, they all retrench in a berthed cargo ship abandoned by captain
and crew, and there Minnie's father finds them, having lost his
hoardings and his health in the gold fields. Minnie and Miss Daisy,
the schoolmarm, nurse him back to health, and together they put the
Ducks to rout. Daisy and Mr. Welden decide to continue their reform campaign as husband and wife.

350. Foley, June. IT'S NO CRUSH, I'M IN LOVE! New York:
        Delacorte, 1972. 215p. Grades 6-9. R+
        Annie Cassidy, 14, is the antithesis of her three fractious
younger sisters. Like her father who died two years ago in an auto
accident, Annie is imaginative and loves to read. Her new high
school teacher calls her "a young woman after my own heart," and
immediately Annie envisions herself playing Elizabeth Bennet to David
Angelucci's Mr. Darcy from her favorite novel, PRIDE AND PREJU-
DICE. Mr. Angelucci encourages her to join the staff of the school
newspaper, but she doesn't hit it off with the editor, Robby Pols.
Her mother, moreover, formerly the perfect and prosaic housewife,
takes a secretarial post and expects Annie to babysit. Annie and
her best friend spend all their spare time spying on Mr. Angelucci,
who spends most of his spare time in the library writing his doctoral
dissertation. Annie volunteers to be his research assistant and endures the long, arduous hours anticipating the moment when he will
declare his love for her. She forgoes a date with Robby to the
school dance to be with Mr. Angelucci, only to discover to her chagrin that he is one of the chaperones and is taking another date.
Her mother, returning from her own first date, senses Annie's an-
guish and confides her own heartbreak after her husband's death
and how proud he would be of both of them. Annie belatedly recognizes Robby's assets and realizes that no one is perfect, least of all
David Angelucci.

351. Fox, Paula. A PLACE APART. New York: Farrar, Straus,
        Giroux, 1980. 184p. Grades 7-10. R+
        Financially unable to remain in Boston after the fatal heart

attack of her husband, a high school principal, Mrs. Finch moves
with her daughter Victoria, 13, to the exurb of New Oxford after
the cremation. Lonely and lost as she starts her freshman year in
a new school, Tory is lured by the friendship of a junior, Hugh
Todd, who is a moody, supercilious, mesmeric perfectionist, disliked
by the other students. Hugh cajoles her into developing a play from
the scenes she has written about her father's death, but when the
project becomes too onerous for her and she abandons it in her
sophomore year, Hugh unceremoniously discards her. Her mother,
meanwhile, has met a man she wants to marry, towards whom Tory
is antagonistic. Her best friend Elizabeth has started dating, causing
Tory further discomfiture. She is empathetically drawn to a new boy
as vulnerable as herself, who has been publicly humiliated both by
Hugh and by Elizabeth's boyfriend. Still carrying a torch for the
treacherous Hugh, Tory is unenthusiastic about returning to Boston
with her mother and Lawrence who are about to wed, but Hugh
moves away and Tory puts their chance encounter behind her.

352. Fox, Paula. PORTRAIT OF IVAN. Englewood Cliffs, N.J.:
       Bradbury, 1969. Illus. by Saul Lambert. 131p. Grades
       5-7. R+
       Scores of photographs of Ivan, 11, adorn the home where
he lives alone with his father, a busy executive and camera buff,
but curiously Ivan has never seen a picture of his mother, who died
when he was a baby. He is obsessed with the need to know more
about his antecedents. All he knows of his mother is that she es-
caped her native Russia at the age of 3 in a horse-drawn sledge.
When he goes to a painter's studio to sit for his portrait, he meets
for the first time imaginative adults who take time to talk to a little
boy and read aloud to him. His father permits him to accompany the
painter and his friend to Florida with the admonition to take plenty
of pictures. There he meets a girl who introduces him to a wonderful outdoor world of boating, swimming, and tropical wildlife. He
takes no photos, but his finished portrait captures his personality
better than any camera. Best of all is the painter's gift, a sketch
depicting his mother's escape party aboard the troika, their faces
modeled by his new friends, thus linking past with present.

353. Fox, Paula. THE SLAVE DANCER. Scarsdale: Bradbury,
       1973. Illus. by Eros Keith. 176p. Grades 5-8. R
       On an errand for his mother, a New Orleans dressmaker,
Jessie, 13, is hijacked, along with his fife, and carried aboard a
slave ship bound for the coast of Africa. His duties are to kill rats,
empty latrine buckets, and pipe music to which the human cargo
exercises. Limber, muscular blacks commanded a better price in
1840 than flaccid ones. On the outbound voyage he is inducted into
the brutality and inhumanity of the captain and crew, but nothing
prepares him for the horrors of the homebound trip. As the con-
signment is about to be sold to Spaniards in Cuba, the ship is
seized by American authorities. In the captain's frenzy to destroy
the evidence, the slaves are all thrown to the sharks. Jessie and

one boy cower in the noisome hold as a storm administers the wages
of sin to vessel and crew. Shipwrecked off the U.S. coast, Jessie
finally plies his way home and the boy to safety in the North.

354. Franco, Marjorie. SO WHO HASN'T GOT PROBLEMS. Boston:
        Houghton Mifflin, 1979. 153p. Grades 6-8. R
        The three friends, all 13, meet on the steps of the Catholic
school in their Chicago neighborhood to watch the new people move
in. Jennifer Davis' father is dead; Dorothy, whose parents are divorced, doesn't get along with her stepfather; while Myra, an only
child in a two-parent family, appears to have no problems at all.
The new girl, Angela, also 13, is aloof and claims to be rich, causing
a rift among them. Myra toadies to Angela and reneges on her invitation to Jennifer to vacation with her, asking Angela instead. Another classmate, Eddie, fills the void and disappointment in Jennifer's
summer by prevailing upon her to decorate his basement walls with a
mural of the city skyline, a project with which Dorothy helps. Eddie becomes Jennifer's first romantic interest, but to their dismay,
Eddie's family announces that they are moving to New York. Jennifer
learns that Angela has lied about her wealth but to her credit does
not divulge the truth to Myra. Dorothy's situation at home, meanwhile, deteriorates, and she wants to run away to join her father in
New York. Jennifer, suddenly faced with the prospect of losing all
her lifelong friends, persuades Dorothy to return home. Dorothy's
father responds by inviting both girls to visit him. There they join
forces with Eddie and have a grand time. Back home they make
peace with Myra and Angela, and the four gather on the school
steps to watch the moving van arriving at Eddie's old house.

355. Gardam, Jane. THE SUMMER AFTER THE FUNERAL. New
        York: Macmillan, 1973. (OP) 151p. Grades 8-10. R
        Mrs. Price, loquacious young widow of the elderly charis-
matic rector, is unconsciously manipulative of her acquaintances.
Energetically and egocentrically she interprets appearances to suit
her own ends and sails along totally oblivious to the divergent needs
of her three children. On the summer after the funeral, while she
seeks a suitable domicile to replace the rectory which they must soon
vacate, she farms out introspective Sebastian, 18, to a monastery
and phlegmatic Phoebe, 12, to a boisterous sailing family. But
dreamy Athene, 16, a classical beauty who thinks she may be the
reincarnation of Emily Brontë, is shunted off to a series of depres-
sing maiden ladies. At the home of the second of these, she is
affronted by the woman's drunken female companion and runs away.
A sheltered and timid girl, she finds the experience of camping out
and dealing with strangers to be psychologically traumatizing. Along
the way she falls in love with an older married man (a la JANE
EYRE) and visits the Brontë home. When her absence is discovered,
she is found up on the roof of the old rectory from which she seems
to make a suicide leap. The deed is averted, but Mrs. Price remains
blissfully ignorant of her daughter's emotional crisis. Tolerantly,
Athene elects to remain with her mother instead of going off to boarding school.

356. Garden, Nancy. FOURS CROSSING. New York: Farrar,
        Straus, Giroux, 1981. 198p. Grades 6-8. NR
          Most of the inhabitants of the small, rural, historic town
of Fours Crossing, New Hampshire, have roots dating back to colonial
times, including Gran, with whom Melissa Dunn, 13, has come to live
since her mother's death of cancer and while her father, an itinerant
fundraiser, is away. Though the calendar indicates it is spring, the
countryside remains in the grip of the most draconian winter in
memory. The annual Spring Festival that has its origins in ancient
pagan rites loses its air of frivolity. At the hut of a mysterious,
misanthropic hermit, Melissa and Jed, her only friend and equally
lonely son of an alcoholic widower, make a connection between the
perpetual chill, the recluse, and Gran's stolen antique silver plate,
engraved with strange runes. Library research about the year 1725
proves their supposition. In an attempt by Melissa and Jed to recover the plate from old Eli, he surprises them and imprisons them
in a cave. They realize then that the crazed curmudgeon believes
himself to be a priest and guardian of the Old Ways and mistakes
them for his betrayers. A concerted effort by the pair's fathers
rescues them. The two fathers promise to do better by their
children, and spring comes at last to the village. Further chilling,
supernatural adventures await Melissa in WATERSMEET.

357. Garfield, Leon. FOOTSTEPS. New York: Delacorte, 1980.
        196p. Grades 5-7. NR
          In the room below his in their English country manor, Wil-
liam Jones, 12, hears his ailing father's footsteps pacing inexorably
night after night. One evening the footsteps stop and William races
down in alarm to find his father dying. To William he confesses
that he is a scoundrel and thief for having cheated his former partner, Alfred Diamond, of part of their fortune. William bravely decides to travel alone to London to right past wrongs. He is informed
that Alfred is dead but has a son John whom he seeks in the city's
noisome slums of the 1700s. John Diamond turns out to be an
amoral parasite who is as consumed with hatred of the Jones family
as guileless William is with guilt toward the Diamonds. John tricks
William into trusting him, then sets his gang of murderous street
urchins upon him, from whom William barely escapes with his life.
Further sleuthing reveals that Alfred Diamond is not dead and harbors no grudge but has disowned his craven, blackguard son.
Meanwhile, John has located the Jones' estate and, failing to exact
revenge on the son, torches the house. William hies home to find
his mother and sister safe but the arsonist trapped in his own conflagration. He saves him at great risk, repaying his father's debt,
laying his ghost to rest, and stirring admiration in his mother and
sisters.

358. Geras, Adele. THE GIRLS IN THE VELVET FRAME. New
        York: Atheneum, 1979. 149p. Grades 5-9. R
          Fallen on impecuniosity because of the death of husband
and provider, the Bernstein family of 1913 Jerusalem is nonetheless

proud and principled. Mrs. Bernstein's single source of shame is
her pampered only son Isaac, who emigrated to America to seek
prosperity but who has failed to communicate with his family. In
her respectability and adherence to tradition, she also looks askance
at her husband's flamboyant, unpredictable, and iconoclastic sister.
But it is the initiative and temerity of Aunt Mimi herself in proposing
that her five stair-step nieces pose for a photograph, and the faith
and ingenuity of the three older girls, Rifka, 13, Chava, 11, and
Naomi, 8, that change their fortunes. A copy of the portrait, accompanied by a poignant letter from each of the girls, even Dvora,
5, and Shoshanna, 3, and an impassioned plea to their rabbi's brother
in New York to find Isaac, inspires the newspaper article that finally
reaches him and guides him to a decent job. In the meantime, Rifka,
shy and sensitive but competent and domestic, is apprenticed to the
baker until it comes time for the marriage that has been arranged for
her, and flirtatious spinster Mimi opts out of marriage to an attractive German to remain in Jerusalem with her nieces. In the end
Mother mellows, and the sisters-in-law are reconciled.

359. Giff, Patricia Reilly. THE GIFT OF THE PIRATE QUEEN. New
         York: Delacorte, 1982. Illus. by Jenny Rutherford. 164p.
         Grades 5-6. R+
         Grace O'Malley, 11, has cared adequately for her hardware
salesman father and her diabetic sister Amy, 9, since their mother
died in a fishing accident a year ago near their rural New York
home. Now Christmas is approaching and Grace is suddenly faced
with new concerns. Her father's cousin from Ireland has arrived
for a visit, and while Fiona Tierney is as comfortable as an old shoe,
Grace, afraid that she will usurp her position in the household, cannot warm up to her. Moreover, Grace has broken her testy new
teacher's prized glass bell accidentally and tries desperately to replace it surreptitiously. She finds a duplicate, and in a gesture of
magnanimity to Lisa Kile, an unpopular classmate who aided her during Amy's last insulin reaction, she wraps the bell as a gift from
Lisa. Her generosity backfires when the teacher accuses Lisa of
stealing the bell and clumsily returning it. Fiona's stories of a brave
and fiery Irish pirate queen of the Elizabethan era inspire Grace to
confess to the teacher, but her feelings of remorse are renewed when
she castigates Amy for ignoring her diet and lapsing into a diabetic
coma. When the crisis passes, Grace begins to appreciate Fiona more
for her staunch, loving support than for her extraordinary housekeeping skills and asks her to stay permanently.

360. Girion, Barbara. IN THE MIDDLE OF A RAINBOW. New York:
         Scribner, 1983. 197p. Grades 7-10. R+
         Corrie Dickerson, 16 and a senior at her Newark high
school, is swept off her feet by Todd Marcus, campus heartthrob,
when he is brought following a soccer injury to the nurse's office
where she works. Although his family is wealthy, Todd is pursuing
an athletic scholarship just as avidly as Corrie is striving for an
academic one out of necessity. Her mother, who has supported them

as a legal secretary while earning her B.A. at night school since
her firefighter husband's death when Corrie was 6, is a strong advocate of self-reliance for women. In fact, she consistently refuses
to marry Steve, a colleague of her husband's, who has been devoted
to her over the years. Corrie allows Todd to buy her an expensive
gown for the winter dance, but her rainbow dissolves when a
jealous ex-girlfriend insinuates that Todd throws the same standard
line at all the girls he dates and is continuing to see her. Corrie's
misery over her fight with Todd and his absence on a skiing vacation is compounded by her mother's anger over the prom dress.
When Mrs. Dickerson confesses her guilt over her husband's death
and her abhorrence of depending on men for material benefits, the
air is cleared and she agrees at long last to marry Steve. And when
Todd returns from Vail he lays to rest the doubts planted by the
venomous sexpot. They decide to wait and see whether their romance
will endure the separation of college years.

361.   Gottschalk, Elin Toona. IN SEARCH OF COFFEE MOUNTAINS.
          Nashville: Nelson, 1977. 203p. Grades 5-8. R
          Having survived fear of wartime bombings and strafings,
German and Russian concentration camps, and especially the brutal
retaliation of German children, Lotukata, her mother, grandmother
and uncle are assigned a tiny room in a houseful of refugees at a
DP camp for Estonians. When she is among others of her own kind,
her nightmares recede and she loses her diffidence, wins the acceptance of the gang she admires, and learns the disillusioning techniques necessary for survival in a hostile, dehumanizing environment.
Her mother is soon evacuated to England where they are to join her,
while debonair, dissolute Unki departs for Brazil. Lotukata and her
grandmother, her last remaining pillar of strength, are left to face
the rigors of interminable boxcar rides to reach a series of appalling-
ly pestilential transit camps. When she becomes separated from her
grandmother, she is saved from panic only by the reassuring herding of her fellow refugees and a sympathetic English soldier. When
they are suddenly reunited, her joy and relief are so unbounded
that she only dimly appreciates the luxuries of soft white bread and
porcelain plumbing fixtures.

362.   Greenberg, Jan. THE PIG-OUT BLUES. New York: Farrar,
          Straus, Giroux, 1982. 121p. Grades 6-10. R+
          Her svelte mother Vanessa's inopportune sarcastic harangues
to shame her into losing weight have the opposite effect on Jodie
Firestone, 15, whose vaguely remembered father died in Vietnam.
It is only when her high school drama coach announces the casting
of a new play that she invokes the will power to slim down. She is
determined to play Juliet opposite her best friend's brother, on whom
she has a crush. Alas, at the audition she faints of undernourish-
ment and her role goes to someone else. Angry and frustrated, she
goes on a binge, regains all the lost weight, and takes a job in a
health-food store to earn money to leave her embattled Connecticut
home for the Great White Way. Then her mother's boyfriend jilts

her for being too aggressive, and suddenly mother and daughter kindle a single spark of dialogue. When Vanessa leaves on a recuperative cruise, Jodie is allowed to stay with Heather and David Simms' warm, supportive family, where she learns that, although David is not romantically attracted to her, she can still be a friend to him. Jodie scores a moral victory when the less talented Juliet can't hack Shakespeare, the play is cancelled, and she salves David's bruised ego. The vegetarian diet at the Simmses has a meritorious effect on her figure, and when Vanessa, a department store buyer, returns relaxed from her vacation, they both agree to make changes but realize that neither can fully live up to the expectations of the other. The wall between them crumbles one brick at a time.

363. Greenberg, Jan. A SEASON IN-BETWEEN. New York: Farrar, Straus, Giroux, 1979. 150p. Grades 7-10. R+

Tall, gangling and pubescent, Carrie Singer, 13, has enough problems of her own at her private school in St. Louis without the awful revelation that her father has cancer. While her mother accompanies him for a month at the Mayo Clinic, Carrie and Sonny, 8, are left in the care of their housekeeper, during which time she gets her period and begins to care for Dewy, a compassionate neighbor boy. She also becomes moody and sarcastic, retreating defensively under her electric blanket when she feels morose. When her dad returns thinner, grayer, older, and wracked with coughs, Carrie deliberately avoids him until Dewy describes the guilt he experienced after his grandmother's death. Dad musters the strength to take the family out to dinner, only to be rushed by ambulance to the hospital later that night. Carrie bargains with God to let him live, but he dies after a final visit from the children. Never close to her seemingly perfect and meticulous mother, Carrie feels more distant than ever as her mother plunges into an orgy of activity. Then her mother, who now runs her father's shoe factory, asks for Carrie's help in the office over summer vacation. During their commute they find a common ground, and when Dewy invites her on a picnic, Carrie starts thinking about life instead of death.

364. Greenfield, Eloise. SISTER. New York: Crowell, 1974. Illus. by Moneta Barrett. 83p. Grades 5-7. R+

Folks notice the physical resemblance between Doretha, 13, and her scapegrace sister Alberta, 16, but fail to note the difference in personalities. Doretha is as proud and positive as Alberta is narrow and negative. Returning home to her black ghetto in Washington, D.C., from a rock concert, Doretha records her sensations in her diary, then reviews the earlier major entries back to the year she was 9 and received the journal from her father. Recorded are her father's death, the story of her great-great-grandfather, a slave, the gift of the flute and another lesson in bereavement, the substitute teacher who almost sowed the seeds of hatred, the day of her resilient mother's second heartbreak, the afterschool African school instilling pride, and the first time her sister ran away. Here is the fabric of her life, the fiber of her heritage that patterned her strength and individuality but sapped her sister's because she failed to perceive its value.

365. Gregory, Diana. THERE'S A CATERPILLAR IN MY LEMONADE. Reading, Mass.: Addison-Wesley, 1980. 123p. Grades 5-7. R+

Samantha never knew her father, who died in military service before she was born. She and her mother, who works in a law office, have always lived amicably and comfortably in their inherited Victorian home. When her exhilarated mom announces that she plans to marry Philip Hooten, a teacher whom she has been dating casually, Sam rejects the whole idea. She resents losing her intimacy with her mother and her privacy around the house, and she fears intervention from Mr. Hooten. Intolerant of organized activities, she nonetheless joins the swim team out of loneliness. All her friends belong, and she feels that her mother has now deserted her. When her archaeologist aunt whom she adores arrives from Greece to stay with her during her mother's honeymoon, Sam confides her misery to her. Aunt Tuckie analogizes that Sam has a caterpillar in her lemonade, meaning that the situation is awkward for both her and Mr. Hooten. Aunt Tuckie reveals that she was fortunate in being able to follow the career to which she aspired but that Sam's mother's dream of being both wife and mother has been only partially fulfilled until now. She reminds her that caterpillars turn into butterflies. Sam remains unconvinced until the day she disgraces her swim team by accidentally disqualifying them from an important competition and is comforted by her empathetic and very human stepfather.

366. Guy, Rosa. THE FRIENDS. New York: Holt, Rinehart and Winston, 1973. 203p. Grades 7-9. R+

When her father transplants the Cathy family from their native West Indies to Harlem to become a restaurateur and get rich, Phyllisia, 14, finds herself cruelly scorned and threatened by fellow black classmates because of her accent and academic achievement. Unlike her sister Ruby, 16, she is unwilling to compromise her intelligence to gain friends, and with the same false pride and hauteur of her strict and domineering father Calvin, she disdainfully rejects the proffered friendship of Edith Jackson until the day Edith saves her life in a street fight. When she comprehends the poverty of Edith's large, motherless family, she can overlook her shabbiness and thievery, but Phyl has to keep her new friendship furtive because of her father's unyielding prejudice against the poor. Edith is forced to drop out of school and take a job when her father deserts, and she and Phyl become estranged. Then Phyllisia's gentle, fragile mother dies, and the grieving Calvin becomes a fanatical, suspicious tyrant, overzealously trying to protect his nubile daughters from the slum's pernicious element. Defiant Phyl starts lying and cutting classes to keep assignations with a boy. When Calvin finds out, he angrily plans to ship the girls back to their island home. Phyllisia, suddenly aware of Calvin's hypocrisy

and contrite over her scurrilous treatment of Edith, finds the courage
to confront her father and resume her friendship with the tragic
Edith.

367. Halvorson, Marilyn. COWBOYS DON'T CRY. New York:
      Delacorte, 1984. 160p. Grades 6-9. R+
      Before dying of injuries sustained in an auto accident in which
her husband was driving drunk, Shane Morgan's mother exhorted
him to be brave. His father Josh continued drinking and was reduced from rodeo cowboy to rodeo clown. When Shane's grandfather
dies, he leaves his ranch in Alberta to Josh, in trust for Shane, 13.
Shane hopes that the pride of owning property will straighten out
his father, but Josh appears drunk in front of Shane's new classmates, and the boy is forced into a fight in his defense. Outclassed
and outnumbered, he, in turn, is defended by a spirited neighbor
girl, Casey Sutherland, whose mom is a vet and tends Shane's
mother's prized mare when she becomes entangled in barbed wire.
The defensive boy and the sensitive girl eventually become friends,
and Shane's father makes an effort to stay dry. One day when he
backslides, however, he makes a scene in front of the Sutherlands.
Shane lashes back by publicly accusing him of killing his mom,
whereupon his father runs out on him, and the boy is placed in the
foster care of the sympathetic Sutherlands. Months later, as a
spectator at a rodeo, Shane is saved from a maverick bull by a rodeo
clown who risks his own life to rescue him. Shane recognizes his
father beneath the makeup. As they begin to patch up their differences, Josh makes Shane a gift of his mother's beloved horse.

368. Hassler, Jon. JEMMY. New York: Atheneum, 1980. 175p.
      Grades 7-12. R+
      The half-breed daughter of an alcoholic white father and a
Chippewa mother, dead six years, Gemstone Opal Stott, 17, is
pilloried by the townspeople of the rural Minnesota community where
she attends high school and is barely tolerated by the Indians of
the nearby reservation. Her father, a former house painter who
now sips vodka and smoke before sleeping the day away and carous-
ing all night, tells her to drop out of school to take care of her
younger siblings, Marty, 11, and Candy, 6. She does so impassively
but feels impelled to return to a high bluff where she used to go
berry picking with her mother in happier days. Caught in an early
blizzard, she is rescued by a famous muralist and his wife, Otis and
Ann Chapman, who are absorbing local color for an Indian legend
Otis has been commissioned to depict. He quickly chooses Jemmy to
sit as his model, and the Chapmans soon become friends, surrogate
parents, and unstinting benefactors to the neglected Stott children.
When the couple returns to Minneapolis, they leave the children in
charge of their farm. The responsibility breeds self-confidence, and
when the Chapmans returns in the spring to pack their belongings
before moving on, Otis, himself a recovered alcoholic, badgers the
weak-willed Mr. Stott into taking control of his life, resuming his
trade, regaining his pride, and earning the respect of his family.

369. Haugaard, Erik Christian. A MESSENGER FOR PARLIAMENT.
     Boston: Houghton Mifflin, 1976. 218p. Grades 5-7. NR
     Named for Oliver Cromwell before his rendezvous with history,
Oliver was born in squalor at Cambridgeshire in 1630 to an illiterate
consumptive mother whom he adores and an incompetent carpenter
with a rudimentary education whom he despises. Squandering his
meager earnings on ale instead of wholesome food and medical treatment for his ailing wife, his father masquerades as a savant when
he is in his cups, prating foolishly and dogmatically for the cause
of Parliament in the British civil war of 1642 and ranting irrationally
against King and Catholicism. When his wife dies, the weak, sanctimonious, self-pitying and insecure dipsomaniac who feigns erudition
enlists in the insurgent army as a scrivener with the boy in tow.
In his uncompassionate loathing of his father, Oliver tries to run
away but is returned to his indifferent and irresponsible sire.
During the course of their first battle they become separated, and
Oliver makes no attempt to find his father; in fact, he is never to
see him again. For survival, he joins forces with a ragtag band
of boys, all unsanctioned camp followers, and learns from experience
and exigency the brutality and pettifoggery of war. His tale is told
in retrospect in old age from the shores of the New World.

370. Hayes, Sheila. SPEAKING OF SNAPDRAGONS. New York:
     Dutton, 1982. 160p. Grades 5-7. R+
     The two of them, both fatherless, have been pals and neigh-
bors since nursery school. Now Marshall's mom is remarrying, and
his stepfather has activities planned for all summer. Heather Mal-
lory, 11, whose mother has run a gift shop since her husband's
death in an auto accident eight years earlier and who has been con-
ditioned to be independent and pragmatic, suddenly finds herself at
loose ends. Ignoring past failures, she decides to plant a flower
garden, and in the course of buying plants she makes the acquaintance of the elderly recluse whom her classmates avoid because he
seems crazy. Duffy, who is actually an eccentric widower, not only
greens her thumb but releases her imagination, and a deep fellowship
develops between them. When Heather's best girlfriend, Lisa, returns
from vacation and belittles Duffy, Heather disloyally stops visiting
him. She tries to seek counsel from her preoccupied mother, who
misunderstands and deems her regressive and clinging. Marshall
returns, disenchanted with his new Superdad, and Heather becomes
sated with Lisa's snobbery. She goes to see Duffy, only to discover that he has collapsed from a stroke. With accustomed self-
reliance she summons help, the story of her clandestine friendship
finally commands her mother's attention, and she gets the reassurance
she needs. Duffy recovers, Heather and Marshall resume their former camaraderie, and Heather makes a valuable new friend to replace
the superficial Lisa.

371. Heide, Florence Parry. GROWING ANYWAY UP. Philadelphia:
     Lippincott, 1976. (OP) 128p. Grades 6-9. R
     Florence's father died when she was too young to remember

him well, but she has remained intense, introverted, and pathologically insecure inside the protective shell she has so deliberately
and painstakingly erected between herself and the threatening world
outside. Her mother's decision to move from their safe routine in
Florida near the soothing sea to a new apartment in Pennsylvania, a
new school, new classmates, and a pompous new boyfriend for her
mother all aggravate her condition because she cannot tolerate the
dangers of change. The spells and incantations she employs to ward
them off give her the appearance of having nervous tics, and she is
suspected of being psychotic. Only her extrovert aunt understands
her and begins to draw her out, but her aunt's sudden departure
threatens to topple her teetering emotional balance while it triggers
a memory of repressed guilt over her father's death. Once articu-
lated, it becomes the bottom rung on Florence's ladder to stability
and maturity.

372.   Hermes, Patricia.   YOU SHOULDN'T HAVE TO SAY GOOD-
       BYE. San Diego: Harcourt Brace Jovanovich, 1982.   117p.
       Grades 6-8.   R++
       She was once voted the best mom in the neighborhood. She
is a lawyer who has maintained her office in the family home since
her daughter Sarah was born so that she could combine motherhood
and a career. Now Mrs. Morrow, with little warning, has developed
a galloping, untreatable melanoma, a death sentence that, as she
puts it, stinks. The impact on the uncommonly close family of three
is shattering. Sarah, 13, reacts first with anger at her mother for
letting this happen to her, then denial of the unthinkable, inad-
missible eventuality. Mom makes her confront the facts, and Sarah
finally gives in to the welling tears. The ache is unmitigated, but
at least they can face their limited future together honestly. Mom
teaches her the mundane household tasks but also attends to the
more sublime considerations, such as selecting books for her now
that she will never be able to give her as she matures. Some days
are more normal than others. Sarah continues practicing for her
gymnastics exhibition; together they paint the breakfast room a sunny
yellow; and just before Christmas they give a party for friends that
is one of the happiest occasions of their lives. On the day of Sarah's
performance Mom is hospitalized for a transfusion, but she elects to
return home for her final days and dies in a paroxysm of pain with
husband and daughter at her side on Christmas Eve. Her legacy
and Christmas gift to Sarah is a handwritten journal in which she
tells the grieving girl to retain in her heart what is important but
to let go of the rest. Sarah begins a journal of her own to chronicle
her seesawing odyssey back from the depths of sorrow.

373.   Hightower, Florence.   DREAMWOLD CASTLE.   Boston: Boston:
       Houghton Mifflin, 1978.   214p.   Grades 5-7.   NR
       Phoebe Smith's father was killed in the Korean conflict, where-
upon her mother returned to college for her teaching credential, accepted a position at a private school in New Hampshire, and is at
work on her master's degree. Phoebe, 13, is unhappy with their

chilly apartment in Miss Tarlton's historic mansion and is acutely
uncomfortable attending Denby School, where the other girls ridicule
her maladroitness. She spends all her free time devouring books on
mountain climbing and is pleasantly surprised when the wealthiest
girl in class shares her passion for mountaineering and invites her
home to meet her twin brother. She soon discovers that Connie and
Harry harbor hatred for their parents for banishing their adored
but unstable older brother Tony. Immediately they begin exploiting
Phoebe's sycophantic friendship by establishing through her an illicit correspondence with Tony. When Tony returns one step ahead
of the law, they conspiratorially conceal him with Phoebe's help.
Because of his carelessness, however, Miss Tarlton's house is incinerated and Phoebe is seriously burned. The story of Tony's
criminality and Phoebe's unwitting complicity is finally bared, and a
rueful Phoebe agrees to buckle down to her neglected schoolwork.

374. Hinton, S. E. TEX. New York: Delacorte, 1979. 191p.
     Grades 6-10. R+
     Texas McCormick, 15, whose mother died of pneumonia when
he was 2, has always gotten along well with his brother Mason, 17,
while their father rides on the rodeo circuit. This time Pop's absence drags on longer and longer, and, when their money runs out,
Mace sells Tex's beloved horse without consulting him. Tex recovers
slowly from his rancor and resumes his lackadaisical, irresponsible
adolescence, getting drunk at the fair, pulling daredevil stunts on a
motorcycle, being apprehended for shoplifting, smoking pot, and
falling in love. He tastes fame when a hitchhiker he and Mace pick
up turns out to be an armed desperado who hijacks them and is
killed in a shootout with the police. The notoriety delivers an additional benefit, for the television coverage brings Pop home. But
nothing changes, and Mason continues to act pedagogical toward Tex
while planning his escape, via a college scholarship, from his tawdry
home. A prank at school leads Tex to the brink of expulsion, and
Mason, outraged to learn that Tex got the idea from Pop, blurts out
the fact that Tex is a bastard, conceived while Pop was in prison.
Stunned, Tex knows then that he will never achieve his goal of
earning Pop's affection and joins an older friend who deals drugs for
a living. Tex is shot in a melee with one of Lem's customers, and
only then, while recuperating, does he begin to appreciate his
earnest, honorable half-brother. He takes a summer job at a stable.

375. Holland, Barbara. THE PONY PROBLEM. New York: Dutton,
     1977. 122p. Grades 5-6. NR
     Every year since she was 6, Jean Monroe, 11, has entered a
magazine's annual pony-naming contest, and finally, on this her final
year of eligibility, she wins. The pony, Hopscotch, is delivered to
the postage stamp lot of their ticky tacky subdivision in suburban
New Jersey. The neighbors fear that the pony will undermine their
property values, and, with winter approaching, Mrs. Monroe, a
widowed museum curator, decrees that Jean must divest herself of
Hopscotch. To save the animal from the clutches of the SPCA, who

will put it to sleep, Jean rides Hopscotch over the hill beyond Dog-
wood Estates and discovers a rundown farm belonging to an eccentric widow. Mrs. Remington, though sympathetic to Jean's plight,
cannot harbor Hopscotch because high taxes are forcing her to sell
her acreage to developers. Seeing the farm's sturdy old stone
tenant house, Jean conceives of an idea that could benefit both Mrs.
Remington and the Monroes. She and her older brother refurbish
the stone house and gamble that their mother will be so enchanted
with the expansive view that she will tolerate the outdoor privy to
live there. Their enthusiasm and perseverance pay off. The rent
that the independent-minded Monroes pay enables Mrs. R. to keep
Highmeadow, and one and all can pursue their individuality.

376. Holland, Isabelle. A HORSE NAMED PEACEABLE. New York:
     Lothrop, Lee and Shepard, 1982. 157p. Grades 5-8. R+
     Peaceable is people to Jessamy Wainscott, 12, whose mother
died two years earlier, but to her unreceptive, strong-willed father,
Episcopal Bishop of West Connecticut, a horse is an indefensible
substitute for the human relationships Jessamy eschews. Accordingly,
while she is away at boarding school, he sells Peaceable. Jessamy
learns inadvertently of the sale and of a fire at the stable which destroyed some of the horses. Frantic with worry, Jessamy sneaks away
to find him while her father is proselytizing in Somalia. She joins
another fugitive, Rudd Fielding, 17, who is as tough and worldly as
she is innocent and naive. The unlikely and often argumentative
pair manage to keep one step ahead of authorities, who are trumpet-
ing Jessamy's disappearance and possible kidnap, as they trace
leads to the lost horse and eventually become friendly and mutually
protective. Peaceable is located at a resort, where Jessamy claims
him and is immediately recognized despite her boyish disguise, effectively thwarting her hope of never having to return home. When
her father arrives, prepared to vent his wrath upon her, a vacationing parishioner opens his eyes to his neglect of his daughter's emotional welfare since the death of his wife, but Jessamy has to shock
him into recognizing how one-sided their relationship has become before they can begin to forge bilateral communication.

377. Hopper, Nancy J. SECRETS. New York: Elsevier/Nelson,
     1979. (OP) 138p. Grades 5-8. R
     Severely traumatized by witnessing the death of her beloved
father in a traffic accident, Lenore James, 14, has retreated into a
shell of silence which she uses to manipulate her teachers, her working mother, her insufferable older brother, and even her psychiatrist, although they do not swallow her ploy of feigning retarda-
tion. Within her transparent box she is a keen observer and overhears a new teacher at her private school plotting to kidnap Sammy
Loudan, the wealthy boy who breathes damply on her neck from the
seat behind her in English class. Sammy doesn't believe her because
the co-conspirator is his bodyguard, her teacher thinks it is a figment of her imagination, and her psychiatrist ignores her. Then on
a museum field trip the abduction takes place, and when she tries

to avert it she is taken too. Locked with Sammy in the basement of
an abandoned building, Lenore has to relearn the art of communication. The trio of abductors tries to kill them by force-feeding them
drugs and whiskey, but Sammy, having had kidnap training, shows
her how to vomit. When they are rescued by authorities, Lenore,
having bared her emotions to Sammy, no longer needs to hoard them
mutely, and when her mother remarries, her stepfather wisely does
not try to take her father's place.

378. Hunt, Irene. THE EVERLASTING HILLS. New York:
         Scribner, 1985. 184p. Grades 6-9. R+
         Embittered by the deaths of his adored wife and promising
elder son long ago, Breck Tydings does not hesitate to inform his
mentally retarded son Jeremy, 12, that the wrong child died. In
their mountain isolation, the bullied and scorned boy's only advocate
and defender is his sister Bethany, 18, who teaches the country
school and labors for her father on their Colorado ranch. When
courteous, aspiring young writer Adam Craine, in search of solitude
and inspiration, comes to visit, he and Bethany strike an instant
chemical and intellectual rapport. As Bethany becomes his editorial
assistant and later his wife, Jeremy, for the first time in his life,
has no one to run interference between himself and his father, and
he grows increasingly anxious and agitated. A particularly rancorous
and spiteful attack by his warped and twisted father drives Jeremy
in desperation to hurl himself down the mountain in escape. A reclusive elderly man who calls himself Ishmael takes him in, binds his
physical wounds and starts to heal the deeper emotional ones. From
their symbiotic relationship Jeremy gains strength, confidence and
independence, while the ailing Ishmael derives youthful assistance,
companionship, and the chance to lay to rest the haunting specters
of his past. Jeremy relaxes enough to conquer the speech impediment that accentuates his handicap and warmly regards the older man
as his true father. The change in him elicits the grudging respect
of Breck Tydings, who again offers him a home upon Ishmael's
death, an offer which he icily declines. It isn't until the traumatic
birth of Bethany's baby that Jeremy can bring himself to forgive
and accept his suddenly humbled father.

379. Hunt, Irene. UP A ROAD SLOWLY. Chicago: Follett, 1966.
         Illus. by Don Bolognese. 192p. Grades 5-8. R+
         Julie is 7 when her mother dies. She and her brother, 9, are
wrenched from their home in town to live in the country with their
reserved, cultivated spinster aunt and suave, sarcastic, alcoholic
uncle, leaving Laura, 17, to keep house for Father, a college professor. Aunt Cordelia is also Julie's school teacher, and Julie is frequently bitterly resentful of her inflexibility and devotion to duty,
longing for a future when she can return to the security of her own
home and family. But when her brother is sent to boarding school,
her sister marries and has children of her own, and Father remarries,
his house is no longer the home she remembers. Over the years she
has become quite fond of her undemonstrative aunt and chooses to

remain with her, commuting to high school in town. An unfortunate infatuation with an exploitative boy almost spoils her relationship with her childhood beau, but Uncle Haskell intervenes before it goes too far, one of his few unselfish and constructive acts. Julie and Danny finally declare their mutual affection, and Julie, class valedictorian, prepares to test wings of independence at the state university.

380. Hunter, Mollie. A SOUND OF CHARIOTS. New York: Harper and Row, 1972. 242p. Grades 6-9. R+

Disabled in World War I, Bridie's father espouses the cause of socialism, stumping for reform for invalided veterans and tenant farmers in postwar Scotland. Bridie, next to the youngest of the family's five children, idolizes her father, grows up in his image, and is the apple of his eye. She is 9 at the time of his death, and her torment knows no bounds. She despises her fundamentalist mother's lachrymose grief and desolation but can find no acceptable channel for her own which surfaces in terrifying nightmares. In trying to explain the finality of death to her little brother, she perceives her own mortality and decides she cannot waste a moment of the time remaining to her. But in trying to find her niche, she only succeeds in understanding and appreciating her mother more. Bridie's poetry is encouraged for its expressiveness but discountenanced because of its unprofitability until one perceptive professor tells her, "You are your father's daughter--live for him!" The exigency of making a living is paramount, but Bridie can devote her spare time to liberating the poetry in her mind.

381. Johnston, Norma. GABRIEL'S GIRL. New York: Atheneum, 1983. 178p. Grades 7-10. R

When Sarah Langham, 17, cannot reach her father Gabriel, a widowed investigative journalist, at the number he left her in Spain, she impulsively flies off to find him. Not only are the hotel personnel and police uncooperative, but she soon finds herself in dire danger. Her luggage and passport are stolen, and a sinister man follows her. The only cohort she can trust is Quent Robards, son of the Canadian ambassador. They determine that Gabriel Langham is trying to expose a terrorist arms smuggling ring that is raising and laundering funds through unsuspecting Americans. Sarah, disguised as Quent's sister, and Quent follow Gabe's trail to London, where two attempts are made on Sarah's life. As stubborn and tenacious as her father, she ignores Quent's advice that she remain sequestered. This time she is kidnapped and taken to the lair of the underworld kingpin, where her foolhardiness also imperils her father. To make amends, she escapes over ledges and rooftops by dint of her gymnastics training and coolly unearths the Libyan's cache of plastic explosives from under their very noses, proving that "Gabe's girl" is a chip off the old block.

382. Jones, Penelope. HOLDING TOGETHER. Scarsdale: Bradbury, 1981. 173p. Grades 5-6. R+

Her mother made her costume for the class play but is too
sick to attend the performance. February, Vickie Stevenson's
favorite month, with the play, Valentine's Day, and her ninth birthday coming in succession, turns out to be a disappointment when
Mommy is hospitalized and has to miss the fabulous sleigh ride party
they have planned for so long. Old-fashioned Mrs. Poudry comes to
keep house for them, but noisy, excitable, impatient, intense, ebullient Vickie needs her mother's soothing influence as a buffer between her and her sister Anne, 10, Vickie's temperamental opposite.
It is sober, observant, thoughtful, industrious Anne who realizes,
on the night that they visit their mother in the hospital, that she
is going to die. Vickie postpones choosing a topic for a research
report at school because she can't bring herself to write about cancer, the subject uppermost in her mind. When her mother comes
home with a nurse, Vickie hopes it means that she is improving, but
her father explains that the only treatment for her now is to control
the pain. Mommy dies in her sleep, and after the turmoil of the
funeral, life returns to a semblance of normal wherein small incidents
trigger sudden tears. Daddy announces a vacation trip to Florida
to draw the three of them closer, and, pulling together for a change,
Vickie and Anne learn a piano duet.

383. Kaplan, Bess. THE EMPTY CHAIR. New York: Harper and
    Row, 1975. 243p. Glossary. Grades 6-8. R
    While lacking material comforts, Becky Devine, 10, and her
brother Saul, 8, savor the innocence of childhood and the solidity
of their Jewish traditions in their Winnipeg home behind the grocery
store that their Russian immigrant parents run. Then their mother
dies in childbirth and Becky's complacency ends. When an uncle
casually sits in Mama's empty chair, Becky angrily moves it to her
room, and that night Mama appears to her and promises to return.
Becky's meddling aunts immediately start matchmaking for Papa,
and when he falls in love with Sylvia Cohen, a schoolteacher, she
is outraged that he would try to replace Mama, who, in one of her
frequent visits to Becky, has specifically stated that she does not
want Papa to remarry. It is difficult to dislike generous, considerate and efficient Sylvia, but when Papa breaks his leg in a freakish
accident Becky knows it is a judgment from Mama. She attributes
Sylvia's morning sickness to Mama's vengeance and is convinced
that Mama's increasingly menacing presence is bent on her own destruction for not halting the nuptials. Papa and Sylvia confront her
when her paranoia becomes obsessive, and Becky blurts out her terrible secret. Papa takes her to the cemetery to show her that Mama
is at peace in her grave, and Sylvia announces that she is expecting
a baby that Becky hopes will be the little sister she lost at Mama's
death.

384. Keene, Carolyn. THE HIDDEN STAIRCASE. New York:
    Grosset and Dunlap, 1959. 182p. Grades 4-8. NR
    The second of 62 formula Nancy Drew mystery adventures in
which the heroine, a wholesome, independent young woman of 18,

interprets clues, solves puzzling cases, brings to justice nefarious
scoundrels, and rehabilitates incipient miscreants for the benefit
of friends and neighbors with the blessing of the local police.
Nancy's father, an attorney, has been widowed since Nancy was 3,
and the two are ministered to by their grandmotherly housekeeper,
Hannah Gruen. Nancy also sustains a chaste and desultory romance
with loyal Ned Nickerson. In this case, Nancy discovers the link
between the kidnapping of her father and the terrorization of a
"haunted" household of women when she finds the secret passage-
way that leads from their old Colonial mansion to its nearby counter-
part.

385. Keith, Harold. THE OBSTINATE LAND. New York: Crowell,
       1977. 214p. Grades 6-8. R
       In the Oklahoma land run of 1893, the Romberg family, im-
migrants from Germany and former Texas sharecroppers, head for a
choice claim their father has scouted in the arid western part of
the territory, only to find that shiftless, illegal Sooners have preempted their land. The lack of law enforcement precludes any legal
recourse. Proud Frederic ignores his wife's pleas to return to their
relatives, and he settles on a nearby section, devoid of water, to
start his farming venture. Award-winning author Keith throws the
full panoply of meticulously researched frontier afflictions at the
stubborn nesters, including hostile ranchers, negligent government,
drought, hail, blizzard, dust storm, prairie fire, outlaws, snakebite,
tetanus, sod dugouts and more. When intrepid Frederic dies of exposure, Fritz, 15, assumes responsibility against overwhelming odds
for his mother and small brother and sister. With enterprise, industry, vision, self-restraint, and main strength, he builds a herd
of cattle from unwanted dogies and becomes a salesman for John
Deere implements and windmills to tide the farm over lean years. He
falls in love with a rancher's daughter, but eventually and pragmatically he chooses as his future wife the waif of his former Sooner
nemesis who has suddenly blossomed like a wild rose. She has the
survival skills necessary to overcome the rigors of pioneer life.

386. Kerr, M. E. HIM SHE LOVES? New York: Harper and Row,
       1984. 215p. Grades 7-10. R
       Henry Schiller's nonchalant banter wins him the regard of
attractive, sophisticated Valerie Kissenwiser when she drops in with
friends at the German restaurant his family has recently opened on
Long Island following his father's murder five years ago in a holdup
of their former establishment in Brooklyn. Valerie's father, Al Kiss,
is less enchanted. A stale comedian who is nervous about his fading
career, he is also possessive of his daughter, defensive about having
to live with his mother-in-law, and a Jew with a lingering hatred of
those of German descent. He puts a damper on the romance but also
exploits it by incorporating it into his new act on national TV, lam-
pooning Henry, 17, whom he dubs Heinrich. The fresh material is an
instant hit, and, while nettling to Henry, it earns him notoriety at
school and draws a brisk business to the restaurant where his mother,

vocalist for the bistro, has begun dating again. Henry and Valerie
continue trysting until Al Kiss discovers him in her bedroom and
delivers an ultimatum. Valerie beseeches Henry to win her father
over, but even his unscripted and applauded appeal during a performance of the school play, with Al Kiss in attendance, fails to
move the father. Then Henry devises a media event so audacious
in scope and concept that it gains the respectful attention of even
that master of showmanship. As soon as Henry secures the approbation of Al Kiss, ironically, Valerie dumps him for other forbidden
fruit.

387.   Kerr, M. E. I'LL LOVE YOU WHEN YOU'RE MORE LIKE ME.
       New York: Harper and Row, 1977. 183p. Grades 7-10. R
       Wally Witherspoon, Jr., is a high school junior in the small
Connecticut town of Seaside where his father, a funeral director,
is grooming his son to take over the family enterprise, an occupation
young Wally loathes. Sabra St. Amour, 18, is a soap opera star who
is coddled and sheltered by her proprietary, twice-widowed mother,
who basks in the reflected glory of her daughter's celebrity and
whose liaisons with a variety of unsuitable show biz swains are an
embarrassment to Sabra. Having developed an ulcer, Sabra is vacationing in Seaside with her mother and contemplating retirement
from acting. She and Wally meet on the beach and are attracted to
one another by the very attributes that make them so different:
Wally by Sabra's glamor and sophistication, Sabra by Wally's All-
American-Boy-Next-Door image. Wally heeds her advice to grab the
reins of his own life and pursue a different career goal, disappointing his father in doing so. Sabra's own resolve to change her lifestyle vanishes, however, when she realizes that she is a compulsive
actress, but she asserts her independence of smother love and
manipulation. Wally and Sabra's unlikely friendship ends as suddenly
and unceremoniously as it began.

388.   Kingman, Lee. THE REFINER'S FIRE. Boston: Houghton
       Mifflin, 1981. 218p. Grades 6-9. R+
       In the four years since her mother's sudden death of dysentery
in India, where her father, a ceramics historian, was studying, Sara
Bradford, 13, has been living with her grandmother in Tennessee.
Now her grandmother has developed emphysema and Sara has been
sent to live with her father, Richard, at the arts and crafts commune
he has colonized in rural New Hampshire. There Sara discovers that
Richard is sharing a bedroom with Kyra, a painter and photographer
he met in Cyprus. At first uncomfortable with their relationship,
Sara soon becomes fond of Kyra and her small son Demetri, hoping
that Richard and Kyra will marry and establish a permanent home in
the huge old barn that serves as living quarters and workshop.
Sara feels maladroit beside her multi-talented, self-confident, temperamental father, but following a calamitous skit at school, the art group
convinces her that her embarrassment is unmerited and that she
should be proud of her fortitude and coolheadedness in other events
over which she exerts more control. Unfortunately she has no control

over the barn burning down at Christmas time or over Kyra's departure for warmer climes, but her father decides to settle down
anyway, face the challenge of rebuilding, and belatedly express his
pride in her.

389. Klass, David. THE ATAMI DRAGONS. New York: Scribner,
      1984. 134p. Grades 5-8. R
      The summer that his high school buddies finally put together
a winning team, Jerry Sanders, the cleanup hitter, is uprooted by
his father, a college professor, while he takes a sabbatical in Japan.
The trip was recommended by Mr. Sanders' psychiatrist as therapy
following his wife's death of cancer a month earlier. Jerry's sister
Carey, 9, joins a cooking club and soon becomes acclimated, but
Jerry, bored with a steady diet of Japanese television, gravitates
toward a high school baseball team in practice and is invited to join
them. His father arranges for him to become a summer school student and regular member of the team. With the addition of Jerry's
skills at batting and fielding, the team becomes proficient enough to
qualify for the fiercely competitive annual all-Japan tournament.
Before the tournament, Mr. Sanders takes the family to climb Mt.
Fujiyama. When he reveals that he met his wife on a ski slope and
wants to say goodbye to her on a mountain, a Buddhist priest suggests that they build a shrine on the mountainside for her spirit.
At the tournament, the American star almost becomes the team's
goat, but on the final pitch he redeems himself and returns home
with a more relaxed and intimate relationship with his lighter-
hearted father.

390. Klein, Norma. BIZOU. New York: Viking, 1983. 140p.
      Grades 7-10. NR
      Elaine's French father, a photo journalist, dubbed her Bizou
or "Little Kiss" before he was killed in Vietnam when she was 3.
Now 13, she has been reared in France by her black American
mother Tranquility, a fashion model and libertarian. Naturally flirtatious like her mother, Bizou has already had two boyfriends by
the time her mother decides to return to the States to acquaint
Bizou with her roots. On the plane they make friends with Nicholas,
a medical school student, and when Tranquility, depressed by the
sexism and racial prejudice she encounters in New York, disappears
to collect herself, she dumps Bizou on Nicholas. The two begin an
odyssey up and down the Eastern Seaboard, finally locating Tranquility's old high school chum Anita and her adopted son. There
Nicholas and Anita fall in love, and Bizou discovers that Anita's
son Duff, 14, is her half-brother, born to Tranquility out of wedlock. Bizou and Duff's grandfather, who lives in a nearby retirement home, confirms the relationship and defends his feud with their
mother for not having fulfilled her potential. When Tranquility suddenly reappears, Bizou demonstrates her anger at the desertion by
jumping from the roof and breaking her leg. Tranquility's reunion
with her father is amicable, but after their return to France it takes
Bizou a long time to comprehend and forgive her mother's bizarre
behavior.

391. Klein, Norma. BLUE TREES, RED SKY. New York: Pan-
      theon, 1975. Illus. by Pat Grant Porter. 57p. Grades 3-6.
      R+
      Valerie Dale, 8, understands that her mother, an artist, has
to work to support the family because her father died five years
before, but she wishes Mom could be home all the time to play with
her and soften the burden of big sister responsibility for Marco, 5.
On the other hand, she values the liberation of her own and her
mother's generations and wonders why her stuffy elderly babysitter
Mrs. Weiss, a former concert pianist, felt constrained to quit her
career when she married and had a family. When Mrs. Dale and
her boyfriend George depart on a week's vacation, Valerie realizes
a deeper appreciation for both Marco and Mrs. Weiss. Upon her return, Mrs. Dale indicates that she and George will marry, but
Valerie's vision of a full-time mom vanishes when her mother says
that she will continue to work as she did even before Valerie's father
died. She explains that meaningful and rewarding occupation is as
important to adults as a favorite toy is to children. Escape into an
enjoyable vocation can be as good as the best fantasy. Then Mom
proves that recreation is important, too, by taking Valerie and her
best friend to play tennis with her.

392. Lee, Mildred. FOG. New York: Seabury, 1972. 250p.
      Grades 7-10. R+
      The caboose of the Sawyer family, Luke, 15, is aware that his
affable but undemonstrative father sacrificed college and a career to
provide a steady but unspectacular income as a hardware store clerk
for him, his mother and two sisters, both now married. Nonetheless,
he feels contemptuous and ashamed of his father's ignoble occupation
and low aspirations, yet he realizes that he is lucky to have a stable,
happy homelife. A flash fire in their clubhouse in which he and two
of his friends are gravely injured gives Luke a new perspective on
his childhood buddies but entrenches his romance with Milo, the
daughter of an uppercrust family in their small Southern town. When
his dad dies suddenly of a heart attack, the boy is not only distraught at his loss but abjectly remorseful that he temporized every
time his dad tried to discuss Luke's future goals with him. Life
without the father he took for granted seems "like River Street in
the fog," and he drifts aimlessly all summer while Milo is away at a
resort. When she changes her mind about their relationship, Luke
desperately and irrationally attempts to hold her by considering a
menial job that would enable them to marry right away, just as his
parents did. Coming to his senses, he decides to pursue the medical
career he really wants with the legacy his father saved expressly for
his eduation.

393. Lee, Mildred. THE SKATING RINK. New York: Seabury,
      1969. 136p. Grades 7-10. R
      Tuck Faraday watched his mother drown when he was a toddler,
and even though his father remarried a kind and sympathetic woman,
Tuck, now 15, remains aloof and uncertain because of his severe

stammering. His problems are exacerbated by the onset of puberty and its maelstrom of emotions, and he plans to drop out of high school. Elva Grimes, the brazen class tease, leads him on and then betrays him. His taunting, tom-catting twin brothers Tom and Cletus, 17, are paragons of virtue in the eyes of Tuck's denigrating father, a defeatist and a fool. Only his younger half-sister Karen and his stepmother Ida defend him. Then construction begins on a skating rink just down the road from the Faraday's rundown Georgia farm, and Tuck, curious, investigates. The entrepreneur, Pete Degley, neither condescends to Tuck nor derides his speech impediment, and Tuck soon becomes friends with Degley and his wife Lily, a skating "artiste." The two teach the gangling, self-deprecating boy to skate, and together they rehearse in secret an intricate routine for opening night. Tuck stuns his incredulous acquaintances with his performance, and with his earnings as skating instructor he buys Ida a new stove, earning his father's grudging respect. With noticeable improvement in his speech stemming from greater self-confidence, he decides to remain in school.

394. Levoy, Myron. ALAN AND NAOMI. New York: Harper and Row, 1977. 192p. Grades 6-8. R
    A target of anti-Semitism by a bigoted classmate and bully in New York City in 1944, Alan Silverman, 12, and his one friend on the block, Shaun Kelly, revel in playing stickball in the streets and flying model planes at a deserted airstrip. When a foreign girl moves into their apartment building, all the boys deride her because of her neurotic behavior, and to his horror, Alan's parents ask him to befriend the pathetic girl who seems totally mute and incessantly tears at paper. He learns that Naomi's father had been beaten to death by Nazis before her very eyes, and Naomi feels responsible for his death by not being quick enough to tear up his incriminating papers. Using his Charlie McCarthy dummy, Alan gradually, with many setbacks, coaxes Naomi into communication, but he is insecure enough to conceal his burgeoning friendship with the "crazy girl" even to Shaun for fear of being ridiculed. But as Naomi progresses to the point where she can attend school, their relationship becomes impossible to hide, and Shaun, stung by Alan's lack of trust, shuns him. Goaded by the bully, Alan retaliates and Shaun comes to his assistance, but the damage is done. Naomi, spotting the blood on Alan's face, has a recurring vision of the Gestapo and lapses into psychosis, for which she must be institutionalized.

395. Lewis, Elizabeth Foreman. YOUNG FU OF THE UPPER YANGTZE. New York: Holt, Rinehart and Winston, 1932. Illus. by Kurt Wiese. 264p. Grades 5-7. NR
    Young Fu, 14, and his mother, a farmer's widow, come to Chungking where he is apprenticed to Tang Coppersmith. The country boy endures the mockery of fellow apprentices, makes bonds of friendship with Small Li, earns the jealousy and animosity of Den, and wins the respect of his employer. Sent on errands about the city, he observes the barbarity of soldiers, the wretchedness of

professional beggars, and the ruthlessness of organized bandits.
Twice in his naivete he is bilked by crafty sycophants, in a pawn
shop and in a gambling den. He saves the missionaries' hospital
from fire and lays to rest his superstitious fear of foreign devils
and dragons of ill fortune. He foils a burglary attempt by a former
disgruntled employee and proves the innocence of another employee
falsely accused of drug trafficking. When his enemy, Den, casts
suspicion of theft on Fu, Tang places his trust in Fu, now 19 and
a journeyman, and adopts him as his son. His mother will never
want again.

396. Lingard, Joan. THE FILE ON FRAULEIN BERG. New York:
        Elsevier/Nelson, 1980. 153p. Grades 5-7. R
        Belfast, North Ireland, is in a boring backwater of World War
II in 1944 to Kathleen Carson, whose mother, "a gentlewoman down
on her luck," supports the two of them as a dressmaker. To Kate
and her best friends, ebullient Sally MacCabe and genteel Harriet
Linton, the arrival of Fraulein Berg to teach German to their fourth
form class heralds the opportunity to forward the war effort and to
gratify their propaganda-fueled hatred of the Hun. Convinced that
the homely, self-effacing, maladroit teacher is a dangerous enemy
agent, they spy upon her in her tiny apartment across from Mr.
MacCabe's butcher shop, dog her every footstep, rebuff her friendly
overtures, and cause the abrupt curtailment of her romance with
another unpopular teacher. On a shopping expedition to Dublin,
they precipitate an embarrassing border incident which backfires on
them, and, following their humiliation, the girls lose the zest of the
chase until Fraulein Berg moves on. A few years after the close
of the war, Kate is deeply chagrined to learn that Fraulein Berg is
a Jew who eventually emigrated to Israel and found happiness there,
bearing no grudge against her thoughtless, childish persecutors.
Kate remembers her mother saying that "not thinking could sometimes be a crime."

397. Lingard, Joan. STRANGERS IN THE HOUSE. New York:
        Dutton, 1981. 131p. Grades 7-10. R+
        Stella Cunningham, 13, and Calum McLeod, 14, are mutually
resentful when Calum's divorced mother Willa agrees to marry Stella's
widowed father Tom and move into the Cunningham's cramped Edin-
burgh apartment. Stella, who formerly kept house for her father,
now has to share her bedroom with Betsy McLeod, 6, while Calum
occupies a storage cubbyhole. Stella wants to move in with her
aunt and uncle who demur. Calum enjoys visiting his father and
his new family in the holidays, but their mobile home is too crowded
to accommodate him permanently. When her father chastises her for
neglecting her chores and overburdening Willa, Stella storms off
and tears a ligament, cancelling an important dance recital. To add
insult to injury, her best friend perfidiously becomes romantically
involved with Calum. When Tom and Willa quarrel over his exces-
sive drinking (he began after his first wife's death), Stella hopes
that they will divorce; and when Calum's father offers him a home

after he and his wife separate, she hopes that he will accept. Instead, Tom and Willa locate a larger apartment, and Stella knows
her hopes are doomed. In protest she runs away. It is Calum who
finds her hiding place and persuades her to try again at making the
melded family work, reminding her that they are both in it together.

398. Little, Jean. MAMA'S GOING TO BUY YOU A MOCKINGBIRD.
      New York: Viking/Kestrel, 1984. 213p. Grades 5-8. R++
      Summer vacation at their cottage on a Canadian lake begins
hollowly for Jeremy Talbot, 11, and his sister Sarah, 7. Aunt
Margery is staying with them while their father has surgery for
cancer. Jeremy learns from adult conversations that his father has
a "fifty-fifty chance," but he doesn't understand its meaning. He
expects their summer fun to start when Dad and Mum return, but
Dad is now an invalid who tires easily. Avid bird watchers, Jeremy
and his father experience a sublime and intimate moment together in
the dark garden when an owl takes wing nearby. On an exhausting
trip to town, Dad brings him a lifelike stone owl to commemorate the
occasion, which he treasures. A premonition of tragedy touches him
when they leave the cottage early and his father is rehospitalized,
intimating that he will never return to work. Jeremy starts acting
more brotherly towards his pesky sister and finds an unexpected
ally in aloof classmate Tess, who is empathetic when Mum confides
in Jeremy that Dad is dying. Tess' formula for sparing herself the
pain of her unwed mother's desertion is to put her out of her mind.
Jeremy agrees that forgetfulness is a convenient panacea, but as
Christmas approaches it is difficult to avoid reminders of his father,
and he knows that Mum, who has returned to school, wants them to
cherish their memories of him. An inspiration to take his dad's
place and fill Mum's half-empty stocking with his precious owl in-
fuses him with a Christmas spirit that he never expected to have.

399. Lutters, Valerie A. THE HAUNTING OF JULIE UNGER. New
      York: Atheneum, 1977. 193p. Grades 6-9. R+
      Julie Unger, 14, has had a chip on her shoulder since her
father died of a heart attack while shoveling snow outside their home
in Pennsylvania, aloofly and sullenly parading the rapport and comradeship she and her father enjoyed like a red flag before her
mother. Now the family, including Amy, 5, has moved to live with
Grandma Eiker in the insular seacoast town in Maine where they
used to vacation. Julie resentfully repels her mother's efforts to
penetrate her stony facade. Her mother, who has taken a clerical
job, wearily sidesteps confrontation with her stoical daughter who
feels so misunderstood. A self-described misfit and outcast at her
new high school because of her defensive attitude, Julie clandestinely
takes up the passionate avocation of photographing wild Canada geese
that she shared with her father. Before long, Julie's father materializes beside her, advising, encouraging, joking, and smoking his
pipe. Soon she lives only for the photography sessions and the re-
sumption of their easy and natural relationship. She dreads the
autumn departure of the geese and lures them with grain long past

178   The Single-Parent Family

their migrating season. One day she returns to find hunters decimating the fowl she has tamed and learns to her horror that she is
largely responsible for their deaths. In an agony of love and remorse she drives away the geese, along with her father's specter,
giving in to the long-denied catharsis of grief. At last she turns
her camera lens forward instead of backward.

400. MacLachlan, Patricia. SARAH, PLAIN AND TALL. New York:
      Harper and Row, 1985. 58p. Grades 3-5. R+
      Mama's last words before her death following childbirth were:
"Isn't he beautiful, Anna?" Anna would have called him "Trouble-
some" instead of Caleb. Papa, who sang with Mama every day, has
remained silent since her death. Anna's sole requisite for the prospective correspondence bride for whom Papa has advertised is that
she sing. Sarah replies that she does sing and adds that she is
plain and tall. She agrees to leave her beloved coastal home in
Maine for a month's trial period at the prairie farm in the spring.
Independent Sarah insists upon helping fix the roof as a storm approaches and learning to plow and drive the wagon. Anna, Caleb
and Papa are utterly captivated by her, but Sarah is homesick and
Anna is terrified that if Sarah learns to drive the wagon she will
use her mobility to leave them. Sarah, however, returns from her
solitary trip to town bringing them pastels in the shades of the sea
for drawing pictures to remind her of the seacoast. She explains
that while she misses her old home, she would miss all of them more
if she were to return. They plan a summer wedding.

401. Madison, Wilfred. CALL ME DANICA. New York: Four
      Winds, 1977. (OP) 203p. Grades 5-8. R+
      With every alluring postcard from her aunt and uncle in Van-
couver, Danica Pavelic, 12, enamored of Western rock 'n' roll, begs
her father to emigrate to that beguiling city, but her father, a
proud, traditional nationalist, will not consider leaving his native
Croatia or the family inn. Because of the dearth of medical care
in their tiny village, he dies shockingly and unexpectedly of appen-
dicitis. Mama shoulders the burdens of head of household and
Danica makes plans to become a doctor until hard times befall them
and they are forced to leave their homeland. Canada is not the land
of milk and honey for immigrants that Danica anticipated. Mama
takes a job as cook in a restaurant; Mirjana, 17, joins a folk dancing
group; and Marko, 8, finds a friend. But Danica, lonely and
alienated, takes up with a tawdry, rudderless young woman of whom
she knows her family would disapprove. When Danica is injured in
a traffic accident, a doctor, who is a client of her dog-walking service and an immigrant himself, learns of her derailed ambition for a
medical career and steers her back on the track. She discovers
that to be a totally assimilated Canadian she does not have to sacrifice her ethnicity. Now 14, she joins Mirjana's dance group, Mama
opens a Croatian restaurant, and they find contentment at last.

402. Madison, Winifred. MARINKA, KATINKA AND ME (SUSIE).

Scarsdale: Bradbury, 1975. (OP) Illus. by Miller Pope.
72p. Grades 3-5. R
The three new girls in class gravitate toward one another on
their first day of fourth grade and soon become inseparable companions, jumping rope, playing dress-up, talking on the telephone,
going to a birthday party, walking their identical puppies, wearing
their identical knit caps, and dancing a special Maidens' Dance at a
school performance. Blonde Marinka's mother is divorced; brunette
Susie's father is dead; while redhead Katinka's father is in prison.
One day a silly quarrel pairs Susie and Marinka against Katinka,
who now walks home from school on the opposite side of the street.
Then Susie and Katinka patch their misunderstanding and it is
Marinka's turn to be odd-man-out. The Ouija board suggests to
Susie and Katinka that Marinka is sad and lonely, and the two agree
that it takes three to jump rope successfully. The olive branch is
extended and the argument forgotten.

403. Mahy, Margaret. THE HAUNTING. New York: Atheneum,
1983. 135p. Grades 5-8. R
When Barney Palmer, 8, whose mother died of a weak heart at
his birth, begins seeing disturbing visions upon the death of Great-
uncle Barnaby Scholar, for whom he is named, there can be no denying that he is haunted. The apparition appears to be that of
Great-uncle Cole, black sheep of the family who died young. Barney's loquacious, inquisitive older sister Tabitha consults the other
great-uncles, who reveal that their inbred family has a penchant
for producing sons with supernatural powers, and they believe that
Barney, too, may be a "Scholar magician." The boy becomes increasingly distracted as foreboding footsteps grow louder and an
insidious force tries to take over his mind. Suddenly, Great-uncle
Cole materializes, very much alive and frightening, having feigned
his own death to escape his bullying mother. He intends to take
Barney away with him forcibly, if necessary, to replace his brother
Barnaby, the only friend he ever had. Barney's beloved stepmother Claire staunchly defends him, but it requires the intervention of his quiet, withdrawn sister Troy, 13, and her shocking
revelation that it is she who inherited the occult powers, not Barney, to restore equilibrium and show Cole how to become more of
an uncle and less of a sorcerer.

404. Mann, Peggy. THERE ARE TWO KINDS OF TERRIBLE.
Garden City: Doubleday, 1977. 132p. Grades 5-6. R+
Nothing is conceivably more disastrous to Robbie Farley than
breaking his tennis arm on the first day of summer vacation. He
can't participate in his favorite sports, nor can he play the snare
drum his mother gave him for his birthday. A suburban homemaker, his devoted, spirited mother is a buffer between Robbie and
his father, a stranger to the boy, whose exchanges are confined to
two-syllable greetings. Leaving the house in the morning before
Robbie rises to commute to his accountancy job in the city and

returning late in the evening, his father's free time is devoted to
politics and finance. Robbie must even restrict music practice because his father is sensitive to noise. Then without warning his
mother is hospitalized for tests, he is told, relating to women's
problems. He sees her only once more prior to her death of a
virulent cancer that metastasized to her liver. Robbie stumbles
through the party-like funeral services and reception afterward,
longing for solitude, but when the guests depart he is again alone
with his uncommunicative father. His grief briefly takes the form
of anger at his mom for leaving him in this predicament. Wrath at
his dad for falling asleep with a lit cigarette turns into a flash of
understanding when he realizes that Dad was poring sorrowfully
over an old photo album. Robbie takes the initiative in meeting his
father half way, and his dad buys him a new set of drums in a
mutual attempt at harmony.

405. Mathis, Sharon Bell. LISTEN FOR THE FIG TREE. New
        York: Viking, 1974. 175p. Grades 7-9. R+
        The dark world of Muffin, 16, blind from glaucoma since 10,
consists of her mother, who finds forgetfulness in a bottle since
her husband's violent death last Christmas Eve; her boyfriend
Ernie, a devout Black Muslim; and Mr. Dale, their upstairs neighbor
who loves her like a father and treats her royally. Her two major
concerns are to guide her mother safely past the anniversary of
her father's death, a seemingly hopeless battle in which their roles
are reversed and Muffin loses some odious skirmishes, and to celebrate her first African Kwanza on Christmas night, a more attain-
able goal even though she lacks a suitable dress. Ernie insists that
it is how you feel, not what you wear, that is important, but Mr.
Dale provides the material and she sews her own stunning costume.
The traumatic attempted rape in which the dress is ruined almost
causes her to miss the Kwanza, but with the support of Ernie and
Mr. Dale she overcomes her fears and experiences the beauty and
unity of the ancient black pageant which instills the strength to
struggle on with her mother.

406. Mays, Lucinda. THE CANDLE AND THE MIRROR. New York:
        Atheneum, 1982. 182p. Grades 6-10. R+
        Anne Simmons' father married her mother, the daughter of a
frontier newspaper publisher, for her spunk and independence, but
when he acquired family responsibilities he expected her to settle
down and become a full-time homemaker. Emily Simmons, however,
continued consciousness raising activities and stumping for women's
suffrage. Anne, 12 in 1895, loves her mother and father Sam, a
Des Moines farm equipment salesman, equally, and is torn between
their diverging expectations of her. Sam dies when Anne is 15, and
her mother joins the lecture circuit, writes articles, and eventually
becomes a union organizer for Pennsylvania coal miners. Anne,
meanwhile, lives briefly with her stultifying grandmother, then attends a conservative upperclass boarding school which prepares her
for a teaching career. When her first job in a reactionary country

school is terminated, she joins her mother in the squalor and oppression of a mining town. There she shares the adversities and
experiences the dangers of opposing the omnipotent mine lords.
Her zealous mother engages her as her secretary while she organizes
a women's march against child labor and the company store policy,
but a devastating flood obliterates the town, and in the emergency
Anne finds her true calling as a public health nurse, dedicated to
the cause of relieving human suffering but free of her mother's
driving fanaticism.

407. McGraw, Eloise Jarvis. THE MONEY ROOM. New York:
      Atheneum, 1981. 182p. Grades 5-7. R
      Scott Holloway, 13, is less than enthusiastic about moving
from the Medford house with its memories of his father, killed three
years ago by a drunken driver, to the farm his great-grandfather
willed to his mother, but the tales of Great-Gramp's fabled Money
Room are intriguing. He and his determined sister Melinda, 9, start
searching for it immediately, but all they find are worthless stocks
and bonds from firms that vanished in the Great Depression.
"Mur," a realtor, believes the room is a myth in spite of the under-
handed efforts of oldtimer Dorrit Suggs to buy the house. Scott's
insular Oregon classmates are hostile and standoffish, but as he
roams the fields, orchards and woods, he develops an intense affection for the farm. When the prospect of expensive repairs plus a
late filbert harvest force Mur to consider selling out, the children
are distraught. The sale agreement is inked on the very day that
Melinda's inquisitive pet parakeet uncovers a room papered in old
stock certificates which have been covered with floral wallpaper.
Mr. Suggs is jubilant, knowing that everything attached to the
house belongs to the buyer. When the certificates are appraised,
however, it is not the stocks on the wall that are valuable but one
of those overlooked in the attic. A disgruntled Mr. Suggs reneges
on the deal, and Mrs. Holloway enters a partnership for harvesting
the nuts with the father of a boy who has become Scott's first
friend.

408. McKinley, Robin. THE HERO AND THE CROWN. New York:
      Greenwillow, 1984. 246p. Grades 6-10. R+
      Aerin, 17, has always suffered the condescension of other
members of Damar's royal family. Her mother, who died in childbirth, was a foreigner from the enemy land to the North and a witch
who some believe beguiled her father, King Arlbeth, into marriage.
Despite her father's love and the devotion of her cousin Tor, Aerin
is a loner who takes pleasure in training her father's retired war
stallion Talat to become a dragon hunter. She tests her skill first
on a small but nasty dragon, earning her father's approbation and
respect. Still, he does not allow her to join him in battle against
the evil forces of the North, but in his absence she engages the far
more menacing black dragon Maur and defeats him at grave personal
injury. While hailed as a heroine, she is also feared as a sorceress
and decides to sneak away to regain her strength. In a mountain

stronghold she finds guru Luthe who nurses her to health and tu-
tors her on her origins and powers. From him she learns that she
must fulfill her mother's hopes that her offspring will seek and destroy the most formidable and cunning dragon of all, her brother
Agsded. Armed with courage, tenacity, perseverance, and the
magical sword Gonturan, Aerin confronts him in his den and vanquishes him, regaining the Hero's Crown. With her army of wild
mythical beasts, she returns to Damar in time to join forces with
her father and Tor in repelling the almost victorious invaders from
the North. Arlbeth dies in the battle, but Tor succeeds him, beseeching Aerin to be his queen. Damar enters into a long period of
peace and prosperity.

409. McLean, Susan. PENNIES FOR THE PIPER. New York:
      Farrar, Straus, Giroux, 1981. 150p. Grades 5-7. R+
      Victoria (Bicks) Purvis, 10, and her mother have been alone
in Minneapolis since the accidental death of her father, a Vietnam
War veteran. Now her mother, too, is dying of a diseased heart,
irrevocably weakened by childhood rheumatic fever. The two have
talked long and ardently of the arrangements made for Bicks when
Mums no longer responds, including the trust fund, the money order to cover funeral expenses, and the bus fare to reach paternal
Aunt Millicent, her only other living relative, in Dubuque. As
Mums grows weaker and Bicks takes on more responsibility, the two,
brimful of love, empathy and compassion, befriend a classmate of
Bicks who is badly abused by his mentally ill mother, and Bicks
decorates untended graves on Memorial Day. The fateful day arrives when Mums dies in her sleep, ending her pain, and Bicks
steels herself to follow the plans. But something is wrong. The
rite of putting Mums to rest will not be complete unless Bicks attends the service and makes a suitable floral tribute. She spends
the rest of the grocery money and most of the bus fare on a funeral
spray, gives in to cathartic tears in a graveside farewell, and then
sets off with resignation and determination for Iowa on foot with all
her worldly possessions in a shopping bag. Starving and exhausted,
she is welcomed at her destination by an anxious and thankful aunt.

410. Milton, Hilary. TORNADO! New York: Watts, 1983. 147p.
      Grades 5-9. NR
      En route to visit her brother Charley in their old home town,
Janet Carson, a recently widowed high school teacher, decides to
leave the interstate highway and take a shortcut. Soon after, she
and the children, Paul, 14, and Lisa, 7, hear a storm warning on
the car radio. The old bridge is already washed out when they
reach it, and when the travellers try to turn the car around it gets
stuck in a ditch. As they abandon the car to seek higher ground,
Janet injures her leg. They have scarcely hobbled a few yards
when Lisa is bitten by a copperhead. Then the tornado is upon
them, and when it passes Paul has to search out and rescue his
womenfolk who have been buried in debris. Together they struggle
on till they reach the deserted hilltop Boy Scout encampment which

is now an island. Paul amost despairs of getting help for Lisa until
he spies the CB radio equipment he doesn't know how to operate.
He fumbles around until he raises Uncle Charley, who manages to
convince someone that the Carsons' plight is worse than that of
others and to send a helicopter after them. Of course the chopper
has no place to land, so Paul, remembering a military training stunt
he saw on TV, courageously straps himself and Lisa to the end of
the rope and is towed, dangling, to the roof of the local hospital.
Paul receives an honorary state trooper badge for his heroism in
this melodramatic cliff-hanger.

411. Moe, Barbara. PICKLES AND PRUNES. New York: McGraw-
Hill, 1976. 122p. Grades 6-8. R++
    In the six years since her father died, Annie Carter's mother
has worked as a nurse in a Denver children's hospital where Annie,
13, an only child, is free to come and go. Suddenly, a new physician, Dr. Abrams, takes a more than casual interest in Mrs. Carter,
which to Annie is a threat to the stability and placidity of their
lives. She decides to act assertive and sophisticated--changing her
name to Anne and embracing a diet of prunes--in an attempt to discourage Dr. Abrams. At the same time, she meets a teenage patient
whose daring she admires in leaving the hospital grounds to buy her
favorite pickles in defiance of the formidable nursing supervisor.
Anne and Laurie become friends and conspirators in thwarting Miss
Gebhard, and Anne soon learns that Laurie is dying of cancer but
is determined to make the most of the time left to her, eventually
leaving the hospital as an outpatient. Anne stubbornly succeeds in
nettling Dr. Abrams but not in deterring his attention to her
mother. When the girls meet again at a friend's wedding, Anne
learns that Laurie is not as brave as she appears and that she herself does not project the trepidation she feels. Laurie tells her
how emotionally unburdening it was to finally discuss her fears and
feelings with her parents. Anne remains unconvinced that baring
her anxieties to adults will help in her case until Elwood Abrams
brings her the news of Laurie's death. She flings her arms around
him for consolation.

412. Morgan, Alison. RUTH CRANE. New York: Harper and Row,
1974. (OP) 244p. Grades 6-9. R
    At the close of a vacation trip to Wales to visit their mother's
girlhood home, the Crane family is involved in an auto accident in
which their father is killed and their mother and the middle child
Patsy are severely injured. Because her mother is a fastidious homemaker, Ruth, 14, has never been taught the rudiments of cooking
or cleaning, but while Auntie Mary keeps vigil at the hospital, Ruth
is expected to keep house for Uncle Sam and Cousin Pete, also 14,
a task to which she warms only after several false starts. Riding
herd on her brother Tony, 9, is more onerous because he is pampered, helpless and whiny. The two of them make friends separately
with Old Mossy, a simple recluse, and when Tony disappears one
morning leaving a cryptic note, Ruth is certain that he must be with

the old man. After searching for him fruitlessly all day, Ruth follows her hunch that he has gone to visit Patsy, who has just come
out of a coma, with Old Mossy to guide him on a shortcut over the
hills. She eventually locates him deep in the woods where Old Mossy
abandoned him. Together they spend the night in a dark and eerie
church. Ruth's crash course in maturity encompasses the knowledge
that the loss of her father is not temporary and that she will be
Tony's primary care giver after her mother recovers and takes a job.

413. Mulford, Philippa Green. THE WORLD IS MY EGGSHELL.
      New York: Delacorte, 1986. 157p. Grades 7-10. R
      Following their father's death of a hemorrhaging ulcer, their
mother accepts a public relations job and starts a new life in Connecticut with fraternal twins Abbey and Sheldon Reilly, 16, and
Joyce, 10. Aggressive and extroverted like his father, Shel adapts
immediately. Abbey, still grieving, unsophisticated, and unable to
live up to her father's expectations, becomes reclusive and fearful
of entering the fiercely competitive and convoluted dating fray at
her new high school. When her mother starts dating again, she
feels that she has no right to be anything but a mother. Abbey
ambivalently runs for editor of the literary magazine and goes out
for track until it becomes obvious that jealous and possessive
Crystal Glass is determined to defeat her at any cost. The challenge inspires Abbey to fight. Crystal underhandedly wins the editorial post which she doesn't really want and later resigns. Abbey
trains hard for the track meet and loses only when Crystal shoves
her. With new confidence Abbey warns Crystal to back off. She
discovers that Shel is not as secure and infallible as he seems in
spite of his drive to excel and his animal magnetism. Abbey accepts
her first date, which proves to be less embarrassing than she
feared, and she bets Shel that when Mom remarries she will handle
that change better than he. She has learned to grapple with life
while eschewing the accepted practice of shifting allegiances and
exploiting acquaintances to gain advantage. She lets her father go.

414. Myers, Walter Dean. IT AIN'T ALL FOR NOTHIN'. New
      York: Viking, 1978. 217p. Grades 6-8. R+
      Devout Grandma Carrie makes a good home in Harlem for
Tippy, 12, on her social security benefits plus occasional daywork
until physical debilities force her into an old people's home. Tippy
goes to live with his father, Lonnie, a virtual stranger to the boy,
his mother having died at his birth. Tippy hates the filthy apartment to which Lonnie brings his tough, sordid friends. Lonnie,
moreover, uses Tippy's welfare money to play numbers and buy booze
and "herb" but no staples for the boy. Lonnie defends his life of
larceny by explaining to Tippy that it is compensation for his emas-
culation by the white establishment. Tippy witnesses a burglary,
and his silence is secured through intimidation. Visiting Grandma
Carrie is no longer any consolation, because the old woman is just
a shadow of her former self, so the lost, unsupervised boy turns to
alcohol himself for solace. Lonnie decides to go straight and get a

job but loses it in short order, returning to crime with Tippy as
accomplice. After a robbery in which one of Lonnie's gang is mortally wounded and has to be sacrificed for the safety of the others,
Tippy overcomes his fear of Lonnie's beatings and goes for help to
a bus driver who befriended him earlier. In his jail cell, Lonnie
holds no grudges and offers hope for a different life after he serves
his term.

415. Naylor, Phyllis Reynolds. THE AGONY OF ALICE. New York:
     Atheneum, 1985. 131p. Grades 5-6. R+
     Alice McKinley, 11, rues all the mortifying moments she has
experienced since kindergarten and blames her humiliations on the
fact that she has had no female guidance since her mother died when
she was 4. She lives in Maryland with her father, a music store
manager, and her brother Lester, 18, neither of whom is of any help
in choosing fashionable clothes or imparting proper etiquette. To
ease her transition into her teens, Alice plans to adopt a female role
model and copy her appearance and behavior. She chooses the popular and glamorous sixth grade teacher, Miss Cole, and is bitterly
disappointed to be assigned to the other sixth grade class taught by
squat and dowdy Mrs. Plotkin. Eventually, however, Miss Cole begins to reveal her impatient and intolerant nature, while Alice comes
to appreciate discerning Mrs. Plotkin for her sympathy and sincerity.
On Valentine's Day, Alice realizes she has a secret admirer in
Patrick, who believes that if one doesn't act embarrassed the teasers
lose interest. At Easter her father sends her to her aunt in Chicago.
While she admires Aunt Sally's self-confidence, she dislikes her regimentation. Alice gets her period on the visit and decides to become
a composite of many women she has appreciated in different ways.
Most of all she wants to be caring like Mrs. Plotkin.

416. Naylor, Phyllis Reynolds. NIGHT CRY. New York:
     Atheneum, 1984. Grades 5-8. R
     Sleet, the horse that was spooked by an electrical storm,
throwing and killing her brother a year ago, has been branded the
devil incarnate, and Ellen Stump, 13, is terrified of him. Her
father, a widower since her mother's death of meningitis five years
earlier, hires a retarded neighbor boy to care for Sleet before leaving on a business trip as a calendar salesman, the last in a string
of unsuccessful endeavors. During his absence a mysterious
stranger appears at their isolated Mississippi mountain home asking
for food in exchange for work. Though Ellen is leery of him and
his hard luck tale, she acquiesces. When the news breaks that the
son of the local benefactor has been kidnapped for ransom, Ellen
first suspects that her father has abducted him out of frustration
with his impecuniosity. Later, when she hears a stifled cry in the
night, she realizes that the sinister stranger is the culprit. Creating a diversionary action, she daringly rescues the boy and hides
him in the last place the kidnapper would think of looking: in the
stable of her nemesis, Sleet. But as the menacing stranger tightens
the noose, she knows that help will not arrive in time and that she

must rely upon the creature she fears to take them to safety. She
becomes a heroine when she is interviewed by the TV newswoman
she idolizes. When her father returns he vows never to leave her
alone again, and Ellen takes pleasure in making friends with Sleet
again.

417. Ness, Evaline. SAM, BANGS AND MOONSHINE. New York:
      Holt, Rinehart and Winston, 1966. Illus. by the author. Unp.
      Grades 2-3. R+
      Samantha invents stories to compensate for the loss of her
mother but can't sort fact from fancy. She tells her very literal
friend Thomas that her mother is a mermaid and that she has a lion
and a baby kangaroo for pets instead of an ordinary cat named
Bangs. When she sends Thomas on a wild goose chase to Blue Rock
to look for the kangaroo, she comes to the sudden realization that
the tide will soon cover the rock and sweep Thomas away with it.
Her fisherman father rescues him but cannot save Bangs, who tagged
along with Thomas. The remorseful Sam sobs herself to sleep, but
bedraggled Bangs belatedly appears, and she ruefully resolves to
separate reality from fantasy without submerging the vivid imagination
her father calls "moonshine." In the morning he presents her with a
gerbil that looks a bit like a baby kangaroo which she in turn bestows on Thomas. She names it Moonshine.

418. Newman, Robert. THE CASE OF THE SOMERVILLE SECRET.
      New York: Atheneum, 1981. 184p. Grades 5-7. NR
      In this third in a series of detective tales featuring Great
Britain's nineteenth-century counterparts to Nancy Drew and the
Hardy Boys, Andrew Tillett, son of a famous actress, and Sarah
Wiggins, daughter of their widowed housekeeper, team up to assist
Inspector Wyatt solve another baffling and heinous crime. Andrew's
mother is on tour, and the two youthful sleuths must be evasive
with Sarah's mother who would be unnerved if she suspected their
dangerous involvement. The "secret" of the title is a human "monster" whom Lord Somerville believes to be his son and from whom it
is his duty to protect the public by locking him away. The witless
creature, now fully grown and a potential menace, is kidnapped for
ransom by a nefarious scar-faced man. Observant Andrew and im-
pulsive Sarah unravel clues with the aid of a terrified chimney
sweep, enabling authorities to close in. With the brute at large and
cornered in a cemetery, Sarah becomes a heroine, and justice is
served in a few wry twists.

419. Nichols, Joan Kane. ALL BUT THE RIGHT FOLKS. Owings
      Mills, Md.: Stemmer House, 1985. 100p. Grades 5-7. R+
      Although his father, a self-confident black magazine photog-
rapher, assimilates into the white community for business purposes,
he makes no secret of his contempt for the white establishment.
When diffident, insecure Marv Johnson flatly refuses to go to summer
camp while his father is on assignment because of the ridicule he receives for his bed-wetting and asthma, his father opportunistically

ships him off to the grandmother he didn't know existed, his
mother's mother, who is white. Marv and Helga strike an immediate
accord. The exercise of learning to bike with Helga improves his
asthma; the acceptance of their New York neighborhood black kids
who don't know about his afflictions eliminates his incontinence; and
karate lessons earn his father's pride and respect. But Marv has a
new and disturbing perplexity: is he black or white? An armed
robbery in which he fails to protect Helga further erodes his fragile
self-esteem. He later redeems himself by confronting, outwitting
and subduing the malefactors. Helga fills in the gaps in his personal history by recounting how his parents met and married as
Civil Rights activists and how his mother died of an accidental drug
overdose in San Francisco, where he now lives with his father.
She confides in him her own confusion about her origins as a half-
Jewish immigrant from Germany, the only member of her family to
survive the Holocaust. Marv concludes that instead of being a blend
of two races he will be a bridge between the black and white worlds.

420. Nixon, Joan Lowery. MAGGIE, TOO. San Diego: Harcourt,
      Brace, Jovanovich, 1985. 101p. Grades 5-6. R+
      When her long-widowed Hollywood director father announces
his intention of marrying a 20-year-old starlet, selling the house that
is filled with memorabilia of her mother, and exiling her for the summer to her maternal grandmother's home in Houston, Margaret Le-
doux, 12, is hurt and angry. No sooner does she arrive than she
quick-wittedly helps foil the hostage-taking of the family next door.
The media coverage brings Grandma Landry's three surviving children and their families rallying in alarm, intent upon convincing her
to give up her commodious house and move into a security high rise.
With the addition of the nervous neighbors and a disobedient mastiff,
the house is bedlam, and Margaret, accustomed to solitude, servants
and boarding schools, enters a radio contest determined to win a
getaway trip to a Mexican resort. The ubiquitous, vociferous and
affectionate relatives make heavy demands on Grandma's time and
energy, but she remains patient and calm, even counseling standoffish Margaret to meet her father halfway when he writes her a
conciliatory letter. Margaret empathizes with her grandmother's desire to stay in her own home and gradually thaws to her uncommon
sense. Perceiving the fragmentation and stress Grandma is bearing
from children and grandchildren, Margaret decides to make her the
recipient of the trip she expects to win. She is incredulous when
the prize goes to someone else, but Grandma appreciates her efforts
on her behalf. She sends all her visitors home and invites Margaret,
who wants to be called Maggie, too, to spend the school year with
her.

420a. Oneal, Zibby. A FORMAL FEELING. New York: Viking,
      1982. 162p. Grades 7-12. R++
      A boarding school student home for the holidays for the first
time since her father's remarriage following her mother's death of a
stroke a year earlier, Anne Cameron, 16, has consciously refused

to indulge her grief, releasing her emotions instead in the physical exertion of long distance running. She is disdainful and resentful of her stepmother Dory, secretary to her university professor father. She considers Dory to be an inept interloper and unattractive affront to the memory of her strikingly beautiful mother, an intellectual who was accomplished in everything she undertook and who expected the same perfectionism from her family. Her brother Spencer, a university student, has little patience for her frigidity towards Dory and looks askance at Anne's recollections of their mother as a paragon of virtue. An ice skating accident triggers sudden subliminal flashbacks, long suppressed, of the year Anne was 8 when her mother abandoned the family, needing "space to think." Anne recalls her anxiety in the belief that she caused the desertion by not measuring up to her mother's expectations. Agonizingly, she must confront the guilty misgiving that she may never have loved her mother at all because of her impossibly lofty and uncompromising standards. While Dory tenderly ministers to her sprained ankle, Anne gradually comes to grips with her inner turmoil and grasps the meaning of Emily Dickinson's words, "After a great pain, a formal feeling comes." She finally unbends, weeps-- and says goodbye.

421. Orlev, Uri. THE ISLAND ON BIRD STREET. Boston: Houghton Mifflin, 1984. Trans. by Hillel Halkin. 162p. Grades 5-8. R
      Before his mother disappeared forever from their ghetto in Warsaw in a German transportation, his parents would not allow Alex, 11, to play in the dangerous bombed out building on Bird Street next to the dividing wall. Before the next selection, however, his father makes plans with Alex to escape their captors and rendezvous there, drilling him in survival techniques and the use of the firearm he provides. Alex is to wait faithfully there alone, constantly threatened by human enemies as well as physical perils, for five full months until his father is able to keep his promise. Early on he is forced to improvise as his supplies dwindle, while Polish looters and Jewish informers, as well as the dreaded German soldiers, restrict his movements ever more tightly. Ingeniously, he rigs a rope ladder to the uppermost floor, hanging precariously in space, where he hides by day in a pantry closet, foraging stealthily by night while risking detection by other furtive scavengers. His loneliness is ameliorated only on the occasions when he daringly sneaks across the wall by secret passage to visit a girl he can see from his high perch. He uses his pistol only once to kill a German in defense of a wounded fugitive. As winter confines him to his cramped hideout, he fights off numbing depression. When at last he hears his father's voice in the rubble, he hardly dares to believe that his deliverance has finally come.

422. Paige, Harry W. SHADOW ON THE SUN. New York: Warne, 1984. 181p. Grades 6-10. R+
      Billy Wade is 14, living with his mother Joline who runs a

boarding house in New Mexico Territory in 1892, when he learns from a pulp western novelist that he is the son of Billy the Kid. Joline has kept the knowledge of his parentage a secret from Billy since his father's death at the age of 21 by the hand of cowardly ex-sheriff Pat Garrett because she abhors the glorification of gun-fighting and the promulgation of her husband's claim to fame. She wants the boy to grow up to be normal, peaceable and law-abiding. Now the avaricious author, J. C. Weatherby, ignites the spark and fans the flames of vengeance in young Billy so that he can write the final chapter in the saga of Billy the Kid. Behind his mother's back, Billy asks his gunslinger friend Wes Wakely, who is also seeking immortality as a legend like Billy's father, to teach him the skill of dueling to the death. At the same time, his mother's boarder Axel Crow, a photographer who is recording the vanishing Old West for posterity, is teaching Billy the creative new art of photography. Wes is ignobly killed by bushwhackers. Even while mourning his friend, Billy, goaded by Weatherby with his lascivious lust for blood and glib rhetoric of honor, nobility and duty, calls out Pat Garrett, now a broken, besotted middle-aged man. When the ex-sheriff fumbles his gun, Billy spares his life, hangs up his pistols, and agrees to go back East with his mother to perfect his proclivity for photography.

423. Peck, Richard. THROUGH A BRIEF DARKNESS. New York: Viking, 1973. 142p. Grades 6-9. R
     The taunting began in the sixth grade--that Karen Beatty's father is a crook, a mobster. That is when Daddy took her out of public school and sent her to a succession of second-rate boarding schools and summer camps. Soon he gave up their large New York apartment, and thereafter her only contact with him was through his highly efficient secretary. Now 16, Karen is a quiet, responsible student with no friends among her peers. Suddenly and inexplicably she is summoned to New York and put on a plane, purportedly to stay with cousins of her long-dead mother in London. Suspicious and mysterious occurrences begin happening immediately, but the sheltered teen does not suspect that something is amiss until she learns that "Cousin" Syd rented his house only the previous week and that he carries a revolver in a shoulder holster. With dawning realization she discovers that she is being held prisoner by her father's underworld rivals, who are trying to force a power play using her as leverage while Daddy is lying seriously injured in pro-tective custody in the States. She makes her escape with the help of a former camp acquaintance, Jay Fielding, who is now enrolled at Eton, and the two begin a suspenseful odyssey of elusion. They are aided by a doughty old dowager who spirits Karen out of the country as her maid while the thwarted thugs turn ugly and violent. With growing self-reliance Karen returns to her father, ready at last to seek and accept the truth about him.

424. Peck, Robert Newton. SPANISH HOOF. New York: Knopf, 1985. 181p. Grades 5-7. R+

Despite the backbreaking labor of cattle ranching during the anxious days of the Great Depression, Harriet Beecher, 11, her teasing brother Dabney, 16, their long-widowed mother, and the two hired hands who consider themselves family take pleasure in life at Spanish Hoof and are fiercely possessive of their piece of Florida real estate. Harry, as she prefers to be called, is overjoyed to receive the pony she requested for her last birthday; Dabney is sweet on their more prosperous but unspoiled neighbor, Trudy Sue; while Mama is optimistic that this year's crop of calves will pay off the worrisome mortgage. But cruel and unjust fate intervenes when a brood cow is killed by an alligator, the hired hands are accosted by drunken hooligans, and worst of all, the new calves contract the dreaded "black leg" and have to be put down. The bankers are unsympathetic, and the doctor orders Mama to retire from active ranching to save her heart. The outlook is bleak for the Beechers, who live by the principle that you don't quit when you're tired but when the job is done. To stay solvent and retain their land, they plant an orange grove, and Harry makes the agonizing decision to sell her beloved pony. The bittersweet year has matured both Harry and Dabney, who now shoulders the brunt of responsibility. New calves drop, giving them hope for the future, and on her twelfth birthday, Harry decides she wants to be called Harriet.

425. Pelgrom, Els. THE WINTER WHEN TIME WAS FROZEN. New
       York: Morrow, 1980. Trans. by Maryka and Raphael Rudnik.
       153p. Grades 5-6. R+
       Refugees from the Nazi occupation of Arnhem in the waning days of World War II, Noortje Vanderhook, 11, whose mother died before the war, and her father find a haven with the warm, generous Everingen family of Klaphek Farm. Their space and provender already overtaxed with son Evert, 12, a retarded daughter, a hired man, and an aging grandmother, the Everingens are also harboring tubercular Theo, a former Resistance fighter, plus another Arnhem family, while providing succor for a young Jewish family hiding in a subterranean shelter in the woods. The farm is a novelty to city-bred Noortje, and she and Evert become boon companions. When a baby is born to the Jewish family, Aunt Janna Everingen takes Noortje along to help with the delivery and later brings baby Sarah home for Noortje to nurture so her lusty cries will not betray the others. In spite of their precautions, the Meyers are discovered and herded off to be killed. The Klaphek pigs are confiscated to feed the beleaguered German army, and even their homestead is commandeered to quarter Nazi soldiers in their last ditch defense. Allied bombers and unmanned German V-1 plane bombs disturb their sleep, but the Everingens remain staunch, serene and patient throughout the ordeal. After the liberation, Noortje must face the inevitability of leaving beloved Klaphek Farm with her father, an insurance agent in peacetime, and taking leave of baby Sarah, who will be sent to relatives in the United States. It is a time she will remember forever.

426. Pevsner, Stella. CALL ME HELLER, THAT'S MY NAME. New York: Clarion, 1973. Illus. by Richard Cuffari. 183p. Grades 5-7. R

Motherless since the age of 2, Heller Hadley, now 11 in 1927, is bold and tomboyish, the antithesis of her ladylike older sister Margaret and her indulgent lawyer father. Then her prim Aunt Cornelia comes for an extended stay, following the death of her husband, and immediately starts to reform Heller and curtail her freedom. Heller's partner in adventure, Walter Wayne, deserts her for the new boy in town. Heller's reaction is to become ever more daring and attention-seeking, attempting to prove her courage to Walter Wayne by paying a midnight visit to her mother's grave and nearly getting caught by bootleggers. When Margaret announces her engagement to Bud, Heller schemes to either keep her at home or to go live with the newlyweds. Bud firmly scotches her manipulative plans, and Aunt Cornelia, her enemy, confirms her intention of staying on permanently. Enraged, Heller tries to discredit her aunt's respectable name by performing at a wild Charleston exhibition and is chastised. Humiliated, she takes the ultimate dare: to walk the railroad trestle. When a train bears down on her, she freezes and is saved only by Walter Wayne's presence of mind. Now overcome with self-pity and remorse, she is comforted by Aunt Cornelia and demonstrates her dependability by helping with the wedding. As she accepts her femininity, she becomes the envy of the girls who formerly despised her. And Aunt Cornelia crops her severe, spinsterish bun into a modish bob.

427. Peyton, K. M. MARION'S ANGELS. Oxford: Oxford University Press, 1979. (OP) Illus. by Robert Micklewright. 152p. Grades 5-8. R

Steeped in the lore of the historic fifteenth-century church by her mother, a classical scholar who died when the girl was 7, Marion Carver has become the self-appointed guardian of the old edifice with its twelve lively and whimsical stone angels flying from the rafters. Living alone with her father, a computer programmer by profession and boat builder by avocation, the sensitive girl indulges in flights of fancy and bears her emotions near the surface. In an emotional outburst during a musical fundraiser for the repair of the church's rotting roof, Marion becomes acquainted with the gifted young pianist whose wife so strongly resembles Marion's mother. The two Carvers and Pat and Ruth Pennington and their infant son soon become friends, and Marion is instrumental in persuading the venerated American violinist Ephraim Voigt to plan a series of benefit concerts for the church with Pat as accompanist. When the concert tour expands to include America, Ruth refuses to accompany Pat and speaks of divorce when he is determined to go without her. Marion dreams of Ruth marrying her father, whom she knows to be in love with her. On a stormy night after the final concert in England, she seeks a miracle to save the Penningtons' marriage and becomes trapped in the church when the ceiling collapses. One of her angels topples across the pews, creating a cave that protects her.

The crisis causes Pat to stay behind, and Marion foreswears further miracles and fantasies.

428.   Platt, Kin. RUN FOR YOUR LIFE. New York: Watts, 1977.
       Photos by Chuck Freedman. 95p. Grades 5-9. Hi-Lo. R
       Lee Hunter, 15, is an insecure borderline member of his Los Angeles area high school track team, practicing daily to better his time in the mile while also holding a part-time job delivering newspapers to sidewalk vending machines and helping to care for his younger siblings, Teresa, 11, Maria, 9, and Dewey, 5. His widowed mother works ten-hour days at a taco and tamale factory. When his newspaper coin boxes are targeted for theft by someone who has a duplicate key, Lee is fired because he is a suspect. He stalks the pilferer and discovers it is Mike Hope, a fellow runner and brother of friendly Connie Hope who encourages Lee's track efforts. Connie reports her brother, who was fired from the same route earlier and has been stealing out of spite ever since. Lee is reinstated but is determined to even the score by beating Mike, a seasoned runner, when he qualifies to compete in the all-city meet. Lee runs his strongest, in spite of Mike's dire threats, and wins, earning Connie's praise. Mike tells him he is only lucky, but with new self-confidence Lee knows that he's the better miler.

429.   Porte, Barbara Ann. HARRY'S MOM. New York: Greenwillow,
       1985. Illus. by Yossi Abolafia. 55p. Grades 1-3. R+
       While doing a vocabulary assignment, Harry Moskowitz is horrified to learn that he is considered an orphan, defined in the dictionary as a person without one or both parents. When he confronts his father with the information, he is told that no one in his large, extended family would deem him an orphan nor feel sorry for him. That evening he asks all his relatives, including his dad, to describe the mother he doesn't remember because she died when he was 1. He discovers that she was a daring sports reporter who participated in everything she wrote about, including mountain climbing, sky diving, scuba diving, and auto racing, at which she died. They also limn a picture of her as a warm and intelligent person who loved animals as a child and adored him when he was a baby. Harry decides that when he grows up he wants to be brave like his mom and a dentist like his dad.

430.   Rabe, Berniece. THE GIRL WHO HAD NO NAME. New York:
       Dutton, 1977. 147p. Grades 5-8. NR
       Although her saintly mother almost died when impetuous Girlie Webster, last of ten daughters, was born, she lived on in frail health for twelve more years. Now that she is in her grave, Girlie's taciturn father, so disappointed that he had no sons to help him on his Missouri farm during the Depression that he refused to give her a Christian name, will not consider keeping her at home with him, even though her cooking and math ability would benefit him. She and her pet cat, the only living being that really needs her, are shunted from the unsuitable home of one married sister to another. In her

sojourns in six different domiciles, she makes many observations
about love, marriage and biology but can't convince Papa to take
her back where she belongs. Then she learns from one sister that
Papa has spurned her because he believes she is the offspring of
an illicit liaison. Another sister debunks that story as a feeble
excuse to assuage his guilt for impregnating his wife once more
against medical advice and thus causing her fragility and premature
death. Girlie importunes him to adopt her, although a book of
genetics from the library proves to her satisfaction that she is truly
his child. That ingenious solution provides a face-saving loophole
for Mr. Webster, who names her Glencora and begins to exercise his
paternal instincts belatedly.

431. Rabin, Gil. CHANGES. New York: Harper and Row, 1973.
    149p. Grades 6-9. R
    Strapped after her husband's untimely death by inadequate
insurance and an outstanding loan that he had made to his older
sister, Jane November has no recourse but to leave South Dakota
with her retired father and son Christo, 14, and move in with her
sister-in-law in her tiny house in Brooklyn while she hunts for work.
Aunt Anna doesn't want them and is hostile and belligerent, but she
cannot repay the loan and so has to accept them. Sensible, stalwart Grandpa is a buffer in the standoff between the two women.
Chris quickly falls in love with frank, worldly, but sympathetic
Peppy, a girl his age, and to help tide them over financially, he
takes a grueling summer job as stock boy to a hat manufacturer.
Then, without warning, Grandpa is felled by a stroke that leaves
him blind. The doctor recommends committing him to a nursing home
for his own good, an idea they resist until Grandpa has a relapse
and Mom lands a sorely needed job as assistant librarian for an en-
gineering firm. Aunt Anna and Mom resolve their differences, but
Chris is powerless to prevent Grandpa from being institutionalized,
even though Peppy warns him, through bitter experience, that the
only escape from the home is to die of neglect. True enough,
Grandpa loses his spirit and becomes disoriented after a futile effort to free himself. The smell of the place so nauseates Chris
that he quits visiting, and upon Grandpa's death he opines that he
died weeks earlier when his mind failed.

432. Reiss, Johanna. THE JOURNEY BACK. New York: Crowell,
    1976. 212p. Grades 6-9. R+
    The war in Europe is over. After spending the past three
years in hiding (see the author's prequel, THE UPSTAIRS ROOM)
from Hitler's dreaded occupational forces in a farmhouse in the Dutch
countryside, Annie and Sini deLeeuw, now 13 and 23 respectively,
are at last free to rejoin their father and older sister and return to
their home in Winterswijk. While reluctant to part with the hearty,
jovial and loving peasant couple who sequestered them, Annie is
nonetheless eager to resume a normal life. But time has not stood
still. Rachel, who was also hidden by a Christian family, has converted to the Catholic faith and has become a sanctimonious spinster

and self-appointed housekeeper to her father, a cattle broker, who
was widowed at the beginning of the war. Sini, having sacrificed
her young adulthood, makes up for lost time by embracing a fast
life, dancing the night away with allied servicemen and infuriating
her father who is unwilling to accept her as an adult. Father, moreover, is planning to marry a refined woman who is critical of
Annie's manners and dress. Annie longs to return to the informal
Oostervelds, who wanted to adopt her. Rachel, displaced by her
father's wife, returns to her sheltering family, and Sini goes to the
city to become a nurse. With maturity and forbearance, Annie
comes to realize that her stepmother's criticism is meant to be constructive and begins to cooperate. Sadly, she knows she has grown
away from the Oostervelds.

433.   Rinaldo, C. L. DARK DREAMS. New York: Harper and
       Row, 1974. 154p. Grades 5-8. R+
       When 12-year-old Carlo's widowed father leaves him in the care
of his grandmother while he embarks for the Pacific in uniform in
1943, the delicate, sensitive boy experiences terrifying nightmares
induced by fear of his weak heart and of the brutal bullies who
prowl the alley. A mentally retarded man across the alley, whom
others fear, befriends and protects him. When Carlo's suspicious
grandmother discovers them playing happily in an abandoned
brewery, however, she has the unfortunate Joey J committed to an
institution. Carlo's anxieties return, and he wishes he were strong
and brave like his father, not fragile like his mother. When disconsolate Joey J escapes, the authorities agree to let him live in
peace with his mother, provided he commits no violence. But when
the hooligans attack Carlo with a knife, Joey J instinctively charges
to his friend's rescue, is remanded to the asylum, and dies shortly
afterward. From his grandmother and his father's letters, Carlo
learns revealing things about both his parents' courage.

434.   Rock, Gail. ADDIE AND THE KING OF HEARTS. New York:
       Knopf, 1976. Illus. by Charles McVicker. 85p. Grades 4-7.
       R
       Billy Wild is sweet on Addie Mills, 13 in 1949 (see 436, 437,
435), but she coyly repudiates his attentions, and when the handsome, urbane Mr. Davenport comes to teach seventh grade history,
all thoughts of Billy vanish. She spends hours after school discussing art and literature with Mr. Davenport and feeling infinitely
more mature and sophisticated than her classmates. At home she
moons over projecting an adult image, remembering that her father
was ten years older than her mother. When she keeps Billy dangling
too long, he asks her arch rival to the Valentine's Day dance, and
she is faced with the dilemma of going alone or staying home. She
and Grandma discuss finding "Mr. Right" and the many disappointments in the quest. Addie finally decides to go, but the dance is
a disaster: Billy is crowned King of Hearts, and Mr. Davenport introduces her to his glamorous fiancee. Addie reacts childishly, is
rebuked by Mr. Davenport, and flees home. To her surprise Billy

follows her, bored with the dance, bringing her a box of candy.
Addie decides to be more tolerant of her father's effulgent new girlfriend.

435. Rock, Gail. A DREAM FOR ADDIE. New York: Knopf, 1975.
      Illus. by Charles C. Gehm. 89p. Grades 4-6. R
      Constance Payne, the famous Broadway actress, is returning
to Clear River, Nebraska, upon her mother's death to sell the big
house in which she grew up. Addie Mills, now 13 (see 436 and
437), is determined to get her autograph and is surprised when
Constance accepts her invitation to dinner and to present the school
style show awards. She appears at the style show drunk, and Addie
and her grandmother are the only two who take compassion on her.
Constance agrees to give Addie and her friends drama lessons, but
at the second one she is besottedly abusive. At first Addie is in-
dignant and humiliated until Grandma calmly persuades her to be
forgiving. They realize that Constance is seriously ill, and Addie
has to convince her intractable father to let Constance convalesce in
their home. Addie remains loyal even when Constance confesses
that she has never been on stage. When they attend Easter services together, Constance regains her pride and decides to begin a
new life teaching piano and drama in Clear River.

436. Rock, Gail. THE HOUSE WITHOUT A CHRISTMAS TREE.
      New York: Knopf, 1974. Illus. by Charles C. Gehm. 87pp.
      Grades 4-6. R
      Strict but sympathetic Grandma acts as buffer between Addie
Mills, 10, and her dour, practical and undemonstrative father.
Growing up in Nebraska in the late 1940s, Addie is embarrassed that
their house lacks a Christmas tree, but Dad remains adamant. Addie
wins the drawing for the classroom tree, and she and her friend
Carla Mae drag it home and set it up with Grandma's help. Dad is
furious with her for accepting charity, and she goes to bed in tears
while Dad and Grandma argue heatedly. In the night, Grandma confides to Addie that her father cannot bear being reminded of her
mother's death at Christmas of the year she was born. In contrition, Addie slips out before dawn and delivers the offending tree
to the town's poor family and experiences the true spirit of Christmas. After the annual Christmas pageant, Dad surprises Addie with
her own Yule tree and even unpacks the precious ornaments made
by her mother. At long last he decides to bury his grief, and the
two of them discuss the past for the first time.

437. Rock, Gail. THE THANKSGIVING TREASURE. New York:
      Knopf, 1974. Illus. by Charles C. Gehm. 91p. Grades 4-6.
      R .
      Addie Mills, now 11 (see 436), has a passion for art, cowboys
and horses. Her father has had an extended feud with the elderly
misanthrope he calls Old Man Rehnquist, and when Addie and her
bosom buddy Carla Mae trespass on his farm to cut cattails, he
threatens them with his shotgun. Spunky Addie is inspired by the

class Thanksgiving pageant to make friends with the old man. When
her father vetoes her idea to have him to Thanksgiving dinner, she
boldly decides to smuggle some turkey and trimmings to him. Her
assertiveness finally succeeds, and soon she wheedles him into letting
her exercise his horse, Treasure. Gradually she erodes his diffidence and irascibility, and he allows her to sketch him. One afternoon she finds him gravely ill and summons a doctor, but it is
too late to save the old widower's life. She confides her furtive
friendship to her grandmother, who gently and wisely assuages her
fear of death. In his will, Mr. Rehnquist makes posthumous reparation for his debt to Mr. Mills and bequeaths Treasure to Addie.
With Grandma's persuasion, her truculent father capitulates and lets
Addie keep the horse.

438. Rockwell, Thomas. HIDING OUT. Scarsdale: Bradbury,
      1974. (OP) Illus. by Charles Molina. 79p. Grades 4-5. R
      Billy Whitson's observant friend Verny is the first to break
the news to him that his mother, a widow, may marry Mr. Wilson,
manager of a local horse farm and himself a widower with two
daughters. Billy has visions of strangers taking over their Vermont
home and bossing him and Mom around. He decides on the spot to
leave home and fend for himself. With Verny's help he builds a
sophisticated hideout high on the ridge which he stocks with supplies from home, and on the eve of the wedding, without confiding
in either his little brother Joe or sister Susie, he goes to elaborate
lengths to conceal his tracks and settle into his fort. Shooting,
skinning and roasting a squirrel for dinner proves more difficult
than he imagined, and nocturnal animal noises are unsettling on his
first night out. Verny gets ill and can't bring provisions as
scheduled, and Billy runs low on canned goods when rain confines
him to his lean-to. Feeling sorry for himself, he sneaks home to
spy on the others snug indoors, then spends the night in the barn
loft. A chance encounter with Mr. Wilson's teenage daughter Mary
makes him realize that she had the same apprehensions as he but
found them groundless. When he returns after four days out, no
one makes a big fuss, but his mother gives him a good, loving
scrub in the tub.

439. Roth, David. A WORLD FOR JOEY CARR. New York:
      Beaufort, 1981. 140p. Grades 6-8. NR
      Since his wife's death at the hands of muggers two years ago,
Joey Carr's father has lived in a vacuum. His most recent live-in
girlfriend, Betty, was a stabilizing influence in both their lives, but
now she, too, is gone and Joey's dad, a plant manager for a stereo
company, has resumed drinking. Joey's efforts at open communication only succeed in infuriating his father, so Joey, 14, decides to
hitchhike from Boston to his maternal grandparents' home in Vermont
for the summer, along with his stray dog Butch. The first motorist
they meet drives an old rundown car and is a young self-proclaimed
witch. Hannah refuses to accept her doctor's diagnosis of incurable
cancer and is seeking a remedy in black magic. Her quest leads

them to sinister, foreboding Abaddon Woods where, far from finding a cure, hapless Butch is set upon and killed by slavering
mastiffs. The evil of the woods follows them, and Joey endures
haunting nightmares induced by Hannah's potions before she can
exorcise the spell. The old car gives up the ghost and they burn
it near Joey's destination. Both pursue their separate ways on
foot after Hannah gives Joey a talisman for finding love. Joey
finds his grandfather impaired by strokes, and after a brief visit
his father comes for him. Having reconciled with Betty, his
father agrees to mend his ways.

440. Sachs, Marilyn. A SUMMER'S LEASE. New York: Dutton,
      1979. 124p. Grades 5-9. R
      Her mother, a factory worker and mother of three whose hus-
band died eleven years earlier, habitually harangues her to take a
commercial course and get a safe office job, but Gloria Rein, 15 in
1943, knows she is an innate writer and is determined to go to
college. It means everything to her to be named assistant editor
of the school literary magazine, knowing that this is the stepping-
stone to full editorship the following year. But Mrs. Horne, the
faculty advisor, recognizing Gloria's arrogance and aggressiveness,
tries to make her more humble and cooperative by naming her as
co-assistant with Jerry Lieberman, a poet scorned by Gloria as an
uncompetitive milksop. To soften the blow, Mrs. Horne invites both
students to spend the summer as mother's helpers to her family at
their vacation home in the Catskills. Gentle Jerry charms the little
girls, while the robust boys gravitate toward Gloria and her organized sporting contests. Gloria adores the bucolic setting, but
her jealousy and contempt of Jerry fester until the end of the
season when the fragile, pampered youngest child dies. Gloria
suddenly feels contrite over her disdainful treatment of the tot and
belatedly makes friends with sensitive Jerry. After a stormy, contentious year as co-assistants, Jerry bows out of the top spot,
leaving the field open to Gloria. In gratitude, she makes a stab at
being more conciliatory to the rest of the staff.

441. Salassi, Otto R. ON THE ROPES. New York: Greenwillow,
      1981. 248p. Grades 5-8. R
      The somber opening of the novel at the rain-drenched funeral
of pious Constance Gains in no way prepares one for the rollicking
farce which unfolds. Unwilling to be adopted by their aunts, quiet
but decisive Squint, 11, and pretty but passive Julie, 17, head for
Dallas in search of the father who deserted them six years before.
They find him promoting rowdy, theatrical wrestling matches, and
he sheepishly agrees to return with them to the East Texas farm
that is about to go into foreclosure. He brings with him his troupe
of wrestlers, including two gentle young hulks, The Claw, whose
hand is missing, and The Mask, whose face has never been seen.
Claudius Gains first resurrects the "tools of the devil," a pool table,
bar, and garish jukebox, that Constance had relegated to the basement, then incorporates a wrestling academy on the premises that he

wickedly dubs the Constance W. Gains Memorial Arena. The lecherous, sanctimonious Deacon lusts for the nubile Julie and tries to
halt the proceedings legally, but the sheriff, a good ol' boy, is in
Claudius' corner. To advertise his enterprise, Claudius stages a
series of winner-take-all exhibitions in which the major challenger
is a monstrous brute whose shifty trainer keeps him caged. He ignominiously declaws The Claw and unmasks The Mask, and all seems
lost until Claudius resorts to some ingenious skulduggery. The de-
feated challenger joins the defenders, and Julie and the now hooded
ex-Mask marry.

442. Sargent, Sarah. WEIRD HENRY BERG. New York: Crown,
      1980. 113p. Grades 5-6. NR
      Since his father, a Vietnam War veteran, killed himself by
drug abuse, Henry Berg has been apathetic and underachieving.
The only entity that fascinates him is his strange, nocturnal pet
lizard Vincent, which hatched from a 100-year-old egg. Meanwhile,
his staunch elderly neighbor has been visited by an alarming and
authentic Welsh dragon that has been combing the Oshkosh area for
the offspring of a peripatetic fellow dragon pair forced to abandon
their egg there at the beginning of its century-long incubation
period. Millie harbors Aelf in her tiny apartment while he makes
nightly forays in search of the infant until he is killed by an incredulous marksman. She then undertakes his mission herself and
soon locates Henry and Vincent. Together they rescue the rapidly
growing reptile from the biology lab where Mrs. Berg's scientist
boyfriend is scrutinizing him. Millie urges Henry to let her return
Vincent to his ancient lair in Wales, but Henry has visions of fame
and fortune from touring with a live dragon. Vincent soon becomes
a liability, however, when he kills people's pets with his poisonous
blood and incinerates his hiding place with his fiery breath. Millie
valiantly spirits him back to Camelot and is rewarded by the dragon
community with an enormous emerald. Henry decides that herpetology
as a career is too tame and takes up astronomy instead.

443. Scott, Carol J. KENTUCKY DAUGHTER. New York: Clarion,
      1985. 186p. Grades 7-10. R
      Her passion for knowledge and self-improvement impels Mary
Fred Pratley, 14, to leave the backwoods Kentucky community in
which she has lived with her mother and three younger sisters since
her father's death in a coal mine accident. In seeking a better education, she petitions her aunt and uncle, who have found work in
the shipbuilding industry in Virginia, to make a home for her. Although she makes friends with classmate Mattie, she is taunted by
another student, Roberta, for her masculine name and unsophisticated
ways. Defensively, she feels ashamed of her industrious mother who
quilts, crafts wooden dolls, and lines caskets for an undertaker.
Disappointing also are her grades in English class. When she
schedules a consultation with her teacher, Mr. Dolsey, he makes
improper advances to her. Fear of jeopardizing her aspirations to
become a teacher inhibits Mary Fred from reporting him to authorities.

She remains in silent agony until she learns that Roberta has also
been molested by Mr. Dolsey. The combined testimony of the two
girls results in the teacher's dismissal. Mary Fred joins the staff
of the high school newspaper not only for the writing experience
but also because she is attracted to the editor, Mattie's older brother,
who is flatteringly attentive. Her mother writes that she has been
offered a clerical job and another one teaching crafts. Mary Fred
reconciles with her family and her origins.

444. Sebestyen, Ouida. WORDS BY HEART. Boston: Little,
     Brown, 1979. 162p. Grades 5-7. R
     Searching for a spot to establish his own identity, Papa has
brought his family, against his second wife Claudie's better judgment, to the small town of Bethel Springs, where they are the only
blacks. The open-mindedness that Papa expects of the Southwest
in 1910 is nonexistent, and he antagonizes the trashy, bellicose
Haney family by taking the job from which their alcoholic father
was fired. Lena, 12, further antagonizes the citizenry by reciting
more Bible verses than her favored rival. Despite harassment, Papa,
with his abiding faith, patience and tolerance, believes in turning
the other cheek and earning the respect of the town by industry
and integrity. Lena finds it difficult to swallow her pride and her
indignation. But when Papa reluctantly exposes the Haneys' theft
of fencing materials from his landlady and employer, the Haneys
plot revenge. When Papa fails to return from a fence-mending expedition, Lena courageously follows him. She finds him dying of a
bullet wound inflicted by young Tater Haney, while the assailant
himself lies gravely injured nearby, having been thrown from his
horse. Before he dies, Papa exacts Lena's promise not to seek
retribution. Stoically, she brings aid to her enemy and refuses to
testify to his villainy, and when Claudie has to decide whether to
stay or leave with Lena and her young stepsiblings, she chooses to
remain and fight Papa's battle for justice and recognition.

445. Shannon, Monica. DOBRY. New York: Viking, 1934. Illus.
     by Atanas Katchamakoff. 176p. Grades 6-9. R
     Young Dobry dreams of being a great artist, and devotes his
spare time to drawing pictures. His grandfather encourages his
ambition, declaring that it has been prophesied that he will grow up
to have the fire of God in him, but his pragmatic mother thinks he
should take his dead peasant father's place in the fields. She
changes her mind when the boy sculpts an inspirational nativity
scene in the snow by the stable, and he is given the job of herding
cows to free him from field work so he can practice his art. Over
the years as he hones his talent, the three of them partake with
gusto in the seasonal events of their Bulgarian village: the annual
journey to the milltown at harvest, the long-anticipated coming of
the Gypsy Bear, Grandfather's victory in the Snow-Melting Game
and his prowess at story-telling. To earn money for his formal
training, Dobry proves his physical endurance by diving in icy
water for the golden crucifix in the traditional February ceremony.

Before his departure for Sofia, he promises his childhood sweetheart
that he will return to her.

446.   Sherburne, Zoa. GIRL IN THE MIRROR. New York: Morrow,
        1966. (OP) 190p. Grades 6-10. R
        Because of her obesity, Ruth Ann Callahan, 16, doesn't like
her reflection in the mirror. A good cook, she has been her own
best customer since her mother died four years ago. Rejected by
her contemporaries because of her weight, she has become a close
companion to her father. Then her dad brings home a trim, well
dressed young nurse, Tracy Emery, and announces their engagement.
Ruth Ann tries to conceal her distress and minimize, unsuccessfully,
Tracy's importance to her father. Kind, sensitive and diplomatic,
Tracy wants to give Ruth Ann time to accept her, and, when that
fails, offers to back out of the marriage if Ruth Ann objects to it.
Ruth Ann, despising her image even more for circumventing her
dad's happiness, assents to the union while still resenting and en-
vying Tracy. There is a terrible accident on the honeymoon; only
Tracy survives, though confined to a wheelchair. To avoid a boarding school life when her housekeeper leaves, Ruth Ann proposes
that Tracy move in with her so they can be crutches for one another. Tracy counters with a proposal for both of them to live in
her small, efficient house while each learns to become self-reliant.
Tracy designs a sensible diet for Ruth Ann, and a fragile friendship is born of their mutual need to conquer their aloneness.

447.   Simon, Shirley. LIBBY'S STEP-FAMILY. New York: Loth-
        rop, Lee and Shepard, 1966. (OP) Illus. by Reisie Lonette.
        Grades 5-8. 191p. R
        Libby Carlton, 13, and her mother, a department store buyer
and long-time widow, have always lived comfortably and companionably
in their East Orange apartment, and Libby sees no reason to upset
the status quo. She is alarmed by her mother's decision to marry
Sam Willis, a recent widower and rare book dealer with two teenage
daughters who are not only resentful of having a stepmother but
also hostile to Libby. Mama says she doesn't have to think of them
as sisters but as friends, but Mildred Willis, 17, lofty, theatrical
and spiteful, makes that impossible. Bertha, 13, is nicer but risks
her sister's wrath by being pleasant to Libby and so plays it safe.
The three are thrown into close proximity when the whole family
flies to Europe on a book-buying and sightseeing expedition. Shy,
artistic Libby, edged out by the Willis girls, makes friends in Paris
with a girl who is also chafing under the onus of a stepfamily. In
Florence her relationship with Bertha chills suddenly. She vents
her pent-up emotions on her mother, who, distracted, is hurt in an
auto accident. Conscience-stricken, Libby blames herself for not
trying harder to like her stepsisters. The shock of the incident
brings their tensions into the open, and the air is finally cleared.

448.   Slepian, Jan. THE NIGHT OF THE BOZOS. New York:
        Dutton, 1983. 152p. Grades 6-8. R+

George Weiss, 13, is a musical and electronics prodigy, a loner whose father was killed in military service and whose mother works long hours as a nurse. His sole companion is his Uncle Hibbie Whipple, 23, who has lived with them since his father abused him for his debilitating stammer. Then the pair meets flamboyant Lolly Jeffers, 14, whose family travels with the carnival in town. She invites them to the show, an event that changes all of their lives. The departure of the Bozo, a clown who goads "marks" into trying to dump him into a tub of water, creates a vacancy that sassy Lolly would like to fill, but her parents vehemently oppose it as they did her ambition to be a tattooed lady. To everyone's surprise, Hibbie makes a bid for the job. The clown disguise enables him to shed his insecurities and inhibitions and with them the stultifying speech impediment, while affording him the chance to compensate for the contumelious treatment he has suffered all his life. When he announces his intention of joining the carnival, George feels abandoned and has his first falling out with his big, simple, genial uncle. On the night that George coordinates the lighting and music for the club dance on the lake, Lolly, believing she is a failure, tries to drown herself, and George is instrumental in saving her. As he pursues his musical opportunities, he philosophically accepts the loss of Hibbie and anticipates seeing Lolly again when the carnival returns next summer.

449. Smith, Alison. HELP! THERE'S A CAT WASHING IN HERE! New York: Dutton, 1981. Illus. by Amy Rowen. 152p. Grades 4-6. R+

Faced with the dire probability of having to sell the family's rambling but rundown home or inviting domineering Aunt Wilhemina to live with them as a paying guest, Henry Walker, 12, agrees to accept responsibility for the first time in his life and take charge of the household while his mother, a widow of three years, concentrates on updating her art portfolio in her attic studio. Orchestrating the morning chores while getting obstreperous Joe, 10, and ingenuous Annie, 6, off to school on time is more difficult than Henry imagines. Then Annie brings home an aggressive overnight visitor who antagonizes Joe, requiring all of Henry's diplomacy, and Aunt Wilhemina drops in for dinner, straining his culinary capacities. When Annie adopts a stray cat, Henry nearly comes unglued because of his lifelong feline phobia, but he carries on nobly, creating a costume for Annie's school play and enduring Aunt Wilhemina's flagrant favoritism for his siblings. His finest hour comes when he volunteers to visit Annie's friend, the holy terror, in the hospital and rescues Annie from peril when she runs away from home one night. In the process he makes peace with Annie's cat and finds a way to keep his meddlesome aunt occupied. Ma lands the book illustrating job she has been grooming for.

450. Smith, Doris Buchanan. THE FIRST HARD TIMES. New York: Viking, 1983. 137p. Grades 5-7. R+

Ancil Witherspoon, 13, loves to visit her paternal grandparents'

home in nearby Juniper, Georgia, because there, occupying the
room that was her father's as a boy and which has not been changed
since he left to marry her mother, she feels close to the parent she
remembers only from others' anecdotes. He has been Missing in Action in Vietnam for eleven years, and her mother, an artist, has only
recently remarried Harvey Hutton, publisher of the Hanover weekly
newspaper. Ancil's three sisters have enthusiastically embraced
Harvey as "Daddy," but redhaired Ancil makes no effort to conceal
her resentment of him. She deliberately flogs her forlorn faith in
her father's survival, because where there is pain there is hope.
She is ignominiously forced to join a beginners' swimming class
where she is exposed to derision. When Harvey publicly humiliates
her by publishing a picture of her with the "Little Fish" class, she
decides to run away to her grandparents. But even they betray
her and their son by redecorating his old room and accepting Harvey as a member of the family. At a family picnic, Ancil finally
recognizes the fun she is missing and begins to relax her rigid,
self-imposed isolation.

451. Snyder, Zilpha Keatley. BLACK AND BLUE MAGIC. New
     York: Atheneum, 1966. Illus. by Gene Holtan. 186p.
     Grades 4-6. NR
     A disappointment to his magician father, Harry Houdini Marco
has always been clumsy. Since his father's death when he was 6,
his enterprising mother has taken boarders into their San Francisco
house. Harry, now 11, has concocted a "Marriage Plan" in which he
hopes to match his mother with Mr. Brighton, a widower and boarder
who runs a sporting goods store and also owns a ranch. His plan
is frustrated when a new female boarder begins monopolizing Mr.
Brighton, and Harry's mom starts acting too chummy with a guest
Harry dislikes. Harry befriends a strange and mysterious man, Mr.
Mazzeeck, who turns out to be a genuine sorcerer under an evil
enchantment. When the grateful Mr. Mazzeeck leaves the boarding
house, he presents Harry with a small vial containing a magic potion.
To his amazement, Harry sprouts wings on his back when he rubs
the potion on his shoulders. He tests his new gift of flight noc-
turnally and, because of his lack of coordination, has several amusing misadventures before mastering the art of aerodynamics. Heroically he saves a pair of toddlers from being swept to sea in a rowboat and miraculously foils a burglary while managing to conceal his
awesome secret. With the last drops of the potion, he fulfills his
plan to frighten off the scheming female boarder and reunite his
mom and Hal Brighton. To his delight, the impromptu flight lessons
have improved his coordination and strengthened his muscles. The
three of them repair to Hal's ranch to live happily ever after.

452. Snyder, Zilpha Keatley. THE EGYPT GAME. New York:
     Atheneum, 1968. Illus. by Alton Raible. 215p. Grades 5-6.
     R
     April Hall, 11, is resentful when her ambitious, war-widowed,
show business mother, awaiting her big break, sends her to live with

her patient paternal grandmother, who works in a university library and whom April condescendingly calls by her first name. In spite of her Hollywood affectations, she makes friends with Melanie because both are imaginative and like to read. Finding a plaster bust of Nefertiti in the cluttered yard of an antiques dealer, they conceive their Egypt Game, recruiting Melanie's little brother Marshall as boy pharaoh Marshamosis and a new girl, Elizabeth, as Neferbeth. When a child in the neighborhood is foully murdered, everyone suspects the gruff old proprietor of the shop in whose yard they play. Two boys, erstwhile bullies, join the Egyptians at Halloween, and the game gets eerier as the Oracle of Thoth begins speaking mysteriously. April almost becomes the murderer's second victim, and the Egypt Game terminates abruptly. When her mother marries her agent, April finally realizes that she never intended to send for her and accepts with dignity her new life with Grandma, whom she has come to respect.

453. Sperry, Armstrong. CALL IT COURAGE. New York: Macmillan, 1940. Illus. by the author. 95p. Grades 4-6. R

Mafatu was christened Stout Heart by his father, a noble Polynesian chief before the days of traders and missionaries, but after the sea claimed his mother and almost snuffed his life when he was 3, the villagers began to mock him as the Boy Who Was Afraid because of his terror of the sea. When all the other youths embark on the annual bonito run, Mafatu, 15, stays behind to craft tools, woman's work. His cowardice shames him, and with sudden resolve he determines to conquer his fear or die trying. With his dog and pet albatross for company, he puts to sea in an outrigger where he is at the mercy of the enemy sea god Moana and the benevolent god of fishermen, Maui. A titanic storm robs him of sail, tools, food and clothing, and he nearly dies of exposure before the albatross directs him to land. There, his tool-making skill proves its value in fashioning weapons and a new canoe. For survival he confronts a shark, octopus and wild boar in mortal combat. Most daring of all is his theft of the sacred spear from the shrine of the eaters-of-men and his hair-raising escape from the fierce and vengeful tribe. He returns to his village victorious, worthy of the title Stout Heart and a credit to his father.

454. St. George, Judith. DO YOU SEE WHAT I SEE? New York: Putnam, 1982. 157p. Grades 6-10. R

Following his father's death in an auto accident nine years ago, Matt Runyon's mother remarried and recently divorced, bringing Matt, now 17, and his half-brother Bucky from their home in Denver to Cape Cod where she takes a job with the local newspaper. Matt despises the cold, windy salt marshes and sand dunes. Even the people seem chilly and obsessed with ecology, especially Julie Chamberlain, his no-nonsense classmate. When an odd couple, the Vosserts, move into a rental house on the bluff, he mistakes them for burglars and calls the law, earning their enmity. He continues to observe the Vosserts and witnesses what he believes to be Mrs.

Vossert's murder by her husband and again cries "wolf." Later he
is convinced that Vossert really did kill his wife and staged the
false alarms to discredit Matt's veracity. When his mother has to
return to Colorado to appear at a custody hearing over Bucky, Matt
is left alone in the creaky cottage, believing that he is being stalked
by Mr. Vossert. He enlists Julie's aid to break into the bluff house
and ascertain the truth. They find the evidence they need, but
Vossert catches them and tries to kill Matt before being subdued.
In learning to curb his belligerence and appreciate the delicate
balance of nature in the salt marsh, Matt also captures Julie's affections.

455.   Stephens, Mary Jo. WITCH OF THE CUMBERLANDS. Boston:
       Houghton Mifflin, 1974. Illus. by Arvis Stewart. 243p.
       Grades 6-9. R
       Dr. McGregor brings his children, cautious Susan, 17, impul-
sive Betsy, 15, and inscrutable Robin, 4, to the peace and tranquility of the Cumberland Mountains of Kentucky because the pressure of life in New York has overwhelmed him since his wife's death.
They are immediately embroiled in a forty-year-old mystery as
catalysts to a suspenseful denouement along with Miss Birdie, the
elderly herbalist and fortune teller; Broughton, the foreboding
figure in black; and the spirit of the dead coal miner who rises
from his dank grave to exact retribution and bare the culpability
for the mine disaster that killed 49 men during the Depression. In
the meantime, they learn to accept and be accepted by "holler"
folk and townfolk alike; understand the alliance of magic, superstition, simple faith, and inspired evangelical oratory that comprise
religion in the hills; deplore the exploitation of the mountain region
and its people; and develop an appreciation for the uncanny gifts
of Miss Birdie and clairvoyant Robin.

456.   Stolz, Mary. THE EDGE OF NEXT YEAR. New York: Harper
       and Row, 1974. 195p. Grades 6-9. R+
       The shattering tragedy of their mother's death in an auto ac-
cident affects Orin, 14, his brother Victor, 10, and their journalist
father differently. Orin is puzzled and resentful of Victor's seeming indifference to their mutual loss in his absorption with his
hobbies, and he is appalled and disgusted by his father's increasing
immersion in alcoholism. Sensitive and introspective, Orin misses
his unique mother despairingly and evokes her memory constantly,
while at the same time shouldering the overwhelming responsibility
for brother, father, home, and personal life. After the disposal of
his mother's effects, he makes a determined effort to control his
sorrow, recalling his mother's words to the effect that emotions
worn on the sleeve are not necessarily more fervent than those expressed in less obvious ways. In the end he summons the courage
to shock his father into seeking help for his drinking problem.

457.   Suhl, Yuri. THE PURIM GOAT. New York: Four Winds,
       1980. Illus. by Kaethe Zemach. 60p. Grades 3-5. R

A poor Jewish widow who sells roasted pumpkin seeds for a meager living in a tiny Eastern European village, Braindel learns that Reb Todres, the sugar merchant, needs a daily quart of goat's milk for his ailing son. With entrepreneuring spirit, she contracts to provide the milk if he will advance her the money to buy the goat. The scrawny goat she procures seems less than a bargain when she discovers that not only does it give but a half-quart of milk per day but also goes on rampages when it is tied up in her hut. Only her son Yossele, 10, can control the perverse creature. Reb Todres sues Braindel for breach of contract, and the rabbi who arbitrates the case decrees that all the townspeople donate their table scraps to fatten the goat. Still the goat gives scant measure, and Yossele fears she will become butcher bait. Then an itinerant dancing bear comes to town, and Yossele sees the glimmer of a reprieve for his pet. Secretly and painstakingly, he and his friend teach the goat to dance on its hind legs, and on Purim day they take their nimble nanny door-to-door, celebrating the story of Esther and collecting more than enough pennies to repay Reb Todres.

458. Talbot, Toby. AWAY IS SO FAR. New York: Four Winds, 1974. (OP) Illus. by Dominique Michelle Strandquest. 91p. Grades 4-5. R+
Despite Pedro's pleas that problems can't be solved by running away from them, his distraught father is driven by grief over his wife's death to leave his farm and village on the Mediterranean coast of Spain and become a wandering minstrel, or tocador. Pedro, 11, remembers his mother's adjuration to live normally after her death, but it does not deter his adamant father. After stopping to buy him sturdy shoes, they strike the open road, sleeping under the stars at night and playing for their meals. They ply their way by train to Paris, where it is rumored that Spanish guitarists are in demand. There his father finds not the forgetfulness he seeks but a return to reason, and he is able to face with equanimity once again the cheerful little house with its myriad memories.

459. Tannen, Mary. HUNTLEY NUTLEY AND THE MISSING LINK. New York: Knopf, 1983. Illus. by Rob Sauer. 121p. Grades 4-6. NR
Persecuted unmercifully by Orson Forest's gang of Skulls because of his short stature, his unusual name, and his devotion to his baby brother Beau, 2, Huntley Nutley, 12, is ten pounds lighter and the same height as the baby. In spite of the fact that his mother died at Beau's birth and that his father is a vague and absent-minded science professor, frequently absent, Huntley, nicknamed Runtley by his tormentors, is an eternal optimist. As his father prepares to leave on another lecture tour, he suggests that Huntley engage a housekeeper, but all potential candidates are intimidated by the Nutleys' ghostly, cluttered mansion. Then Huntley and Beau discover in the ravine behind the house a simian creature who seems to adapt well to domesticity, in a crude way, and whom Huntley passes off to the near-sighted Dr. Nutley as the new housekeeper,

Mrs. Link. Huntley tries to keep his hairy houseguest a secret,
but the Missing Link is hard to hide, especially on forays through
the supermarket. Orson sees an opportunity for more cruelty and
publicity by turning Link over to science to be poked and prodded,
but a video game duel between him and the Link, in which beast
trounces boy, binds the bully to silence and a truce with Huntley.
With the advent of spring, the restless antediluvian primate moves
on.

460. Taylor, Theodore. TEETONCEY. Garden City: Doubleday,
      1974. Illus. by Richard Cuffari. 153p. Grades 5-6. R
      The independent, insular folk indigenous to North Carolina's
Outer Banks in the 1890s have witnessed the foundering of count-
less vessels on their treacherous shoals, but being the descendants
of castaways themselves they have not been inured to human suffering. When Ben, 11, finds a half-drowned girl, sole survivor of
yet another shipwreck, on the beach one stormy night, his mother,
who lost a husband and son to the sea, insists upon taking her in
and caring for her. The girl recovers physically but her mind remains in a catatonic trance, blocking out all memory of the tragedy
in which her parents perished. Nicknamed Teetoncey, meaning small
in the peculiar Banks patois, she is mutely and unemotionally docile
and allows Ben, her reluctant escort, to lead her about. But when
she wanders off alone and becomes a danger to herself, Ben's
mother devolves on him a desperate scheme for restoring her to
reason. On a violently stormy night, he leads her back to the
beach. The re-creation by demonic wind and wave of the initial
trauma breaks the barrier, and her emotions flood forth in normal
reaction.

461. Taylor, Theodore. TEETONCEY AND BEN O'NEAL. Garden
      City: Doubleday, 1975. Illus. by Richard Cuffari. 185p.
      Grades 5-7. R
      When the castaway Teetoncey girl is catapulted from her
catatonia (see 460) and reveals that she has no living relatives,
Ben's mother is determined to keep her for the daughter she has always wanted, and Ben sees the opportunity to cut the apron strings
and go to sea as did his brothers and father before him. He
changes his mind when Teetoncey discloses to him privately that she
is a British heiress whose fortune lies under the shallow waters and
shifting sands of the shoals where she was shipwrecked. The
youths' effort to recover the legacy goes awry and doesn't remain
secret for long. Soon a full-scale salvage operation is mounted,
with the spoils hotly contested. Ben's mother sees to it that if the
fortune cannot be restored to the rightful owner, no one shall profit
by it, but the effort costs her life. Ben and Tee have grown fond
of one another but know they must part: Teetoncey to return to
England, Ben to fulfill his destiny at sea.

462. Terris, Susan. NO SCARLET RIBBONS. New York: Farrar,
      Straus, Giroux, 1981. 154p. Grades 6-9. R+

When harpist Rachel Nolan, 13, plays matchmaker between her
photographer mother Ginger and her San Francisco English teacher
Norman Ross, she envisions a readymade, unified family (including
Norm's son Sandy, 14) who enthusiastically embrace the spontaneous
and original diversions that she and her parents invented before Fa
died of lung cancer two years ago. Instead, Norm proves to be
stodgy and unadventurous, while Sandy flees in embarrassed resentment from his aggressive and frenetic stepsister. Then Sandy hurts
his leg in basketball practice and, in his enforced idleness, becomes
more tolerant of her, but Ginger and Norm pair off and Rachel's
solid foursome becomes two fractions. In jealousy and perversity
Rachel reacts bizarrely, and Ginger bitingly accuses her of trying
to sabotage her marriage. With everyone irritated at her, she feels
that her only recourse is to drive Norm away and at least salvage
her close relationship with her mother, however it is not Norm who
stalks off after a fight but Ginger. When Rachel perceives the magnitude of Norm's despair and anger at her, she realizes that she has
gone too far and tries to make amends. She knows that she must
learn to let things happen instead of trying to make them happen.
And Norm shows that he is trying to love and please her even if
he can't instinctively anticipate and fulfill her every need.

463. Tolan, Stephanie S. A TIME TO FLY FREE. New York:
        Scribner, 1983. 163p. Grades 5-7. R+
        Although he is bright and inquisitive about the natural
science in his backyard, Chesapeake Bay, Joshua Taylor, 10, is
an indifferent student who is not fulfilling his capabilities because
of his teacher's humorless regimentation, condescending textbooks,
and his fellow students' callousness. When threatened with a tutor,
he flees his private school and discovers gruff, retired Rafferty
who operates a licensed wildlife rehabilitation shelter for injured
migratory birds. When Josh proposes that he drop out of school
to assist Rafferty and learn from him, his mother, a freelance
artist with whom he has good rapport, will not even consider the
idea. His stepfather George Forbes, whom his mother married after
his father's death in a motorcycle accident long ago, is a history
professor who is steady, logical and reasonable. He supports the
concept of a leave of absence from school, as if Josh were con-
valescing from an illness, and the proposition of an alternative
education from Rafferty who is firm yet fair and who takes his avocation seriously. Under Rafferty's tutelage the boy is exposed to
a broad curriculum, but against his wisdom and experience Josh
sneaks off to try to save a badly wounded blue heron and is injured himself in the abortive attempt. As he recovers, his mother
asks him to keep an open mind about enrolling in a different
school with individualized instruction.

464. Turner, Ann. A HUNTER COMES HOME. New York: Crown,
        1980. 118p. Grades 5-8. R
        After his father and brother froze to death while seal hunting,
Jonas' Inuit Eskimo mother becomes overprotective of her last son

and exacts a promise from his grandfather, a dauntless and proficient hunter who wants to teach the boy the timeless skills of survival, to let Jonas finish school and then decide his future for himself. In the meantime, the old man, 70, becomes the family provider.
Jonas discovers that the BIA boarding school is condescending, mon-
grelizing and humiliating, and he endures the year stoically. Back
at home, he finds that Grandfather is just as uncompromising as his
teachers and is contemptuous of the boy's inexperienced attempts to
master the traditional ways. Smarting from Grandfather's criticism
of his clumsy seal hunting technique, he vents his frustration by
wantonly slaughtering a herd of caribou and feeling great remorse.
In his third endeavor to earn the old one's respect, the two depart
on a comradely fishing expedition, but in trying to draw in the
turgid nets, Grandfather is swept away in the spring freshet. At
first Jonas panics but later redeems himself and recovers the valiant
warrior's body. He decides that the finest tribute he can offer to
Grandfather's spirit is to bear his body home with dignity and responsibility, along with their bountiful catch, as a true hunter
would do.

465. Turner, Ann. THE WAY HOME. New York: Crown, 1982.
      116p. Grades 6-8. R
      A pestilence sweeps Medieval England in the year 1349. Anne,
afflicted with a harelip and unmarriageable, lives with her father,
a widowed farmer, and Gran, a herbal healer. Her friend Hugh has
been driven from Lord Thomas' estate for poaching a single dove,
and Anne herself is beaten for taming one of his falcons. Angry
at the injustice, she curses Lord Thomas and is branded a witch.
When he subsequently dies of the plague, Anne is forced to leave
her family and flee to the great marsh to evade his vengeful retainers. Resourcefully, she makes a thatched shelter, subsists on
mussels, hatches chicks for companionship, and survives a flood.
After four months, when she feels that the furor will have subsided,
she decides to return home but is captured along the way by a
vicious brigand who takes her upriver to his remote cottage to be
wife to his son Jem. Following many weeks of captivity, abuse and
forced labor, she manages to escape in their boat during a wild
storm. She is horrified and remorseful upon her return to find the
village deserted and overgrown. All its inhabitants are dead, and
even the great manor house is empty and still. Grieving for Gran
and Da, Anne is afraid she will go mad in the solitude even as she
harvests the neglected crops and pens the errant livestock. Then
down the road she espies the faithful Hugh returning.

466. Uchida, Yoshiko. THE BEST BAD THING. New York:
      Atheneum, 1983. 120p. Grades 5-6. R
      Rinko Tsujimura, 11, is horrified when her mother asks her
to spend two weeks of summer vacation as mother's helper to Mrs.
Hata, whose husband has just died of tuberculosis. Mrs. Hata is
reputedly crazy, lives in a dilapidated house without plumbing or
electricity in rural East Oakland, California, and, worst of all, has

two sons, Zenny, 10, and Abu, 8, who pull practical jokes and test
her patience at every turn. But Mrs. Hata is not crazy; unlike other
Japanese-American women of 1935, she is assertive, non-conforming,
drives a truck like a man, and sells home-grown cucumbers for a
living. Rinko earns the respect of the boys and becomes friends
with an elderly Japanese alien who lives in the Hata barn and makes
fabulous kites. Then a trio of misfortunes befalls them. Rinko
sprains her ankle, Abu requires surgery to save his arm after a
daredevil leap from a freight train, and Mrs. Hata's truck and produce are stolen from in front of the hospital. Rinko decides to stay
on beyond her two weeks. An officious social worker deports the
old kitemaker and threatens to evict the Hatas and place them on
public welfare. Rinko's parents find a job for Mrs. Hata as housekeeper for the Japanese bachelors in their church dormitory so that
she can be self-supporting and retain her home and pride. Rinko
decides that being sent to the Hatas was the best bad thing ever to
happen to her.

467.   Ullman, James Ramsey. BANNER IN THE SKY. Philadelphia:
       Lippincott, 1954. 252p. Grades 6-9. R
       Rudi's father, the greatest mountaineer in Switzerland, died
while attempting to scale the Citadel, the last unconquered Alp.
Rudi, 16, dreams of completing his father's quest, but his mother
and uncle have forbidden him to climb. By concealing his rude
equipment he manages to practice clandestinely, and when he saves
the life of a great British alpinist, the astute veteran recognizes
the boy's spirit and potential. Rudi's fearful mother remains im-
mutably opposed to his ambition, and he resorts to subterfuge to
join the Englishman's expedition. Against all odds, the lad finds
the elusive route that even his father failed to discern fifteen years
before and leads the party against the panoply of dangers a
chimerical mountain can hurl at mere mortals. He is bitterly
thwarted yards short of the summit in coming to the aid of an injured adversary, but the adulatory Englishman plants Rudi's father's
pennon atop the peak and predicts that Rudi will climb it often,
while his mother ruefully removes her opposition.

468.   Wallace-Brodeur, Ruth. THE KENTON YEAR. New York:
       Atheneum, 1980. 93p. Grades 4-6. R+
       One day Mandy's father leaves for work and doesn't return,
the victim of an intoxicated truck driver. The stricken girl, 9,
clings to her mother like a shadow and refuses to go to school.
Anne McPherson decides to take her daughter away from familiar
surroundings with their painful memories and spend summer vacation
in a remote house in Vermont where Anne stayed in her childhood,
taking a leave of absence from her Boston job. The rural life and
friendly people appeal to them both. Shandee, the old recluse, and
Carrie Marquand become Mandy's special friends, while the patroniz-
ing hardware store owner is her only nemesis. At summer's end,
Anne McPherson plans to buy the cozy cottage and remain in Kenton,
which has been so salubrious to Mandy's mental health. Mandy

celebrates a memorable birthday and starts school in the tiny schoolhouse, while Anne takes a job on Martin Wechsler's weekly newspaper. A classmate's gossip about the relationship between Martin
and her mother disturbs the girl until she has a frank talk with
Anne. Mandy, a novice skier, is obsessed with excelling in the
winter carnival ski race, and when she places high after colossal
effort, it is the cathartic that releases her tightly reined emotions.
On the anniversary of her father's death, she erects a memorial to
him in her favorite place and relaxes into her new life.

469. Wellman, Alice. THE WILDERNESS HAS EARS. New York:
    Harcourt, Brace, Jovanovich, 1975. 141p. Grades 7-9. R
        Luti, 14, has grown up in the bush of Angola where her
father, an American geologist, is employed. Because he is often on
field trips, she is left in the care of the native Nduku, who taught
her to speak his dialect before she could speak English. When
Nduku is grievously wounded by a leopard, he insists on returning
to the healer and diviner in his Kimbutu village instead of going to
a modern hospital. Luti accompanies him but is scorned and spat
upon for her sunburned white skin. Only the wise old diviner
Onavita welcomes her and tends her burns after treating Nduku
with her ancient remedies. When a sacred chameleon takes refuge
in Luti's hair, the villagers believe that she harbors the spirit of
an Old Soul and finally accord her reverence and respect.
Marooned in the bush till her father comes for her, she shares the
deprivation of the Long Dry that brings hunger-crazed hyenas to
the very gates of the stockade and participates in old rites that
forbid sacrificial goats to be eaten even in the teeth of starvation.
The rain that ends the drought brings flash floods that threaten
the Kimbutu's holiest relics, and Luti valiantly saves them.

470. Wells, Rosemary. NONE OF THE ABOVE. New York: Dial,
    1974. 184p. Grades 9-12. R
        The Van Dam and Mills families have been friends for many
years, and at the death of Mr. Van Dam and Mrs. Mills, their surviving spouses marry. It is extremely awkward for Marcia Mills, 13,
and her older sister Sharon to make the transition from their
lower-middle-class milieu to the upper-middle-class Van Dam home
where their stepsiblings Christina, 13, and law school student John
are ambitious, social-conscious overachievers. Sharon soon escapes
her critical, undemonstrative stepmother by marrying a serviceman,
but Marcia, who is content watching TV and making barely passing
grades, is forced into competition with active, intellectual Chrissy
by the stepmother who doesn't disguise the fact that she is trying
to make a silk purse of a sow's ear. By studying doggedly and
conforming to pressure, Marcia qualifies for the college prep class
and by her senior year has been conditionally accepted at Sarah
Lawrence. Yet she keeps her own social identity by dating Raymond
Siroken, an auto mechanic of whom her stepmother disapproves.
When she flunks a crucial English final and is offered the opportunity of working doubly hard to make it up, Marcia opts for a safe,

steady and unthreatening marriage over the successive challenges
of academia and career.

471. Wersba, Barbara. RUN SOFTLY, GO FAST. New York:
      Atheneum, 1970. 205p. Grades 9-12. R+
      On the night of his father's funeral, David Marks, 19, begins
a testament of revilement against the parent he once revered as a
tower of strength. Leo Marks, an impoverished Jewish immigrant,
capitulates to crass materialism and even avarice and marital infi-
delity as he pursues financial success and the American dream of
upward mobility. Professing love for his son and wife, he plies
them with the worldly luxuries and opportunities he never enjoyed
but robs them of their sense of self-worth. David's mother accepts
her new fate and fortune docilely and dutifully, but David, with
developing self-awareness and the loss of innocence of an adolescent
of the 1960s, rebels. Where his father's goals for him are to prepare for an academic and business career, David with equal fervor
plans to be an avant-garde artist. His disillusionment reaches its
zenith when his father banishes from the house his best friend and
mentor who is a long-haired intellectual, conscientious objector, and
bisexual. In a rage, David leaves the Riverside Drive apartment
and moves in with hippie drug culturists in the East Village. When
the life of a dropout palls, he finds true love, if illicit, with Maggie
Carroll and becomes serious about his art. But conventional father
and recalcitrant son remain implacable and antagonistic in their
polarized value systems. When his father develops cancer, David
cannot even render him the courtesy or consideration of visiting him
in the hospital. It is only in retrospection that he concedes that if
his father was fallible, so is he, and that he will probably also repeat the mistakes of the past.

472. Westall, Robert. SCARECROWS. New York: Greenwillow,
      1981. 185p. Grades 6-9. R+
      Simon Wood, 13, maintains a low profile at the British military
academy he attends in order to avoid the attention of the rapacious
dormitory bully, but when Bowdon makes sport of Simon's mother,
the boy attacks him with reckless ferocity to avenge her honor as
would his father, a flying ace and war hero who died at Aden. Then
his mother takes a job at an art gallery where she meets Joe Moreton,
a paunchy pacifist and political cartoonist, the antithesis of Simon's
spit-and-polish father. Simon is furious when his mother betrays
his father's memory by marrying Joe, even though his little sister
Jane adores him. He doesn't try to hide his hostility when he
spends the summer with them at the old millhouse Joe has bought,
taking refuge in the derelict mill nearby. A hole in his closet floor
allows him to overhear intimacies between his mother and Joe, and in
reprimand he places his father's old uniform on a chair in their bedroom. Joe manhandles him for hurting Mum's feelings, and in rage
Simon tries to invoke his father's spirit. He only succeeds in conjuring three specters who died violently at the mill many years before and who now advance menacingly upon the house. He is

impotent to halt the scarecrows, who are bent upon destruction of
the interlopers in the millhouse, until an old friend intervenes and
convinces him in the nick of time to regain control of his passions.

473. Whitehead, Ruth. THE MOTHER TREE. New York: Seabury,
      1971. (OP) Illus. by Charles Robinson. 149p. Grades 5-7.
      R
      Tempe's mother's death from pneumonia changes her life
radically, compelling her at 10 to be housekeeper for her father and
brother Phil, 14, and nursemaid for her sister Laurie, 4, on their
Texas farm at the turn of the century. The burden of responsibility, crowned by Phil's needling and jocular superiority, frays
her young nerves to the breaking point. When Father and Phil depart to follow the harvest across the Southwest for extra cash, she
leaps at the opportunity to stay with her grandparents, enabling
her to be a little girl again. Under their gentle guidance she still
tends to chores and to Laurie, but the primary responsibility is no
longer hers. With her best chum and nearest neighbor she constructs a playhouse in a lofty old mesquite which she calls the
Mother Tree because its branches enfold her like a surrogate mother.
When Father and Phil return at the end of the summer, she is reluctant to leave the comfort and security of Grandma's house and
the sanctuary of her tree, but through Laurie's dependence on her
she realizes that she has more strength than she supposed.

474. Willard, Barbara. STORM FROM THE WEST. New York:
      Harcourt, Brace and World, 1963. Illus. by Douglas Hall.
      189p. Grades 5-9. R
      Twelve years after their father's death as a war correspondent,
English boarding school students Nicholas and Charlotte Lattimer, 16
and 14, are surprised but not displeased when their mother Sarah,
a London artist, announces that she is marrying American attorney
Robert Graham, who was more recently widowed in an auto accident.
Their trepidation lies in the knowledge that he has four children.
News of the Lattimer children is equally disquieting to Nan, 16,
Alan, 12, Roderick, 11, and Lucy Graham, 10, especially when they
learn that all of them will be sharing the Lattimers' small Scottish
croft for the summer. Although Lucy, initially petulant, adapts
rather quickly, the older children are tense and defensive. When
the Grahams, who are of Scottish descent, propose being outfitted
in tartan kilts, the jealousy and resentment of the Lattimers turn
the uneasy situation into an ugly altercation. Sarah Graham is so
distressed that her husband whisks her off on an extended motor
trip, leaving the children behind till they learn how to coexist.
With Nan and Nicholas in charge, the six establish fair if crude justice, and when Lucy is saved from a dangerous fall, they savor their
first heady sense of unity. Their squabbles are far from over, however. It takes a titanic storm in which Lucy is marooned in dire
peril to forge the disparate elements into a cohesive whole and una-
nimously summon their parents to return to the helm.

475. Wisler, G. Clifton. THUNDER ON THE TENNESSEE. New
     York: Dutton, 1983. 153p. Grades 6-9. R
     At the outbreak of the Civil War, Colonel Bill Delamer, veteran
of the Mexican War who also helped drive the bellicose Comanches
from the ranchland on the Brazos River that he calls home, reenlists
with the Confederacy in defense of home, family, way of life, and
freedom of choice, even though he eschews slavery. His middle son
Willie, 15, also heeds the call to arms, following in his family's
proud tradition of duty and honor, leaving behind his sweetheart
Ellie Cobb, 14. The new Texas recruits are soon blooded. After
the carnage of their first encounter at the battle of Pittsburg Land-
ing, later called Shiloh, Willie, a corporal, finds himself second in
command. The survivors help themselves pragmatically to their
dead opponents' rifled muskets and boots, and Willie comforts a
dying Yank drummer. In their second engagement, Willie's father
is mortally wounded leading a charge and dies following surgery.
Willie scarcely has time to mourn as a third assault is mounted.
Out of ammunition and outnumbered, their retreat nearly turns into
a rout until another officer rallies the Texans to stand their ground
with fixed bayonets. Willie is wounded and evacuated on a charnel
wagon. Given the option of an honorary discharge to return to
home and Ellie, Willie stubbornly elects to honor his commitment and
fights on as a lieutenant.

476. Wojciechowska, Maia. "HEY, WHAT'S WRONG WITH THIS
     ONE?" New York: Harper and Row, 1969. Illus. by Joan
     Sandin. 72p. Grades 3-4. R
     Three rambunctious motherless boys, Harley, Davidson, and
little Mott Elliott, 7, inadvertently create a domestic crisis that
causes the last of a succession of housekeepers to defect quite suddenly. Despairing of ever finding another acceptable one, the boys
connive to supply their father with a perfect new wife--and themselves with the ideal mother. In a crowded supermarket Mott spots
several possible candidates and causes considerable consternation
and confusion for his father and a pretty young lady, but all's well
that ends well, and the boys learn to cooperate and control themselves to please the lady who pleases all four Elliotts.

477. Wojciechowska, Maia. SHADOW OF A BULL. New York:
     Atheneum, 1964. Illus. by Alvin Smith. 165p. Grades 5-7.
     R
     At 9, Manolo is aware that he bears a striking physical re-
semblance to his father, the legendary torero who put the town of
Archangel on the map; that all its citizens expect him to emulate his
father so that they can once more bask in reflected glory; and that
he, Manolo, is a coward. Six aficionados and the Count, who have
supported him and his mother since his father's death by goring
before Manolo was born, begin grooming him at this age for his in-
exorable tienta, or public debut, when he is 12, the age at which
his father began his short career. Assisting the doctor who attends a novice matador who has been gored, he realizes that he

wants to save lives, not take them. He promises his friend's
brother Juan, who lives only to fight bulls and has an unerring in-
stinct for it but who lacks financial support and opportunity, that
he will intercede with the Count on his behalf. On the day of the
corrida, he capes the bull for a few passes so as not to disgrace
his mother but hands the sword to Juan, who demonstrates his bril-
liance in the denouement.

478. Wolitzer, Hilma. TOBY LIVED HERE. New York: Farrar,
      Straus, Giroux, 1978. 147p. Grades 5-8. R+
      "You just have to live," Ellen Goodwin temporizes when her
friends remark upon her courageous reconcilement to her husband's
death in an auto accident and the subsequent loss of her mother.
Now, two years later, the bottled grief has seeped out like acid to
erode her sanity. Toby, 12, and Anne, 6, watch in bewilderment
and fright as their cheerful and energetic editorial assistant mother
reverts to infantilism. The girls are placed in the foster care of
elderly Mr. and Mrs. Selwyn, whose extended family includes dozens
of former homeless children. One is Constance, who once carved
her name on the nightstand in Toby's room and who now, about to
be married, facilitates Toby's transition into her teens. At her new
school in Queens she becomes chums with Susan Schwamm, whose
friendly curiosity Toby parries with lies, ashamed to acknowledge
that her mother is institutionalized and that she and her sister are
wards of the court. Her frequent, wistful letters to her mother go
unanswered, and the social worker is evasive about her progress.
The fabrications increase exponentially until Toby almost believes
them herself and begins to hate her mother for necessitating them.
Observant Mrs. Selwyn recognizes the symptoms of trouble and arranges for the girls to visit their mother. When she sees her
mother on the mend, Toby's amorphous fears evaporate. Before
she and Anne move with their mother back to Brooklyn, Toby carves
her name below that of Constance.

479. Wolitzer, Hilma. WISH YOU WERE HERE. New York: Farrar,
      Straus, Giroux, 1984. 180p. Grades 6-9. R+
      Self-described "half-orphan" Bernie Segal, 13, whose father
died of a heart attack, dislikes his mother's fiance Nat Greenberg
for his chronic, disgusting cheerfulness and just for existing. When
they marry in April he intends to be far away from New York, living with his beloved paternal grandfather, a retired commercial
fisherman who now resides in Florida. Hampered by asthma from
taking a well paying job, Bernie babysits twins he loathes and rehearses his sister Celia, with whom he constantly bickers, for her
high school play in order to earn his airfare. His acquisitive little
sister Grace, 7, will not loan him any of her savings, so Bernie reluctantly accepts Nat's offer of a job helping him pack and move.
He finds himself beginning to like Nat, whom both of his sisters
adore, in spite of himself, but that does not weaken his resolve to
leave. An unexpected windfall enables him to buy the ticket, but
on the eve of the wedding his grandfather derails his plans by

coming north for the nuptials, and Bernie's mother, a buyer at
Macy's, discovers his intentions inadvertently. In a private discussion she tells him he needn't feel disloyal to his dad's memory
in accepting Nat, expalining that his father would expect them to
carry on lives of their own. With his grandfather's blessing,
Bernie adopts his father's name as a middle name in a Hebrew ceremony and agrees to give away the bride.

480. Yep, Lawrence. CHILD OF THE OWL. New York: Harper
     and Row, 1977. 217p. Grades 7-9. R+
     Casey, 12, has learned to be tough, streetwise, and brashly
American by following her father, Barney, a compulsive, debt-
ridden gambler, the length and breadth of California. When he is
hospitalized as the result of a mugging, she is farmed out to her
maternal grandmother, Paw-Paw, who lives in penury in San Francisco's Chinatown. The ambience is alien to her, and she is scorned
because she doesn't speak the language. Gradually Paw-Paw steeps
the lonely outcast in the lore and traditions of her Chinese heritage.
Barney continually promises her by postcard that he will come and
deliver her from her purgatory but just as regularly reneges. His
sudden reappearance, coupled with the theft of Paw-Paw's valuable
old owl charm and her injury in the robbery, injects an aura of
mystery and intrigue that leads to Casey's bitter disillusionment in
her dad. In the end, the owl charm must be sold to a museum to
pay Paw-Paw's hospital bills and to rehabilitate Barney through
Gamblers Anonymous. Casey elects to stay with proud Paw-Paw
and her newly won friends in Chinatown.

481. Zindel, Paul. PARDON ME, YOU'RE STEPPING ON MY EYE-
     BALL. New York: Harper and Row, 1976. 262p. Grades
     9-12. R
     The two alienated teens meet in their high school group
therapy class. Louis "Marsh" Mellow, 15, lives with the mother he
hates who gets drunk and passes out every night at 7:00. The
father he loves, he confides to Edna, is in a Los Angeles asylum
about to be lobotomized, and he is desperate to get him released.
Edna Shinglebox is hectored and disparaged by her ambitious,
manipulative, tunnel-visioned parents for her lack of social aspirations and apparent indifference to boys. Pathologically shy, she
recognizes that Marsh is far more disturbed than she, not only because of his wild talk and his dependence on his pet racoon, but
especially because she learns that his father was killed by a bus
while drunk before Marsh's eyes, and that his ashes are kept in
an urn under Marsh's bed. With conflicting hostility and compassion toward him, she only accedes to his pathetic plea to join him
on an expedition to free his father after a disastrous drug and
drink orgy in which the host's home burns to the ground and Rac-
coon is incinerated. They get as far as Washington, D.C., before
Marsh wrecks his mother's car on a bridge embankment. It is Edna
who retrieves his father's remains from his suitcase and dumps them
in the Potomac, but she knows that the ghost must still be exorcised.

They squeeze through the gates into Arlington National Cemetery, and, using the eternal flame from Kennedy's grave, they ignite the rocket that Marsh has been carrying for a special occasion.

UNWED MOTHERS

482. Anderson, Mary. STEP ON A CRACK. New York: Atheneum,
      1978. 180p. Grades 6-9. R+
      As long as she can remember, Sarah Carpenter, 15, has been
plagued by a recurring nightmare in which she kills her beloved
mother, followed by a compulsion to shoplift some inconsequential
item. That is perturbing enough, but suddenly, following the news
that the peripatetic, bohemian artist aunt whom she has never met
is coming to visit, Sarah begins sleepwalking. Terrified of losing
her sanity, she consults her New York private school classmate
Josie, a would-be psychologist. Sarah and her down-to-earth mother
tolerate Aunt Kat's flighty, impatient, egotistical presence, while
Josie secretly probes Sarah's earliest memories for clues to her irrational symptoms. When her mother breaks a leg, Sarah is certain
she subconsciously caused the accident, and Aunt Kat stays on to
help. A visit to a city park with Josie triggers the traumatic recollection that releases the subliminal knowledge that Sarah's parents
have never divulged. Aunt Kat is, in reality, her unmarried
biological mother who abandoned her when she was a toddler. The
only parents she has ever consciously known are Kat's stable older
sister and brother-in-law who adopted her. In her dreams Sarah
has been retaliating against Aunt Kat, and after Kat's departure,
Sarah enters teen group therapy to comprehend and accept her
past.

483. Anderson, Mary. TUNE IN TOMORROW. New York: Athene-
      um, 1984. 179p. Grades 6-9. R+
      Short, overweight Josephine Kaputkin, 14, who lives vicarious-
ly through the storyline of her favorite soap opera, meets a kindred
spirit in tall, skinny Peggy McKale at the New York TV studio she
haunts after school, hoping for glimpses of tube lovers Fern and
Travis. Peggy's mother is institutionalized, and Josephine worries
that her mother Francine, a former flower child who has no inkling
of the identity of her daughter's father, is a potential mental case
also. Now a psychic, Francine is unmaternal, vague about money, and
dependent on Jo for fixing meals. Peggy and Jo collaborate on writing a script for "Quest for Happiness" in which Fern and Travis
share a romantic idyll. They are devastated when their idea is rejected and the characters are killed off on the show. Aunt Gert ar-

arrives from California to take them to Fire Island on vacation, and
their fantasy is rekindled when they discover that Fern and Travis
are real-life lovers also vacationing, incognito, on the island. They
spend all their waking hours tracking down the actors, but their
daydream irrevocably collapses when they learn that their idols are
crass, conceited cocaine snorters. In the meantime, Francine has
met a herbologist at a psychic convention and begins taking an
interest in nutrition and reality. Jo, having lost weight, is attracted to a local boy who likes her as she is. She muses that she
will have to tune in tomorrow to learn how her life will evolve.

484. Branscum, Robbie. TOBY, GRANNY AND GEORGE. Garden
     City: Doubleday, 1976. Illus. by Glen Rounds. 105p.
     Grades 4-6. R
     A bastard left on her grandmother's doorstep, enterprising
October (Toby), 13, grows up in an atmosphere of subsistence and
quiet acceptance, along with her canine companion George, among
their neighbors in the Ozarks, where life revolves around crops and
church. Complacency dissolves when an obese parishioner drowns
during baptism. One faction, led by penurious Deacon Treat, believes that Preacher Davis maliciously held the victim under. The
other faction, led by sensible and respected Granny, an herbalist,
maintains that Deacon Treat was negligent in dredging the baptismal
hole. Then Deacon is discovered dead and the Treat baby missing.
Toby is bound to solve the mystery and absolve Preacher. She makes
friends shyly with the mute eldest of the Treat tribe, whose father
had starved and enslaved them for his own gain. When she hears
Granny's tale of child abuse and finds the small grave hidden deep
in the woods, she knows intuitively that her new friend killed his
father in defense of the baby. Preacher Davis assures them that the
boy will not be prosecuted. When her mother comes to visit, Toby
is afraid of having to go live with her in the city, but strict and
loving Granny reassures Toby that she will always have a home with
her, to be the succor of her old age.

485. Byars, Betsy. THE TWO-THOUSAND-POUND GOLDFISH. New
     York: Harper and Row, 1982. 152p. Grades 5-6. R+
     Fourth grader Warren Otis thinks of his mom as a Joan of Arc.
A militant antinuclear activist, she has been a fugitive from the FBI
since bombing a chemical plant when he was a baby. She communicates with him only by postcards that can't be traced. Never married, she only bore Warren and his high-school-aged half-sister
Louise because she is also an antiabortionist. The children are being
reared by their grandmother, who disowned her daughter long ago.
A devotee of monster movies, Warren spends every waking hour, to
the detriment of his schoolwork, creating his own highly imaginative
horror films featuring radioactive cows, carnivorous snails, monstrous
skunks, and, his favorite, a grotesquely overgrown goldfish that in-
gests humans whole. When his grandmother confiscates his mother's
postcards, Warren angrily makes her the victim in his next plot. His
guilt when she suffers a stroke is tempered by joy in his conviction

that his mother will have to return if she dies. His expectations
are unfulfilled; moreover, he only begins to appreciate his grandmother when she is gone. The realization that Mom will never return, long accepted by Louise, jolts him back to earth, and he
deals "Bubbles" a coup de grace. Louise confides in him her own
daydream of becoming a lawyer and defending Mom in court.

486. Chetin, Helen. HOW FAR IS BERKELEY? New York: Har-
      court, Brace, Jovanovich, 1977. 122p. Grades 6-8. R
      In this potboiler of a contemporary problem novel, Michael,
12, named for the father her unwed mother refused to marry because of differences in nationality and religion, has been living a
stable and secure life with her conventional middle-class grandparents in Los Angeles when her mother decides to return to graduate school at Berkeley. There they move into a house shared by
Al, an ex-Ph.D. candidate who now peddles orange juice and cookies
on campus, and by three lesbian feminists. Open-minded Mike makes
friends with sensitive, physically handicapped David who lives next
door with his alcoholic mother and senile grandmother. Another acquaintance, precocious, sexually conversant DeeDee, resides with
her libertine psychologist father and his POSSLQ because her mother
is a promiscuous hippie living in a houseboat commune. While her
mother struggles with her studies, Mike pursues her obsession with
Aztec history because it helps her identify with the Mexican father
she has never met. When she gets her first period, the friendly
feminists throw a party for her to celebrate the rites of puberty,
agreeing that men are jealous of women for their menstrual cycles.
Then a fire in David's house precipitates the removal of his mother
to a sanatorium and his grandmother to a retirement home. Michael's
mom's intensifying friendship with the Orange Juice Man threatens
to turn into a permanent relationship, and Mike responds by childishly defacing his pushcart. Her grandparents come to visit and
give reserved acquiescence to their new lifestyle, and Mike puts the
compulsion to find her father on a back burner.

487. Cleaver, Vera, and Bill Cleaver. I WOULD RATHER BE A
      TURNIP. Philadelphia: Lippincott, 1971. 159p. Grades 5-7.
      R+
      Ostracized by her erstwhile friends when her sister's illegiti-
mate child comes to live with her and her pharmacist father in their
small Southern town, Annie, 12, is stultified and covered with con-
tumely. Rebellion, revenge, and retreat fail to restore her self-
respect. Attempts at expressing herself in prose and poetry are
unsatisfactory. A triumphant piano recital and her heroic rescue
of her bright, studious nephew from a mad bull offer only temporary
respite from her despondency. It is 8-year-old Calvin himself who
introduces her to the world of literature and the knowledge and
solace it imparts. Words written by Helen Keller inspire her to look
beyond "the fixity of limitations" through books. She discovers that
William the Conqueror was illegitimate yet became king of England in
spite of benighted bigots.

488. Colman, Hila. TELL ME NO LIES. New York: Crown, 1978.
      74p. Grades 5-7. R++
      On the eve of her mother's marriage to Larry Brandon, with
whom they live in New York and who wants to adopt her, Angela
Dunoway, 12, learns that she is illegitimate. Her never-married
mother, a designer, weaned her on the elaborate fiction that when
her husband took a job in Saudi Arabia she refused to accompany
him, and when he failed to return she divorced him. Angela presses
her to reveal that her true father is a Portuguese fisherman, Jose
Avillar, whom her mother met as a tourist in Provincetown and who
doesn't know that Angela exists. The girl is furious with her mother
both for lying to her and for robbing her of the fictitious paternal
image of "Robert Grey" whom Angela has fleshed out in her imagination. She is determined to find her father, against her mother's
better judgment, in hopes of establishing a filial relationship. After
promising to be discreet, she is allowed to visit her mother's old
friend Margaret in the seaside village. She is disappointed on meeting Jose, because he shows no flash of recognition or warmth in
spite of their physical resemblance. When Margaret arranges for
her to spend a day with the Avillars, she feels like a fish out of
water. Jose gently tells her that as an independent young woman
with a loving stepfather, she doesn't need a biological father, just
as he, having a wife and three sons, does not need a daughter.
Finally, Angela feels free to be adopted by Larry and to forgive her
mother.

489. Eyerly, Jeannette. HE'S MY BABY NOW. Philadelphia: Lip-
      pincott, 1977. (OP) 156p. Grades 7-12. R
      When his mother, a legal secretary since the desertion of
Charles Elderbury's father many years ago, points out the newspaper
statistic that a former girlfriend of his has just had a baby out of
wedlock, Charles, 16, realizes that the infant is his. Daisy, the
baby's mother, declined an abortion and bore the child in rebellion
against her punitive father and intolerable homelife, but she has also
rejected the baby and is putting him up for adoption. Daisy and the
social worker expect him to sign the release form, but Charles, who
has always been sensitive about his own abandonment, experiences a
kindling of fatherly instincts and decides to rear the child alone.
With a friend's connivance, he discovers the location of the foster
home, and Charles daringly kidnaps the infant and pumps a fellow
employee of the supermarket where he stacks groceries to learn what
supplies he needs. He reasons that because his mother is soon to
marry her boss and retire, she will have plenty of time to care for
the baby while he is at school or work. The trauma of the first
diaper change causes him to recant with alacrity, however, and he
returns the baby and signs the adoption papers. As he begins to
date a new girl, the memory of Daisy and his son starts to fade.

490. Gaeddert, Lou Ann. DAFFODILS IN THE SNOW. New York:
      Dutton, 1984. 114p. Grades 7-10. R
      Born late in life to a pious Kansas farmer and his wife, saintly

Marianne is not permitted to date as a teenager; her sternly protective father drives off her only suitor. With her beatific face
and singing voice she attracts the attention of the featured evangelist, glib Billy Jim Johnson, at an old-fashioned Midwest revival. In
a rhapsodic state, she faints at his feet and is carried off to his
trailer. Weeks later her girlhood friend Eleanor learns that Marianne
is pregnant. When her father demands that she name the baby's
father, Marianne declares that it is God's child. The rigid, sanctimonious man denounces her publicly and disinherits her. A newcomer to town, compassionate disabled veteran Joe Holt, harbors and
marries her. The baby is born during a blizzard while daffodils
bloom incongruously in the farmyard. Word spreads quickly, and
other miracles are soon attributed to mother and baby. The family
is beleaguered by hysterical mobs of people seeking blessings and
cures, besieged by reporters, and badgered by ecclesiastics clam-
oring to ascertain baby Christopher's paternity. Coincidentally,
Billy Jim Johnson is shot and killed by a man whose wife he seduced.
To escape the hectoring crowds, the Holts move west so that Christopher can have a normal childhood. Eleanor loses touch with her
old friend but learns years later of a commune in Oregon whose
spiritual leader has a widowed mother who sings angelically and plays
the Autoharp, as Marianne did.

491. Gripe, Maria. THE NIGHT DADDY. New York: Delacorte,
      1971. (OP) Illus. by Harald Gripe. Trans. by Gerry Both-
      mer. 150p. Grades 4-6. R
         A young writer answers a newspaper advertisement for sleep-
while-you-work night babysitting and discovers his charge to be a
lonely, precocious girl whose unwed mother is a nurse on night
shift. With his sensitivity and tact, he overcomes the independent
child's resentment at having her autonomy curtailed and calls her
Julia when she refuses to divulge her real name. They soon become
fast friends, along with the Night Daddy's pet owl Smuggler. Together they engage in philosophical discourses over midnight snacks,
exchange dreams, share the magical moment of the blooming of an
exotic tropical plant, and worry over Smuggler's disappearance.
Julia and the Night Daddy, who is writing a book on rocks and
minerals, pen alternate chapters of the narrative.

492. Hall, Lynn. THE HORSE TRADER. New York: Scribner,
      1981. 121p. Grades 7-10. R++
         When she discovered at the age of 11 that her unwed mother,
a former rodeo queen, had to sell her palomino parade horse when
she was born, Karen Kohler, now 15, believing that she was not
worth the sacrifice, approached Harley Williams, the horse trader to
whom he was sold, to try to recover him. The palomino was long
gone, but in the four years since, Karen, yearning for a father
figure, has developed a heavy crush on Harley, who has done nothing to discourage her. At 53 he is still handsome and dashing but
has the reputation in their Colorado environs of being an unscrupu-
lous philanderer. He takes her life savings to procure for her a

chronically foundered mare, but Karen refuses to acknowledge that
he cheated her. She loves Lady Bay and tirelessly nurses her back
to health. When Lady Bay throws a palomino foal, Karen offers it to
her mother. The gesture elicits her mother's guilt at having tried
to abort her pregnancy after being disavowed by Karen's father, a
cowboy on the rodeo circuit. But Della Kohler has since atoned for
her wild youth and has become a devoted mother, studying diligently
to become a licensed insurance salesperson and improve their lifestyle. Then Harley's fortunes take a plunge when he is shot by a
jealous husband, and he tries to exploit Karen's infatuation, reeling
out more facile lies to recapture her affections. A sadder but wiser
Karen now recognizes his glib palaver for what it's worth and walks
away from the treacherous horse trader.

493.   Hellberg, Hans-Eric. GRANDPA'S MARIA. New York: Mor-
       row, 1974. (OP) Illus. by Joan Sandin. Trans. by Patricia
       Crampton. 189p. Grades 4-6. R
       This is the astute and empathetic observation of 7-year-old
Maria's abstractions, emotions and exploits, captured by her grandfather, who has the expert eye of the professional photographer
focused fondly upon his favorite subject. The perplexities of childhood appear humorous to him, but his amusement is always in rapport with Maria. The small Swedish girl has been christened Maria
Charlotta, and though the usually obedient and poetic Maria pre-
dominates, sometimes her naughty alter ego Charlotta surfaces.
Maria believes that Grandpa is her father until a neighbor girl
blurts out that she has no daddy. Then Mama has to go away to a
rest home because of a nervous breakdown, causing further bewilderment. Adults' explanations of these unsettling situations are
most mystifying, but Maria takes comfort in Grampy's solid and
philosophical presence. Mama sends her a gift certificate for a bicycle, and Grandpa helps her pick one, though she must teach herself to ride it (with occasionally comical and chaotic results) because
Grandpa has a lame leg. One day she meets her biological father
and a half-brother she didn't know existed, which adds to her
bafflement. Finally Mama returns, and Grandpa's photos chronicle
for her Maria's development in her absence.

494.   Howker, Janni. THE NATURE OF THE BEAST. New York:
       Greenwillow, 1985. 138p. Grades 6-9. NR
       The specter of destitution following the closing of the mill
upon which the community of Haverston depends for its livelihood
affects different men in different ways. Bill Coward's father, who
has reared the boy since his common-law wife's defection at his
birth, travels to Glasgow in search of work. His grandfather,
Chunder, cries in despair and drinks more heavily, though he is
otherwise rational. Both are forced to swallow their pride and go on
the dole. When a mysterious predator begins decimating livestock
in the district, a newspaper offers a reward for a photograph of
the beast. In hopes of improving the family finances, Bill nicks a
camera and spends an unnerving night on the desolate moor with

his mate Mick before capturing it on film. Angered when the sarcastic editor refuses to glance at the dark and indistinct image,
Bill resolves to go out alone and kill the marauder, which he has
identified from its shape and color as a black panther. Armed only
with an air rifle, the terrified hunter quickly realizes he is being
stalked by the vicious creature and nearly falls prey to it before
witnessing its death in a peat bog. Safely home, he is incredulous
to learn that his experience is attributed to hysteria and hallucina-
tions. Welfare officials disclose that his father has been jailed for
assaulting a police officer and that they deem Chunder an unfit
guardian. Before he will submit to foster care or institutionalization, the fiercely independent and alienated boy decides to become
a predator himself and live off the land like the Haverston Beast.

495. Jones, Hettie. I HATE TO TALK ABOUT YOUR MOTHER.
     New York: Delacorte, 1980. 248p. Grades 7-9. R+
     Fay Prince is an unwed mother, a Polish-American who is
voluptuous, promiscuous, an ex-hippie, and normally either drunk
or hungover. She is despised by her biracial daughter Alicia, 13,
whose father was Dominican. Fay, who has briefly held a variety
of jobs in New York City, has been offered the use of a vacation
home on the Jersey Shore for an off-season weekend, and Alicia
has no choice but to accompany her. While her mother carouses in
the bar of the old hotel, Alicia is left to explore the deserted summer colony. She soon makes the acquaintance of Gary Willis, with
whom she develops a strong, mutual, glandular attraction and is
immediately horrified that she may be as licentious as Fay. She
also makes friends with Lena, the wild, rebellious, illegitimate, and
reputedly lesbian granddaughter of the hotel's staid, sanctimonious
proprietor. The two plan an abortive runaway attempt. Alicia is
caught in the lifeless Fun House, accused of a theft that Lena committed, and exposed to a humiliatingly intimate search by Lena's
grandmother. Attention is diverted from her when the historic hotel
burns and Fay's dissipation is disclosed. When the local constabu-
lary asks them to leave town as personae non gratae, Fay blames
Alicia, who suddenly realizes that there will be many options in her
future. She is eager to investigate the possibilities.

496. Klein, Norma. MOM, THE WOLF MAN AND ME. New York:
     Pantheon, 1972. 128p. Grades 5-7. R+
     Eleven-year-old Brett's unorthodox photographer mother never
married her father (Brett doesn't even know who he is--or care to),
and both of them like their casual, independent New York lifestyle,
although Brett's grandmother has conventional qualms about the arrangement. Brett's friend Evelyn, on the contrary, wants to have a
father. Her divorced mother is a compulsive husband-hunter who is
neurotically domestic and attempts suicide when her latest matrimo-
nial hope miscarries. Brett and her mother are both immediately attracted to Theo, owner of a Russian wolfhound, whom they meet on
assignment. But Brett is alarmed to learn that Mom and Theo plan
to wed, fearing that marriage will spoil her relationship with her

224

mother and shatter their autonomy. She is gradually mollified, especially when they promise her the master bedroom in their new apartment.

497. Levitin, Sonia. BEYOND ANOTHER DOOR. New York: Atheneum, 1977. 174p. Grades 6-9. R
Daria Peterson, 13, and her mother are frequently at odds, because while Daria is a dreamer, Peg Peterson is a practical, plodding, suspicious, overprotective, terse, unsentimental, and rigidly conventional bank teller. Daria's curiosity about her origins in Missouri, which they left when she was a baby, particularly about her father and grandmother, both now dead, is quickly parried by Peg. On a visit to a street carnival in her coastal California town, Daria wins a cheap dish which seems to come to life in an alarming manner, frightening off her former best friend Kelly but attracting the comradeship of Rob, her first boyfriend, and Nan, who is fascinated with the occult. The face in the dish tries to communicate with her, informing her that she is a "love child." It is only after a visiting aunt supplies information about her grandmother, a reputable psychic, and her father, who died tragically before Daria was born out of wedlock, that Daria understands her mother's fear of the unknown and uncontrollable. She opens her mind to her grandmother's spirit and establishes contact, forestalls a premonitory disaster to her old friend Kelly, and musters courage to seek parental permission to explore her gift of prescience to its full potential.

498. Mazer, Harry. THE DOLLAR MAN. New York: Delacorte, 1974. 204p. Grades 7-9. R+
Though overweight and given to flights of wild fancy, Marcus Rosenbloom, 13, is secure in the love and respect he shares with his mother Sally, a New York City social worker who has reared him since birth without benefit of marriage. His most obsessive fantasy involves the identity of his father, whom he imagines to be a benevolent man who dispenses money liberally to the needy, but Sally steadfastly refuses to discuss him. As Marcus enters junior high, he draws away from his former grammar school friends and toadies to the sophisticated, unsavory ninth-grader Dorrity, who seems to defend him from those who torment him about his weight. His trust in Dorrity is misplaced when the older boy casually betrays him at a hearing on marijuana charges at which Marcus is censured for refusing to testify against his new acquaintance. He is expelled and sent to a different school from which he launches a concerted investigation to find his father. Eventually he locates him, a successful businessman with wife and family in a wealthy exurb, but under the handsome, prosperous veneer is a superficial, materialistic, vain, selfish and insincere man, all qualities Sally has taught him to abhor. He returns to the loyalty and support of Sally and his old chums and leaves behind on the bus the bribe money and watch given to him by the father who never cared.

499. Paterson, Katherine. THE GREAT GILLY HOPKINS. New

York: Crowell, 1978. 148p. Grades 5-7. R+
    Galadriel Hopkins' young unwed mother named her for a Tol-
kien character and then decamped for California when Gilly was 3,
foisting her off on the social welfare system while still sending postcards fanning Gilly's hope of a reunion. Now 11 and bitter and resentful of foster care, Gilly has developed a tough, aggressive,
profane crust that tells both adults and children who is in control
and to keep their distance. Labeled incorrigible, she is sent to a
foster home of last resort in a Maryland suburb of Washington run
by Maime Trotter, fat and slovenly but patient, tolerant, and
fiercely loyal and protective of her other charge, the vulnerable
William Ernest, and of her elderly, blind, black neighbor Mr. Randolph. Neither Trotter nor the new sixth grade teacher is intimidated by Gilly, and, nonplussed, she steals money from Trotter and
Mr. Randolph to go and join her mother. She is caught and returned,
and when the rest of the "family" contracts flu, Gilly tackles the
task of nursing them to health and later of teaching self-defense to
little William Ernest. Just as she becomes reconciled to life at
Trotter's, her grandmother arrives to take Gilly to her home in Virginia, dispatched by the daughter she hasn't seen in thirteen years.
Gilly's hopes of being reunited with her mother are raised again,
only to be dashed irrevocably during a brief, impersonal visit.
Kindly Trotter encourages Gilly to remain with the lonely grandmother who needs her.

500. Peck, Robert Newton. MILLIE'S BOY. New York: Knopf,
        1973. (OP) 195p. Grades 7-10. R
    The scattergun attack that kills his mother, a dipsomaniac and
scarlet woman in Cornwall, Vermont, in 1898, badly wounds bastard
Tit Smith, 16. Sympathetic Sheriff Gus Tobin pulls him through,
but Tit, now an orphan and pauper, is afraid of being sent to the
county poor farm and is obsessed with solving the riddle of his
antecedents. He sets out in deep snow for Ticonderoga, following
the only clue he has to his mother's name and birthplace. Along
the way he is set upon by savage coydogs but is saved in the nick
of time by an Amazonian nurse practitioner, Fern Bodeen. After a
third brush with death on a half-frozen lake, she takes him to live
with her and her spunky teenage niece, Amy Hallow, who plans to
become a doctor. Hearty Fern, who is both cook and surgeon to
the loggers at George Washington Ostrander's lumber camp, divulges
part of what she knows of his mother Millie Sabbathday's background
after he mistakenly accuses her of the murder. As soon as Tit sees
Ostrander's flaming red hair, identical to his own, he knows who
his father is. But before he can declare himself, he learns the
bitter truth about Ostrander's hatred of Indians and his cruel and
contemptible treatment of women when Ostrander tries to rape Amy,
with whom Tit has fallen in love. Ostrander's violent death and
Sheriff Gus' solution to his mother's murder finally free Tit to relinquish the past and plan a future for himself that includes loving
and supportive Amy, Fern and Gus.

501. Pevsner, Stella. LINDSAY, LINDSAY, FLY AWAY HOME.
       New York: Clarion, 1983. 184p. Grades 6-10. R+
       Suspecting that her widowed and remarried father, an inter-
national businessman with whom she has resided in India for most of
her life, is sending her back to the States to break up her romance
with a Hindu, Lindsay Collins, 17, is highly resentful of her Aunt
Meg, the Chicago radio personality with whom she has come to live.
Her British accent and protective cloak of hauteur heighten her cul-
ture shock and serve to alienate her from her classmates until an
old family friend, Jess, also 17, tries to acclimatize her. She plots
to return to India until the news that Rajee has become engaged to
someone else sends her spinning into deep depression and a bleak
sense of expatriation. A summer trip spent laboring on a farm down-
state with Jess restores her self-esteem until she suffers a broken
leg. Half conscious, she dreams that her mother is alive and comforting her. She awakens to find Meg solicitously tending her and
comes to the incredible realization that Meg is her biological mother.
Meg confesses that as a young, unmarried college student, she re-
linquished Lindsay to her childless brother and sister-in-law to
rear. When her sister-in-law died, Meg longed to reclaim Lindsay
but couldn't bring herself to disrupt their lives. It was only Lindsay's standoffishness that deterred Meg from declaring herself earlier, now that her brother has married again. When Lindsay has a
chance to digest the startling information, she finds herself ready to
accept a permanent home with a loving new mother.

502. Rodowsky, Colby. EVY-IVY-OVER. New York: Watts, 1978.
       153p. Grades 5-7. R
       Her mother named her Mary Rose before boarding a Trailways
bus and disappearing. Her grandmother, Gussie, renamed her Slug-
a-bed. Slug has always enjoyed their special way of communicating,
their daily forages through the Virginia community's garbage cans
in search of colored glass or pieces of metal, and their impromptu
dancing. She has taken for granted the castoffs they wear, their
outlandishly decorated house, and Gussie's prescience. When she
enters sixth grade, however, she becomes self-conscious of their
eccentric lifestyle, goaded by a vicious classmate, Nelson, and a
teacher who discriminates against her. Like a jump rope in one of
the incessant schoolyard games, Slug's emotions flop from fierce
fealty to acute embarrassment when Nelson brands Gussie a witch
and a thief on cruelly contrived evidence. He also terrorizes his
own senile grandmother, but it is only when Gussie is beaten senseless that Nelson's psychosis is diagnosed. A sympathetic new
teacher helps Slug through the trauma of Gussie's convalescence
and shows her that being different is nothing to be ashamed of.

503. Rodowsky, Colby. JULIE'S DAUGHTER. New York: Farrar,
       Straus, Giroux, 1985. 231p. Grades 7-10. R++
       Julie Wilgus, who has not seen her daughter Slug, now 17,
since infancy (see 502), impetuously volunteers to care for her following her grandmother Gussie's death, but only until her brother

returns from abroad to make a permanent home for her. Mother and
daughter hold one another at arm's length, and Slug is shocked to
learn that Julie, promiscuous in her youth, is not even sure of the
identity of Slug's father. Even though Julie explains that she ran
away to start a new life for herself because she couldn't live down
her reputation in their small town after the birth of her baby, Slug
is still bitter that the death of her mother's best friend was more
tragic for her than abandoning her child. Julie eventually made
something of herself and is now a school nurse in Baltimore, where
Slug is attracted to an elderly artist neighbor who, because of her
eccentricity, reminds her of Gussie. Harper Tegges is brilliant,
creative, driven and forthright. When she is diagnosed as having
an inoperable brain tumor, she reacts with anger and denial. To
spare her the indignity of being placed in a nursing home, Julie
organizes the neighbors to care for Harper in her own home. During
one of Slug's shifts, Harper reveals that she, like Julie, left husband
and daughter to follow her muse. In coming to terms with her sudden revulsion for the stubborn, restless old woman, Slug realizes
that she can also forgive her mother for her long ago desertion.
After Harper's death, mother and daughter agree to remain together.

504. Sachs, Marilyn. CLASS PICTURES. New York: Dutton,
      1980. 138p. Grades 6-9. R+
      Upon high school graduation, Pat Maddox, nearly 18, pores
over her photo album and reminisces upon the significant events of
her life and her dynamic and volatile friendship with Lolly Scheiner
from the day they met in kindergarten, when Pat bit Lolly's cheek
because it resembled a rosy apple, to the threshold of Pat's promising
college career. At one time, Lolly was plump, timid, and tormented
by her peers though pampered by her affluent family, while Pat was
bold and friendly, a natural leader, living over a San Francisco
store with her job-hopping mother, grandmother and younger half
brothers. Later Pat learns that her mother, now a widow, was
seduced at a school dance and never knew the name of Pat's father.
It is Pat's third grade teacher, Mr. Evans, who becomes a surrogate
father to her and encourages her serious pursuit of science. Somehow, her loyalty to Lolly survives emerging class consciousness
among their classmates and Lolly's sudden metamorphosis into a social butterfly, a gorgeous but giddy magnet for both sexes. Pat
also weathers her grandmother's remarriage, though it causes an un-
breachable rift between her mother and grandmother and burdens
Pat with responsibility for the household. Overlooked by the boys
in high school and snubbed by most of the girls but Lolly, Pat immerses herself in academics and develops a crush on Mr. Evans,
whose son she babysits. Proud of her scholarship to MIT, Pat
faces the future and her parting from Lolly with determination and
optimism.

505. Smith, Doris Buchanan. LAST WAS LLOYD. New York:
      Viking, 1981. 124p. Grades 5-6. R+
      Born when his mother was only 14, Lloyd Albert, 12, has been

hopelessly coddled and protected because of his mother's overanxious-
ness to prove herself a good parent and keep her child. A crack
batter, practicing daily with his mother's softball team, he hides his
light under a bushel and is always picked last when his class
chooses teams because his corpulence causes derision when he runs
the bases. He overreacts to his Georgia sixth grade classmates'
needling so that he can sit aloof from them at the detention desk.
He even loosens his own shoelaces so his mother will have to tie
them when she picks him up after school on her way home from her
shrimp plant job, and he invents an imaginary illness to excuse his
maternally indulged gluttony and garner sympathy. It is only when
an erstwhile tormentor learns of his covert athletic aptitude and
urges him to walk unescorted to the park and learn to ride a bike
that Lloyd even conceives of disengaging himself from the apron
strings. Uncharacteristically, he defends the pugnacious new girl
in class, the only one lower on the totem pole than he, and when
the opportunity arises to display his new self-confidence, in spite
of his mother's misgivings, he discovers that he can make friends
and summon the willpower to go on a diet.

505a. Smith, Doris Buchanan. RETURN TO BITTER CREEK. New
      York: Viking/Kestrel, 1986. 174p. Grades 5-8. R+
      After spending all but two years of her life in Colorado,
where her unwed mother Campbell fled from her domineering mother,
Lacey Bittner, 12, is returning to the Bittner family compound in
rural North Carolina, where Campbell's current lover David Habib,
a blacksmith, has been offered a commission at a mountain crafts
school. The imperious matriarch immediately tries to exert control
over both Campbell and Lacey, subjecting her daughter to sarcasm
and contempt for her illicit relationships. Campbell reacts by obstinately rejecting the entire family. Lacey learns that her grandmother once instituted legal proceedings to gain custody of her.
Their only common bond is their love of wildflowers, but that drives
a wedge between her and her nearest cousin Tam, the favored
grandchild and chief idolater. Through the discord and dissention,
fair, rational and pragmatic David, though aspersed by Mrs. Bittner
as an Irani, maintains a Solomonic stance. Lacey loves him as a
father and feels no attachment toward her biological father, Campbell's high school sweetheart. David's sudden death in an auto accident plunges Campbell into deep depression and lassitude, while
Lacey channels her grief into energetically building the cabin David
started. Grandmom Bittner's attempt to bully her black sheep
daughter into submission finally goads Campbell, a skilled crafts-
person herself, into snapping out of her lethargy and accepting the
challenge of finishing David's commission to keep the two of them solvent and independent. Cousin Tam courageously switches allegiance to
Campbell and Lacey, breaking the genteel despot's stranglehold of
power and forcing her to accept Campbell on the latter's terms.

506. Snyder, Zilpha Keatley. THE BIRDS OF SUMMER. New York:
      Atheneum, 1983. 195p. Grades 7-10. R++

Born of her mother Oriole's brief dalliance with a medical student in San Francisco's Haight-Ashbury in the halcyon days of the 1960s, Summer McIntyre, 15, has inherited her anonymous father's sense of responsibility and desire for achievement and security. It is she who picks up the pieces when Oriole is fired for use of recreational drugs and she who cares for her half sister Sparrow, 7. Now living in a house trailer on mountain property belonging to her best friend Nicky Fisher's family, lonely Summer writes unmailed diary-style letters to the father who is unaware of her existence and whose address is unknown. Unwilling to depend on welfare, she takes a job as housekeeper with the Olivers, who own a horse ranch, and as a mother's helper to a sympathetic teacher, Alan Pardell, and his wife. She is appalled when Oriole establishes a new liaison with a menacing man, Angelo, who works for the Fishers and whom she suspects of raising marijuana and killing her dog. Her fears are confirmed when Nicky tells her that Angelo is an international drug dealer and terrorist who is holding his family hostage. When police raid the pot farm, Summer is petrified that Oriole will be caught in the crossfire. Oriole is arrested, and Summer and Sparrow are placed in a foster home. Pragmatically, Summer arranges for Sparrow's adoption by the wealthy Olivers, who are moving to Connecticut, but with Alan Pardell's guidance, Summer decides to remain behind out of loyalty to her fickle, irresponsible parent.

507.   Stanek, Lou Willett. GLEANINGS. New York: Harper and
       Row, 1985. 184p. Grades 7-10. R+
       Illegitimate, irreverent Pepper Marlan scandalizes the insular
Long Island farming community with her punk hairstyle and tough, aggressive posturing. She has come from California, where she lived with her bon vivant father, to stay with the kindly grandmother who overindulged her only son and now lives in poverty. Pepper singles out timid, ingenuous Frankie Banning, also 14, to be her friend and foil. Mortified at first, he is quickly mesmerized by her creative imagination and audacious unconventionality. Observantly, he comes to comprehend her artful and defensive prevarication. She claims that her father Zack is amassing wealth in California and will soon return to deliver her and Granny from penury, while her hopes of security and stability are actually pinned on her carefully orchestrated expectation that her father will marry her English teacher. Frankie perceives the truth: that Zack Marlan is an egocentric, profligate Lothario. Both are stunned to learn that Zack once had an affair with Frankie's playful older sister, who hastily married a stodgy dentist when she learned she was pregnant. Frankie's rigid fundamentalist parents fear that history will repeat itself when he and the precocious girl develop a romantic attachment. When Granny is hospitalized with a fractured hip, Pepper's dreams die slowly. To cover medical and nursing home expenses, they reluctantly agree to sell Granny's property. Resilient Pepper shoulders her precious guitar and catches the Greyhound for California to seek her fortune.

508. Thorvall, Kerstin. AND LEFFE WAS INSTEAD OF A DAD.
     Scarsdale: Bradbury, 1971. (OP) Trans. by Francine Lee
     Miro. Illus. by Kees deKiefte. 131p. Grades 4-6. R+
         Until he was 8, Magnus and his unwed mother, who gave birth
     to him at 16, lived with his grandparents. Then Mom, a hairdresser,
     moves into an apartment, but both of them are lonely until Mom falls
     in love with Leffe, who moves in with them. Magnus suddenly has
     a pal and a dad who is much more of a father to him than the bi-
     ological one who only sends support payments. Leffe, moreover, is
     a status symbol for the diffident, insecure boy, having served time
     for bank robbery with bullet scars to prove it. On probation now,
     he is a photographer, next to his mom the kindest person Magnus
     knows and a good cook who always has dinner waiting for them in
     the evening. When Leffe suddenly disappears without warning, Mag-
     nus is crushed and Mom becomes a nervous wreck. He returns dead
     drunk and shortly thereafter absconds with their savings. Days
     later they read in the news of a bank robbery and are convinced that
     Leffe committed it. Mom goes to see him in jail, where he appears
     demoralized and remorseful. Magnus realizes that his forlorn young
     mother will continue to anguish over Leffe in spite of his track
     record, and he resolves to take up the slack and become the man of
     the family.

509. Townsend, John Rowe. DAN ALONE. New York: Lippincott,
     1983. 214p. Grades 6-8. NR
         Grandfather Purvis, stern, ascetic, sanctimonious, has one
     virtuous daughter, Aunt Verity, and one licentious daughter, Prue,
     who is Dan Lunn's mother. When Mum, a shop clerk, runs off with
     her "fancy" man, Dan goes to live with his grandfather and his
     parsimonious new wife Hilda, but when Grandfather suffers a heart
     attack and dies, he overhears Hilda saying that she will have to
     place him in an orphanage. Dan, 12 in 1922, flees in search of the
     father whose identity he doesn't know and goes into hiding in a
     tough, seedy part of town with an abused, homeless girl named
     Olive. After following one clue to a dead end and being relieved
     of his nest egg by thieves, Dan is forced to throw in with a
     Dickensian "family" of professional crooks and tarts. They set him
     to begging because of his cherubic face. The house is raided by
     the constabulary, and Dan is eventually apprehended and turned
     over to Aunt Verity, who doesn't want him and blames his mother
     for their father's death. Then Dan learns that unfortunate Olive
     has been taken in by Benjy, the cruelly ridiculed Jewish glazier.
     Deductively and intuitively Dan concludes that Benjy is his own
     father, barred from marrying Mum by her Christian fundamentalist
     father's irrational hatred of Jews. Dan's mother, whose affair has
     now ended, confirms his suspicions when he locates her waiting
     tables. Dan helps reunite Benjy and Prue, and the foursome re-
     treats to the country to live happily ever after.

510. Voigt, Cynthia. DICEY'S SONG. New York: Atheneum,
     1982. 196p. Grades 6-10. R+

Having reached the sanctuary of Gran Tillerman's Maryland
farm and exacted her promise to adopt the four of them in light of
their mother's institutionalization (see 511), Dicey, 13, is content
to doff her mantle of authority, start high school, work at a part-
time job to help with expenses, and restore the old sailboat she
finds in a shed. But Gram insists that Dicey share responsibility
with her for James, 10, who is not working up to capacity in
school, Maybeth, 9, who is failing because of a learning disability
but who displays great musical promise, and Sammy, 6, who is trying unsuccessfully to curb his pugnacity. Accustomed to being
tough and masking her emotions, Dicey is defensive with her peers
but eventually makes friends with Jeff, a junior, and Mina, a self-
assured black classmate. She is stunned to be accused of plagiarism
on a biographical essay by a teacher who finds her personal experiences incredible. Gram, always pragmatic and still laconic, does
not tell her why the two of them are journeying to Boston in the
dead of winter. Later she reveals that she has been summoned by
doctors because her daughter, Dicey's mother, is in a coma and
dying. Their pilgrimage draws them closer, and together they bear
home the dead woman's ashes. Dicey, like her grandmother, is complex, often contradictory, but proud, independent, spirited, intu-
itive, tenacious and dauntless.

511. Voigt, Cynthia. HOMECOMING. New York: Atheneum, 1981.
312p. Grades 6-9. R+
When Momma loses her supermarket checker's job in Provincetown, she loads the four children into the old car, heading for her
Aunt Cilla's home in Bridgeport, but early on she parks the car at
a shopping mall and vanishes. Their instincts warn them to elude
the law or face separation in foster homes, so practical Dicey, 13,
and bright James, 10, marshal stubborn, rambunctious Sammy, 6,
and shy, imaginative Maybeth, 9, for the trek to Connecticut.
When their tiny hoard of money runs out they live by their wits,
plodding ever onward. Great-aunt Cilla has died, but her passive,
punctilious spinster daughter hesitantly but dutifully takes them in.
There they learn that their mother is in a mental hospital, and
Dicey, fearing that their diverse personalities will become submerged
at Cousin Eunice's, squires them back on the road to their only
other known living relative. Grandmother Tillerman lives on Maryland's Eastern Shore on a farm which their mother left to elope with
their seaman father whom she never married. Steering her siblings
safely through the numerous adventures and misadventures that befall them, Dicey finds her grandmother, who turns out to be curt,
acerbic, asocial and unwelcoming. The farm, however, is ideally
suited to the children, and Dicey makes it her formidable mission to
convince the surly but sensible widow that they are indispensable to
her in running it. Both are worthy adversaries, but Dicey eventually wears down the older woman, who mellows and agrees to adopt
the lot.

512. Wilkinson, Brenda. LUDELL. New York: Harper and Row,

1975. 170p. Grades 6-8. R+
    Growing up poor in the segregated South at midcentury holds
its share of rewards for Ludell, who has lived with her grandmother,
whom she calls Mama, since birth when her unwed mother left for
New York to take a live-in service position. Her grandmother does
day work to support them, and there isn't much loose cash for
frills, but Ludell and her irrepressible friends manage to share
lighthearted fun, endure embarrassing moments, make occasional
mischief, and take adversity in stride. The narrative follows her
from the fifth grade, when boys start teasing girls, through the
seventh grade, when they begin getting serious, under the watchful
eye of "Mama." Ludell describes in lyrical patois her personal
nadirs and zeniths at school, on Sunday School picnics, picking cotton, celebrating Christmas, hoping for a TV set, doing the laundry
out-of-doors, and just fooling around.

513. Wilkinson, Brenda. LUDELL AND WILLIE. New York: Harper
      and Row, 1977. 181p. Grades 8-12. R+
    To Ludell and her sweetheart Willie, both 17, it is a foregone
conclusion that they will marry following high school graduation when
Willie will join the army to support them, but Mama, Ludell's grandmother and guardian, is overprotective, belaboring her with her
mother's past transgressions (see 512) and men's age-old designs on
women. It is increasingly difficult to snatch time alone together or
even to attend school functions when Mama retires from her housekeeping job because of failing health and becomes a tenacious watch-
dog, growing increasingly querulous and punitive as senility encroaches. Sometimes Ludell thinks aloud in the black idiom of the
South that she hates Mama, but eventually, when the deteriorating
old lady takes to her bed, opportunities to sneak trysts become
more abundant. Suddenly Mama dies and Ludell's biological mother
arrives to take her back to New York with her, even though neighbors offer to make a home for Ludell for the last few months of
school. Ludell rails against such injustice to no avail and transfers
her resentment to Dessa, whom she refuses to call mother. While
she mourns Mama, her grief in parting with Willie overshadows it.
They exchange poignant letters declaring their undying affection.

514. Wilkinson, Brenda. LUDELL'S NEW YORK TIME. New York:
      Harper and Row, 1980. 184p. Grades 7-10. R+
    Dessa spirits a protesting and grieving Ludell off to Harlem to
finish her senior year (see 512 and 513), convinced that Ludell will
benefit from metropolitan opportunities and sophistication. But vir-
tuous and naive Ludell sees New York as a den of iniquity and its
denizens as scandalously licentious. Dessa tries to promote friendship between Ludell and the girl upstairs, but Regina's indulgence
in smoking, drinking, partying, and premarital sex bores Ludell,
who gravitates increasingly to the young married woman with three
children whom she met on the train coming North and with whom she
attends church. She confides her anger, confusion and frustration
to her journal and lives for the infrequent communications from

Willie, back in Waycross, who is working to save for their marriage. Dessa, a factory worker, has conflicting plans for Ludell to start college in the fall. In the meantime, following graduation, Ludell learns firsthand that racial prejudice limits employment opportunities for blacks. She finally lands a typing job and makes friends with a freedom marcher from Mississippi. Willie's nest egg dwindles under the exigency of twin medical emergencies, including his sister's attempted abortion, and wedding plans have to be postponed. Suddenly, Willie is drafted and sends for Ludell to come home to Georgia and be married right away, and Ludell, over the strenuous maternal objections of Dessa, follows her destiny.

515. Alexander, Anne. TROUBLE ON TREAT STREET. New York:
Atheneum, 1974. Illus. by John Jones. 128p. Grades 5-7.
R
Clem gets off to an inauspicious start when he moves to the
San Francisco ghetto with his grandmother after the accidental death
of his parents. Manolo, a boy his age, lives in the same building
but takes an instant dislike to Clem simply because Clem is black,
not a Chicano like himself. In school they are paired together in
fifth grade but maintain their unsheathed hostility until a gang of
older toughs of mixed race tries to play the two against each other.
Just as they achieve one another's trust and friendship, Clem's
grandmother and Manolo's mother jump to the erroneous conclusion
that the other's boy is a bad influence on hers through circumstantial evidence. Only after Clem's Granny saves the life of Manolo's
baby brother does the true story unfold. Mrs. Gomez, in gratitude,
invites the newcomers to a party, and Clem stands up to the bullies.

516. Angell, Judie. DEAR LOLA. Scarsdale: Bradbury, 1980.
166p. Grades 4-6. R
Subtitled "How to Build Your Own Family," this poignant,
amusing but implausible tale concerns six disparate orphans, un-
adoptable for varied reasons, who run away from St. Theresa's
Home under the competent leadership of Arthur Beniker who has
just turned 18 and is legally free to go. Possessed of rare wisdom,
maturity and insight learned in the school of hard knocks, Arthur
writes a syndicated advice column and is called Lola, his by-line,
by the kids, James, 13, Annie and Al-Willie, 10, Edmund, 9, and
Ben, 5, who regard him as their big brother. Under Lola's enlightened parenting and tutelage, which consists chiefly of the time-
honored public library variety of education, they learn practical
as well as theoretical skills and settle in an idyllic fixer-upper cottage in a small town. The choice of location leads to their eventual
undoing, because the cloistered neighbors are inquisitive, meddlesome and officious. When the news media divulge that "Dear Lola"
is a mere boy, he loses the job with which he supported his numerous dependents, and the sympathetic judge is reluctantly obliged to
remand them to the orphanage. In a desperate attempt to remain
free together, they make their getaway in Lola's van and go under-

234

ground as itinerant fruit pickers, adopting another waif along the
way to be a sister to Annie, the narrator of their odyssey.

517.   Baird, Thomas. WALK OUT A BROTHER. New York: Har-
       per and Row, 1983. 278p. Grades 6-10. R
       His father, a widowed pilot navigator on Puget Sound during
the winter, acts as a buffer between prickly, outspoken Don Rennie,
16, and his brother Keith, 22, a law school student. Now their
father has just died in a riding accident at their summer home in
the Wyoming mountains, and, on top of his grief, Don chafes at
being subservient to Keith, his guardian, until he receives his inheritance seven years hence. Apprehensive about living with Keith
and his girlfriend, he decides to run away, covering his getaway
by purporting to take a short backpacking trip for breathing space.
In the wilderness he encounters a tenderfoot camper whom at first
he naively does not suspect to be the killer who is reportedly at
large. But the man, Lester Pratt, volatile and temperamental, soon
tips his hand, and Don realizes that Lester plans to use the information he innocently divulged to kill Keith and steal his car in
which to escape. As resentful as he is of his overbearing brother,
blood is thicker than water, and Don tries to outflank Lester to
warn Keith. Instead he becomes trapped in the Rennie cabin where
he is stalked by the ruthless murderer, and only his quick wit
saves him from death. The brothers bury the hatchet, but Don
still insists upon making a life of his own--this time with Keith's
blessing.

518.   Bawden, Nina. THE WITCH'S DAUGHTER. Philadelphia:
       Lippincott, 1966. 181p. Grades 5-8. NR
       Orphaned in infancy, Perdita, 11, has been reared by kind,
elderly Annie on a tiny island off the coast of Scotland where she
has run as free and wild as the wind and grown as shy and stunted
as the flowers in their rocky crevices. Annie acts as housekeeper
for the enigmatic Mr. Smith, who does not allow Perdita to attend
school or make friends. Hence she is taunted and feared as a witch
by the other island children. When the steamer brings a vacationing
family and a mysterious stranger to Skua, Perdita finds her first
friends in blind Janey and her imaginative brother Tim. The
children pool their extraordinary capabilities to solve an almost perfect crime and save one another from the brink of death. Tim's inquisitive mind provides the impetus, Perdita's clairvoyance rescues
Tim from peril, but Janey, who has developed acute senses of touch
and hearing, emerges as the heroine when the trio is stranded in
the Stygian depths of a cave by jewel thieves. Mr. Smith has been
kind to Perdita in his clumsy way, and when his complicity is revealed, she warns him to escape and grieves when he loses his life
in the attempt. Her new friends promise to return, and in the meantime she will start school.

519.   Bellairs, John. THE FIGURE IN THE SHADOWS. New York:
       Dial, 1975. Illus. by Mercer Mayer. 155p. Grades 5-7. NR

When chubby, timorous Lewis, 11, expresses shame at being the brunt of bullies without the spunk or fortitude to defend himself, his Uncle Jonathan, a practicing wizard, shows him the contents of his great-grandfather's Civil War chest and tells the story of how that peaceable ancestor avoided combat. Lewis asks to keep the coin his forebear wore as a good-luck charm and soon discovers that it is a magic amulet capable of conjuring up new strength, courage, and sudden respect. But it also summons forth a frightening figure in dark robes that lunges at him unexpectedly, and his best friend Rose Rita takes the amulet and hides it for his own protection. He ferrets it out by stealth, and only quick thinking and fast action on the part of Mrs. Zimmerman, the witch next door, Uncle Jonathan and Rose Rita save him from being possessed by the shadowy haunt from the past.

520. Branscum, Robbie. CHEATER AND FLITTER DICK. New
      York: Viking, 1983. 106p. Grades 5-8. R
      The story goes that Grabapple Barnes adopted her at birth when she was given to him by a family with 18 children. He named her Cheater because she turned out to be a girl instead of the boy he wanted. He earned his own nickname as a scavenger in their Arkansas hill country. Though he is an otherwise shiftless sharecropper generally besotted with moonshine, Cheater, 14, loves him and her family of bizarre pets which includes the cowardly rooster, Flitter Dick. To pay the rent, she works as day help for their landlord's priggish, patronizing wife, Mrs. Hanson. One day, "the Missus" insults her by suggesting that she is leading her son Bradley astray. The next day a tornado levels the Hansons' pretentious house, and they are forced to move into the Barnes' ramshackle cabin. Though ill, the raving woman continues to besmirch Cheater's dawning womanhood with accusations of incest against her and Grabapple. Bradley explains to her that his mother's mental attitude is caused by losing nine children in infancy; she now regards sex as a means of filling graveyards. Still, Cheater remains implacable in her hatred of the unfortunate woman. Grabapple takes the pledge of sobriety, but the specter of privation dogs them. Mrs. Hanson is on the verge of starvation when Cheater offers the ultimate sacrifice of her beloved Flitter Dick. The menfolks' firewood-cutting enterprise saves him in the nick of time, and Mrs. Hanson recovers and apologizes for her shrewish imputations.

521. Brooks, Ron. TIMOTHY AND GRAMPS. Scarsdale: Bradbury,
      1978. Illus. by the author. Unp. Grades K-2. R+
      Timothy lives alone with his grandfather in a quaint old English cottage. While he and Gramps are inseparable companions on fishing expeditions, tramping the countryside and telling stories to one another, Timothy is ambivalent about school because of his difficulty in making friends. One day he brings his grandfather for Show and Tell, but the occasion is awkward and strained. The next time, Gramps comes prepared and regales the class with a cracking good story. Timothy's appreciative classmates beg him for more details

about his grandfather's fascinating life of adventure, and in obliging them he emerges from his shell.

522. Bulla, Clyde Robert. WHITE BIRD. New York: Crowell, 1966. (OP) Illus. by Leonard Weisgard. 79p. Grades 3-5. R
        John Thomas is rescued and reared in the Tennessee wilderness by reclusive, taciturn misanthrope Luke Vail after his cradle is carried Moses-like down the flooding river in which his pioneer parents perished. Denied a pet because he might become emotionally attached to it, John adopts a wounded albino crow and nurses it to health, only to have it stolen by scoundrels. Restrained from following them by impassive Luke, John runs away and eventually finds his bird dead. He returns voluntarily to Luke, bringing to him a subliminal lesson in love and trust.

523. Burch, Robert. SKINNY. New York: Viking, 1964. Illus. by Don Sibley. 126p. Grades 4-6. R
        Skinny is the descriptive sobriquet of the naive but engaging Georgia orphan boy who has reached the age of 11 without learning to read and write because his shiftless father, an alcoholic sharecropper, saw no value in education. When Pa dies he is offered a home by benevolent Miss Bessie, who operates the local rustic hostelry. She wants to adopt him legally, but the town fathers look askance upon a single woman assuming the responsibility of motherhood. For a while it appears that their dreams will materialize when Daddy Rabbit takes up residence at the hotel and takes a shine to Miss Bessie and Skinny, but hopes go aglimmering when the lure of the road again beckons him. Skinny accepts his fate with a certain aplomb, makes friends his own age at the orphanage, goes to school, and looks forward to holidays and summer vacation with Miss Bessie and the rest of the hotel "family."

524. Burnett, Frances Hodgson. THE SECRET GARDEN. Philadelphia: Lippincott, 1962 (c1911). Illus. by Tasha Tudor. 256p. Grades 5-8. R
        Three tragic, unloved and unloving parallel lives gradually change course, eventually to bond in joy and affection, when orphaned Mary is sent to her uncle's estate in England upon her parents' death in India and discovers the magical secret garden that becomes the catalyst in dispelling her uncle's bitterness, her cousin Colin's fears, and her own rancor. Industry, exercise, fresh air and determination become nature's panacea for both physical and emotional maladies.

525. Byars, Betsy. AFTER THE GOAT MAN. New York: Viking, 1974. Illus. by Ronald Himler. 126p. Grades 4-6. R+
        Three single-parent situations occur in this story: Figgy lives with his grandfather, Ada with her father, and Harold with his mother. Harold is a self-indulgent, egocentric, obese boy who takes lugubrious pleasure in wallowing in his own misery. His only

friend is Ada, who is totally unselfconscious, tolerant, thoughtful and sympathetic. Then diffident, defensive Figgy moves in, and Harold, with Ada's guidance, learns to become sensitive to the misfortunes of others. Figgy's grandfather is the taciturn "Goat Man," an eccentric recluse whose cabin has been condemned to make way for a superhighway. The broken old man cannot adjust to city life in the row of concrete block houses where he has been relocated, and he returns to the cabin to defy the bulldozers. Figgy's injury in a bike mishap en route with his new friends to his grandfather's defense forces his grandfather to abandon his campaign but not his dignity. Ada's father promises to find them a more suitable domicile.

526. Byars, Betsy. THE HOUSE OF WINGS. New York: Viking, 1972. Illus. by Daniel Schwartz. 142p. Grades 4-6. R+
    Youngest of eight children, Sammy, 10, has just been abandoned by both parents to live in Ohio with his mother's long-widowed father at his sprawling, derelict house where odd fowl roam indoors at will. Incredulous and outraged at the perfidy, the boy visits his anger and frustration on the grizzled old man, calling him names and leading him on a gruelling chase through a culvert and up a rocky hillside. His desperate flight is halted by the haunting cry of a stranded and injured crane. His grandfather's determination to save the afflicted creature puzzles but fascinates the callous, self-centered boy. Because the bird is blind, it must be hand fed while their personal comfort waits. Sammy learns that while his grandfather cannot distinguish among his own children, he has no problem recalling each of his succession of avian acquaintances. He finally makes peace with his grandfather, whose unorthodox lifestyle he finds appealing, especially his disregard of bathing and changing clothes. He hopes that when he eventually tries his own wings, his grandfather will remember him as he has the other wildfowl in his temporary custody.

527. Clark, Ann Nolan. SECRET OF THE ANDES. New York: Viking, 1952. Illus. by Jean Charlot. 130p. Grades 5-7. R+
    Cusi has lived for 8 years, as long as he can remember, high in the Andes in the solitude of Hidden Valley with Chuto, his mentor, herding the sacred flock of Incan llamas. From an overhanging rock he can look down and see a family with three children like ants far below, and he yearns to be part of a family. Two unexpected visitors to their mountain sanctuary change his pastoral life and give him the opportunity he seeks. Cusi wears the golden earplugs of Incan royalty and is being groomed as keeper of the ancient treasure and traditions. The time has come for him to make his pilgrimage to Cuzco, bringing the symbolic gift of llamas. His dream comes true when he is asked to join a large, rollicking Indian family on holiday in the city, but he is quickly disillusioned with their Spanish corruptions and habit of sleeping indoors. He recognizes that his place is with Chuto, father of his choice, as guardian of the gold and llamas. He returns home, takes the vows, is shown the secret cave and told the story of his blood parents.

528. Cleaver, Vera, and Bill Cleaver. TRIAL VALLEY. Philadel-
     phia: Lippincott, 1977. 158p. Grades 5-8. R
     With Devola now married to Kiser Pease, some of Mary Call
Luther's problems are solved, but her youngest siblings Romey, now
12, and Ima Dean, 7, to whom she has been sole parent since her
father's terminal illness in the backwoods of North Carolina (see
529), are growing lazy and rebellious. Mary Call, now 16 and having beaux of her own, remains implacable and uncompromising in
insisting that the younger children shoulder their share of the
family's wildcrafting enterprise and absorb the lessons in botany
and history she gleans from books and tries to impart to them. She
has inherited a new responsibility, moreover, in the form of win-
some Jack Parsons, 5, an abandoned child. Kiser and Devola want
to adopt him, but little Jack will let no one but Mary Call approach
him. Accustomed to sacrifice, she nevertheless feels a fluttering of
resentment and exasperation toward her unappreciative and demanding dependents for stealing her own youth. She tries to wean Jack
away from her, but he runs away in a thunderstorm and is nearly
drowned in the flooding creek before Mary Call finds him and he is
rescued. Bowing to her fate, Mary Call adopts him to rear as she
has the others and without regret sends her impractical suitor away.

529. Cleaver, Vera, and Bill Cleaver. WHERE THE LILIES BLOOM.
     Philadelphia: Lippincott, 1969. Illus. by Jim Spanfeller.
     174p. Grades 5-7. R+
     Under the shadow of the Great Smoky Mountains, Roy Luther
lies dying, and Mary Call, 14, has promised him that she will keep
the family intact, not accept charity, and never permit childlike
Devola, 18, to marry importuning Kiser Pease, the instrument of
their oppression and poverty. With proud fortitude and grim determination she takes the helm, buries her father up on the mountain as he desired, exploits Kiser Pease with Machiavellian cunning,
and launches a family enterprise of wildcrafting, the gathering of
medicinal roots and herbs for sale. Her brave but shaky ship of
state founders during the demoniacally inclement winter when
Pease's sister arrives and threatens to evict them from their
crumbling cabin. In the end she cannot prevent the suddenly
mature Devola from marrying the mellowed and repentant Pease,
whose love for Devola proves to be salvation also for Mary Call,
Romey, 10, and Ima Dean, 5.

530. Clymer, Eleanor. THE GET-AWAY CAR. New York: Dutton,
     1978. 149p. Grades 4-6. R+
     Maggie, 11, has lived contentedly for six years with her ma-
ternal grandmother, whose motto is Fun First, Work Later, in her
inner-city apartment. Now her paternal Aunt Ruby, a self-proclaimed expert on child development, is getting married and wants
to put Grandma in a retirement home and give Maggie a proper
suburban home and education. To escape Aunt Ruby, Grandma
quits her job and borrows an old touring car to visit her cousin on
her New York estate, bringing along Maggie and a motley lot of

multi-cultural neighbor children for company. They are certain
Aunt Ruby is on their trail when they hear a description of their
car broadcast on the radio, so they leave the beaten track. They
find the estate derelict and cousin Esther cynical, but with a lot of
teamwork from friends made along the way and a run of good luck
(antiques in the attic and thieves' booty stashed in the car, for
which there is a handsome reward), they restore the estate to its
former opulence. Cousin Esther agrees to let Grandma and Maggie
move in permanently, and even Aunt Ruby puts her seal of approval
on the new arrangement.

531. Corcoran, Barbara. THE LONG JOURNEY. New York:
     Atheneum, 1970. Illus. by Charles Robinson. 187p. Grades
     5-7. R
     Laurie makes her home with her tough and independent grand-
father in an Eastern Montana ghost town. Grandpa has taught her
self-reliance, grooming, etiquette, fine arts, and especially love,
while a correspondence school has handled her lessons. But because
of Grandpa's abhorrence of institutions and the authorities who might
place her in an orphanage, Laurie has had no experience with human-
kind or civilization. Now Grandpa is losing his sight and charges
Laurie with the awesome task of riding her horse the breadth of the
state to summon Uncle Arthur from Butte. Being alone against the
elements of nature does not alarm her, but the novelties of modern
plumbing and restaurant meals are perplexing, and the encounters
with a religious fanatic and a trigger-happy rancher are terrifying.
She meets generous and sympathetic individuals also, who try to be-
lay her mistrust. She finally reaches Butte, where Uncle Arthur
arranges surgery for Grandpa's cataracts. Afterward Laurie declines
a comfortable home with her aunt and uncle in order to resume the
rigors of the primitive life with her beloved grandfather, but she
promises to visit them often to continue her acculturation.

532. Fleischman, Sid. CHANCY AND THE GRAND RASCAL. Bos-
     ton: Little, Brown, 1966. Illus. by Eric von Schmidt. 179p.
     Grades 5-8. R+
     Chancy lost both parents during the Civil War, and he and
his younger sisters and brother were parceled out to whoever would
make a home for them. Now that he's grown, Chancy sallies forth
to reunite the family, trundling his worldly possessions in a wheel-
barrow, intending to board a steamer for Paducah to collect his
sister Indiana first. Two days later he is duped out of all his money
by a villainous old jackanapes and left with a suitcase of eggs hatch-
ing like popcorn. He and the chicks make camp on an island in the
Ohio River where he joins forces with his uncle, an audacious ad-
venturer, roguish raconteur, and jack-of-all-trades. Together they
pursue their quest, flummoxing their adversaries and regaling their
confederates with wits, whoppers, and derring-do. They deliver
Indiana, 11, from the penurious scoundrel who has held her in ser-
vitude and trace Jamie, 9, and Mirandy, 7, to Kansas just in time
to save the town histrionically from jayhawkers disguised as Indians.

A grateful citizenry offers Uncle Will the mayoralty, he accepts it
as a challenge, and the reunited family decides to stop rambling.

533. Gage, Wilson. BIG BLUE ISLAND. Cleveland: World, 1964.
       (OP) Illus. by Glen Rounds. 120p. Grades 5-6. R
       After his father's desertion and his mother's death from tuber-
culosis, Darrell, 11, is sent from Detroit to live with his only known
relative, a great-uncle who lives alone on a river island in Tennessee
with no plumbing or electricity. Darrell resents the lack of amenities,
the imposed solitude, and especially the old codger's acerbity. He
plans to run away to Florida where living is easy, but he lacks both
money and opportunity, being a virtual prisoner on the island because the old man padlocks his rowboat. When his uncle bets him a
dollar that he can't catch one of the great blue herons that winter
there, he sees his chance to earn pocket money and sets about the
task with determination until he learns, when his uncle stumbles on
his snares and hurts his back, that it is impossible, illegal, and
dangerous to trap the creatures. A ranger convinces the boy that
it is actually desirable to live on an island, like a sort of permanent
camping trip, and persuades the curmudgeon to buy the boy an old
motorboat so he will have some mobility.

534. Goffstein, M. B. TWO PIANO TUNERS. New York: Farrar,
       Straus and Giroux, 1970. Illus. by the author. 65p. Grades
       3-5. R+
       Reuben Weinstock, who has tuned pianos for the immortals,
takes on a new vocation, that of ably parenting his small granddaughter, Debbie. He is grooming her to be a concert pianist, but
she wants nothing so much as to follow in his footsteps. She tags
along on all his jobs, alertly observing. One day Mr. Weinstock is
scheduled to tune the concert grand for Isaac Lipman, with whom
he formerly toured, but he remembers that he has also promised to
tune a neighbor's piano. He sends Debbie with a message for Mrs.
Perlman, but Debbie, with childish confidence, decides to tune the
piano herself with her grandfather's discarded instruments. When
Grandpa and Mr. Lipman come to collect her, they find that it is
only the antiquated instruments that have betrayed her efforts.
Mr. Lipman invites her to play for him, and he and Mrs. Perlman
agree that her talent lies in tuning, not playing, as she has always
known. Mr. Weinstock is in accord.

535. Gordon, Shirley. THE BOY WHO WANTED A FAMILY. New
       York: Harper and Row, 1980. Illus. by Charles Robinson.
       90p. Grades 3-5. R+
       One of his few possessions is a battered suitcase, because
Michael, 7, is an orphan who has bounced from one foster home to
another. Like a wish come true, his social worker tells him there
is someone who wants to adopt him. Miss Graham turns out to be
a single, aging writer who asks him to call her Mom. Michael likes
having a room to himself and a large yard to play in at her suburban Southern California home, but he's afraid that he will miss the

camaraderie of other children. He is also anxious that his new mom
will not find him acceptable. The older boys down the block are
sometimes impatient with him, but the boys in his class like him immediately. Mom, moreover, has many fascinating friends, including
the retired Navy man who builds ships in bottles. Mom, who has
imagination and a good sense of humor, plans many Saturday adventures for the two of them. After a year in which he acquires a cat,
wins a goldfish at the school carnival, celebrates an intimate
Christmas and an extraordinary birthday, his adoption becomes final, and all his doubts and reservations are expunged. His old
suitcase will prove useful on a round trip to meet his new grandfather.

536.   Greaves, Margaret. STONE OF TERROR. New York: Harper
       and Row, 1972. 215p. Grades 6-10. NR
       Sent by his dying mother in Cromwellian England to live with
his grandfather on an isolated channel island with links to its Breton
past, Philip Hoskyn, 15, learns that his grandfather and the zealot
minister, Mr. Noel, are the only educated persons among the native
fisherfolk and are engaged in a war of wills with a self-proclaimed
sorceress and priestess of the primitive heathen monolith known as
the Grandmother Stone who hold the island in their terrible thrall.
Enlightened Grandfather, alone, believes that the execrable woman,
Annette Perchon, is more the victim of circumstances than the agent
of Beelzebub. Philip befriends Annette's wild and alienated niece,
Marie, but makes enemies among the brutal and ignorant islanders.
On the night of a pagan festival, Mr. Noel rallies his small force of
church officials to destroy the Grandmother Stone and thus break
Annette's stranglehold of superstition. The tormented woman, robbed
of her cult and her sanity, leads the vengeful villagers against
Philip. The mob then turns on Annette, bent on burning her for
witchcraft, but she flings herself to her own destruction, and Philip
consoles the girl he has tamed and fallen in love with.

537.   Hartling, Peter. OMA. New York: Harper and Row, 1977.
       Illus. by Jutta Ash. Trans. by Anthea Bell. 95p. Grades
       4-6. R++
       Kalle is 5 when he is orphaned and goes to live in the tiny,
old Munich apartment of his paternal grandmother. The events of
their lives for the next five years are chronicled from Kalle's point
of view in fifteen chapters, following each of which Oma briefly
soliloquizes, soul-searchingly and heart-warmingly, her views of the
same events. They consist of the confrontation at the welfare office
for Kalle's orphan's allowance to augment Oma's meager pension; her
modesty at bath time; her need of an occasional relaxing nip of
brandy when she is concerned about inflation; Kalle's embarrassment
when Oma breaks up his fight with a playmate; Oma's inability at
helping him with homework; her defense to the officious welfare
worker who comes to investigate; and her interest in his soccer
team. Their only serious clashes occur over the memory of Kalle's
mother, whom he sanctifies. Still, their love and affection are

palpable. Oma, though he has kept her young in spirit, knows she
must prepare Kalle for a time when she is gone. He copes very
capably when she is hospitalized for angina, and on his tenth birthday they discuss seriously but not morbidly the prospects that may
lie ahead for both of them.

538. Hest, Amy. MAYBE NEXT YEAR. New York: Clarion, 1982.
      153p. Grades 5-8. R
      Since the boating accident that killed her parents when she
was 4, Kate Newman, now 12, and her sister Pinky, 9, have lived
with their Jewish grandmother, two years widowed, in her comfortable old Manhattan apartment. Nana Stein encourages both girls to
study the arts, but Pinky does not have the zeal or aptitude for
piano lessons that Kate brings to her ballet classes. Dance is the
consuming passion of Kate's best friend Peter, 14, whom she is beginning to see with maturing eyes. When the opportunity arises to
audition for the National Ballet Summer School, he urges her to attend extra practice sessions with him, and her avocation suddenly
becomes serious business. Meanwhile, Nana has invited their lonely
upstairs neighbor, a lawyer recently forced into retirement, to move
in with them. The girls like Mr. Schumacher, but Kate fears the
loss of her privacy and her intimacy with her grandmother. Her
reservations fade when Max Schumacher is persuaded to market his
special chocolate chip cookies, establishing a thriving cottage industry in their home. Kate is increasingly ambivalent about the audition, feeling too inexperienced to succeed yet fearful of losing handsome, sympathetic Peter to her formidable rival if she retreats. She
is further distressed when Nana and Mr. Schumacher announce wedding plans, until Nana explains that he will not displace her in their
family group. More confident, Kate decides to postpone auditioning
for a year or two and quit worrying about Peter's fealty.

539. Lexau, Joan M. BENJIE. New York: Dial, 1964. (OP)
      Illus. by Don Bolognese. Unp. Grades K-2. R
      Benjie is the most bashful boy his granny has ever seen, and
she despairs of him when he starts school in a few weeks. Tongue-
tied, he always peeks out to see if the coast is clear before ventur-
ing outside alone. He is especially intimidated by the formidable
bakery lady. One Sunday after church Granny loses one of her
keepsake earrings. While she is napping, he goes out in search of
it. He is about to give up when he remembers that nobody looked
in the bakery where they stopped after church, and he slips in the
back room while the bakery lady is engaged. When she discovers
him, he is compelled to explain his mission to prevent her from
calling the police. Then she even helps him sift through the trash,
and the earring is found. Granny is overjoyed to get it back but
notes with a twinkle that something else is missing: Benjie's bash-
fulness.

540. Lexau, Joan M. BENJIE ON HIS OWN. New York: Dial,
      1970. Illus. by Don Bolognese. Unp. Grades K-2. R+

When Benjie's grandmother is not there to meet him after
school as usual (see 539), he is concerned about her but not sure
he can find his way home alone through the ghetto streets. He is
chased by a dog and accosted by teenage toughs but finally arrives to find Granny desperately ill. Resourcefully, he calls for an
ambulance from the police emergency box. He doesn't want to
leave her alone while he waits to guide the ambulance, but he has
no one to turn to. Finally in desperation he yells, "HELP! Please
somebody HELP!" At last the impassive neighborhood rallies round,
and helping hands reassure Granny that he will be well cared for
while she is hospitalized.

541. McHugh, Elisabet. KAREN'S SISTER. New York: Greenwil-
      low, 1983. 149p. Grades 5-6. R+
      Adopted by single veterinarian Barbara Bergman when she
was 4, Karen, now 11, is anticipating becoming big sister to another
Korean orphan whom they name Meghan (see 542). Though small
and slight, Meghan, 5, is energetic, inquisitive, imitative, ravenous,
perverse, and given to sleeping in Karen's bed. In spite of the
constant vigilance of Karen, Mom, and Grandmother, who is visiting
from California, Meghan is either innocently or deliberately making
mischief. Karen is gratified when she is influential in getting
Meghan to attend kindergarten without a fuss and relieved when
Meghan learns to accept her own bed. While Grandmother needles
Mom about her unmarried status and the need for a husband to provide for her, Karen is quietly scouting for a mate for Mom, who
dates desultorily. But she is appalled when Mom announces that
she is going to marry a widower she has only known for four weeks,
the father of Marcus Carlson, Karen's obnoxious 13-year-old schoolmate. She is stunned when Mom tells her firmly that she will marry
John Carlson in spite of her objections, even though she loves
Karen very much. Because of that love, Karen decides not to fight
the radical changes it will bring in her complacent life.

542. McHugh, Elisabet. RAISING A MOTHER ISN'T EASY. New
      York: Greenwillow, 1983. 156p. Grades 5-7. R+
      Karen Bergman's mother is thoroughly competent in her veteri-
nary profession, but at home she is disorganized and absent-minded.
Pragmatic Karen, 11, a Korean orphan, has been looking after her
and their menagerie since she was adopted at the age of 4. Recently she has been searching for a suitable husband for Mom to take
over the responsibility. The most likely candidate is the new
bachelor in town, Brian Roberts, a teasing, witty, divorced man
without children who teaches forestry conservation at the university.
Mom plays tennis and enjoys a casual rapport with him but doesn't
seem serious until the day they go off together without her. Karen's
curiosity is piqued, and she imagines that they are eloping and depriving her of the pleasure of being bridesmaid. Her disappointment
is keen when Mom begins dating others and encourages Brian to do
the same. The mystery of their day's disappearance is solved when
she learns that Brian is buying a horse, something Karen has always

yearned for, and has made arrangements for Karen to care for it
and take riding lessons. An even greater surprise is in store for
her: Mom has transacted the adoption of another Korean orphan.
Karen decides that getting a new sister is more fun than finding a
mate for her mother (see 541).

543. Paige, Harry W. JOHNNY STANDS. New York: Warne,
       1982. 136p. Glossary. Grades 6-9. R+
       His grandfather, Stands Alone Against The Enemy, is the only
parent, mentor and role model Johnny Stands, 14, has known since
his parents were killed in an auto accident long ago. Now an officious social worker has declared that the old man is too infirm to
remain his guardian in their tarpaper shack on the Lakota Sioux
reservation and has arranged for him to live with his aunt in Denver. Johnny adamantly refuses to abandon his grandfather. Taking
the advice of the animal spirits with whom he communes, Grandfather
leads them to Broken Bow where they take refuge in a church, only
to be taken hostage by a band of militant young Indians demanding
concessions for past oppression and injustice. Johnny stages a daring escape, and he and Grandfather make their way to an urban
ghetto where they are welcomed by earlier emigres from the reservation whose demoralizing existence is a degradation of their proud
ancestry. Johnny and his grandfather participate in a flesh-
sacrificing ritual symbolizing tribal unity. Feeling caged himself,
Johnny tries to free an eagle, sacred to the Lakota people, which
is en route to the zoo. He is arrested, but a sympathetic judge releases him after listening to a plea, eloquent in its simplicity and
pride, from Grandfather. Johnny, in a rite of manhood, makes a
Vision Quest which reveals to him that he must leave Grandfather
to acquire the education he needs to help his people in a constructive way.

544. Somerlott, Robert. BLAZE. New York: Viking, 1981. 221p.
       Grades 5-7. NR
       When David Holland, 10, lost his parents in an auto accident
two years earlier, his paternal grandfather sent him to live with an
aunt and uncle in San Francisco along with one of the prize German
Shepherds he breeds on his desert ranch. Afraid of dogs, Uncle
Arthur gives Blaze away to a man who inadvertently brutalizes him
in making him a vicious guard dog. Now Aunt Nadine is about to
have a child of her own who David fears will supersede him in their
affections. When his grandfather, Cappy Holland, comes to collect
the mistreated dog, David, who everyone thinks is bound for camp,
stows away in Cappy's old camper heading for the San Pascual
ranch. Cappy discovers his presence only when Blaze nearly
slaughters him. The boy begs to be allowed to spend the summer
on the ranch and aid in Blaze's retraining and rehabilitation. When
Blaze nearly dies at the hands of a poisoner, David suspects the
vapid lady at the ranch next door, but when he and the woman become lost in the mountains in the path of a raging forest fire, he
learns differently. Blaze heroically saves them both, and at summer's

end, Cappy realizes that it would be cruel to separate the boy, the
dog, and the grandfather who dotes on both. While the boy and
the dog have been growing up, the man has been growing younger.

545.   Spyri, Johanna. HEIDI. New York: Messner, 1982 (c1880).
       Illus. by Troy Howell. 336p. Grades 5-6. R+
       The beloved classic in which Heidi, 5, comes to live with her
grandfather, the truculent Alm-Uncle, endears herself to him and to
Peter, the goatherd, and his blind grandmother, only to be spirited
off to the city to be companion to the wealthy invalid Clara. Her
homesickness is physically and mentally debilitating in spite of her
love for Clara, and the discerning doctor prescribes a return to her
natural habitat. There she repatriates her grandfather into human
society and brings light into Peter's grandmother's darkness. When
Clara pays a visit to the Alm, Peter's jealousy precipitates a crisis,
but he atones by assisting Heidi and her grandfather in restoring
the afflicted girl to health. Clara's grateful father bestows bene-
ficences on all.

546.   Streatfeild, Noel. THE CHILDREN ON THE TOP FLOOR. New
       York: Random House, 1964. (OP) Illus. by Jillian Willett.
       248p. Grades 5-8. R
       Suave, bachelor TV personality Malcolm Master acquires an
instant family following an emotional Christmas Eve performance:
four infants whose mothers left them on his doorstep as gifts. In
reality, small children terrify the great star, so the four babes are
spirited off to the top floor of his London house to grow up in
sheltered solitude where he seldom sees them. Their needs are
ministered to by old-fashioned Nannie, "Mistermaster's" secretary
Aunt Mamie, the cook, and the chauffeur. They attain immediate
notoriety as the Master Quads, on which Mamie cannily capitalizes
by hiring an agent and signing the children for TV endorsements.
The advertisers keep the kids supplied with their products, and
they only venture from the house to be driven to and from the TV
studios until the arrival of Mrs. Comfort, the new governess, who
begins normalizing their cloistered existence. Meanwhile, Mr. Master
is shipwrecked in the South Seas and feared dead, and Thomas,
eldest of the four 10-year-olds, injures his back, terminating the
Quads' commercial career. It appears that they will have to go to
an orphans' home until Mr. Master suddenly returns to be a real
father to them.

547.   Talbot, Charlene Joy. A HOME WITH AUNT FLORRY. New
       York: Atheneum, 1974. 200p. Grades 5-7. R+
       Accustomed to the accoutrements of wealth and ease, twins
Jason and Wendy, 12, orphaned by their parents' plane crash, are
appalled when they come to live in New York in a derelict newspaper
plant with their bohemian, iconoclastic Aunt Florry. She is an inveterate junk collector who never cleans house and keeps pigeons in
the loft. Robbed of the security of order and regulation in their
lives, the twins are first frightened and then resentful at having to

help with chores which consist of opening cans or heating TV din-
ners, hanging the laundry on the roof, feeding and exercising the
pigeons, and scavenging in trash bins for wood to stoke the pot-
bellied stove. When Aunt Florry is hospitalized for a fractured hip,
the two must practice self-reliance, and they begin to appreciate
their independent and unorthodox lifestyle. But the day of their
eviction to make way for urban renewal quickly approaches. Resourceful Aunt Florry, however, has already planned an alternative
home which satisfies both the children's bourgeois attorney and her
own idiosyncrasies.

548. Wier, Ester. THE BARREL. New York: David McKay, 1968.
      (OP) Illus. by Carl Kidwell. 136p. Grades 5-7. R
      For seven years Chance has been shunted from one foster
home to another after his father abandoned him to a child welfare
agency. Now, at 12, he is being sent to family he didn't know
existed in the Florida Everglades: his maternal grandmother and
his brother Turpem, 15. Their father was a braggart who instilled
in his older son the idea that courage and daring are all that count,
and Turpem swaggers and boasts before Chance, who inherited his
dead mother's gentle disposition and slight build and who, as a city
boy, nurtures a healthy respect for the alligators, wild boars and
poisonous snakes that infest the swamp. Chance soon realizes that
Turpem's bravery is nothing but bravado. He later proves that he
and his doughty runt pup are no cowards when a hurricane blocks
their normal egress to civilization and they must detour through
dreaded Doomsday Slough, Turpem's nemesis. Resentment is forgotten as the boys finally become friends, to the delight of their
wise but simple granny.

549. Wier, Ester. THE LONER. New York: David McKay, 1963.
      (OP) Illus. by Christine Price. 153p. Grades 5-7. R
      The boy has known no life but that of itinerant crop picker,
has had no friend but the golden-haired girl with whose family he
has been traveling. When she is killed, the grieving boy strikes
out blindly on his own and is found starving and exhausted in
sheep-grazing terrain in the Montana foothills by Boss, the Amazonian rancher who has brought her flock to winter pasture by herself in order to track down the grizzly that killed her beloved grown
son Ben. The boy selects the name David at random from Boss'
Bible, and she sets about teaching him the intricacies and rigors
of herding sheep, subconsciously comparing him to her flawless Ben.
The laconic woman and the willful loner misunderstand one another's
motives, but David quietly learns. When Ben's widow Angie tells
David to use his own good judgment, he summons the confidence to
save the ranch foreman from a bear trap and kill the behemoth, his
personal Goliath, to win his own place in the family and his first
home.

550. Armstrong, William H. SOUNDER. New York: Harper and
      Row, 1969. Illus. by James Barkley. 116p. Grades 4-6. R+
      The deep-baying mastiff adopted the man when he was just a
pup, and the two are inseparable. Now the man has six mouths to
feed, but the coons and possums have gone to earth with the coming
of chill winter winds. One morning the oldest boy wakens to the
smell of cooking pork for only the second time in his life. Before
the day is out, the sheriff has come to arrest his father for stealing
a ham and some sausage links. As deputies take him away in
shackles, Sounder bursts from the boy's grasp, tries to follow his
master, and is shot down in the road. With half his head and
shoulder missing, he drags himself into the woods to die. The boy
visits his father in jail and experiences the law's contempt for the
human dignity of blacks. The father is sentenced to hard labor and
taken away. But Sounder does not die. One day he reappears,
missing an eye, ear and leg, hideously scarred and also mute. The
boy tries vainly to locate his father but finds instead the opportunity
for education. Years later the father returns, crippled, and the
aging Sounder gives voice once more. Both old veterans soon go to
their final reward, but Sounder has kept the faith.

551. Bauer, Caroline Feller. MY MOM TRAVELS A LOT. New York:
      Warne, 1981. Unp. Grades K-1. R
      A young girl weighs the pros and cons of her mother's fre-
quent absences. On the debit side is the fact that Mom is not there
to kiss her goodnight, share the birth of puppies, attend her school
play, remind her to water the plants, or locate her missing boots.
On the credit side are the trips to the airport, the long distance
telephone calls, the postcards and presents from abroad, dining out
with Dad, staying up late on occasion, and not having to make her
bed every day. But the best thing of all about Mom's travels is the
joyous day of her return.

552. Benary-Isbert, Margot. THE ARK. New York: Harcourt,
      Brace and World, 1953. Trans. by Clara and Richard Winston.
      246p. Grades 5-8. R+
      Two frigid attic rooms with a dour landlady look palatial to the

248

four Lechow children and their mother, homeless refugees in post-
war Germany, optimistic for the safe return of their father who has
been held in a Russian prison camp. Mother's ingenuity, generosity
of spirit, and sewing skill help fend off destitution, and the younger
children make friends and attend school. An affinity for animals
and an auspicious Christmas-caroling odyssey into the countryside
bring jobs for the older children at Rowan Farm, where they set up
housekeeping in an old railway car they dub "The Ark." It is
there that the entire family is eventually reunited. Shy Margret,
14, makes friends, in turn, with the petulant landlady and with
Marri, the reclusive "bee witch," from whom she learns the secret,
not of how to forget sorrows in the aftermath of war, but of how
to "remember differently."

553. Blume, Judy. STARRING SALLY J. FREEDMAN AS HERSELF.
      Scarsdale: Bradbury, 1977. 298p. Grades 5-7. R
      Bright, imaginative Sally Freedman, 10, concocts fantasies
that she and her friends act out, usually adventures involving her
favorite post-World War II movie stars. When her brother Douglas,
13, develops nephritis following an injury, their overanxious mother
decides to take the family to Florida for the winter, leaving their
dentist father at home in New Jersey. Adjustment to a fatherless
homelife, cramped apartment, strange school, and new friends is
stimulating. Triggered by her mother's anxieties and her grandmother's accounts of relatives who died at Dachau, Sally jumps to
the conclusion that an elderly Jewish retiree who offers them candy
is a resurrected Adolph Hitler in disguise. Correspondence with
her father and special holiday visits from him do not distract her
from her pursuit of evidence against the innocuous greybeard, and
she fills her keepsake box with poison pen letters to Mr. Zavodsky
until his death of natural causes anticlimactically ends that specula-
tion. As her father approaches his forty-second birthday, Sally
becomes increasingly haunted by the fear that he will die as his two
older brothers did at that age. An intimate talk with him plus other
revelations about life and death dispel some of her fears and pique
her natural curiosity about growing up.

554. Burch, Robert. QUEENIE PEAVY. New York: Viking, 1966.
      Illus. by Jerry Lazare. 159p. Grades 4-7. R+
      Rebellious Queenie, 13, defensive of her incarcerated father
in their rural Georgia town during the Great Depression, vents her
aggressions in destructive rock throwing and causes her chief tormentor to break his leg. No one believes her protestations of innocence when she is unjustly accused of breaking windows in the
church, and she is on the brink of being sent to the reformatory.
Given a chance to redeem-herself when a classmate collapses from
malnutrition, Queenie decides to turn over a new leaf. Her father
comes home on parole and reveals his true character, and Queenie
learns to handle her disillusionment and rely on her own aptitudes.
Exculpated of the charges against her, she gains the acceptance of
her junior high classmates.

555. Cleaver, Vera, and Bill Cleaver. HAZEL RYE. New York:
       Lippincott, 1983. 178p. Grades 5-7. R+
       Millard Rye and his daughter Hazel, 11, are cut from the same
bolt: incurious, phlegmatic, stubborn, argumentative, but very devoted to one another. Hazel's fondest desires are to get her ears
pierced, drop out of school and be a taxi driver like her married
brother. Normally indulgent Millard has different ideas. He deeds
to her a Central Florida grove of frost-damaged orange trees, with
a cabin in its midst, as an investment. When Mrs. Rye, who suffers from a nervous disorder, joins her parents in Tennessee to escape the dissension between Hazel and her father, Hazel decides to
cash in on her nest egg as soon as possible. She rents the little
house to the itinerant but industrious and erudite Poole family with
the understanding that Felder Poole, a budding horticulturist at 12,
will renovate the grove so she can sell it for the cash to buy a car.
Millard is jealous of Felder over Hazel's attention but does not
rescind his gift. In her impatience to capitalize on the grove,
Hazel grudgingly assists Felder with the work, but as she gets increasingly involved, she becomes obsessed with the restoration and
possessive of the trees. She decides not to sell. The Pooles move
on in the middle of the night, but Felder has left her a legacy of
curiosity, an itch for understanding that will ultimately catapult her
beyond the comfortable rut in which she and Millard are entrenched.

556. Collier, James Lincoln. GIVE DAD MY BEST. New York:
       Four Winds, 1976. 219p. Grades 6-8. R
       The fortunes of the Lundquist family have been declining
steadily since the onset of the Great Depression, when their musician father lost his steady employment but refused to soil his
hands with menial labor. Their mother lost her mind from anxiety
and had to be institutionalized. Now there is no money to feed and
clothe the three children or pay rent and utilities, yet Dad spends
what little he makes on expensive records, beer and cigarettes for
himself, exhorting the kids to "look on the bright side." Fearing
bankruptcy and scattering of the family, while juggling boyish
dreams of becoming a baseball star with adult schemes to make
money, Jack, 14, takes part-time jobs and frequently contemplates
larceny. Facing eviction, he finally summons the nerve to steal the
ill-gotten gains of his employer but salves his conscience by making
partial restitution when he realizes that dissolution of the family is
inevitable because his dad's personality will never change.

557. Dupasquier, Philippe. DEAR DADDY. New York: Bradbury,
       1985. Unp. Grades K-2. R++
       The top portion of each double page spread in this picture
book shows Sophie's seaman father performing shipboard and dock-
side activities on a year's voyage on a freighter to ports on the opposite side of the globe. The lower portion resembles a stage set
depicting the facade of Sophie's house, the yard, garage and street
outside. It changes with the seasons to show Sophie, her mother
and baby brother engaged in the pursuits of daily life as Sophie

describes the highlights of her year in letters to her dad which also
express her yearning for his return. On the final pages the two
scenes dovetail as Daddy steps off the bus in front of the house and
sweeps the exultant girl into his arms.

558. Greene, Constance C. STAR SHINE. New York: Viking/
      Kestrel, 1985. 150p. Grades 5-8. R
      The summer that their youthful, animated and gregarious
mother is offered her dream of touring with a summer stock company,
Jenny and Mary Chisholm, 11 and 13, start quarreling. Their
father, a stolid geologist, begins smoking again, and Jenny reverts
to sucking her thumb. Jenny wonders why it's an asset for a
mother to be young for her age but a debit for her children. When
their inexperienced cooking and fast food meals pall, they accept a
friend's invitation to dinner, but boredom is harder to overcome.
Without maternal sanctions they stay up too late, frightening themselves with R-rated movies, and allow an unsupervised, impromptu
party to get out of hand. The sisters wish they had greater re-
strictions but refuse to stay with their grandmother. The news that
a movie is to be filmed in their small town spurs them to interview
for work as extras, and Jenny is chosen when she exaggerates her
ice skating ability. Her gamin looks and new punk hairstyle catch
the eye of the director, who expands her role, earning her the admiration of all their acquaintances. When Mom returns, shaken and
bitter at being told she is too old to play the part she has been rehearsing, Mary fears that she will be further upset that Jenny's
star has eclipsed her own. The fear is unfounded, and Mary is
also able to dismiss her concern that Dad, too, might decide to ab-
dicate his family responsibilities. Each sister has attained greater
self-reliance and maturity.

559. Grohskopf, Bernice. CHILDREN IN THE WIND. New York:
      Atheneum, 1977. 190p. Grades 5-8. R
      Lenore Pickel, 14, thinks her mother is selfish for wanting
to uproot the family from New York City and move to Stamford,
where her firm is relocating. As she starts the year at her private
school, she makes friends with Chris, the new girl from California
whose life seems so glamorous but who in reality is lonely and
alienated. Chris' mother is neurotic, and an aura of mystery
shrouds her father's very existence. Lenore's other friend Marah,
whose psychiatrist father treats Chris' mother, harbors a deep and
puzzling antipathy for Chris and tells Lenore that Chris' father is
alive, contradictory to the information in her school records. Another classmate, Howie, unhappy and frustrated in his homelife,
joins a religious cult, and Chris is about to follow suit when suddenly her missing father appears and the two drop quietly out of
sight. Marah finally reveals to Lenore that Chris' father is a former
Nazi who has been living underground and who has come to claim
Chris now that her mother is hospitalized with a nervous breakdown.
Even Marah, who seems so supremely self-confident, has her own
hangups and family problems. Lenore receives a reassuring letter

from Chris in Argentina, and her own mother decides to commute to
Stamford.

560. Langford, Sondra Gordon. RED BIRD OF IRELAND. New
        York: Atheneum, 1983. 175p. Glossary. Grades 6-10. R
        Ireland in 1846 is a fetid, seething broth. English landlords,
who confiscated all rural properties in the 1600s, keep their tenants
tax-poor, ignorant and subservient. In County Kerry, Aderyn
Moynahan's father is a schoolmaster who is prohibited from teaching.
In the school he runs clandestinely, he foments rebellion among the
farmers' sons. When his tyrannical landlord's barns are burned, he
is forced to flee to the New World with a price on his head, leaving
Aderyn, 13, and her mother Kincora behind. Mother is a herbal
healer and midwife, respected second only to the priest who depends
upon her for her strength and wisdom. Quick-wittedly, she feigns
illness to avoid being raped by the landlord's lecherous agent. A
potato blight poisons the farmers' sole food crop, forcing them to
eat their rent grain. The landlords seize this as an excuse to evict
all their tenants so they can introduce more profitable sheep. Passage to America is arranged for them aboard pestilential "coffin
ships." The entire community, led by Kincora, make the arduous
trek to the sea, scourged by starvation, scurvy and typhus. Both
the priest and Aderyn's betrothed, Michael, 17, succumb. The
Moynahans discover that Father has providentially procured private
passage for them to Canada. When they are reunited with him and
bound for the U.S., he warns Aderyn to expect hostility and
prejudice, but after her other ordeals she is prepared to face any
setback.

561. L'Engle, Madeleine. A WRINKLE IN TIME. New York: Farrar,
        Straus and Giroux, 1962. 211p. Grades 5-8. R+
        With the help of three unearthly beings, Mrs. Whatsit, Mrs.
Which, and Mrs. Who, the two most sensitive of the four Murry
children, Meg, 14, and Charles Wallace, 5, along with Calvin, a
high school friend of Meg's, travel a tesseract, or wrinkle in time,
to new planets beyond their galaxy which exist in a fifth dimension.
They go in search of their father, a physicist who disappeared abruptly while on a secret and perilous government mission. There
they consult the Happy Medium and are directed to the planet of
Camazotz, ruled by the Dark Thing. The children find themselves
in a menacing world of regimentation and mechanization. A disem-
bodied brain called IT mesmerically tries to control their minds.
Charles Wallace succumbs, but Meg and Calvin resist long enough to
rescue her father from the transparent column in which he is imprisoned and "tesser" to a safe planet. Alone, Meg returns to
Camazotz to wrest Charles Wallace's mind from the clutches of IT
with love as her sole weapon.

562. Levitin, Sonia. JOURNEY TO AMERICA. New York:
        Atheneum, 1970. Illus. by Charles Robinson. 150p. Grades
        5-8. R

In the year 1938, Hitler is on the ascendency in Europe, and many Jews no longer feel safe in Germany. Papa had seen the handwriting on the wall years earlier and had taken the entire Platt family to Brazil, but the effects of the tropical climate forced them to return. Now he has seized his last opportunity and emigrated alone to the U.S. where, accustomed to wealth and respect, he has to labor as a janitor to earn enough to send for the family. They receive word from him to abandon everything at once and travel to Switzerland to wait in relative safety. It is wrenching to leave behind family, friends and all valuables, and nerve-wracking to cross the border under the punitive eye of the Gestapo. But their real hardship begins in Zurich when they run out of money, have no source of income (for refugee women are not eligible for employment), and Mama contracts pneumonia complicated by malnutrition. Ruth, 14, and her older sister Lisa are sent to an orphanage where the cruel and avaricious director starves the children. Later, all three girls, including little Annie, are farmed out to individual Catholic families where they are loved and treated kindly and generously. Mama recovers but is stunned by the murder of her sister and brother-in-law in their Berlin home. Finally, they receive their passports and board ship for America and the reunion with the father whom Annie scarcely remembers.

563. McCutcheon, Elsie. SUMMER OF THE ZEPPELIN. New York: Farrar, Straus, Giroux, 1985. 168p. Grades 5-8. R
In the weary waning days of World War I, Elvira Preston feels oppressed by her stepmother Rhoda, who tolerates her out of duty, not love, while her father is missing in France. At home in southern England, Rhoda saddles Elvira with heavy household chores and the care of her half-brother Arthur, 2, while she works in an aircraft factory. Aggrieved, Elvira transfers her resentment to the German prisoners who are assigned to local farmwork. With her friend Clarry, a mistreated orphan who was evacuated to the countryside when Zeppelins started bombing London, she discovers a derelict house hidden deep in a copse which serves them as a sanctuary from their misery. To their alarm, they learn that one of the German soldiers is also using the house as a retreat. "Bill," who was conscripted as a medical student, quickly allays their fears, and they agree to help him escape. A spy is known to be active in the neighborhood, and when a Zeppelin ineptly bombs their community, circumstantial evidence leads Elvira to suspect Bill briefly. Elvira tirelessly nurses Rhoda through the influenza epidemic, and the latter finally shows her appreciation. When Elvira is implicated in Bill's abortive escape attempt, Rhoda defends her against defamatory neighbors. A sanctimonious shopkeeper betrays himself as the real spy, and Bill is repatriated to Germany. A benevolent family adopts Clarry, and Elvira's father turns up safely.

564. Pearce, Philippa. THE WAY TO SATTIN SHORE. New York: Greenwillow, 1983. Illus. by Charlotte Voake. 182p. Grades 5-7. NR

The mysterious disappearance of the tombstone she believes to be that of her father, who supposedly drowned on the day of her birth ten years ago, rouses Kate Tranter's curiosity. Her first quest to Sattin Shore in search of information about him is fruitless. Her mother, who works in a confectionery store, and her formidable maternal Granny Randall, with whom they and her two older brothers live, tell her to forget him. Though she tries to heed their advice, she believes that she sees her father's ghost in the house. During the holidays, her brother takes her on another pilgrimage to Sattin Shore where she meets a lovable lady, Grandmother Tranter, of whose existence she was unaware because of Granny Randall's implacable antipathy toward all Tranters. She learns that her father, accused unjustly by Granny Randall of drowning his brother so long ago, left his family, and that Granny Randall intends to bribe him with a suitcase full of money she has been saving for that purpose to secure his absence permanently. Again Kate pedals to Sattin Shore to find her father and implore him to confront his malicious mother-in-law. When Kate's mother realizes that her husband has been falsely maligned by her mother all along, she agrees to a reunion, and the family, sans Granny Randall, emigrates to a new life in Australia.

565. Ransome, Arthur. SWALLOWS AND AMAZONS. Philadelphia: Lippincott, 1931. Illus. by Helene Carter. 343p. Grades 6-8. R
        Seafaring father cryptically cables permission for the four eldest Walker children to spend an adventurous amphibious summer vacation on an "uninhabited" island in the English Lake Country, sailing their own craft, the Swallow, while Mother and baby remain on the mainland. Alternately at war with or in league with the rival Amazon pirates, an equally nautical pair of sisters, the siblings subdue unfriendly natives (adults), peacefully co-exist with the friendly ones, especially Mother, and even ferret out treasure buried by real pirates. Lemonade becomes grog, a family squabble is a full-scale mutiny, and able-seaman Titty emerges the heroine.

566. Sachs, Marilyn. FOURTEEN. New York: Dutton, 1983. 116p. Grades 7-9. R
        Rebecca Cooper, 14, will not conduct normal telephone conversations because she knows that her mother, an author of children's books, is eavesdropping to collect material for her latest story. Now Mrs. Cooper is starting her first teen romance, and Rebecca is more sensitive than ever, even though she is not dating yet. Then Jason Furst, also 14, moves into the adjacent San Francisco apartment. He is an exceedingly sheltered and emotional boy, a living horticultural encyclopedia who is anxious over the mysterious disappearance of his amateur botanist father. His mother is a nervous wreck who is hostile to Rebecca and her parents, whom she accuses of prying. Jason and Rebecca puzzle over the cryptic postcards he has been receiving from his father, postmarked in Europe, and theorize initially that he is either a CIA agent or getting a divorce. Rebecca

conceals her budding friendship with Jason from her parents so that
her mother will not embellish it for her book. It is Rebecca who
makes the fateful discovery that Jason's father is in prison, arrested
for arson with the intent to collect insurance to bankroll his hobby.
Jason's overprotective mother successfully kept the truth from him
with postcards planted with international business associates. Con-
fronted with the facts, Jason's mother stops coddling him, and Rebecca is smug in the knowledge that her romance is entirely different
from the one her mother is composing.

567. Sharmat, Marjorie Weinman. I WANT MAMA. New York:
      Harper and Row, 1974. (OP) Illus. by Emily Arnold McCully.
      Unp. Grades K-3. R
      When the little girl's mother goes to the hospital for surgery,
her promise to return soon seems to stretch on interminably. The
girl and her father mope about at loose ends. Because she's too
young to visit in the hospital, she writes her mother letters instead,
talks to her on the telephone, and makes lots of crafts projects for
Dad to take to the hospital. She begins to worry whether Mama will
ever return or whether she herself could suddenly get sick and have
to be hospitalized too. When Daddy finally brings the good news of
her release, the girl wonders whether Mama will be different in any
way. She busies herself cleaning house and making welcome home
signs. When Mama finally arrives, they cuddle together in Mama's
rocking chair.

568. Shotwell, Louisa R. MAGDALENA. New York: Viking, 1971.
      Illus. by Lilian Obligado. 124p. Grades 5-6. R
      When shy Magdalena, 11, whose father is away at sea, is trans-
ferred to the intellectually gifted sixth grade class, some of her
classmates deride the long, thick braids her old-fashioned Puerto
Rican grandmother makes her wear. When her friend, odd old Miss
Lillie, provides the opportunity, she wastes no time in having her
hair cropped, causing her horrified grandmother to think she has
been bewitched by American frippery. In the meantime, another
Puerto Rican girl, an incorrigible with a wretched homelife whom
everyone calls Spook, is transferred into her class. The principal
asks Magdalena to befriend her, a monumental task that seems
doomed to failure. The girls' mutual respect for Miss Lillie and
Magdalena's grandmother, Nani, eventually draws them together and
modifies Spook's behavior, but Nani remains intractably suspicious
of Miss Lillie and her Americanizing influence. Miss Lillie's collapse
from malnutrition reconciles the two women, and Magdalena and
Spook write the two best stories for the class literary magazine.

569. Stecher, Miriam B. and Alice S. Kandell. DADDY AND BEN
      TOGETHER. New York: Lothrop, Lee and Shepard, 1981.
      Illus. by Alice S. Kandell. Unp. Grades K-3. R
      The illustrator's black-and-white photographs chronicle the
special rapport between Ben and his dad from the time the toddler
is able to shuffle around in his father's oversized shoes to the

after-school and weekend jaunts to the city, the country, or to
Daddy's office. Now Mommy's new job takes her out of town for
several days, and Ben's relationship with his father is strained
when Ben accidentally drops eggshells in the omelette and interrupts
Daddy's reading. Suddenly, Ben remembers his mother's parting
admonition to "laugh a lot." He succeeds in distracting his tired,
intense and preoccupied parent, who breaks the tension by proposing a picnic and later a pillow fight. When it is time for Mommy
to return, the two pals dress to the nines to please her.

570. Taylor, Sydney. A PAPA LIKE EVERYONE ELSE. Chicago:
      Follett, 1966. (OP) 159p. Grades 4-6. R
      Papa left Hungary for America in 1914, intending to send for
Mama and the girls within a year, but World War and an influenza
epidemic intervened. Mama and Szerena, who is old enough to remember Papa fondly, are eager to join him in a better life in America. Gisella, who was only 1 when he left, does not want to leave
her familiar homeland and friends. In the meantime, they continue
to operate their humble subsistence farm, raising geese, flax, silk-
worms and plums. They also relish traditional Jewish and Slovakian
festivals and holidays, suffer the depredations of marauding gypsies
and foxes, and savor folk food and fairy tales. When Papa finally
forwards tickets for their passage, they soberly face the upheaval
of leave-taking and stalwartly meet the challenge and adventure of
new technology, an ocean voyage, and alien cultures.

571. Wisler, G. Clifton. WINTER OF THE WOLF. New York:
      Elsevier/Nelson, 1981. 124p. Grades 5-8. NR
      On the Texas frontier in the year 1864, Pa and his two grown
sons discharge their duty to fight for the Confederacy in Tennessee,
leaving Thomas Jefferson Clinton, 14, in charge of the farm, five
younger siblings, their mother and grandmother. Marauding Comanches are spotted, and the neighboring landowners set up a preemptive ambush. In the aftermath of the slaughter one Indian
youth survives, and T.J., refusing to execute him, takes him home
despite the misgivings of the others to nurse him back to health.
The grateful Yellow Feather becomes a boon companion and willing
worker about the homestead. When a monstrous, supernatural wolf
begins raiding the livestock, concerted efforts by the settlers to
kill it prove fruitless. Armed by T.J., Yellow Feather disappears,
to the alarm of the other pioneers. Throughout that long, arduous
winter T.J. struggles alone to provide for his family, and when the
wolf reappears to threaten their very lives, T.J. knows he must
confront it. He tracks it to its rocky lair, where he finds that
Yellow Feather has also been stalking the beast. The two battle it
to the death, fulfilling the prophecy of Indian legend that only two
warriors of pure heart and courage can vanquish the demon. Yellow
Feather is mortally wounded, but the bounty tides the Clintons over
till Pa returns.

572. Yep, Laurence. DRAGONWINGS. New York: Harper and

Row, 1975. 248p. Grades 7-9. R+

Moon Shadow is only 8 when he is reluctantly sent by his mother from their home in China to join his father and the other male family members in California, the Land of the Golden Mountain. There they are earning money to send to their families back home by working first on the railroad, later at trades in San Francisco's Chinatown. Moon Shadow's father had been a master kite builder at home, but in America he helps in the family laundry. A dream reveals to him that in another incarnation he had been physician to the Dragon King, possessed of the ability to fly, and he longs to fulfill his destiny. Events following the San Francisco earthquake plus his innate mechanical ability polarize his ambition, and he and the boy leave the family establishment to build Dragonwings, a biplane inspired by the Wright brothers' flight. Over the course of seven years they make firm friends with an American couple with whom they exchange cultural traditions, and finally they are able to send for Moon Shadow's mother.

573. Brelis, Nancy. THE MUMMY MARKET. New York: Harper
and Row, 1966. (OP) Illus. by Ben Schecter. 145p.
Grades 4-6. NR
The Martin children, Elizabeth, 11, Jenny, 10, and Harry,
6, are cared for by the crabby housekeeper they call The Gloom.
Unable to endure her stifling rules and regulations any longer,
they appeal to old Mrs. Cavour, whose fabled garden seems enchanted, for occult intervention. She conjures up a "Mummy Market" where unsuitable mothers can be exchanged for more satisfac-
tory models. The Mummy Market consists of stalls where prospective mothers display themselves to their best advantage with the
trappings of their trade. The children's first choice is the fretful,
squeamish sort who likes to be called Mimsey. The second, who
calls herself Mom, has a physical fitness fetish. The third is a
permissive authority on child psychology who nearly turns the
youngsters into juvenile delinquents. Their fourth and final choice
occupies a bare stall with no gimmicks. She wants to start with a
clean slate and let herself grow with the children as imagination and
circumstance dictate. Here is a real mother they feel comfortable
in calling Mummy.

574. Carlson, Natalie Savage. ANN AURELIA AND DOROTHY.
New York: Harper and Row, 1968. Illus. by Dale Payson.
130p. Grades 4-5. NR
Her mother's new husband doesn't like her, so Ann Aurelia
has been consigned to a succession of foster homes. Her new foster
mother Mrs. Hicken is an old dumpling who seems genuinely fond of
her and even joins the PTA, so Ann Aurelia no longer needs her
real mother. She has found her first bosom buddy in Dorothy, a
black girl in her fifth grade class, and she likes her new school.
She and Dorothy have fun concocting weird snacks, shopping in the
supermarket, being in the Safety Patrol together, saving a teacher
from drowning on a field trip, making a spooky Halloween mask, and
staging a surprise party for their teacher. When her mother turns
up unexpectedly, having divorced Mr. Lacey and avowing her mistake, Ann Aurelia initially refuses to forgive her or go to live with
her until Dorothy helps her to empathize with her mother's loneliness. Mrs. Hicken finds them an apartment near school, and Ann
Aurelia and Dorothy go to visit Mrs. Hicken and her new foster child.

575. Cleary, Beverly. OTIS SPOFFORD. New York: Morrow,
      1953. Illus. by Louis Darling. 191p. Grades 4-6. R
         His penchant for "stirring up a little excitement" earns Otis
the reputation of scapegrace of Room 11 at Rosemont School in his
Oregon town. His mother, Valerie Todd Spofford, when she isn't
busy teaching tap and ballet at Spofford School of the Dance, has
more tolerance than most for his shenanigans. His classmates, especially Ellen Tebbits whom he teases unmercifully, and even his
teacher Mrs. Gitler, are just waiting for him to go too far so he will
finally reap his "comeuppance." He changes the script for the bull-
fight his class is staging for the school fiesta by having the bull
(of which he is the front half) turn the tables on the toreador. He
throws spitballs, invalidates the science project by being overly
sympathetic to the control rat, salvages the academic standing of
the high school football hero by completing an assignment for him,
and creates a riot when Mrs. Gitler is out of the room by "scalping"
Ellen of a lock of her precious hair. Ellen wreaks her vengeance on
the day the lake freezes over by grabbing his shoes and boots
while he is on the ice, forcing him to stump home painfully on his
skates. Knowing Otis, one can be sure he will live down his humiliation and rise again to bait Ellen.

576. Cooper, Margaret. CODE NAME: CLONE. New York: Wal-
      ker, 1982. Illus. by Christopher Bigelow. 121p. Grades
      4-6. R
         In the prequel to this sci-fi thriller, SOLUTION: ESCAPE,
Evonn and Stefan, who have been reared separately for experimental
purposes for 13 years, learn that they are identical brothers cloned
from the skin cells of the severed finger of Grigory Metvedenko,
former Soviet military hero and academician who lost his digit in a
plane crash while defecting to the U.S. and who is now under CIA
protection. The boys, with the aid of a sinister accomplice, escape
the U.S.S.R. disguised as statues to search out the father who does
not know of their existence. Once in the U.S., their collaborator
shows his true colors, and the boys are forced to flee from his
nefarious clutches. They join a girl named Rosa and her grandmother, who, along with other poor, disenfranchised people, live in
a subterranean labyrinth beneath a futuristic American city, while
the boys seek their father. But they, too, are sought and have one
harrowing escape after another from their relentless pursuers while
establishing contact with the CIA. Eventually Evonn is captured
and the existence of a third clone, Niko, still manipulated by the
Soviets, comes to light, part of mad scientist Dr. Zorak's plan to
destroy the father through his own offspring. Evonn's heroic rescue
and the dramatic reunion of the three with their father, Mr. Griggs,
who is also their CIA contact make gripping and heartwarming reading.

577. Delton, Judy. MY MOTHER LOST HER JOB TODAY. Chicago:
      Whitman, 1980. Illus. by Irene Triva. Unp. Grades K-2.
      R+

The young, briefcase-toting mother is both angry and lachrymose when she arrives home to announce to her bewildered daughter
that she lost her job. Barbara Anne tries to console her with an
offering of dandelions, but Mom is too pensive to notice. She is uncommunicative at dinner and doesn't even scold the girl for kicking
the table leg. The child wonders whether her birthday will be celebrated next week or whether they'll have any festive occasions in
the future. As she prepares for bed alone, she has visions of the
two of them begging on a street corner and offers to get a job
shoveling snow, cutting grass or babysitting. At that Mom emerges
from her somberness and reassures her that she will eventually find
a new job, possibly better, and Barbara Anne knows that everything
will be all right.

578. Delton, Judy. ONLY JODY. Boston: Houghton Mifflin, 1982.
      Illus. by Pat Grant Porter. 95p. Grades 4-6. R
      Just as he has been accepted on his new school's wrestling
team, Jody's mother arbitrarily transfers him to St. Gertrude's,
where the students wear uniforms and attend religious classes. Already disgruntled about having a girl's name and being the only boy
in a family of three females, including Jill, 16, Joana, 12, and his
mother, Jody, 10, rails to no avail at having to attend his eighth different school. He is acutely embarrassed at having to wear hand-me-
down girls' boots until he discovers that another boy in class shares
his plight, and instantly he makes his first friend since moving to
St. Paul. His initial misadventure with Otto is to track down drug
abusers for a reward, but they only land in trouble for destroying
his sister's prescription medication. Their scheme to sell compost
nearly ends when Jody's mother learns that all the neighbors are
donating their refuse to the project. But she is not unfair and locates a buyer who relieves them of their effluvia. She even convinces the children that they need a pet. The standard poodle she
acquires proves almost too obstreperous, but eventually he becomes
Jody's second friend and playmate.

578a. Drescher, Joan. MY MOTHER'S GETTING MARRIED. New
      York: Dial, 1985. Illus. by the author. Unp. Grades K-2.
      R+
      The countdown to her mother's imminent marriage is distress-
ful and traumatic for Katy, who would rather maintain the status quo
of impromptu picnics at the beach and Saturday night TV parties a
deux. When Ben is around, Katy feels like a fifth wheel, and she
fears that life will become more regimented for her while Mom and
Ben have all the fun. The teasing of her classmates and adults' ex-
pressions of delight only enhance her anxiety. Projections of sharing the bathroom and breakfast table with Ben are not palliated by
his proffered assistance in learning to ride a two-wheeler or designing wedding invitations for her classmates. Her resentment almost
triumphs on the day of the wedding when she surreptitiously wears
jeans under the pretty flower girl dress her grandmother made, but
she quells it for the ceremony. As Mom and Ben prepare to leave

on their honeymoon, however, Katy blurts out her concealed anger
and unhappiness to her astonished mother, who reassures her of
her love and the continuation of some of their private times together.

579. Estes, Eleanor. THE HUNDRED DRESSES. New York: Har-
      court, Brace, 1944. Illus. by Louis Slobodkin. 80p. Grades
      3-4. R
      The fashionable girls in Room 13 poke pernicious fun at Wanda
Petronski, who lives on the wrong side of the tracks, has a funny
name, and wears the same clean but faded blue dress to school every-
day while claiming to have a hundred more at home in her closet.
Their ridicule turns to remorse when they learn that Wanda's drawings of one hundred dresses have taken the prize in the school art
contest, but they cannot make amends because Wanda, her brother
and father have moved to the city to escape their gibes. Their
guilt is finally absolved when Wanda writes a letter to her former
tormentors at Christmas, making them gifts of the choicest of her
hundred dresses.

580. Gray, Elizabeth Janet. ADAM OF THE ROAD. New York:
      Viking, 1942. Illus. by Robert Lawson. 317p. Grades 5-7.
      R
      Roger the minstrel calls for his son Adam, 11, at the abbey
school at St. Albans in 1294. On the retired warhorse Bayard they
accompany Sir Edmund's entourage to London for the wedding of
the nobleman's daughter. After the wedding all the minstrels are
given purses, but Roger loses his at dice, and the horse as well,
to the minstrel Jankin. The boy and his insouciant father are
paupers once more who must ply their trade for meals. The villainous Jankin lames Bayard and absconds with Adam's beloved
spaniel Nick in the middle of the night. Father and son set off in
pursuit but are separated before reaching St. Giles' Fair, precipi-
tating a hue and cry that carries them all over England. After
numerous adventures, including an encounter with brigands, father,
son and dog are reunited in Oxford, where Adam forgoes an opportunity to continue his education in order to follow the road with his
father.

581. Griffiths, Helen. THE DOG AT THE WINDOW. New York:
      Holiday House, 1984. 123p. Grades 5-7. R
      Lonely Alison, 12, is a latchkey kid who is as disorganized,
untidy, casual and pragmatic as her mother is extravagant, immacu-
late, glamorous and hedonistic. When Alison expresses her wish
for a German Shepherd like the one she admires in an apartment
window, her mother buys her an expensive but inanimate china dog.
Curious about the dog in the window, Alison introduces herself to
Mrs. Bailey, the eccentric old woman who is keeping the neglected
and unloved dog Wolf for her institutionalized grandson. She begs
the beleaguered woman to let her groom and exercise the feral animal and gradually earns his confidence, obedience and love. Her
success with Wolf overwhelms Mrs. Bailey, who cannot control him

in Alison's absence. When the despairing woman commits suicide, the dog is remanded to the SPCA. Alison desperately wants to adopt him but knows that her mother would veto the idea. While her mother, a travel agent, is on a business trip, Alison appeals for help to her mother's fiance, Uncle Reg, the first sincere and caring man Mum has ever dated. Alison longs to tell him how much she approves of him but is constrained by embarrassment. Uncle Reg comes through anyway. Through complicated negotiations he acquires Wolf for her and convinces Mum to accept him after they move into his house. Beyond her wildest fantasy, Alison has gained both an adoring dog and a companionable father.

582. Keats, Ezra Jack. LOUIE'S SEARCH. New York: Four
     Winds, 1980. Illus. by the author. Unp. Grades K-2. R
     What does it take for a small boy to get noticed in his teeming city neighborhood? Louie dons a bizarre costume to attract attention in his quest of a father, but it fails to elicit any curiosity from the melange of extraordinary adults he passes. He stops to recover an old music box that falls from a passing junk truck, only to be accused of theft by the wild, bearded driver. Louie runs home to his mother, pursued all the way by Barney the junk dealer. The man apologizes when he is informed of the misunderstanding and offers the music box to Louie as a gift. Louie's mother Peg invites Barney for a cup of tea, and a friendship ensues that results in a wedding and plenty of attention and excitement for shy, lonely Louie.

583. Maury, Inez. MY MOTHER THE MAIL CARRIER. Old West-
     bury, N.Y.: Feminist Press, 1976. Illus. by Lady McCrady.
     Trans. by Norah Alemany. 32p. Grades K-3. R+
     Lupita is proud of her urban mother's occupation. She has to be strong, brave, helpful and gregarious to deliver mail, but she also feels angry when sexists criticize her vocation. Among her mother's other attributes are being tall, loving bright colors, cooking well, and enjoying intimate picnics. When Lupita grows up she doesn't want to be a mail carrier, however; her ambition is to be a jockey. "Right on!" says her mother's boyfriend Jose.

584. Schick, Eleanor. CITY IN THE WINTER. New York: Macmil-
     lan, 1970. Illus. by the author. Unp. Grades K-2. R+
     Jimmy wakes up in the morning to find that schools are closed because of the blizzard, but his mother still must go to work while he stays at home with Grandma. After breakfast he helps Grandma straighten the apartment and makes a barn out of a cardboard box. He eats his prepacked school lunch as an indoor picnic and feeds the bread crumbs to the birds on the windowsill. Jimmy and Grandma make a sortie through the drifts to the corner grocery but find that it is closed. Jimmy prepares the vegetables and sets the table for their supper of soup, and when his mother gets home he recounts the day's events for her while she tucks him tenderly into bed.

585. Schick, Eleanor. NEIGHBORHOOD KNIGHT. New York:
    Greenwillow, 1976. Illus. by the author. 64p. Grades 1-3.
    R+
    In the absence of a father, a small city boy pretends that he
is a knight errant, gallantly protecting and defending his mother (the
queen) and older sister (the princess) from the imagined dangers
lurking about their apartment castle. When the queen goes off to
work and the princess to school, he, too, mounts his steed and gal-
lops off to school, pragmatically parking it and his derring-do outside the postern gates so as not to divulge his true identity to his
classmates. At play time he builds a fortress of blocks, and when
a playmate topples it and two others laugh, he is so angry that he
engages them all in a scuffle to avenge his honor. To add insult to
injury, the teacher punishes all four of them. That evening, the
queen and princess are puzzled by his moodiness. He repairs to
his donjon keep to do battle royal with invading forces. Victory
over them restores his elan, the imperial family dines convivially,
and their conquering hero retires to bed deserving of the sleep of
the just.

586. Shyer, Marlena Fanta. STEPDOG. New York: Scribner, 1983.
    Unp. Grades K-2. R+
    The first two times that Terry meets his father's friend Mari-
lyn, she races him around the block, letting him win, and brings
him a stuffed animal. Naturally, when Dad announces that he is
marrying Marilyn, Terry whoops for joy. The only cloud on the
horizon is Marilyn's dog, who she assures him is friendly. But
when she introduces him to his new stepdog at their summer cottage,
the dog not only snubs Terry but dunks his stuffed toy in the lake.
Terry learns why the dog is called Hoover (for the vacuum sweeper)
when he bolts Terry's hamburger on a cookout and makes off with
his new hiking boots. Marilyn punishes Hoover by chaining him to
his doghouse for the night, but his howls disturb Terry, who re-
lents and takes him into his room. Terry dreams that he is a dog
who has been superseded by a little boy and banished to the doghouse, unable to communicate his jealousy. When he awakens, he
empathetically showers affection upon Hoover, who responds by
sharing with him his collection of assorted missing shoes.

587. Sonneborn, Ruth A. I LOVE GRAM. New York: Viking,
    1971. (OP) Illus. by Leo Carty. Unp. Grades 2-3. R
    Ellie's mom works late and her big sister is always busy with
homework, so it is Gram who is always there to meet Ellie after
school, give her snacks and play with her. But one day Gram is
hospitalized, and the bewildered and frightened black inner-city
child wonders if she might die like her friend Joey's grandmother
did. The days drag hollowly as the three try to cope without Gram,
but when Mom announces that Gram is coming home tomorrow, Ellie
exultantly draws her a welcoming picture and asks the preschool
teacher to emblazon her message across the top.

588. Sonneborn, Ruth A. THE LOLLIPOP PARTY. New York:
      Viking, 1967. (OP) Illus. by Brinton Turkle. Unp. Grades
      K-3. R
      Every morning Mama takes Tomas to nursery school on her
way to work, and every afternoon his big sister Ana picks him up
on her way home from high school. When Mama gets home, Ana
leaves again for her babysitting job. One day, however, Mama
isn't home on schedule, but Ana must leave anyway, believing that
Mama will be there momentarily. Tomas waits patiently, playing with
his cat and listening anxiously for Mama's footsteps. Finally someone knocks at the door, but he knows it must be a stranger, for
Mama always uses her key. While he is in a quandary about opening
the door, the caller announces herself as Miss Sibil, his teacher.
He welcomes her joyfully, remembering his manners and offering her
refreshments--a lollipop. When a worried Mama finally arrives, delayed by a stalled subway train, she finds that Tomas has been
taking care of Miss Sibil instead of the other way around.

589. Steptoe, John. MY SPECIAL BEST WORDS. New York:
      Viking, 1974. (OP) Unp. Grades K-2. R
      Some of Bweela's favorite phrases are "Whatshappeninman,"
"Iwantsomewaterdad," "Prettyful" and "Idontwanttotakeanap." When
she is annoyed with her little brother Javaka, her special best word
is "Youadummy." Bweela, 3, and Javaka, 1, live with their black
dad, who sends them off to their devoted babysitter every morning
before he goes to work and picks them up before dinner each
evening. One night during their after-supper bath, Bweela proudly manages to toilet-train Javaka all by herself to her daddy's delight, and after he reads them a bedtime story, he rewards them
with a kiss, hug, and his special best word, "Iloveyou."

590. Thurber, James. MANY MOONS. New York: Harcourt,
      Brace and World, 1943. Illus. by Louis Slobodkin. Unp.
      Grades K-3. R
      When Princess Lenore, 10, takes to her bed from "a surfeit of
raspberry tarts," her anxious father, the King, promises her anything she wants. She asks for the moon. The King summons the
Lord High Chamberlain, the Royal Wizard, and the Royal Mathema-
tician, all of whom have procured, conjured and computed various
and sundry items for him in the past, but they all agree, if not
about the composition of the moon, at least that its size and distance prohibit its procurement. Only the Court Jester has the
presence of mind to ask the Princess for her conception of the
moon. She describes it as being smaller than her thumbnail, no
higher than the tree outside her window, and made of gold. The
Jester promptly commissions that such a trinket be struck by the
Royal Goldsmith, and the Princess is happy. But now the Royal
brains and even the Jester are stumped on how to conceal the
real moon when it rises again. They need not have worried; Lenore
also has a logical explanation for the moon's reappearance in the
night sky.

591. Turkle, Brinton. THE SKY DOG. New York: Viking, 1969.
      (OP) Illus. by the author. Unp. Grades K-2. R
      The boy and his mother are vacationing at the beach. In the
cloud patterns the boy sees a shaggy white dog in many attitudes
and activities. His mother looks and looks but never sees the sky
dog. One day late in the season, the boy finds a real shaggy white
dog. He insists that it is his sky dog, but his mother knows it is
someone's lost pet. For weeks the boy and dog play companionably,
but there is a dilemma when it is time to go home. A policeman suggests that since the beach is nearly deserted by now and no one
has come to claim the dog, the boy might as well keep it. But the
boy knows that Cloudy has been his dog right along.

592. Williams, Vera B. A CHAIR FOR MY MOTHER. New York:
      Greenwillow, 1982. Illus. by the author. Unp. Grades K-2.
      R++
      When a fire guts their old apartment, compassionate friends,
neighbors and relatives help them set up housekeeping in another,
but they lack a comfortable easy chair where Mama can relax after
a hard day's work as a waitress at the Blue Tile Diner. Since then
Mama has saved every coin from her tips in a huge jar toward the
purchase of a new armchair. The girl and her grandmother, who
lives with them, contribute to the collection whenever they have
spare change. A year later, when the jar is full, they count the
money, wrap it, and exchange it at the bank for bills. The three
feel like Goldilocks when they make their shopping expedition to the
furniture stores. At last they find the perfect chair, and while
Mama rests her weary feet with the girl nestled on her lap after
supper, Aunt Ida takes a picture of them to memorialize the auspicious occasion.

593. Williams, Vera B. MUSIC, MUSIC FOR EVERYONE. New
      York: Greenwillow, 1984. Illus. by the author. Unp.
      Grades 1-3. R+
      Her mother's big chair (see 592) sits empty now because
Grandma, who cares for Rosa while her mother is at work at the
diner, lies sick upstairs. Rosa cheers her by playing her new accordion, bought with the change from the purchase of the chair.
(The story of how Rosa got her accordion is related in the author's
SOMETHING SPECIAL FOR ME, Greenwillow, 1983.) But now the
jar of savings is depleted because of Grandma's illness, and Rosa
devises an ambitious plan for replenishing it. With three friends
who also play instruments, she forms the Oak Street Band. The
girls practice until they are proficient enough to be hired to
serenade at a block party. The music, dancing and camaraderie
act as a tonic for Rosa's grandmother, who recovers, while Rosa's
share of the profits goes directly into the family coffers.

594. Wrightson, Patricia. A RACECOURSE FOR ANDY. New York:
      Harcourt, Brace and World, 1968. (OP) Illus. by Margaret
      Horder. 156p. Grades 5-6. R

The circle of five friends plays a sort of verbal Monopoly in
their Sydney suburb, claiming and swapping properties around town.
Fatherless, mentally retarded Andy, 12, does not comprehend the
sporting nature of the game, and when an old wino offers to sell
him Beecham Park racetrack for three dollars, he liquidates his
hard-earned savings to buy it in good faith. His friends try to
let him down gently, but his bubble refuses to burst. He takes a
more and more proprietary interest in his investment, helping with
the gardening and sweeping. The caretakers, concessionaires,
horse and dog trainers, and patrons indulge the boy, encouraging
his harmless fiction, until he becomes a celebrity. When he begins
painting bleachers, tampering with the mechanical hare, letting
stray dogs loose inside, and decorating with streamers, the actual
owners take a dim view and offer to buy it back from him. Andy
turns a tidy profit and is none the wiser.

595. Young, Miriam. KING BASIL'S BIRTHDAY. New York:
      Watts, 1973. (OP) Illus. by Victoria Chess. Unp. Grades
      K-2. R
      King Basil the Sad is never happy, even on his birthday,
and can think of no wish for the Birthday Fairy to grant him, so
she surprises him with three children, Richard, 8, Alison, 7, and
Jennifer, 4, plus Jennifer's imaginary playmate Googie. The introduction of three lively, imaginative, trusting and ingenuous moppets
into the royal household does not improve the king's disposition,
and he tries in vain to invoke the Birthday Fairy, who appears
only on his birthday, to remove his bane. When cold weather arrives, however, concern replaces consternation in the expostulating
potentate, and he starts playing the parent against his regal inclinations. His mortification is boundless when he inadvertently
acknowledges the presence of Googie at a formal state function, but
he has been so involved with his instant family that he is unaware
of his approaching birthday. When the Birthday Fairy pops in to
grant his wish, he is no longer pale, thin and gloomy. He realizes
that he can't part with the tykes, and this time she surprises him
with a queen who agrees to accept all five of them--including
Googie.

596. Zolotow, Charlotte. THE SUMMER NIGHT. New York:
      Harper and Row, 1974. Illus. by Ben Schecter. Unp.
      Grades K-2. R+
      The little girl's father cares for her all day and in the evening
bathes her and puts her to bed, but she isn't sleepy. He brings
her a snack and opens the window to the soft night air, but still
sleep eludes her. In sympathetic understanding he carries her
downstairs, reads her a story and plays her a nocturne, but they
are not soporific enough. He takes her for a walk in the dark
garden among fireflies, rabbits, and the moon reflected in the pond.
An owl hoots as they go inside for warm milk and bread. He carries her up and tucks her in tenderly, and when the owl hoots again
she doesn't hear it because she is sound asleep.

NONFICTION BOOKS

Nonfiction books are not individually evaluated.
All are highly recommended.

597. Andrew, Jan. DIVORCE AND THE AMERICAN FAMILY.
New York: Watts, 1978. 138p. Bibliography. Index.
Grades 9-12.
This liberal view of the contemporary family begins with the
iconoclastic premise that marriage need not be the goal of every normal adult and that divorce is not necessarily a failure and may even
be the salvation of the modern family. The author traces the history of divorce from primitive societies to the present, the changes
that transpired to create the ideal of the middle-class marriage, and
the legalities of dissolution practices. She states that divorce reform began with the elimination of guilt from the courtroom and that
the same must follow in the counselor's office. Once the decree has
been granted there is a serious lack of guidance for the ranks of
the formerly married, who must rely on support groups. Problems
to be addressed for the children of divorce are the destigmatization
of "broken homes" and creation of security in the one-parent home
through childcare facilities and flexible working schedules. To complete the cycle, Ms. Andrew lists the reasons and probability of
success for second marriages. Radical and experimental alternative
lifestyles are explored, including open-, serial-, and group-marriage.
In conclusion she states that the concept of divorce as a "right" is
changing the future of the family and should not be regarded as a
failure but as a challenge to grow.

598. Berger, Terry. A FRIEND CAN HELP. Milwaukee: Raintree,
1974. Illus. by Heinz Kluetmeier. 31p. Grades K-2.
Since the divorce, the narrator, an only child, has moved
across town from her best friend Susan, but her dad drops by to
drive her over for a visit. The girl confides in Susan her sadness
and forlornness over her dad's living apart. She recollects the
chores they used to share that she now handles alone. She admits
that life is more peaceful now that her parents are no longer fighting
and that her time spent with both parents is quality time. Susan
listens like the good friend she is.

599. Berger, Terry. HOW DOES IT FEEL WHEN YOUR PARENTS
      GET DIVORCED? New York: Messner, 1977. Illus. by
      Miriam Shapiro. 59p. Grades 2-4.

      Each page of this photographic narrative describes a situation
from predivorce battling to post-divorce dating and portrays the
sensitive daughter's emotional reaction to each circumstance. She
feels frightened by the fighting, guilty at the split, angry and unloved at her father's departure. Her unhappiness, loneliness and
disappointment turn to worry over the possibility of something happening to her mother, then anger at both parents, and shame among
her friends. When she starts helping her mother with the chores
she begins to feel important, but when Dad doesn't appear when he
promised she resents him for that. When she visits him at his
apartment she is surprised that he can take care of himself (and
maybe even of her), but when she sees his new friends she feels
excluded. She is sad when she and her mother have to give up
their familiar home for an apartment and Mom takes a job, and when
Mom has a date she is jealous and begins fretting about a stepfamily.
When both parents visit her at camp she feels loved again, and as
she develops outside interests and activities with friends she is
happy at last.

600. Berman, Claire. "WHAT AM I DOING IN A STEP-FAMILY?"
      Secaucus, N.J.: Lyle Stuart, 1983. Illus. by Dick Wilson.
      Unp. Grades K-3.

      Cartoon drawings, large type, and straightforward text explain
that unlike in fairy tales, a family may not be a once-upon-a-time
family that lives happily ever after. Adults, like children, change
as they get older, and the child may unexpectedly become a member
of a stepfamily. If it happens by divorce, it is important to remember that the parents did not divorce the child--they will always be
his parents no matter what. If it happens by the death of a parent,
no amount of wishing will make life the way it was, but having a
stepparent doesn't mean that one is expected to forget the parent
who has died. Real stepparents are not like wicked storybook stepparents. They probably worry how they will be treated, too. The
book discusses what to call stepparents; what to expect of stepsibling relationships, including possible favoritism; the reasons for
following new rules; compromising and communicating; and how to
handle feelings of disloyalty. Practical tips are given for dividing
time between two households, including the need for privacy and
space of one's own. Belonging to a stepfamily means that there are
more people in one's life--the more the merrier.

601. Bienenfeld, Florence. MY MOM AND DAD ARE GETTING A
      DIVORCE. St. Paul: EMC, 1980. Illus. by Art Scott. 38p.
      Preface, epilogue and appendix for parents, teachers and
      counselors. Grades K-2.

      In this simple, stream-of-consciousness story in cartoon format,
Amy, a small blonde girl, informs her friends that she doesn't feel
like playing soccer because she's despondent over her parents'

divorce announcement. While she explains divorce, in voice balloons, to a friend who is ignorant of the subject, picture balloons show what she is thinking. Another friend, Dan, a black boy, announces that his parents have been divorced for some time and shares with the others his feelings about the dissolution, confiding that his mother works, is about to remarry, and that he goes to day care after school. Amy reveals that her parents are going to share custody of her and that her mother is job-hunting but that their future is unpredictable. Verbalization of her concerns and conflicts and of her parents' discussions with her helps her to reconcile her misgivings. She concedes that she is fortunate to have two parents even if they are separated. Then she is ready to play ball with the others.

602. Boeckman, Charles. SURVIVING YOUR PARENTS' DIVORCE. New York: Watts, 1980. 133p. Index. Grades 5-9.

A thorough and serious compendium for the older child, unrelieved by "cute" illustrations, this book is designed to minimize the pain and confusion of family dissolution and to offer him specific and practical advice, as well as emotional support, for taking charge of his or her own life. It enables the adolescent to choose options instead of reacting viscerally, and it answers questions he may feel too awkward to ask. The psychological tool of "choice awareness" is applied to the subjects of fighting and/or abusive parents; divorce proceedings; adjustment to a new life, including dating parents and possible sexual molestation by the parent's partner; visitation with the noncustodial parent; and, inevitably, remarriage and stepfamilies. Numerous organizations and agencies are introduced throughout the text and in a separate chapter as referrals for assistance.

603. Booher, Dianna Daniels. COPING WHEN YOUR FAMILY FALLS APART. New York: Messner, 1979. 126p. Bibliography. Index. Grades 5-8.

An expansive, non-technical index as well as a no-nonsense table of contents make the material in this well organized book highly accessible to young people facing the disaster of divorce. Vividly illustrated with examples, it offers a pragmatic approach to surviving the hostilities and anxieties of a shattered life, shifting family groups, and stepfamilies. Children who are just experiencing the shock and disbelief of the divorce announcement will relate easily to the chapters entitled "Hearing the News" and "First Reactions." They will learn what to expect later on with the chapters "Second Thoughts," "Rules, Rituals, and Restraints," "Games Parents Play," and "Games Kids Play." The importance of coping mechanisms is the subject of another chapter, as is parental dating, remarriage and the instant family. The final chapter, "Turning the Bad into Good," shows how to use emotions and pain in positive ways to grow as a human being.

603a. Brown, Laurene Krasny, and Marc Brown. DINOSAURS

DIVORCE: A GUIDE FOR CHANGING FAMILIES. Boston:
Atlantic Monthly, 1986. Illus. by the authors. 32p. Glossary. Grades K-3.
A cartoon-format introduction to family dissolution and restructuring for young children but with a twist: the characters
are anthropomorphic, pea-green, potato-headed, benign dinosaurs.
Vicariously, they lead the child through all the common situations
and emotions surrounding divorce and remarriage, including the
reasons for divorce, the expectations of living with one parent and
visiting the other, the advantages and disadvantages of joint custody arrangements, how to cope with holidays divided between two
homes, how to break the news to friends, what to expect when
parents start dating again, and how to handle stepparent and stepsibling relationships in more crowded and often less affluent households. The expressive seriocomic illustrations flesh out the spare
text, successfully conveying abstract concepts while avoiding many
big words. A short glossary of divorce terms, not all of which appear in the text, provides further succinct explanations. The
authors, whose family has experienced divorce and remarriage firsthand, have consulted professional counselors in their joint effort
to offer reassurance and sound advice to the small child, reduce
anxiety, dispel misconceptions, and encourage expression of fears
and feelings when difficulties arise.

604. Cain, Barbara S., and Elissa P. Benedek. WHAT WOULD
     YOU DO? A CHILD'S BOOK ABOUT DIVORCE. Indianapolis:
     Saturday Evening Post, 1976. Illus. by James Cummins.
     Unp. Grades K-2.
     The authors, a social worker and a medical doctor, pose hypo-
thetical questions for children in strife-torn homes whose parents
decide to divorce. Typical candid, poignant answers are provided
by other children who themselves have experienced the incompre-
hensible and emotionally distressing ordeal of having parents get
"unmarried" and move apart. They express their feelings upon
seeing Dad only once a week, fear of abandonment when custodial
parent is delayed in getting home, trepidation upon moving to new
neighborhoods, jealousy over parents' dates, and reconciliation to
having two peaceful households with undivided attention from
separate but loving parents.

605. Cottle, Thomas. CHILDREN'S SECRETS. Garden City:
     Anchor Press/Doubleday, 1980. 273p. Bibliography. Grades
     9-12.
     This is a compilation of revealing and candid observations
elicited by the sociologist/clinical psychologist author from child
clients who have survived family crises, the trauma of desertion,
neglect and abuse. The deeply personal, moving dialogues show
rich insights into the myths of harmony and decency surrounding
the family. One case history describes the psychosomatic manifestations of a girl whose mother maintains that her husband is dead,
when in reality he abandoned the family, while the girl harbors the

terrible knowledge of having seen her father alive in the company
of her mother.

606. Craven, Linda. STEP-FAMILIES: NEW PATTERNS IN HAR-
      MONY. New York: Messner, 1982. 186p. Index. Grades
      7-10.
      Part of the "Teen Survival Library," this book deals with such
recurrent problems as loyalty conflicts, blame-placing, role and name
confusion, stepparent/stepchild disagreements, lack of family unity,
sexual issues, stepsibling friction, and discipline difficulties. Nine
case studies outline the problems (both sides of them, if there are
two), followed by commentary by the author, a stepmother herself,
counselor, and editor of the national journal, STEPFAMILY BULLETIN,
on methods of solving them from a practical and positive standpoint.
An appendix of organizations and hotlines offering aid to children,
adults, and total families is included.

607. Fayerweather Street School. KIDS' BOOK ABOUT DEATH AND
      DYING. Boston: Little, Brown, 1985. 119p. Bibliography.
      Grades 6-9.
      The second undertaking of "The Unit" at Fayerweather Street
School in Cambridge, Massachusetts, by and for children, this
volume was born of the need to help a classmate through the emotional crisis of his father's terminal illness and took the form of a
large discussion group comprised of fourteen children aged 11 to 14.
Guided by teacher Eric E. Rofes, the group also participated in
dramatic improvisations, read books and articles, and interviewed
other children, parents, and adults engaged in suicide prevention
services, hospices, hospitals, funeral homes, churches and ceme-
teries who could give them new perspectives on death and dying.
Their written reports became chapters for the book and include
such topics as learning to talk about death, life-threatening diseases,
brain death and euthanasia, autopsies, funeral customs, organ dona-
tion, cremation, and wills. The relative degree of trauma surrounding the death of pets, older relatives, and parents is scrutinized
in other chapters. Under this heading are discussions of
how children should be informed of the death, whether they should
attend the funeral, and schoolmate reactions. Final chapters deal
with the death of children, violent deaths, and life after death.
The summary of this year-long research project propounds the
Kubler-Ross definition of the five stages in the acceptance of death
and the need to treat death as part of the life cycle.

608. Fayerweather Street School. THE KIDS' BOOK OF DIVORCE.
      Lexington, Mass.: Lewis, 1981. Eric E. Rofes, ed. 123p.
      Bibliography. Grades 4-9.
      Twenty children between the ages of 11 and 14, most of whom
experienced divorce in their families and who are enrolled in a
Cambridge, Massachusetts, school, contributed to this book, which
is subtitled, "By, For and About Kids." Each chapter was compiled
by a team from material collected in interviews with family members,

professional counselors and clergymen. Illustrated with expository
photographs and students' artwork, the book is intended to be
read by parents and children together. Chapters describe nuclear
and extended families; the causes of conflict in the household; how
the decision to separate is made, including why and how children
should be told; the emotional and financial impact of separation and
custody of minors; and the legal aspects of alimony, support, custody, decrees, name changes and no-fault divorce. Also addressed
are the various types of counseling obtainable; divorce ceremonies
and innovative living and visitation arrangements; taking sides and
"weekend Santas;" dating parents, stepparents and gay parents;
and finally, the long-range effects of divorce on children. A brief
annotated bibliography of fiction and nonfiction titles for and about
children of divorce completes the volume.

609. Gardner, Richard A. THE BOYS AND GIRLS BOOK ABOUT
     DIVORCE. New York: Science House, 1971. Illus. by Alfred
     Lowenheim. 159p. Grades 4-6.
     With a foreword by Louise Bates Ames of the Gesell Institute
and an introduction for parents and children, this book, written by
a practicing psychiatrist who derived his material from his therapeutic work with children, has become the standard for divorce hand-
books and was a pioneer in the field of realistic, practical and sensible information and guidance. Dr. Gardner differentiates between
constructive and destructive anger and demonstrates methods of
dealing with unloving parents after first determining what unloving
behavior is. He examines the vicissitudes of getting along better
with both parents, including those who work, date, spoil their
children, fail to visit, and use children as spies or weapons against
the other. Additional chapters are devoted to improving relationships with stepparents, the destigmatizing of professional counseling,
and the extra duties and responsibilities required of children of
divorced parents. He attempts to allay the child's fear of losing
both parents by introducing the possibilities of boarding schools
and foster homes. The thoroughly outlined table of contents compensates for the lack of an index.

610. Gardner, Richard A. THE BOYS AND GIRLS BOOK ABOUT
     STEPFAMILIES. New York: Bantam, 1982. Illus. by Alfred
     Lowenheim. 164p. Grades 4-6.
     The most unique element of Dr. Gardner's popular handbook
is its chapter on a parent living with a partner to whom (s)he is
not married and how to cope with meddling moralists. The practicing child psychiatrist discusses five of the major anxieties and
wishful thoughts that arise when a parent remarries, as well as the
sensitive subject of how to address stepparents. He explores the
emotions of anger, loyalty, and especially of love, realistically citing
the possibility that the child may not come to love the stepparent
and vice versa. One chapter is devoted to better relationships with
stepparents and includes some specific advice for boys with step-
fathers. Another chapter deals in depth with improving relationships

with half siblings and stepsiblings. The issue of adoption by a stepparent is untangled, as well as what to expect if and when professional
counseling is indicated. The author concludes with a short check-
list of important things to remember and an analogy drawn between
the legendary phoenix and the rebirth of a new family from the
ashes of an old one.

611. Getzoff, Ann, and Carolyn McClenahan. STEPKIDS: A SUR-
     VIVAL GUIDE FOR TEENAGERS IN STEPFAMILIES. New York:
     Walker, 1984. 171p. Index. Grades 7-12.
     While conceding that rebellion is a normal part of maturation,
the authors explain why teens feel rebellious and demonstrate how
to rebel without deliberately evoking negative reactions from parents
or stepparents. They aver that communication employing "assertive
language" is as constructive as active listening. An exploration of
adolescents' feelings about their parents' divorce, their attempts at
reconciling the two, living with a single parent, and the complexities of love and remarriage is followed by a thorough analysis of the
dynamics of stepfamilies and personalities. The well organized chapters are in the style of a practical handbook with abundant examples.
Also covered are visits with noncustodial parents, absent parents
who never call or visit, sex in the stepfamily, and homosexual relationships. Five appendices indicate how to hold family councils,
ways for adults and kids to become friends, when to seek professional help, and further advice from print sources and the Stepfamily Association of America.

612. Gilbert, Sara. HOW TO LIVE WITH A SINGLE PARENT. New
     York: Lothrop, Lee and Shepard, 1982. 128p. Bibliography.
     Index. Grades 6-12.
     Written specifically for teens aged 10 to 18 in single-parent
situations of all causes (divorce, death, and never-married), this
book begins with exploring, acknowledging and controlling the common emotions of anger, fear, grief, feeling cheated, and being relieved that the fighting is over. It proceeds to adjusting to change,
coping with unanticipated change, and dealing with parents' moods
and susceptibilities while confronting the problems of adolescence.
The author suggests rights and options that are available to teens
who are unhappy with their living arrangements, enabling them to
exercise greater responsibility and independence. But she also
outlines deeper problems, such as psychological games parents play,
court battles, abuse, neglect, addiction, and mental illness, that
are more difficult to solve and may require legal recourse. Phony
fears are contrasted with real fears, including the derision of peers,
financial insolvency, losing contact with the noncustodial parent,
and death of the sole parent. The author also deals with the
double standard in dating for teens and parents and the need to be
prepared for the remarriage or serious liaison of the parent with its
attendant confusion and mixed emotions. The necessity for keeping
an open mind, being empathetic, iterating problems, overcoming
self-pity, and curbing rebellion is stressed. A chapter for parents,

a fiction and nonfiction bibliography, and a list of support organizations complete the book.

613.   Glass, Stuart M. A DIVORCE DICTIONARY. Boston: Little,
       Brown, 1980. Illus. by Bari Weissman. 72p. Grades 3-6.
       This useful lexicon was developed by an attorney who noticed
that while children of divorce have considerable psychological re-
sources and guidance available to them through books, their need
to understand the legal terminology that is changing their lives has
been overlooked. Most of the 58 definitions, from Abandonment and
Adultery to Visitation and Visitation Rights, are short and simple,
but several, because of their complexity, run conversationally from
two to eight pages. Illustrated copiously with self-explanatory char-
coal drawings, definitions incorporate straightforward examples and
answer typical questions that may trouble children, such as, "Do
grandparents have visitation rights?" (Yes, by statute, in several
states.) Entries are cross-referenced for accessibility.

614.   Hazen, Barbara Shook. TWO HOMES TO LIVE IN: A CHILD'S-
       EYE VIEW OF DIVORCE. New York: Human Sciences, 1978.
       Illus. by Peggy Luks. Unp. Grades K-2.
       Niki, a preschooler, describes her parents' gradual alienation
beginning with their one-home, one-family life through their disagreements and fights to their mutual decision to separate. Both parents,
though they no longer love one another, reassure her that they will
always love her even if she's naughty, but still the situation is
strange and unsettling to Niki. At home she misses her father; at
Daddy's new place she misses her mother. When she cries, Mommy
says that "tears wash away sad feelings and let good feelings grow,
the way rain makes flowers grow." She discovers that wishing
won't make her parents remarry, hiding won't cause her dad to
stay when he comes to pick her up, and throwing a tantrum won't
keep her mother from dating other men. Outside activities begin to
supersede her preoccupation with the divorce, and eventually Niki
becomes reconciled to having two families, two homes and two different ways of doing things.

615.   Krementz, Jill. HOW IT FEELS WHEN A PARENT DIES. New
       York: Knopf, 1981. Illus. by the author. 110p. Grades
       4-9.
       Eighteen children from 7 to 16, black and white, Christian
and Jew, share their thoughts, reactions, and emotions in taped interviews with the author/photographer on the loss of one of their
parents. Causes of death include seven accidental, two cardiovas-
cular, five cancer, two suicide, and one of multiple sclerosis. While
all the children experience the same emotions and stages of grief in
varying degree, each individual handles his sorrow differently according to his own personality. Some, but not all, of the children
feel the need to discuss the events candidly with adults, to cry,
and to relive memories. Most of them feel awkward accepting sympathy from classmates, agree that time helps heal the pain, and

express the hope that the surviving parent will not remarry but
that they expect to adjust to a stepparent when faced with the
exigency. A few benefit from professional help.

616. Kreimentz, Jill. HOW IT FEELS WHEN PARENTS DIVORCE.
      New York: Knopf, 1984. Illus. by the author. 115p.
      Grades 4-8.
      Nineteen children aged 7 to 16 agreed to be photographed and
interviewed for this intimate portrait of divorce from children's perspectives. One lives primarily with his father in a joint custody
arrangement. One expresses fear that her mother will remarry even
though she likes her live-in boyfriend. One sees more of his father
on weekends than he did before the divorce but would feel jealous
if his dad had another child. One vows not to marry young and
risk divorce herself. One was kidnapped by his mother after custody was awarded to his father, who hired detectives to recover him.
One still feels awkward over her parents' sleepover dates. One
wishes that the Catholic church would liberalize its tenets on divorce
and remarriage to reduce the stigma. When one's parents were first
divorced, the kids stayed put while the parents switched homes.
One's father abused his mother; he has since been paired with a Big
Brother. One still retains hope that his parents will reconcile after
six years' separation. One girl and her brother rotate homes weekly.
One has lived with his grandparents since he was a baby because
both parents were immature. One's mother tried to turn her against
her father; she benefitted from psychiatric counseling. One's
parents never stopped fighting--even after the divorce. One did
not benefit from counseling but was grateful for having a sister with
whom to share his burden. One believed she was to blame for her
parents' breakup and is envious of her half sister for having a full-
time father. The last changes homes semi-annually and has become
friends with both parents.

617. LeShan, Eda. LEARNING TO SAY GOOD-BY: WHEN A PARENT
      DIES. New York: Macmillan, 1976. Illus. by Paul Giovano-
      poulos. 85p. Bibliography. Grades 4-6.
      The noted educator/writer/counselor guides the child from the
initial nightmarish disbelief phase of an immediate loss, whether the
death was expected or not, through all the normal stages of grief.
While helping the child understand contradictory and often misguided
adult behavior through the funeral period, she warns that the most
intense grief comes later with the realization of the loss. Reassuring
the child that there is no right or wrong way to mourn, she elabor-
ates, through example and illustration, upon the concomitant emotions
the child is liable to encounter: terror and anger which can lead to
the belief that loving is dangerous; the fear of losing the remaining
parent or anxiety over personal illness or injury; guilt and shame
over resentment of the living parent or the inability to mourn after
a long terminal illness. She stresses that open communication is essential in assuaging these feelings. During the recovery, memories
will fade in and out until they return without pain or morbid fixation.

Some children will experience a desire for immediate change such as
remarriage or relocation, while others will resist it. She prepares
the child for such adult decisions and again counsels bilateral dialogue. Through the process, she emphasizes the importance of
seeking sympathetic, supportive friendship among both adults and
other children. The signal that sorrow has passed is the ability
to look forward and express joy in being alive. For those who can't
put grief behind them, she recommends professional counseling.

618. LeShan, Eda. WHAT'S GOING TO HAPPEN TO ME? WHEN
      PARENTS SEPARATE OR DIVORCE. New York: Four Winds,
      1978. Illus. by Richard Cuffari. 134p. Bibliography.
      Grades 4-8.
      The author of LEARNING TO SAY GOOD-BY: WHEN A
PARENT DIES tells intermediate children that the worst time in the
divorce process may be the earliest stages because of uncertainties,
divided loyalties, and lack of parent/child communication. While explaining the standard causes and effects of divorce, she also plumbs
the acute heartache of desertion. She equates divorce with the
death of marriage, requiring the same rites of grief as dying, and
describes gently the emotions and changes the child is likely to experience, including the effects of divorce on the adults. She warns
children against taking advantage of parents while they are vulnerable and that unpleasant things happen inevitably in nuclear families
also. She stresses that adjustment takes time and that there is no
stigma to talking about one's parents' divorce with outsiders. Inter-
actions among various family members are aired, and the pitfalls to
be aware of as time passes are enumerated, such as the false hope
of reconciliation and the manipulation of parents. The complexities
of new family combinations comprise the concluding chapters, embracing the need for patience and practice in the formation of new
relationships. Ms. LeShan cautions children about deciding prematurely never to marry, suggesting that children of divorce can
profit from their parents' mistakes.

619. Mayle, Peter. DIVORCE CAN HAPPEN TO THE NICEST
      PEOPLE. New York: Macmillan, 1979. Illus. by Arthur
      Robbins. Unp. Grades 2-4.
      Humorous, whimsical color cartoon decorations punctuate the
three mustn'ts: (1) Don't think your parents don't love you because
they're getting divorced; (2) Don't think it's your fault because it
never is; (3) Don't blame one parent, because it's never just one
person's fault. Conversational chapters are entitled, "Why Your
Parents Got Married," "What Goes Wrong," "Other Men and Other
Women," "Living with Half Your Parents" and "Who's Right? Who's
Wrong; Who's to Blame?" The final chapter targets the good news
or consolation prizes that follow divorce, such as regarding one's
parents as friends rather than authority figures and caretakers, the
fact that two homes are less boring than one, and the case for cooperation and taking the initiative in adult/child relationships. The
book offers reassurance, sympathy and sound advice in a simple,

honest and objective format, as well as sensible suggestions for
coping with crisis. It can be used as a departure point for further
discussion. The author is a divorced parent who has been through
it all with his own children.

620.   Richards, Arlene, and Irene Willis. HOW TO GET IT TO-
       GETHER WHEN YOUR PARENTS ARE COMING APART. New
       York: McKay, 1976. 170p. Grades 6-9.
       Somewhat limited by lack of an index, this book is a pioneer
in its field and a gold mine of information and advice. It is designed to convey to adolescents "which parts of a divorce concern
you and what you can do about them; which parts do not concern
you and how to stay out of them; how to find people to talk with
and be with when your world is changing; how to get professional
help if you feel more is happening than you can handle alone; how
to turn feelings into energy that moves you forward instead of
holding you back; (and) how to build your own life no matter what
your parents or other people do with theirs." It was written with
the collaboration of dozens of professionals in the field of law,
medicine, religion, psychology, and sociology. The ultimate goal
of the book is to protect and foster the youngster's image of himself as an effective person and to forestall many serious difficulties.

621.   Sinberg, Janet. DIVORCE IS A GROWN-UP PROBLEM. New
       York: Avon, 1978. Illus. by Nancy Gray. Unp. Bibliog-
       raphy. Grades K-1.
       Available only in paperback, this book explains divorce for
the preschool child in the most simplistic terms and full-page pen-
and-ink line drawings. It iterates and reiterates that divorce is
a problem between adults and not the fault of the child. The
author describes the emotions, false hopes and confusions that
come with the territory and how to deal with them. ("Daddy says
it's better to hit a pillow than it is to hit him.") She emphasizes
the love of the individual parents for the child in spite of all the
upheavals in his or her young life.

622.   White, Ann S. DIVORCE. New York: Watts, 1979. 55p.
       Index. Grades 4-6.
       Unique among divorce books for children, this is not a how-
to-cope manual. It offers simple, solid, clinical information on all
phases of divorce from causes and reconciliations to the fact that
most divorced people remarry. No-fault and adversarial divorces
are explained, as well as the step-by-step process of dissolution.
Elements of the divorce contract are discussed, including custody
of the children and visitation privileges. The author suggests that
the changes incumbent upon divorce are actually new beginnings,
especially those involving relocation, mothers returning to the work
force, improved relationships with both parents, and dating parents.
Illustrative examples of many situations are given, and an excellent
index provides access to the material.

Numbers in parentheses refer to entries, not to pages

ADAM OF THE ROAD: Insouciant troubador and son travel length
   and breadth of 13th-century England in pursuit of Dame Fortune.
   (Gray--580)
ADDIE AND THE KING OF HEARTS: Young teen, whose father
   dates a woman she dislikes, spurns teenage admirer and develops
   crush on teacher. (Rock--434)
AFTER THE GOAT MAN: Two disparate children of single parents
   help a third one and his grandfather/guardian adapt to urbani-
   zation. (Byars--525)
AGONY OF ALICE, THE: Pre-teen ponders mortifications she has
   suffered through lack of maternal guidance and seeks female role
   model to emulate. (Naylor--415)
ALAN AND NAOMI: Jewish girl traumatized by father's violent
   death in WWII is befriended by insecure boy who derives strength
   from their encounter. (Levoy--394)
AL(EXANDRA) THE GREAT: Adolescent acquires new sensitivity
   and earns admiration of divorced parents by making a sacrifice
   for her mother's sake. (Greene--91)
ALL BUT THE RIGHT FOLKS: Motherless boy of mixed race resolves his identity crisis while spending the summer with his maternal grandmother. (Nichols--419)
ALL US COME CROSS THE WATER: Confusion over origins prompts
   motherless black boy to consult family members who give him different answers. (Clifton--305)
ALWAYS, ALWAYS: Young daughter ponders joys and sorrows of
   custody shared by geographically and philosophically distant
   parents. (Dragonwagon--66)
AMAZING MEMORY OF HARVEY BEAN, THE: Believing that neither
   of his divorcing parents wants him, boy runs away and is befriended by older couple. (Cone--48)
AND LEFFE WAS INSTEAD OF A DAD: Ideal prospective stepfather
   dashes hopes of Swedish boy and mom when he lapses back to
   alcoholism and crime. (Thorvall--508)
AND PHILIPPA MAKES FOUR: Rivalry and resentment ensue when
   girl's widowed father sets up housekeeping with divorcee and her

279

flawless daughter. (Derman--330)

ANGEL IN CHARGE: While single mother is vacationing and sitter
is hospitalized, young girl undertakes care of brother with mixed
results. (Delton--59)

ANGEL'S MOTHER'S BOYFRIEND: Intense, imaginative girl objects
to mother's friendship with clown until he disarms her with kindness and attention. (Delton--60)

ANIMAL, THE VEGETABLE AND JOHN D JONES, THE: It takes a
near-tragedy to reconcile two sisters and an only son whose single
parents are cohabiting. (Byars--288)

ANN AURELIA AND DOROTHY: Mother consigns daughter to foster
care upon her remarriage. (Carlson--574)

ANYWHERE ELSE BUT HERE: Mature young teen tries to convince
widowed father to declare independence from his sister with whom
they live. (Clements--303)

ARK, THE: Refugee family in postwar Germany awaits return of
POW father while establishing livelihood and friendship. (Benary
Isbert--552)

ARROW IN THE WIND: Boy and mother are resourceful in coping
with financial straits, natural disaster, and a bully when father
deserts them. (Dexter--62)

ASK ANYBODY: Naive small town girl is mesmerized, then disillusioned, by worldly new classmate while living in father's temporary custody. (Greene--92)

ASK FOR LOVE AND THEY GIVE YOU RICE PUDDING. Insecure
senior learns to know father who abandoned him through a journal
he left behind. (Angier--13)

ATAMI DRAGONS, THE: Sojourn in Japan following mother's death
brings peace to boy's grieving father and glory to himself on
baseball diamond. (Klass--389)

AWAY IS SO FAR: Spanish father tries to escape pain of wife's
death by taking to the road with son as troubadors. (Talbot--
458)

AXE-TIME/SWORD TIME: WWII high school graduate battles intellectually snobbish divorced mother over right to take defense
plant job. (Corcoran--50)

BACK HOME: Americanized by her evacuation to U.S. during WWII,
British girl returns to England alienated from her equally liberated
mother. (Magorian--152)

BACK YARD ANGEL: Burden of baby-sitting lively toddler brother
weighs heavily on shoulders of young daughter of working mother.
(Delton--61)

BANNER IN THE SKY: In defiance of mother's opposition, Swiss
boy resorts to stealth in order to scale peak that killed his father.
(Ullman--467)

BARREL, THE: Gentle, urban boy is out of his element when he
joins custodial grandmother and fractious older brother in their
swamp home. (Wier--548)

BEARS' HOUSE, THE: Head of household because of desertion and mental illness, schoolgirl retreats into fantasy when anxieties overwhelm her. (Sachs--209)

BEAUTY QUEEN, THE: Against her inclinations, teen enters beauty pageants to satisfy her divorced mother's unfulfilled ambitions. (Pfeffer--192)

BEFORE THE LARK: Suffering the stigma of a harelip, 19th-century girl entreats custodial grandmother to renounce society and go to father's farm. (Brown--280)

BELOVED BENJAMIN IS WAITING: Foster care becomes inevitable for victim of double desertion who takes refuge from hoodlums in cemetery. (Karl--128)

BENJIE: Introverted black pre-schooler loses his shyness while bravely recovering his grandmother/guardian's lost earring. (Lexau--539)

BENJIE ON HIS OWN: Black kindergarten boy keeps his head and summons aid when he finds his grandmother/guardian incapacitated. (Lexau--540)

BEST BAD THING, THE: Depression-era Japanese-American girl at first deems it a penance to serve as mother's helper to independent widow. (Uchida--466)

BEST CHRISTMAS PAGEANT EVER, THE: Modern miracle transpires when incorrigible, streetwise fatherless kids muscle their way into Sunday School play. (Robinson--208)

BEYOND ANOTHER DOOR: Psychic phenomena and her mother's taciturnity fire young teen's curiosity concerning her obscure origins. (Levitin--497)

BEYOND THE DIVIDE: Amish father and daughter become victims of inhumanity as the rigors of the Gold Rush drive sane people irrational. (Lasky--142)

BIG BLUE ISLAND: Belligerent urban orphan and misanthropic great-uncle/guardian bristle when thrown together on latter's isolated island. (Gage--533)

BIRDS OF SUMMER, THE: When perpetual hippie mother becomes involved with drug ring, mature teen arranges the adoption of her impressionable younger sister. (Snyder--506)

BIZOU: Improbable story in which widowed black mother returning to U.S. for reunion with her estranged father temporarily abandons teen daughter. (Klein--390)

BLACK AND BLUE MAGIC: Boy's altruism to magician is rewarded with gift of flight which he uses to make a match for widowed mother. (Snyder--451)

BLAZE: Magnificent dog melds lonely boy and uncompromising custodial grandfather into the family unit that both need. (Somerlott--544)

BLIMP: Counseling helps teen understand subconscious reasons for overeating after mother's death and father's remarriage while urging suicidal friend to seek same. (Cavallaro--298)

BLISSFUL JOY AND THE SATs: Teen's preoccupation with exams takes detour around dog, disappointing romance, and divorced parents' convoluted involvements. (Greenwald--98)

BLOWFISH LIVE IN THE SEA: Teen turns disillusionment in reunion

with long-absent alcoholic father into constructive effort to rehabilitate him. (Fox--79)

BLUE TREES, RED SKY: Fatherless girl ambivalently wishes her
employed, feminist mother could also be a full-time homemaker like
her aging baby sitter. (Klein--391)

BOOK FOR JODAN, A: Divided by distance, girl and her beloved
father exchange scrapbooks of memorabilia and minutiae. (New-
field--175)

BOY IN THE OFF-WHITE HAT, THE: Boy is sexually molested by
the man his mother is attempting to entice into marriage. (Hall--
104)

BOY ON THE RUN: Oversheltered teen plots elaborate escape from
neurotic divorced mother's plush prison. (Bradbury--26)

BOY WHO COULD MAKE HIMSELF DISAPPEAR, THE: Emotionally
abused by both divorced parents, boy lapses into schizophrenia,
befriended only by outsiders. (Platt--196)

BOY WHO WANTED A FAMILY, THE: Orphan's joy at being adopted
by single woman is tempered by anxiety that she will change her
mind. (Gordon--535)

BUT IN THE FALL I'M LEAVING: Divorced parents' mysterious,
self-serving secret deprives teen of normal relationship with
grandmother. (Rinaldi--205)

C. C. POINDEXTER: Self-conscious teen's confusing role models
are her clinging vine mother and her feminist aunt, both divor-
cees. (Meyer--165)

CAGES OF GLASS, FLOWERS OF TIME: Battered teen conceals sordid life with mother because the alternative, living with grandmother who abuses them both, is worse. (Culin--55)

CALL IT COURAGE: Ancient Polynesian lad, traumatized by
mother's drowning, steels himself to conquer fear of the sea.
(Sperry--453)

CALL ME DANICA: Fatherless European emigree discovers unanticipated stumbling blocks to her acculturation as a Canadian.
(Madison--401)

CALL ME HELLER, THAT'S MY NAME: Aggressive 1920s tomboy
resists being feminized by aunt who comes to keep house for her
and widowed father. (Pevsner--426)

CANDLE AND THE MIRROR, THE: Daughter of militant suffragette
seeks career that is a compromise between wishes of activist
mother and deceased father. (Mays--406)

CAPTIVE THUNDER: Headstrong teen, stifled by mother's expectations, discovers that her immature hopes and plans are unrealistic and disappointing. (Butler--30)

CARDBOARD CROWN, THE: Two children of uncaring single
parents circumvent Dickensian tedium and woe through fantasy.
(Bulla--282)

CARTOONIST, THE: Boy escapes sordid strife between embittered
mother and irritating grandfather by obsessively pursuing his
avocation. (Byars--31)

CASE OF THE SOMERVILLE SECRET, THE: Clever British pair
  helps Scotland Yard close a case with no assistance from either
  one's single mother. (Newman--418)
CASSANDRA-JAMIE: Pre-teen hand-picks model stepmother only to
  learn that both her father and designated woman have different
  plans. (Ames--255)
CAT-MAN'S DAUGHTER: Only child becomes unwilling foil in egocentric showbiz parents' custody duel. (Abercrombie--1)
CHAIR FOR MY·MOTHER, A: Dispossessed by fire, three-genera-
  tion family of women saves every penny to replace their fur-
  nishings. (Williams--592)
CHANCY AND THE GRAND RASCAL: Civil War orphan sets out to
  reunite scattered siblings under the aegis of his outrageous
  uncle/guardian. (Fleischman--532)
CHANGEOVER, THE: Young teen's passage to puberty, coinciden-
  tal with her conversion to witchcraft, helps her understand
  mother's need of sexual intimacy. (Mahy--153)
CHANGES: Teenage boy must deal with loss of father, followed by
  relocation, first romance, and grandfather's debilitating stroke
  and death. (Rabin--431)
CHEATER AND FLITTER DICK: Distraught woman wrongly accuses
  mountain girl and unorthodox adoptive single father of incest.
  (Branscum--520)
CHILD OF THE OWL: Compulsive gambler abandons daughter to
  care of her grandmother in Chinatown, where she learns new way
  of life. (Yep--480)
CHILDREN IN THE WIND: Quartet of teens, including one whose
  mother is unstable and whose absent father is a fugitive, struggle
  with a variety of family problems. (Grohskopf--559)
CHILDREN ON THE TOP FLOOR, THE: Bachelor video celebrity acquires ready-made family he doesn't want and is unprepared to
  handle. (Streatfeild--546)
CHLORIS AND THE CREEPS: Dedicated to the glorification of divorced father who committed suicide, sullen girl impedes mother's
  bid to remarry. (Platt--197)
CHLORIS AND THE FREAKS: Jealous, hostile teen orchestrates
  mother's second divorce in punishment for divorcing her father
  and triggering his suicide. (Platt--198)
CHLORIS AND THE WEIRDOES: Bitter teen derails her twice-divorced
  mother's every attempt to establish new relationships with men.
  (Platt--199)
CHRISTMAS WITH IDA EARLY: Peerless hillbilly housekeeper employs zany diversions to ease family's sorrow through first holiday since mother's death. (Burch--285)
CITY IN THE WINTER: When schools are closed by blizzard, young
  boy stays home with grandmother while single mom is at work.
  (Schick--584)
CLASS PICTURES: College-bound daughter of unwed mother reviews
  checkered friendship with classmate and the fickle fate leading to
  their forking paths. (Sachs--504)
CODE NAME: CLONE: Cloned sons of Soviet defector seek their

father in U.S. while pursued by KGB bent on his destruction. (Cooper--576)

COUNTRY OF BROKEN STONE: Summer spent at stepmother's archaeological dig brings British girl unlikely friendship and insight into father's remarriage. (Bond--24)

COWBOYS DON'T CRY: Father's grief and remorse over wife's death exacerbate his alcoholism, costing him his son's love and respect. (Halvorson--367)

CRACKER JACKSON: Schoolboy singlehandedly endeavors to aid battered woman when his divorced parents won't get involved. (Byars--32)

CRAZIES AND SAM, THE: Lonely latchkey boy breaks one of father's safety regulations and becomes kidnap victim of alienated old woman. (Morris--170)

CRAZY QUILT: Adolescent changes contribute to ambivalence of girl whose loyalties are divided between institutionalized mother and the grandmother who committed her. (Riley--203)

CURSE OF THE BLUE FIGURINE, THE: Malevolent shade menaces boy whose widowed airman father is serving in Korean conflict. (Bellairs--265)

DADDY: Young black girl anticipates with pleasure Saturday outings with her divorced father. (Caines--33)

DADDY AND BEN TOGETHER: Young boy's natural rapport with father is strained when his mother leaves town on business. (Stecher--569)

DADDY'S NEW BABY: Father's new responsibilities detract from shared time on weekends, but older half sister learns to enjoy her role in entertaining baby. (Vigna--237)

DAFFODILS IN THE SNOW: Suggestible, sheltered teen, who claims that God fathered her out-of-wedlock baby, is actually victim of seduction by suave evangelist. (Gaeddert--490)

DAN ALONE: When British boy's unwed mother deserts him for a new lover, he goes in search of unknown father to avoid orphanage. (Townsend--509)

DANCE TO STILL MUSIC, A: Deaf runaway from mother's remarriage and threat of institutionalization is befriended by mellow recluse. (Corcoran--51)

DANNY THE CHAMPION OF THE WORLD: British boy and single father share with pillars of the community the time-honored sport of game poaching. (Dahl--326)

DAPHNE'S BOOK: Insecure adolescent from fatherless home fears ostracism when she is paired on assignment with class misfit. (Hahn--103)

DARK DREAMS: Frail boy left in grandmother's care by widowed serviceman father is plagued by doubts of his own courage. (Rinaldo--433)

DE DE TAKES CHARGE: Daughter of divorced parents tries, with mixed results, to match mother with shop teacher. (Hurwitz--121)

son makes grandson all the more determined to find his missing father. (Fenton--345)

EDGE OF NEXT YEAR, THE: Grief over mother's tragic accidental death affects teen, younger brother, and father in vastly different ways. (Stolz--456)

EGYPT GAME, THE: Resentment at being farmed out to grandmother by show biz mom fades when girl makes friends and becomes embroiled in mystery. (Snyder--452)

EIGHT MULES FROM MONTEREY: With children's aid, intrepid widowed librarian establishes library outposts in desolate, lawless wilderness. (Beatty--262)

ELIZA'S DADDY: Before meeting her father's new stepdaughter, small girl is jealous of stepsister she fantasizes to be perfect. (Thomas--233)

ELLEN GRAE: Given to grisly fabrication, daughter of divorced parents is disbelieved when she unveils a true tale of murder. (Cleaver--41)

ELLIE'S INHERITANCE: Jewish-American Princess evolves from passive materialism to independence and activism during pre-Holocaust era. (Colman--316)

ELLIOTT AND WIN: Young teen suspects his cultured, role model Big Brother of being a homosexual. (Meyer--166)

EMILY AND THE KLUNKY BABY AND THE NEXT-DOOR DOG: Miffed because divorced mother has no time for her, pre-schooler runs away to find father. (Lexau--145)

EMPTY CHAIR, THE: Her mother's spirit appears to Jewish-Canadian schoolgirl and instructs her to oppose her father's remarriage. (Kaplan--383)

EMPTY HOUSE, THE: When custodial father is incarcerated for tax fraud, teens, convinced of his innocence, solve mystery to exonerate him. (Holland--114)

EVERETT ANDERSON'S CHRISTMAS COMING: While lamenting dead father and gifts he might have received from him, black boy savors spirit of Christmas with mom. (Clifton--306)

EVERETT ANDERSON'S FRIEND: New girl in next apartment makes as good a friend as a boy when lonely black son of working mother gives her a chance. (Clifton--307)

EVERETT ANDERSON'S GOODBYE: Pathos of grief is simply and realistically portrayed through eyes of young black boy who wrestles with loss of father. (Clifton--308)

EVERETT ANDERSON'S 1-2-3: Small black boy resists widowed mother's sympathetic friend who wants to make a trio out of their cozy duo. (Clifton--309)

EVERETT ANDERSON'S YEAR: For black child the months are filled with seasonal activities, memories of his father, and hope for the future. (Clifton--310)

EVERLASTING HILLS, THE: Retarded boy, emotionally abused by contemptuous widowed father, finds love and acceptance with elderly recluse. (Hunt--378)

EVY-IVY-OVER: Abandoned at birth by unwed mother, girl suffers cruel ridicule over eccentricity of custodial grandmother. (Rodowsky--502)

EYES IN THE FISHBOWL: Son of indolent father has higher ambitions for himself and incidentally becomes embroiled in occult adventure. (Snyder--224)

FAITHFULLY, TRU: Reappearance of long absent agnostic father causes teen grave doubts about her mother's uncompromising morality. (Baehr--16)

FALSE START: Ghetto boy refuses to let humble, sordid environment sap his drive and integrity as it did his alcoholic, self-pitying father. (Rabin--201)

FAMILY TRAP, THE: Incompatible with sister/guardian, teen petitions to become emancipated minor after father's death and mother's incapacitation. (Colman--317)

FAMILY UNDER THE BRIDGE, THE: Homeless, fatherless French waifs beguile indolent old indigent into becoming family's protector and provider. (Carlson--297)

FAMOUS STANLEY KIDNAPPING CASE, THE: Stepsister is target of abductors when she boasts that the estranged father she adores is wealthy. (Snyder--225)

FAT GIRL, THE: Divorced mother's gnawing, neurotic self-pity infects teenage son in his relationship with social outcast. (Sachs--210)

FATHER EVERY FEW YEARS, A: When his stepfather abandons them, pre-teen boy is fearful that he and his mother will founder without a man. (Bach--15)

FATHER FIGURE: Role model for younger brother since dad's desertion, teen develops rivalry with father when he resumes paternal duties. (Peck--188)

FATHER LIKE THAT, A: Fatherless boy describes the ideal parent he would like to have--or to be himself someday. (Zolotow--250)

FIGURE IN THE SHADOWS, THE: Timid boy, ashamed of his weaknesses, is given frightening magical powers by his custodial uncle, a wizard. (Bellairs--519)

FILE ON FRAULEIN BERG, THE: Fatherless WWII Irish girl and callow chums seek excitement by harassing German teacher they imagine to be enemy spy. (Lingard--396)

FINDING FEVER: Teen recalls dying dad's advice to overcome antipathy for peer with whom he is investigating dogs' disappearance. (Baird--259)

FIRST HARD TIMES, THE: Daughter of remarried mother is alone in believing obsessively that her MIA father is still living. (Smith--450)

FIRST STEP: Teen loyally minimizes mother's alcoholism until humiliation and threat of personal harm force her to seek help. (Snyder--223)

FISHMAN AND CHARLY: Rejected by impersonal widowed military father, boy seeks friendship among pet fish and marine mammals.

(Davis--328)

FOG: After father's sudden death, teen realizes that his parent's
wasted occupational potential was a sacrifice to his son's own
future. (Lee--392)

FOOTSTEPS: Heir to tainted family fortune tries to make restitution to injured party and becomes prey to knavery worse than
dead father's. (Garfield--357)

FOOTSTEPS ON THE STAIRS: Stepdaughter and biological daughter
vie for father's affection while investigating vacation home mystery. (Adler--251)

FORMAL FEELING, A: Intellectual teen wrestles with perfectionist
mother's ghost which strains family relationships and her personal happiness. (Oneal--420a)

FOUR-STORY MISTAKE, THE: Misgivings over moving to the
country are dispelled for widower's children when new home
proves intriguing. (Enright--334)

FOURS CROSSING: Following mother's death, daughter of traveling
salesman stays with grandmother and becomes catalyst in occult
adventure. (Garden--356)

FOURTEEN: Teens become romantically involved as they strive to
solve mystery of boy's father's mysterious disappearance. (Sachs
--566)

FRIENDS, THE: Black teen overcomes snobbery and the opposition
of tyrannical widowed father to make friends with impoverished
girl. (Guy--366)

GABRIEL'S GIRL: Gothic potboiler of international intrigue whose
dauntless, imperiled, motherless heroine is a chip off the old
block. (Johnston--381)

GARDEN IS GOING FINE, THE: Young teen agonizes through classic stages of grief--denial, anger, bargaining, sorrow and ac-
ceptance--when father dies. (Farley--343)

GARDEN OF BROKEN GLASS: Young white slum teen makes friends
with black classmates when alcoholic mother makes life unbear-
able. (Neville--174)

GARDINE VS. HANOVER: Jealous stepsisters' baneful brawling
nearly delivers knockout punch to their parents' marriage.
(Oppenheimer--181)

GATHERING OF DAYS, A: The year her father remarries, her best
friend dies, and she aids a runaway slave is reflective and apoc-
alyptic for 19th-century girl. (Blos--266)

(GEORGE):   Schizophrenia is suspected by stepmother when boy's
conscientious alter ego verbalizes mistrust of a schoolmate.
(Konigsburg--140)

GET-AWAY CAR, THE: To avoid institutionalization and custody
battle with relatives, grandmother and orphaned granddaughter
take flight. (Clymer--530)

GETTING RID OF ROGER: Hyperactive little brother is an acute
embarrassment to high-achieving daughter of divorced mom.
(Matthews--155)

GIFT OF MAGIC, A: Clairvoyance is mixed blessing to adolescent rebellious over parents' divorce and mother's impending remarriage. (Duncan--67)

GIFT OF THE PIRATE QUEEN, THE: Motherless girl resents relative who comes to relieve her of responsibility for father and diabetic sister. (Giff--359)

GIRL CALLED AL, A: Lonely daughter of working, dating mother and absent, divorced father seeks attention through exhibitionism. (Greene--93)

GIRL IN THE MIRROR: Teen must cope with beloved father's remarriage, his subsequent death, and the need to deal with resented stepmother. (Sherburne--446)

GIRL WHO HAD NO NAME, THE: Product of an unplanned pregnancy, a tenth daughter is rejected by her father after his wife's untimely death. (Rabe--430)

GIRL WITH THE SILVER EYES, THE: Her odd powers and appearance cause consternation, uneasiness and fear among associates of fatherless girl. (Roberts--207)

GIRLS IN THE VELVET FRAME, THE: A studio portrait helps reunite fatherless Jerusalem family with their emigrant brother before WWI. (Geras--358)

GIVE DAD MY BEST: Improvident musician of Depression era refuses to accept responsibility for supporting his three children. (Collier--556)

GLEANINGS: Resilient teen tries unsuccessfully to fulfill her dreams and create stable, conventional homelife for her wastrel father. (Stanek--507)

GO AND CATCH A FLYING FISH: Adored, extravagant mom, resentful of pragmatic husband's nagging criticism, leaves home and family. (Stolz--229)

GOLDEN VENTURE, THE: Widowed 49er's courageous daughter retains femininity while learning street wiles in frontier San Francisco. (Flora--349)

GOOD-BYE PINK PIG: Dominated by her driven, uncompromising mother, insecure girl invents fantasy world she can manipulate. (Adler--3)

GOODBYE SUMMER, THE: Uninhibited Vietnam-orphaned girl has difficulty relinquishing important people and paraphernalia she holds dear. (Bonsall--270)

GOOSEBERRIES TO ORANGES: Grown woman relates her impressions of immigrating to the U.S. from war-torn Europe when she was young and motherless. (Cohen--312)

GRANDPA'S MARIA: While her unwed mother is hospitalized with nervous breakdown, girl is cared for by her photographer grandfather. (Hellberg--493)

GREAT BURGERLAND DISASTER, THE: Youthful gourmand muddles through divorced parents' change in lifestyles while earning culinary kudos. (Levine--143)

GREAT GILLY HOPKINS, THE: Embittered child of unwed mother develops bellicose defense against foster care while yearning for reunion with mom. (Paterson--499)

GRIP, A DOG STORY: Devotion of motherless boy and pit bull pup
    obverts the brutality that has been bred into both of them.
    (Griffiths--100)
GRIZZLY, THE: Virile, noncustodial father takes sensitive, shel-
    tered boy into the wilderness to make a man of him. (Johnson--
    122)
GROVER: Terminally ill woman's suicide plunges husband into self-
    pity while son internalizes his grief. (Cleaver--300).
GROWIN' PAINS: Believing that mother's frugality caused father's
    desertion, ambitious girl also strives to leave impoverished town.
    (Blount--39)
GROWING ANYWAY UP: Neurotic girl's precarious balance is threat-
    ened by relocation and repressed guilt over father's long ago
    death. (Heide--371)
GUY LENNY: Adolescent feels betrayed when his custodial father
    palms him off on his estranged mother to enable him to remarry.
    (Mazer--156)

HALF NELSON, FULL NELSON: With girlfriend as accomplice, teen
    abducts his sister to attempt reconciliation of separated parents.
    (Stone--232)
HAPPILY EVER AFTER...ALMOST: Self-confident girl enjoys com-
    patibility with both new stepparents but develops instant antipathy
    for shy, supercilious stepbrother. (Wolkoff--248)
HARRY'S MOM: Elementary school boy learns from relatives about
    his courageous mother who died before his recollection. (Porte--
    429)
HAUNTING, THE: British boy is stalked by necromancer intent
    upon harnessing the powers he may have inherited from his dead
    mother. (Mahy--403)
HAUNTING AIR, A: Only child of preoccupied father makes friends
    with elderly woman, young widowed mother, and Victorian ghosts.
    (Freeman--81)
HAUNTING OF JULIE UNGER, THE: Grieving teen imposes self-
    isolation and evokes the living image of her father in denial of
    his death. (Lutters--399)
HAZEL RYE: Girl's mundane aspirations change with acquisition of
    land from her custodial father and the prodding of a new friend.
    (Cleaver--555)
HE NOTICED I'M ALIVE ... AND OTHER HOPEFUL SIGNS: Teen,
    thrust into premature sophistication by mother's abandonment in
    midlife crisis, yearns for romance. (Sharmat--216)
HEADLESS CUPID, THE: Audacious girl tries to unnerve large new
    stepfamily with her command of the occult. (Snyder--226)
HEADS YOU WIN: TAILS I LOSE: Overweight pawn in parents'
    marital strife, teen falls into drug spiral in attempt to increase
    popularity with peers. (Holland--115)
HEIDI: Misanthropic, reclusive grandfather learns to love again
    through orphaned moppet for whom he grudgingly makes a home.
    (Spyri--545)

dad's failure to observe Christmas customs until she learns it's
connected to mother's death. (Rock--436)

HOW FAR IS BERKELEY? Pubescent daughter of unwed mother undergoes radical change in lifestyle when latter enrolls at bohemian
university. (Chetin--486)

HOW I PUT MY MOTHER THROUGH COLLEGE: Starting junior high
as her divorced mother starts college, unsure girl has double
adjustment to make. (Gerson--85)

HOW MANY MILES TO BABYLON? In search of hospitalized single
mom, young black boy is victimized by gang of rowdies. (Fox--
80)

HUGO AND THE PRINCESS NENA: City girl learns to control her
qualms about beach life with grandfather when divorced mother
returns to school. (Ellis--69)

HUNDRED DRESSES, THE: Scorned motherless immigrant girl triumphs over supercilious classmates after moving away to escape
their taunts. (Estes--579)

HUNTER COMES HOME, A: Eskimo widow, who wants son to be
educated, and grandfather, who wants boy to follow tradition,
vie over his future. (Turner--464)

HUNTLEY NUTLEY AND THE MISSING LINK: Australopithecine
visitor both creates and solves problems for son of single,
absent-minded professor. (Tannen--459)

I AND SPROGGY: Arrival of his new British stepsister, a veritable
Wonder Woman, bruises New York boy's ego. (Greene--94)

I HATE TO TALK ABOUT YOUR MOTHER: On weekend trip with
promiscuous, alcoholic mother, illegitimate teen worries about her
own sexual appetite. (Jones--495)

I HAVE TWO FAMILIES: Young girl's trepidations about parents'
divorce are ameliorated by shared custody and open communication.
(Helmering--111)

I KNOW YOU, AL: Adolescent waxes emotional over attending absent
father's wedding and over her own physiological development.
(Greene--95)

I LOVE GRAM: Daughter of working, single black mother misses
companionship of live-in grandmother when latter is hospitalized.
(Sonneborn--587)

I MET A TRAVELER: Transplanted from U.S. to Israel by libertine
mother, lonely adolescent makes friends with elderly immigrant
and pines for home. (Hoban--113)

I, TRISSY: When her father divorces her mother, precocious girl
vents her hostilities through her new typewriter. (Mazer--157)

I WANT MAMA: Mother's hospitalization for surgery is unsettling
for her small daughter. (Sharmat--567)

I WISH I HAD MY FATHER: Approach of Father's Day painfully
reminds small boy of void left by divorced father whose whereabouts are unknown. (Simon--218)

I WOULD RATHER BE A TURNIP: Sensitive to small town conventionality, motherless girl is stigmatized when illegitimate nephew

comes to stay. (Cleaver--487)

IDA EARLY COMES OVER THE MOUNTAIN: A hoosier Mary Poppins
marshals an unraveling motherless mountain family. (Burch--286)

IF I LOVE YOU AM I TRAPPED FOREVER? Perturbed teen ponders
meaning of love, loyalty, and role changes as he loses girlfriend
and meets his father and wife. (Kerr--131)

I'LL GET THERE. IT BETTER BE WORTH THE TRIP: Adolescent
returns to estranged alcoholic mother at critical stage in his
sexual and emotional maturation. (Donovan--64).

I'LL LOVE YOU WHEN YOU'RE MORE LIKE ME: TV starlet daughter
of inveterate single stage mother and rebellious son of prosaic
family exert their independence. (Kerr--387)

IN SEARCH OF COFFEE MOUNTAINS: When refugee girl becomes
separated from widowed mother, grandmother becomes last bastion
of defense. (Gottschalk--361)

IN THE MIDDLE OF A RAINBOW: Teen's romance becomes tug-of-war
between boyfriend's possessiveness and widowed mother's obsession
for female independence. (Girion--360)

IN THE WINGS: Parents' trial separation and divorce triggers
teen's spiraling depression while rehearsing for school play.
(Goldman--88)

INNKEEPER'S DAUGHTER, THE: The inn her widowed mother
manages is home and firm anchorage to self-conscious teen until
fire destroys it. (Cohen--313)

IOU'S: Loyal, loving relationship of independent divorced mother
and son weathers crises of a death in the family and boy's test-
ing of parental values. (Sebestyen--215)

IS THAT YOU, MISS BLUE? Sheltered teen comes to terms with life,
injustice and maturation at boarding school upon feminist mother's
desertion. (Kerr--132)

ISLAND ON BIRD STREET, THE: Jewish fugitive subsists covertly
in Warsaw ghetto awaiting reunion with captive father after
mother's deportation to death camp. (Orlev--421)

IT AIN'T ALL FOR NOTHIN': Grandmother's incapacitation pitches
black inner city boy into battle to retain integrity against degenerate single father. (Myers--414)

IT'S AN AARDVARK-EAT-TURTLE WORLD: Can teens' friendship
survive transition to sisterhood as custodial father and mother
decide to cohabitate? (Danziger--57)

IT'S JUST TOO MUCH: Mother's remarriage and the addition of
stepbrothers to their menage exacerbates adolescent's growing
pains. (Okimoto--178)

IT'S NO CRUSH, I'M IN LOVE! When teen's infatuation with teacher
inevitably leads to disillusionment, she learns to compensate as
mother did when father died. (Foley--350)

IT'S NOT THE END OF THE WORLD: Pre-teen tenaciously endeavors
to keep family intact until she opens her eyes to parents' misery.
(Blume--23)

IT'S NOT WHAT YOU EXPECT: Young teens open restaurant to
occupy themselves during parents' summer-long separation.
(Klein--136)

J.T.: Suspicious black inner city mother fears that son will become delinquent like felon father who deserted them. (Wagner--239)

JAKE: Impudent young black's passion for baseball is clouded by threat of foster home and disbandment of team unless custodial uncle shapes up. (Slote--219)

JEMMY: Stoical, disenfranchised half-Amerind daughter of alcoholic father develops self-respect through attention of renowned artist. (Hassler--368)

JOHNNY STANDS: Orphaned Amerind youth decides to chart course between gentle grandfather/guardian's traditional insularity and militancy of young radicals. (Paige--543)

JONATHAN DOWN UNDER: Lore of Australian gold rush of 1851 unfolds through adventures of impractical, ill-fated Yankee widower and steadfast son. (Beatty--263)

JOSHUA FORTUNE: Son of divorced hippies, young teen learns to mitigate frustration at change and nonconformity by rolling with the punches. (Grant--90)

JOURNEY BACK, THE: Motherless survivors of Holocaust try to reassemble jigsaw puzzle of their lives into frame that has been warped by war. (Reiss--432)

JOURNEY TO ALMOST THERE: With infirm grandfather in tow, rebellious teen, asserting independence from mother, runs away in search of father. (Guernsey--102)

JOURNEY TO AMERICA: WWII Jewish refugee family is stranded in Switzerland while waiting to join foresighted father in America. (Levitin--562)

JOURNEY TO AN 800 NUMBER: Class-conscious boy's disdain of father's itinerant life is slowly dispelled during summer's sojourn with him. (Konigsburg--141)

JULIA AND THE HAND OF GOD: Antagonism between temperamentally disparate grandmother and granddaughter results when widow moves in with mother. (Cameron--294)

JULIE'S DAUGHTER: When teen comes to live with unwed mother who abandoned her at birth, reality does not match her fantasy expectations. (Rodowsky--503)

JUMP SHIP TO FREEDOM: Slave boy whose father died as Revolutionary War veteran seeks emancipation for mother and himself and is witness to history. (Collier--315)

JUST LIKE SISTERS: Only child's hope for a sister vanishes when visiting cousin from broken home turns out to be her diametrical opposite. (Gaeddert--82)

KAREN'S SISTER: Single woman's adoptive daughter, who perennially plays matchmaker for her, is stunned when she chooses someone unacceptable to her. (McHugh--541)

KENTON YEAR, THE: Girl's reaction to shock of father's accidental death prompts mother to relocate in healing rural surroundings. (Wallace-Brodeur--468)

KENTUCKY DAUGHTER: Daughter of widowed craftswoman is ashamed of backwoods origins when she attends school in the city. (Scott--

443)

KICK A STONE HOME: Androgynous style affected by girl after parents' divorce is difficult to dismantle when she becomes a teen. (Smith--221)

KILLER SWAN, THE: Young teen bottles up a volatile brew of emotions after father's suicide and mother's remarriage. (Clifford--304)

KILLING TREE, THE: Young adult is imperiled in defending dead father's integrity while resenting the mother who divorced him earlier. (Bennett--21)

KING BASIL'S BIRTHDAY: Despondent single monarch is presented with ready-made family who inveigle themselves into the resistant royal heart. (Young--595)

LADY CAT LOST: Diverse family deserted by father experiences difficulty adjusting to new life sharing quarters with another family. (Dixon--63)

LADY ELLEN GRAE: Divorced parents ship diamond-in-the-rough daughter to punctilious relatives to be polished. (Cleaver--42)

LAST WAS LLOYD: Physically, socially, emotionally crippled by smother love, pre-teen boy learns to assert independence and gain self-esteem. (Smith--505)

LATCHKEY MYSTERY, THE: Alone after school for various reasons, group of children establishes Neighborhood Watch to foil burglaries. (Clark--299)

LAUGHTER IN THE BACKGROUND: Her mother's spiraling alcoholism prompts pre-teen to overeat and in final desperation to seek foster care. (Dorman--65)

LEAP BEFORE YOU LOOK: Young teen bitterly resents unforeseen divorce of contentious parents and its deleterious effect on her life. (Stolz--230)

LENNY KANDELL, SMART ALECK: Son of overprotective war widow is certain of his Thalian talents but unsure if his courage matches his father's. (Conford--320)

LIBBY'S STEP-FAMILY: It is odd-man-out when teenage girl's mother marries widower with two resentful daughters of his own. (Simon--447)

LIBERATION OF TANSY WARNER, THE: Young teen agonizes over disappearance of her mother, a quasi-slave to rigid husband and peremptory older children. (Tolan--235)

LIKE JAKE AND ME: Physical and temperamental antithesis of new stepdad, little boy feels overshadowed until he learns that the man is not perfect. (Jukes--126)

LILLAN: Victim of paternal desertion fears loss of mother's love also, especially when mom begins dating seriously. (Norris--176)

LINDSAY, LINDSAY, FLY AWAY HOME: Father's motive in sending balky teen to U.S. is not to sever her bi-racial romance but to reunite her with birth mother. (Pevsner--501)

LION IN THE BOX, THE: Christmas appears bleak for turn-of-century working widow's family until benefactor sends them mysterious box. (DeAngeli--329)

LION TO GUARD US, A: Three intrepid Elizabethan children seek
their father in the New World after their mother's death in England. (Bulla--283)

LISTEN FOR THE FIG TREE: Black teen's maturity is forged by her
widowed mother's alcoholism and her own blindness and attempted
rape. (Mathis--405)

LITTLE DESTINY, A: Spurned suitor exacts vengeance thirty years
later by contributing to rival's death and persecuting his widow
and family. (Cleaver--301)

LOCKED IN TIME: Suspense and foreboding grip teen as she joins
widowed father and secretive new stepfamily on isolated plantation. (Duncan--332)

LOLLIPOP PARTY, THE: When working mother is late getting home,
small inner city Hispanic boy recalls lessons on safety and etiquette. (Sonneborn--588)

LONER, THE: Orphan of migrant workers sinks roots and finds a
family with uncompromising woman rancher. (Wier--549)

LONG JOURNEY, THE: When grandfather/guardian is incapacitated,
orphaned teen undertakes wilderness journey to summon assistance.
(Corcoran--531)

LONG SECRET, THE: Sheltered girl reared by grandmother shows
spirit when reclaimed by jet set mother who has long neglected
her. (Fitzhugh--77)

LOOKING ON: Adolescent daughter of working mother is enticed
into maturing too fast by proximity to fascinating and sophisticated newlyweds. (Miles--167)

LOUIE'S SEARCH: Serendipitous turn of events rewards inner city
black child's quest for a father. (Keats--582)

LOVE ALWAYS, BLUE: Teen who hates superficial life with social-
conscious mother temporarily fulfills desire to live with manic-
depressive father. (Osborne--184)

LOVE IS A MISSING PERSON: Father's flamboyant favorite leaves
his custody to return to conventional mother and sister with whom
she is incompatible. (Kerr--133)

LUCKY WILMA: Lockstep Saturday visitations lack spontaneity until
unexpected occurrence boosts small girl and dad out of their rut.
(Kindred--135)

LUDELL: While unwed mother works as domestic in the North,
black daughter is reared in the South by exacting grandmother.
(Wilkinson--512)

LUDELL AND WILLIE: Black teen pursues romance behind back of
overprotective grandmother who doesn't want her to repeat unwed
mother's mistake. (Wilkinson--513)

LUDELL'S NEW YORK TIME: While pining for Southern sweetheart,
black teen battles her mother and the gravid metropolis to a
standoff. (Wilkinson--514)

LUKE WAS THERE: Victims of paternal desertion rely for physical
and emotional stability on black counselor during mother's hospitalization. (Clymer--45)

MADELINE AND THE GREAT (OLD) ESCAPE ARTIST: Repugnant
move to small town following divorce is aggravated by adolescent's
humiliating epileptic seizure. (Jones--123)
MAGDALENA: Suspicion of American customs creates friction between
Hispanic grandmother/guardian and granddaughter's new friend.
(Shotwell--568)
MAGGIE, TOO: Defensive, resentful girl is exiled to perceptive,
diplomatic grandmother while father marries a Hollywood starlet.
(Nixon--420)
MAGIC EYE FOR IDA, A: Craving attention from preoccupied single
mother, small girl runs away and is reassured by benevolent for-
tune teller. (Chorao--38)
MAMA: How can a boy convince his mom to stop stealing from her
employers to supplement her income without losing her love?
(Hopkins--118)
MAMA AND HER BOYS: Kleptomaniac mother turns over a new leaf
when she accepts a better job and receives a marriage proposal.
(Hopkins--119)
MAMA'S GOING TO BUY YOU A MOCKINGBIRD: The anatomy of
loss is poignantly probed from son's point of view when his
father succumbs to cancer. (Little--398)
MAN IN THE BOX, THE: Atrocities of war which killed father
prompt principled Vietnamese boy to desert family to aid captive
American. (Dunn--333)
MAN WITHOUT A FACE, THE: Rudderless son of oft-married
mother gets paternal guidance from disfigured paragon with feet
of clay. (Holland--116)
MANY MOONS: All the king's men cannot produce for his beloved
daughter the moon, which is in the eye of the beholder anyway.
(Thurber--590)
MARINKA, KATINKA AND ME (SUSIE): Petty quarrel temporarily
splits triumvirate of unrelated fatherless schoolgirls. (Madison--
402)
MARION'S ANGELS: Emotional British girl's devotion to ancient
church has unexpected consequences for her, her father, and
their new friends. (Peyton--427)
MARLY THE KID: Teen begins to form her own personality after
leaving mother's repressive custody to live with remarried father.
(Pfeffer--193)
MARRYING OFF MOTHER: Austrian girl's schemes to find mate for
mom in order to escape grandmother's oppressive domicile have
amusing and unexpected results. (Nostlinger--177)
MATT GARGAN'S BOY: Boy who expects divorced parents to reconcile when his father gives up baseball career is doomed to disappointment. (Slote--220)
MATTER OF SPUNK, A: Compelled by divorce to fend for themselves, mother and daughters seek new life in bohemian enclave
during 1920s. (Jones--124)
MAYBE NEXT YEAR: Adolescent frets about relationship with a boy,
a dancing career, and her grandmother/guardian's remarriage.
(Hest--538)

ME AND JIM LUKE: Ozark boys attempt to solve suspenseful murder mystery for the reward that could reunite one of them with his mother. (Branscum--273)

ME AND MR. STENNER: Militantly loyal to divorced dad, girl tests future stepfather's forbearance by nettling him at every opportunity. (Hunter--120)

ME, CALIFORNIA PERKINS: Frontier mother mutinies when husband uproots family to become silver prospector in lawless, cultural wasteland. (Beatty--19)

ME DAY: Inner city boy fears his divorced father has forgotten his birthday as he waits in vain all day for a message. (Lexau--146)

ME TOO: Pre-teen is obsessed with educating her mentally retarded twin to entice their intolerant divorced father back home. (Cleaver--43)

MESSENGER FOR PARLIAMENT, A: Cromwellian era son has only contempt for the inebriate father who was so undeserving of his dead mother's love. (Haugaard--369)

MIDDLE MOFFAT, THE: Earnest and imaginative middle child of fatherless family creates her own humorous diversions. (Estes--338)

MILLIE'S BOY: Harlot mother's murder propels turn-of-century teen into sanguinary search for her killer and his own father. (Peck--500)

MIMOSA TREE, THE: Backwoods family is demoralized by move to big city, exacerbated by father's blindness and stepmother's desertion. (Cleaver--302)

MISSING FROM HOME: Runaway siblings attempting reconciliation of separated parents become kidnap victims. (Clewes--44)

MISSING PIECES: Widow's inability to verbalize grief drives wedge of silence between her and teen whose only confidant is her boyfriend. (Asher--258)

MITZI AND FREDERICK THE GREAT: Jealous, headstrong girl thinks stepbrother is unjustifiably cautious and superior until he saves her life. (Williams--242)

MITZI AND THE ELEPHANTS: Daughter of newly remarried mother discovers a special talent at which stepbrothers cannot overshadow her. (Williams--243)

MITZI AND THE TERRIBLE TYRANNOSAURUS REX: Girl's one prospective stepbrother is overbearing; the other is a precocious little monster. (Williams--244)

MITZI'S HONEYMOON WITH NANA POTTS: While mom is honeymooning, resentful girl's home is preempted by assertive stepbrothers and their domineering grandmother. (Williams--245)

MOFFAT MUSEUM, THE: Widowed seamstress' creative children collect artifacts memorializing family life in early 1900s New England. (Estes--339)

MOFFATS, THE: Resourceful fatherless family survives impoverishment, disease, deprivation and ennui with style and elan. (Estes--340)

MOM OR POP: Fat Albert and the Cosby kids befriend shy, sad

newcomer whose combative, separated parents are using her for
a football. (Levy--144)

MOM, THE WOLF MAN AND ME: Content with their independent
lifestyle, pre-teen is leery of unwed mother's decision to marry
a man they both like. (Klein--496)

MONEY CREEK MARE, THE: After mother's desertion, determined
girl tries to help father and siblings by agreeing to adoption by
wealthy couple. (Calvert--34)

MONEY ROOM, THE: City boy's tepid acceptance of farm life ignites when rural neighbor conspires to force his widowed mother
to vacate. (McGraw--407)

MONTH OF SUNDAYS, A: Divorced child syndrome strikes boy suffering from strained visits with father and working mother's
chronic fatigue. (Blue--22)

MOONLIGHT MAN, THE: Vacationing with intemperate, unconventional, noncustodial father, teen comes to appreciate his strengths
and tolerate his weaknesses. (Fox--80a)

MOTHER TREE, THE: Mother's premature death catapults young
1900s girl into domestic, maternal role long before she's ready.
(Whitehead--473)

MOTOWN AND DIDI: Two black teens unite in romance and a campaign to conquer vice in Harlem that destroys girl's single mother
and weak brother. (Myers--171)

MOVE OVER, BEETHOVEN: Adolescent musical prodigy finds it
hard to live up to widowed mother's expectations when social
distractions beckon. (First--347)

MOVES MAKE THE MAN, THE: Mixed race friendship collapses with
the growing cynicism of idealistic teen whose mother is institutionalized. (Brooks--279)

MUMMY MARKET, THE: Dissatisfied with dour housekeeper, children
choose a model stepmother by trial and error in humorous fantasy.
(Brelis--573)

MUSHY EGGS: When beloved babysitter returns to her homeland,
preschool sons of divorced mother mourn her departure. (Adams
--2)

MUSIC, MUSIC FOR EVERYONE: Single waitress' small daughter
enterprisingly replenishes family savings depleted during grandmother's illness. (Williams--593)

MY BROTHER ANGE: Fatherless British boy cannot appreciate
vexatious brother he babysits until the child is hurt through his
carelessness. (McCaffrey--160)

MY DAD LIVES IN A DOWNTOWN HOTEL: Boy who experiences
classic divorce syndrome decides to form a club for others of
his ilk. (Mann--154)

MY MOM TRAVELS A LOT: Compensations of more relaxed lifestyle
with father balance drawbacks of girl's businesswoman mother's
absences. (Bauer--551)

MY MOTHER IS NOT MARRIED TO MY FATHER: Miffed at not being
consulted in divorce decision, resentful, bewildered girl tries to
manipulate both parents' new lives. (Okimoto--179)

MY MOTHER LOST HER JOB TODAY: Until reassured, daughter of

young, single, professional woman mirrors mother's anxiety over loss of her job. (Delton--577)

MY MOTHER THE MAIL CARRIER: Hispanic girl is proud of her feminist single mother's occupation but would rather be a jockey herself. (Maury--583)

MY MOTHER'S GETTING MARRIED: Elementary school girl feels threatened by the inevitable changes in her life when mom re-marries. (Drescher--578a)

MY OWN PRIVATE SKY: Timid, fatherless boy and individualistic aging woman learn to surmount fear of physical handicaps. (Beckman--264)

MY SPECIAL BEST WORDS: Black tot earns praise of single father by personally potty-training her baby brother. (Steptoe--589)

MY WAR WITH MRS. GALLOWAY: Imaginative mischief-maker and her fussy, old-fashioned babysitter are mutually suspicious of the other's motives. (Orgel--183)

NAME A STAR FOR ME: Young teen and her married mother flirt with temptations of illicit romance on summer vacation fling. (Gerber--83)

NATURE OF THE BEAST, THE: Single father's unemployment im-pels British boy to seek reward involving deadly peril from wild beast. (Howker--494)

NEIGHBORHOOD KNIGHT: Imaginative, fatherless boy plays neo-knight, chivalrously defending fair damsels (mom and sis) in their contemporary urban castle. (Schick--585)

NIGHT CRY: Young teen disloyally and mistakenly suspects im-provident, widowed father of kidnapping child for ransom. (Naylor--416)

NIGHT DADDY, THE: Lonely daughter of night shift nurse de-velops mutually rewarding relationship with grown, male sitter. (Gripe--491)

NIGHT OF THE BOZOS, THE: Son of working mother learns to broaden his horizons when his handicapped uncle/sitter leaves to join carnival. (Slepian--448)

NIGHT SWIMMERS, THE: Girl assumes maternal role over younger brothers by default when widowed father shirks burden of parenthood. (Byars--289)

NO BEASTS! NO CHILDREN! Children and custodial father fight guerilla war against eviction by fastidious landlord who hates pets. (Keller--130)

NO ONE IS GOING TO NASHVILLE: Sympathetic stepmother con-vinces girl's father to let her keep a dog at their home for her weekend visits. (Jukes--127)

NO PLACE FOR MITTY: Unconventional grandmother delivers Gay Nineties girl from stultifying life with prudish aunt after parents' divorce. (Young--249)

NO SCARLET RIBBONS: Uninhibited stepdaughter tries and fails to tailor her new family into carbon copy of her old one. (Terris--462)

America. (Taylor--570)

PAPPA PELLERIN'S DAUGHTER: Beleaguered Swedish girl tries but
fails to hold fatherless family together when mother forsakes them
to work abroad. (Gripe--101)

PARDON ME, YOU'RE STEPPING ON MY EYEBALL: Severely disturbed teen relies on another to overcome emotional problems inflicted by father's death and mother's alcoholism. (Zindel--481)

PAUL'S KITE: Unwanted, unloved British boy tries to make the best
of returning to live with egocentric mother who abandoned him as
a baby. (Morgan--169)

PENNIES FOR THE PIPER: Heartrending story of girl's lonely, resolute vigil during mother's terminal illness and final rites and her
journey to a new home. (McLean--409)

PERSON IN THE POTTING SHED, THE: Defensive stepfather believes children are trying to humiliate him when they report a
murder he is skeptical of. (Corcoran--324)

PHILO POTTS: Lonely boy's longing for dog inadvertently invokes
vexatious problems and a startling revelation about his "deceased"
mother. (Ames--8)

PICKLES AND PRUNES: Diffident young teen tries changing her
image to thwart her mother's suitor and makes friends with
courageous dying girl. (Moe--411)

PIECE OF THE WORLD, A: When girl's parents divorce, she draws
strength from massive boulder until it, too, is "riven asunder."
(Walker--240)

PIG-OUT BLUES, THE: Obese daughter of slim, nagging widow
learns to break vicious circle of overeating to compensate for
frustration. (Greenberg--362)

PISTACHIO PRESCRIPTION, THE: Mother with martyr complex saps
asthmatic teen's self-confidence and sours her own marriage.
(Danziger--58)

PLACE APART, A: At loose ends after her father's death, teen
accepts friendship of chimerical boy who manipulates, then spurns
her. (Fox--351)

PLACE TO COME BACK TO, A: Bitter teen must go to live with
career-oriented divorced mother and stepfather when custodial
uncle dies. (Bond--25)

PLANET OF JUNIOR BROWN, THE: Driven to the brink of psychosis
by neurotic mother and obsessive piano teacher, adolescent is
succored by black classmate. (Hamilton--106)

PLAYING BEATIE BOW: Angered Australian victim of paternal desertion gets new perspective on love when she reverts one century in time. (Park--186)

PLEASE DON'T KISS ME NOW: Feminist mother's preoccupation with
self-fulfillment drives teen into welcoming arms of superficial,
opportunistic boy. (Gerber--84)

PONY PROBLEM, THE: Winning the pony she pines for poses problems for fatherless girl living in suburbia. (Holland--375)

PORTRAIT OF IVAN: Boy's sterile life with executive father is
ameliorated by friendly artist who encourages his curiosity about
dead mother. (Fox--352)

PRIVATE MATTER, A: Schoolgirl adopts elderly neighbor as sur-
    rogate father after parents' divorce and is shattered when he
    moves away. (Ewing--71)
PURIM GOAT, THE: Son of poor widow teaches terpsichorean tricks
    to pet goat to save its life and repay mother's debt. (Suhl--457)

QUEENIE PEAVY: Daughter of imprisoned father cultivates tough
    image in compensation for peer harassment. (Burch--554)

RACECOURSE FOR ANDY, A: Retarded son of Australian mother be-
    lieves he has bought his own race track to consternation of real
    owners. (Wrightson--594)
RACHEL VELLARS, HOW COULD YOU? Divorce and relocation con-
    tribute to diffident girl's quandary over choice of friends.
    (Fisher--74)
RACHEL'S LEGACY: Mettlesome Jewish immigrant matriarchy attains
    mixed fortunes in New York's early 1900s melting pot. (Colman--
    318)
RADIO ROBERT: Among other changes in his adolescent life, boy's
    divorced celebrity father moves back to town and puts him on the
    air. (Fisher--75)
RAINBOW JORDAN: Bewildered black teen is caught in three-way
    tug-of-war among promiscuous mother, conservative foster parent,
    and boyfriend's sexual pressure. (Childress--37)
RAISING A MOTHER ISN'T EASY: Korean daughter of single adop-
    tive mother believes she has found perfect mate for disorganized
    mom. (McHugh--542)
RAT TEETH: Triple stigma of buck teeth, two homes, and embar-
    rassing performance on baseball diamond drive boy to alienate the
    world. (Giff--86)
REALLY WEIRD SUMMER, A: Distressed by parents' impending di-
    vorce, boy discovers enchanted time warp with idyllic family he
    longs to join. (McGraw--163)
RED BIRD OF IRELAND: Teen's mother becomes heroine during
    Ireland's potato famine after father precedes them to America.
    (Langford--560)
REFINER'S FIRE, THE: Suddenly reunited with assertive, ac-
    complished father four years after mother's death, young teen
    feels subdued and inept. (Kingman--388)
REFUGEE SUMMER, THE: War-orphaned Greek boy gains insights
    into the war, the world, the mighty and the meek when he makes
    international friends. (Fenton--346)
REMEMBERING THE GOOD TIMES: Two young teens of single-
    parent homes ponder events leading to suicide of third member
    of their triumvirate. (Peck--189)
RETURN TO BITTER CREEK: Unwed mother's unorthodox lifestyle
    polarizes matriarchal mountain family when she returns with
    daughter and lover. (Smith--505a)
ROADSIDE VALENTINE: Once errant teen tries to regain respect of

pejorative single father and capture affections of childhood girl-friend. (Adler--4)

ROBBERS, THE: British boy, who has lived with grandmother since mother's death, is resentful when father remarries and sends for him. (Bawden--261)

ROBBIE AND THE LEAP YEAR BLUES: Son of frequently re-paired parents ponders social and sexual responsibilities of contemporary urban adulthood. (Klein--137)

ROBOT BIRTHDAY, THE: Functioning robot made by electronics whiz mom assuages children's pain over divorce and relocation. (Bunting--29)

ROCK FEVER: Alcoholic personality change in divorced mother drives distracted teen to seek tranquility in prescription drugs. (Rabinowich--202)

RONNIE AND ROSEY: The shock of her husband's sudden death transforms effervescent mother of teen into unreasonable despot. (Angell--256)

ROOM MADE OF WINDOWS, A: Early teen embellishes memories of father and tenaciously resists changes in status quo, including mother's remarriage. (Cameron--295)

RUFUS M.: Spirited youngest child finds rewards in fighting WWI on the homefront and helping his fatherless family through crisis. (Estes--341)

RUN FOR YOUR LIFE: Fatherless track athlete refuses to be intimidated by older competitor who bullies him to throw race. (Platt--428)

RUN SOFTLY, GO FAST: Vietnam-era teen chronicles growing disillusionment with once-idolized deceased father's materialism, conventionality and hypocrisy. (Wersba--471)

RUTH CRANE: Coddled teen is unwillingly harnessed to housework and care of brother when father is killed and mother injured in accident. (Morgan--412)

SAM, BANGS AND MOONSHINE: After mother's death, young girl's escape into fantasy nearly costs friend and pet their lives. (Ness--417)

SARAH, PLAIN AND TALL: Papa's prospective mail order bride is homely but brings a song to the hearts of motherless 1800s prairie family. (MacLachlan--400)

SASHA, MY FRIEND: City teen has difficulty adjusting to wilderness isolation where her father moves upon wife's tragic death. (Corcoran--325)

SATURDAYS, THE: Memorable experiences befall creative motherless children who spend pooled allowances on one big adventure for each. (Enright--335)

SCARECROWS: Defensive of military father's memory, British boy allows hatred of his usurper to overcome reason when his mother remarries. (Westall--472)

SEASON IN-BETWEEN, A: Awkward adolescent experiences despondency over father's death and ambivalence toward perfectionist

stepfather comes to a boil after he finds and tames a wild dog. (Corbin--323)

SO WHO HASN'T GOT PROBLEMS: Innocuous early teen soap opera of shifting allegiances, first romance, and two disparate one-parent homes. (Franco--354)

SOLITARY BLUE, A: Self-serving mother who abandoned boy when he was small re-enters his life as teen and tries to exploit him as she did his father. (Voigt--238)

SOLITARY SECRET, A: Following her parents' separation, unwanted and unloved young teen is brutally carnalized by her custodial father. (Hermes--112)

SOLOMON SYSTEM, THE: Fear of parents' impending divorce casts shadow over close-knit brothers, while adolescent changes drive wedge between them. (Naylor--172)

SOME OF THE DAYS OF EVERETT ANDERSON: Imaginative black inner city boy enlivens his week, waiting for widowed mom to come home from work. (Clifton--311)

SOMEONE SLIGHTLY DIFFERENT: Addition of unconventional grand-mother is an asset to household of pre-teen and divorced working mother. (Mearian--164)

SOMETHING TO COUNT ON: Occasionally obstreperous black girl worries that her behavior deters her divorced father from visiting her. (Moore--168)

SOMETIMES I DON'T LOVE MY MOTHER: Obsessive grief over hus-band's death impels dependent wife into unwelcome intimacy with grown daughter. (Colman--319)

SOMETIMES I THINK I HEAR MY NAME: On unannounced visits to divorced parents, boy who lives with relatives confronts bitter reality that he is unwanted. (Avi--14)

SON OF SOMEONE FAMOUS, THE: Homely daughter of small town widow and unachieving motherless son of public figure form un-likely alliance of losers. (Kerr--134)

SORROW'S SONG: Boy helps mute, fatherless friend to save en-dangered wildfowl from human predators. (Callen--293)

SOUND OF CHARIOTS, A: Scottish adolescent finds outlet for an-guish at loss of father during WWI in composing poetry. (Hunter --380)

SOUNDER: Faithful son and dog keep vigil during poor black Southern father's long, unjust incarceration for minor offenses. (Armstrong--550)

SPANISH HOOF: The fruits of industry and enterprise elude widowed Depression ranching family that never loses hope or hu-mor. (Peck--424)

SPEAKING OF SNAPDRAGONS: Self-sufficient daughter of working mother must reassess old friendships when she makes new ones on summer vacation. (Hayes--370)

SPIDERWEB FOR TWO: Older children away at school create riddles-by-mail to entertain younger, homebound motherless siblings. (Enright--336)

SPORT: Quasi-humorous adventure befalls boy who is abducted from father's custody by haughty, avaricious mother. (Fitzhugh

SUMMER OF THE SWANS, THE: Disappearance of mentally retarded
brother puts awkward, motherless teen's personal problems into
perspective. (Byars--291)

SUMMER OF THE ZEPPELIN: WWI British girl blames unlikely scape-
goats for stepmother's indifference and military father's disappearance. (McCutcheon--563)

SUMMER'S LEASE, A: Aspiring writer with prickly personality
battles single mother over college plans and school advisor over
editorial assignment. (Sachs--440)

SUNDAY FATHER: Teen reacts belligerently to father's planned remarriage because it rings death knell on her hopes of parents'
reconciliation. (Neufeld--173)

SUSAN'S MAGIC: Loss of adored father to divorce spurs girl's
compulsive possessiveness, materialism and selfishness. (Agle--6)

SWALLOWS AND AMAZONS: Children embark on summerlong voyage
of discovery in English Lake Country in emulation of seafaring
father. (Ransome--565)

SWEET WHISPERS, BROTHER RUSH: Forced by single mother's
employment to assume adult responsibility, black teen blames her
when retarded brother dies. (Hamilton--107)

SWITCHAROUND: Resentful of peremptory summons to visit long-lost
father, brother and sister wreak vengeance that they later regret.
(Lowry--150)

TAKING SIDES: Adolescent prefers living with father until his mild
heart attack necessitates her return to working mother. (Klein--
138)

TAKING TERRI MUELLER: Stunning revelation that she was kidnapped by father and that mother is not dead as she presumed
taxes teen's loyalty to dad. (Mazer--158)

TEETONCEY: Cheated of husband and elder son by the remorseless
sea, widowed mother adopts a castaway waif. (Taylor--460)

TEETONCEY AND BEN O'NEAL: Widow and son fiercely defend the
rights of castaway orphan they have unilaterally adopted. (Tay-
lor--461)

TELL ME NO LIES: When illegitimate daughter locates father, she
realizes why her mother fictionalized him to her--and forgives
her. (Colman--488)

TELLTALE SUMMER OF TINA C., THE: When mother returns with
new husband, insecure teen is reluctant to leave custodial father
to spend summer with them. (Perl--190)

TENNIS REBEL: Uprooted, homesick teen overcomes resentment of
broken home and stepparents by immersing herself in champion-
ship tennis. (Sanderlin--213)

TEX: While older brother pursues respectability and achievement,
younger one seems to emulate ne'er-do-well single father.
(Hinton--374)

THANK YOU, JACKIE ROBINSON: Only male in household of
women, baseball enthusiast welcomes companionship of elderly
black man. (Cohen--314)

TINA GOGO: To survive adversity, daughter of incompetent mother
  cloaks vulnerability with aggression through years of foster care.
  (Angell--11)
TO LIVE A LIE: Angry and stigmatized by mother's desertion, girl
  tells new acquaintances that mom is dead. (Alexander--7)
TO RAVENSRIGG: Eighteenth-century girl loses widowed stepfather
  in shipwreck and learns that her biological sire is rapacious slave
  trader. (Burton--287)
TO THE GREEN MOUNTAINS: Early feminist and civil rights activist inadvertently triggers tragedy for black family she and
  daughter both love. (Cameron--35)
TO THE TUNE OF A HICKORY STICK: In absence of children's
  widowed mother, avaricious uncle/guardian abuses them and ap-
  propriates their support checks. (Branscum--275)
TOAD ON CAPITOL HILL, THE: Federal period provides backdrop
  for story about independent young girl and her irritating new
  stepfamily. (Brady--271)
TOBY, GRANNY AND GEORGE: Girl who lives with pragmatic
  backwoods granny solves mystery and has traumatic meeting with
  birth mother. (Branscum--484)
TOBY LIVED HERE: Young widow's pent emotions propel her into
  mental institution and her daughters into a foster home.
  (Wolitzer--478)
TOO HOT FOR ICE CREAM: When divorced dad can't keep their
  Saturday beach date, young girl takes toddler sister to the park
  instead. (Van Leeuwen--236)
TORNADO! One natural disaster after another strikes hapless
  fatherless family whose survival is dependent on young teen.
  (Milton--410)
TOUGH CHAUNCEY: Foster care becomes only recourse for teen
  brutalized by grandfather and rejected by beloved but promiscuous mother. (Smith--222)
TRAPPED ON THE GOLDEN FLYER: Momentous train trip turns into
  frigid nightmare for uprooted boy whose mother has recently
  died. (Fleming--348)
TRIAL VALLEY: Teen philosophically bears trials and tribulations
  of rearing orphaned siblings and an abandoned waif. (Cleaver--
  528)
TROUBLE ON TREAT STREET: Interracial misunderstanding plagues
  black orphan and loyal, defensive grandmother/guardian after
  move to Chicano barrio. (Alexander--515)
TUNDRA: Teen is distraught when the dog her mother buys her to
  compensate for divorce gets lost and suffers grave perils.
  (Hallstead--105)
TUNE IN TOMORROW: Voyeuristic teen escapes into soap opera fantasy to avoid the anxiety of life with immature unwed mom.
  (Anderson--483)
TURKEYLEGS THOMPSON: Belligerent pre-teen develops reputation
  as aggressive roughneck after parents' divorce but comes un-
  strung upon sister's death. (McCord--161)
TV KID, THE: Tube-obsessed fatherless boy substitutes TV

adventure for dull reality until near-fatal accident gives him new perspective on life. (Byars--292)

TWO GUYS NOTICED ME ... AND OTHER MIRACLES: Teen is emotionally embroiled in love triangle involving her parents while experiencing one of her own. (Sharmat--217)

TWO PIANO TUNERS: Orphaned girl convinces grandfather who is rearing her that she should emulate him in choice of career. (Goffstein--534)

TWO PLACES TO SLEEP: After parents' divorce, young boy stays at home with father and housekeeper and visits mother's apartment on weekends. (Schuchman--214)

TWO SPECIAL CARDS: Primary schoolgirl can't find appropriate divorce card so she makes her own, expressing love for both parents. (Lisker--148)

TWO-THOUSAND-POUND GOLDFISH, THE: Denied maternal attention he craves, son of absent, unwed activist creates imaginary world of poetic justice. (Byars--485)

TWYLA: Mentally and socially handicapped fatherless teen tries optimistically to boost self-esteem by clinging to hopeless, illusory romance. (Walker--241)

UNCLE MIKE'S BOY: Child, burdened by divorced father's alcoholism, mother's neuroses and sister's tragic death, is lifted from despair by wise uncle. (Brooks--28)

UNDER THE HAYSTACK: When mother masochistically runs off with man who mistreats her and abuses them, abandoned sisters try to cope alone. (Engebrecht--70)

UN-DUDDING OF ROGER JUDD, THE: Sensitive, insecure teen is brought to brink of suicide by needling stepsister and mistrustful father. (Luger--151)

UNMAKING OF RABBIT, THE: While living with caring grandmother, diffident boy yearns for normal relationship with his indifferent mother. (Greene--96)

UP A ROAD SLOWLY: Following his wife's death, professor father sends daughter to be reared by punctilious aunt. (Hunt--379)

VERONICA GANZ: Tallest girl in class, whose mother has remarried a temporizer, reigns as school bully until humbled by diminutive new boy. (Sachs--211)

VISITORS WHO CAME TO STAY, THE: Small girl's complacent routine with father is disrupted when his avant-garde girlfriend and her obnoxious son move in. (McAfee--159)

VIVA CHICANO: Delinquent Hispanic youth's bid for redemption despite intolerable homelife and peer pressure is aided by subconscious memories of father. (Bonham--269)

WALK OUT A BROTHER: Independent teen rebels against guardianship of older brother following widowed father's accidental death.

(Baird--517)

WATCHERS, THE: Boy who masks sensitivity with toughness because of parents' dissolving marriage finds solace in befriending
handicapped youngster. (Rinkoff--206)

WAY HOME, THE: Deformed motherless girl displays resourcefulness
in fleeing superstitious villagers in plague-wracked Medieval England. (Turner--465)

WAY TO SATTIN SHORE, THE: Vindictive, tyrannical grandmother
misleads British girl into believing that her absent father is
dead. (Pearce--564)

WEEKEND SISTERS: Envy, enmity, misunderstanding, and lack of
communication stratify a father's two families. (Colman--47)

WEIRD HENRY BERG: Tuned out, turned off son of drug suicide
father loses apathy when pet lizard turns out to be bona fide
dragon. (Sargent--442)

WHAT A WIMP! Timid boy becomes target of older bully after
mother's divorce and family's relocation. (Carrick--36)

WHAT ARE FRIENDS FOR? Two lonely girls from divided homes develop symbiotic relationship in spite of one's warped, negative
personality. (Ames--9)

WHAT IT'S ALL ABOUT: Pre-teen is perplexed by conflicting
loyalties over divorced parents' revolving door marriages and
liaisons. (Klein--139)

WHAT TIME OF NIGHT IS IT? The arrival of family's meticulous,
meddling grandmother is a mixed blessing when their mother deserts. (Stolz--231)

WHAT'S BEST FOR YOU: Children's fair, sensible, considerate
parents make flexible custody arrangements to benefit everyone.
(Angell--12)

WHEN THE SAD ONE COMES TO STAY: After custody switch,
intimidated girl complies with overbearing mother's inducement
to forget happy past with her father. (Heide--110)

WHEN THE WIND BLOWS HARD: Cultural shock ensues when schoolgirl moves with mother from New York City to Alaska following
divorce. (Orenstein--182)

WHEN WE LIVED WITH PETE: Lonely boy who cannot relinquish
memories of simple, meaningful life with mother's former flame,
effects a reconciliation. (Buchan--281)

WHERE IS DADDY? Toddler is traumatized when insufficiently prepared for parents' divorce, mother's new job, and family relocation. (Goff--87)

WHERE THE LILIES BLOOM. Proud and resolute young teen assumes
responsibility for dirt-poor mountain family after father's death.
(Cleaver--529)

WHICH WAY TO THE NEAREST WILDERNESS: Pre-teen who hates
peacemaker role between warring parents and prickly sibs plans
escape a la Thoreau. (Springstubb--228)

WHISTLE DOWN A DARK LANE: Middle-aged mother's platonic relationship with husband in pre-contraceptive era prompts him to
seek separation. (Jones--125)

WHISTLING BOY, THE: On summer's respite from young new

drinking father, boy experiences chilling encounter with witchcraft. (Roth--439)

WORLD IS MY EGGSHELL, THE: Introverted since father's death,
teen learns to play treacherous, convoluted game of life that
comes naturally to her twin. (Mulford--413)

WORLD OF ELLEN MARCH, THE: Stunned by parents' divorce and
smarting from its imagined stigma, teen makes desperate reconciliation attempt. (Eyerly--73)

WRETCHED ROBERT: Following his parents' divorce, normally cooperative boy decides to become perverse and attract attention.
(Fisher--76)

WRINKLE IN TIME, A: With extraterrestrial assistance, children
rescue missing father from mental imprisonment in fifth dimension. (L'Engle--561)

YEAR IN THE LIFE OF ROSIE BERNARD, A: In remarrying, widowed
father seems to break a second promise to his distressed and resentful daughter. (Brenner--276)

YEAR THE DREAMS CAME BACK, THE: Teen's mother's suicide in-
duces subconscious fears that surface only when her father decides to remarry. (Feagles--344)

YOU CAN'T GET THERE FROM HERE: Cast adrift when father deserts and mother enters marketplace, vulnerable teen falls prey
to exploitative mentor. (Anderson--10)

YOU SHOULDN'T HAVE TO SAY GOOD-BYE: Close-knit family lives
day by day through physical and emotional ordeal of beloved
mother's terminal cancer. (Hermes--372)

YOUNG FU OF THE UPPER YANGTZE: Mixed adventures await boy
apprenticed by widowed mother to coppersmith in corrupt Chinese
city. (Lewis--395)

YOUR OLD PAL, AL: Intense adolescent tries patience of best
friend while awaiting letters from her stepmother and a boy she
likes. (Greene--97)

75, 76, 166
Bienenfeld, Florence 601
BIRACIAL CHILDREN 368, 390, 419, 486, 495
BLACKS 33, 37, 80, 106, 107, 146, 147, 168, 171, 219, 239, 305,
    306, 307, 308, 309, 310, 311, 315, 364, 366, 390, 405, 414,
    444, 512, 513, 514, 515, 539, 540, 550, 582, 587, 589
BLENDED FAMILIES 24, 162, 178, 225, 226, 242, 243, 244, 245,
    248, 251, 271, 288, 327, 330, 397, 462, 470, 474
Blos, Joan W. 266
Blue, Rose 22
Blume, Judy 23, 267, 553
BOARDING SCHOOLS 34, 80a, 82, 116, 132, 152, 253, 272, 324,
    325, 331, 363, 376, 379, 406, 420a, 423, 472, 474
Boeckman, Charles 602
Bond, Nancy 24, 25, 268
Bonham, Frank 269
Bonsall, Crosby 270
Booher, Dianna Daniels 603
BOY AS MAN OF THE FAMILY 385, 508, 571, 585
Bradbury, Bianca 26
Brady, Esther Wood 271
Bragdon, Elspeth 272
Branscum, Robbie 273, 274, 275, 484, 520
Brelis, Nancy 573
Brenner, Barbara 276
Bridgers, Sue Ellen 27, 277
Brink, Carol Ryrie 278
Brooks, Bruce 279
Brooks, Jerome 28
Brooks, Ron 521
BROTHER AS GUARDIAN 517
Brown, Irene Bennett 280
Browne, Anthony 159
Buchan, Stuart 281
Bulla, Clyde Robert 282, 283, 284, 522
Bunting, Eve 29
Burch, Robert 285, 286, 523, 554
Burnett, Frances Hodgson 524
Burton, Hester 287
BUSINESS TRIPS (1 PARENT FROM 2-PARENT HOME) 551, 569
Butler, Beverly 30
Byars, Betsy 31, 32, 288, 289, 290, 291, 292, 485, 525, 526

Cain, Barbara S. 604
Caines, Jeannette 33
CALDECOTT MEDALISTS 417, 590
CALIFORNIA 1, 8, 9, 19, 40, 68, 69, 72, 84, 90, 108, 124, 151,
    158, 181, 197, 198, 199, 213, 227, 249, 255, 262, 264, 269,
    281, 294, 295, 296, 348, 349, 419, 428, 451, 462, 466, 480,
    486, 497, 504, 506, 515, 535, 566, 572

Callen, Larry 293
Calvert, Patricia 34
Cameron, Eleanor 35, 294, 295, 296
CANADA 80a, 367, 383, 398, 401
CAREER ASPIRATIONS OF CHILDREN
    ACTRESS 10, 192, 194, 235
    ARTIST 31, 55, 77, 368, 445, 471
    BIOLOGIST 242, 243
    CLOTHING DESIGNER 316
    COMEDIAN 320
    DANCER 538
    DOCTOR 392, 401, 477
    JOCKEY 583
    MOUNTAIN CLIMBER 467
    MUSICIAN 27, 106, 202, 347, 448, 462, 593
    NURSE 406
    PALEONTOLOGIST 149
    PHOTOGRAPHER 399
    PIANO TUNER 534
    POET 16, 39
    PSYCHOLOGIST 98
    SCIENTIST 504
    TEACHER 443
    VETERINARIAN 127, 221
    WRITER 295, 296, 380, 440
Carlson, Natalie Savage 297, 574
Carrick, Carol 36
Cavallaro, Ann 298
CELEBRITIES, CHILDREN OF 1, 75, 134, 195, 220, 420, 546
Chetin, Helen 486
CHILD ABUSE (see also SEXUAL ABUSE; INCEST) 54, 55, 196,
    222, 238, 269, 275, 378, 393
CHILD ACTRESS 194, 387
CHILD SUPPORT/ALIMONY 40, 124, 168, 223, 237, 508
CHILDCARE/MOTHER'S HELPERS (see also HOUSEKEEPERS) 2, 8,
    29, 59, 104, 111, 183, 264, 266, 299, 391, 440, 448, 466,
    491, 589
    BY HALF SIBLING 150, 504, 506
    BY SIBLING 28, 43, 61, 107, 145, 160, 161, 203, 204, 209, 229,
        289, 350, 412, 428, 449, 473, 506, 563
    BY STEPSIBLING 24
CHILDREN'S SHELTERS 45, 103
Childress, Alice 37
CHINA 395
CHINESE AMERICANS 480, 572
Chorao, Kay 38
Christian, Mary Blount 39
CLAIRVOYANCE (see also SUPERNATURAL STORIES) 67, 226,
    296, 331, 455, 497, 518
CLAIRVOYANT MESSAGE FROM DEAD PARENT (see also HALLUCINA-
    TION OF PARENT'S SPIRIT) 296, 331, 383, 399

EMPLOYMENT OF SINGLE MOTHERS BY OCCUPATION (cont.)
  DESIGNER 47, 74, 488
  DOCTOR 183
  DOMESTIC 39, 101, 147, 284, 346, 418, 512
  EDITOR 80a, 99, 479
  ENTERTAINER 386
  FARMER/RANCHER 424, 466
  FOOD SERVICE 30, 40, 51, 55, 187, 241, 254, 592, 593
  HEALTHCARE 258, 264
  HEIR TO HUSBAND'S BUSINESS 363
  HERBAL HEALER 560
  HORSE TRAINER 104
  INNKEEPER 35, 270, 292, 313, 314, 422, 451
  INSURANCE AGENT 123, 155, 492
  INTERIOR DECORATOR 1, 27, 56, 105, 235
  JOB HOPPER 118, 495, 504
  JOURNALIST 288, 454, 468
  LIBRARIAN 103, 108, 262, 431
  MAIL CARRIER 583
  MODEL 96, 169, 390
  MUSIC TEACHER 46
  MUSEUM CURATOR 375
  NIGHT SHIFT 329, 448
  NURSE 43, 107, 210, 212, 329, 411, 448, 491, 503
  PARALEGAL 259
  PART-TIME JOB 61
  PHOTOGRAPHER 92, 462, 496
  PHYSICIST 109
  PINK COLLAR (CLERICAL) 30, 62, 65, 155, 161, 204, 206,
    214, 365, 399, 495
  POET 236
  PROSTITUTE 500
  PSYCHIC 483
  PUBLIC RELATIONS 131, 413
  REALTOR 15, 36, 71, 76, 407
  RECEPTIONIST 10
  RESTAURATEUR 386, 401
  RETAIL SALES/MERCHANDISING 59, 63, 91, 93, 97, 121, 153,
    160, 161, 163, 168, 177, 199, 213, 362, 447, 479, 564
  RODEO RIDER 290
  SEAMSTRESS 318, 338, 339, 340, 341, 346, 353, 396
  SECRETARY 227, 234, 299, 350, 360
  SHOP OWNER 186, 370
  SOCIAL WORKER 498
  SOCIOLOGIST 99
  STEWARDESS 32
  TEACHER 16, 29, 84, 90, 137, 182, 252, 373, 410
  TOUR GUIDE 117
  TRAVEL AGENT 111, 581
  UNSPECIFIED 22, 60, 87, 89, 118, 119, 138, 140, 166, 176, 198,
    207, 307, 311, 320, 329, 472, 584, 585, 587, 588

ACCUSATION OF   520
INDIANA   123
INNER CITY   22, 37, 80, 144, 146, 171, 174, 201, 239, 269, 302,
     305, 306, 307, 308, 309, 310, 311, 364, 414, 515, 539, 540,
     582, 587, 588, 592, 593
INSECURE/DIFFIDENT CHILDREN   3, 28, 36, 38, 40, 69, 77, 80,
     96, 103, 122, 124, 126, 151, 167, 174, 193, 246, 260, 264,
     268, 328, 388, 393, 413, 419, 428, 433, 505, 508, 518, 519,
     521, 535, 539
INSTITUTIONALIZED PARENT (2-PARENT FAMILY)   27, 279, 556
INSTITUTIONALIZED SINGLE PARENT   27, 54, 200, 203, 209, 317,
     478, 493, 510, 511
INTERGENERATIONAL MISUNDERSTANDING   215, 231, 294, 390,
     505a
INTERRACIAL MISUNDERSTANDING   35, 444, 515, 568
INTOLERABLE HOMELIFE   31, 55, 65, 68, 106, 174, 187, 193, 222,
     269, 506
IOWA   150, 406
IRELAND   396, 560
ISRAEL   113, 358
ITALY   117, 225

JAPAN   389
JAPANESE-AMERICANS   466
JEWS   28, 113, 172, 201, 312, 313, 314, 316, 318, 358, 363, 383,
     394, 421, 432, 457, 479, 534, 553, 562, 570
Johnson, Annabel   122
Johnston, Norma   381
JOINT CUSTODY   12, 48, 56, 66, 86, 92, 98, 111, 133, 138, 141,
     143, 172, 248
Jones, Adrienne   124, 125
Jones, Hettie   495
Jones, Penelope   382
Jones, Rebecca C.   123
Jukes, Mavis   126, 127

Kandell, Alice S.   569
KANSAS   280, 321, 322, 490
Kaplan, Bess   383
Karl, Jean E.   128
Katz, Welwyn   129
Keats, Ezra Jack   582
Keene, Carolyn   384
Keith, Harold   385
Keller, Beverly   130
KENTUCKY   83, 443, 455
Kerr, M. E.   131, 132, 133, 134, 386, 387
Kindred, Wendy   135
Kingman, Lee   388

249, 253, 303, 342, 379, 430, 431
TENNESSEE 529, 533
TERMINAL ILLNESS 343, 363, 372, 382, 398, 409
Terris, Susan 462
TEXAS 39, 420, 441, 473, 571
Thomas, Ianthe 233
Thompson, Paul 234
Thorvall, Kerstin 508
THREE-GENERATIONAL FAMILIES 31, 87, 102, 123, 131, 164, 177,
    189, 230, 239, 249, 294, 305, 399, 431, 434, 435, 436, 437,
    464, 493, 504, 564, 584, 587, 592, 593
THRIFT 592, 593
Thurber, James 590
TOILET TRAINING 589
Tolan, Stephanie S. 235, 463
Townsend, John Rowe 509
TRIAL SEPARATION 17, 19, 88, 125, 136, 144, 163, 177, 216, 217,
    229, 231
TRUANCY/TARDINESS 106, 161, 219, 239
Turkle, Brinton 591
Turner, Ann 464, 465

Uchida, Yoshiko 466
Ullman, James Ramsey 467
UNCLE AS GUARDIAN 25, 54, 219, 275, 519, 524, 532
UNDEMONSTRATIVE/INSENSITIVE PARENTS 21, 100, 104, 238,
    254, 258, 261, 272, 282, 328, 352, 404, 430, 436, 437, 522,
    546
UNDEMONSTRATIVE STEPPARENT 563
UNDERACHIEVERS 116, 134, 292, 374, 442, 463, 485
UNEMPLOYED FATHERS (FATHER AS SINGLE PARENT) 224, 316,
    368, 414, 416, 507, 520, 556
UNFIT PARENTS 11, 169, 222, 289, 368, 414, 506, 556
UNORTHODOX LIFESTYLES 80a, 90, 117, 141, 388, 505a, 506,
    520, 526, 547
UNRELATED ADULT AS GUARDIAN 516, 518, 520, 522, 527, 535,
    546, 549
UNSUPERVISED MINORS (see also LATCHKEY CHILDREN) 59, 70,
    101, 128, 209, 283, 289, 290, 409, 416, 421, 459, 474, 506,
    511, 528, 529, 558
UNWANTED CHILDREN 14, 37, 48, 70, 83, 96, 100, 169, 196, 282,
    328, 378, 430, 452, 516, 526

VACATION STORIES 52, 83, 125, 240, 251, 257, 288, 337, 342,
    389, 419, 440, 447, 474, 565, 591
Van Leeuwen, Jean 236
VERMONT 5, 134, 240, 438, 439, 468, 500
VIETNAM 333
Vigna, Judith 237